DISCOVERING BUDDHISM

DISCOVERING BUDDHISM

DOMINIQUE SIDE

Matador
Unit E2 Airfield Business Park,
Harrison Road, Market Harborough,
Leicestershire. LE16 7UL
Tel: 0116 2792299
Email: books@troubador.co.uk
Web: www.troubador.co.uk/matador
Twitter: @matadorbooks

ISBN 978 1803131 122

British Library Cataloguing in Publication Data.
A catalogue record for this book is available from the British Library.

Printed and bound by CPI Group (UK) Ltd, Croydon, CR0 4YY
Typeset in 10.5pt Minion Pro by Troubador Publishing Ltd, Leicester, UK

Matador is an imprint of Troubador Publishing Ltd

May these pages open
thousands of hearts and minds
to the truth within

FOREWORD

Introducing any kind of spiritual system, and especially one like Buddhism that comes to the West from an alien culture, requires a lot more than passing on information and hearsay. So, no matter how many footnotes or how much academic research a presentation has, Buddhism would still be better presented by someone who actually lives as a Buddhist and practises the Buddha dharma. After all, at the end of the day, what we call 'practice' is really nothing other than in-depth study and research.

As long as I have known Dominique Side, she has not only been a critical searcher and academic, but she has also personally seen the value of the Buddhist path and encountered many great masters of this century. That's why her book is not like most introductory books that present Buddhism as a religion along with lots of facts, figures and logical arguments.

Instead, it presents a different way of looking at life and the world, and it encourages the kind of critical exploration, questioning, and reflection that can actually enrich the reader's personal understanding. That's why I'd sooner recommend this book than some compilation of materials based primarily on academic credentials and references.

Dzongsar Jamyang Khyentse,
author of *What Makes you Not a Buddhist*

ACKNOWLEDGEMENTS

I gratefully acknowledge all the many people who have explained Buddhism to me over the years. For this book I am indebted to Professor Peter Harvey, now retired from the University of Sunderland, UK, who kindly commented on the text of my first book, *Buddhism,* on which this one is based. I am also grateful to Karl Brunnholzl for his comments on Chapter 21 and to Dzongsar Jamyang Khyentse for the dynamic way in which he upholds the Buddhist teaching and for his consistent encouragement and support.

Contents

Chapter 1

THE INDIAN CONTEXT

The story of Buddhism begins over 2,500 years ago in northern India. It is the story of an extraordinary man who lived in one of the greatest civilisations in human history, and whose genius led him to share a wisdom so profound and so timeless that it set free millions of people in the past, is doing so right now in the present, and no doubt will continue long into the future.

Buddhism did not develop in a vacuum. This Chapter provides the historical context into which the Buddha was born. It explores the main factors that influenced the Buddha's thinking and shaped the way the religion developed after his death.

A Turning Point in Human History

At the time the Buddha lived in India, that is, between the sixth and fourth centuries BCE, there occurred possibly the most profound and widespread intellectual and spiritual transformation the world has ever seen. People in different corners of the Earth, from China to Europe, had come to find that the spiritual practices of their ancestors were no longer working for them. An extraordinary number of geniuses made supreme efforts, separately, to find a new solution that would meet people's needs. The result is that many of the main religions of the world as we know it today took root during that time. That is why the period that extends from about 800 to 200 BCE is called the Axial Age because it is an axis or turning point in the development of humanity. This new movement had already begun in India before the Buddha.

Between the seventh and fifth centuries BCE, across the world, intellectual life was in ferment. The Axial Age saw the great Hebrew prophets of Judaism between the eighth to sixth centuries; in China it saw Confucius in the sixth century and Lao Tzu in the fifth century who respectively gave birth to Confucianism and Taoism; sixth century Iran probably saw the sage Zoroaster and the development of the Zoroastrian religion, while in ancient Greece the thought of Socrates and Plato in the fifth to fourth centuries lay the foundation for European philosophy as well as important aspects of Christian thinking. Meanwhile, in India, the writing of the *Upanishads* from the seventh century BCE onwards lay the cornerstone of modern Hinduism. It was also during this period, in the sixth and fifth centuries, that Mahavira gave birth to Jainism and Shakyamuni Buddha gave birth to Buddhism.

One of the most striking characteristics of this new religious movement is the emphasis on the inwardness of spiritual life, the realization that it is by looking within ourselves that we can find the fulfilment we are looking for. These new religions sought inner depth rather than magical control of the external world. Instead of animal sacrifice to external nature gods people gradually turned their minds to the inner 'sacrifice of the ego'. Morality, rather than ritual, became central. In this period, too, religion became less social and more personal, and to a great extent less worldly and more other-worldly, meaning that religion was less about ensuring good circumstances in this life and more about ensuring happiness after death. Furthermore, religious teachings were no longer the exclusive preserve of the priestly class but a way of transmitting a faith to people at large.

The cultural history of northern India

Indian civilisation is one of the oldest continuing cultures in human history, along with that of China. Some scholars, such as Klaus K. Klostermaier, believe that India

Figure 1.1 – Comparative Dates for the Period Leading to the Emergence of Buddhism

All dates are BCE and approximate

2650	Oldest Egyptian pyramid
2500	Indus Valley civilisation
2000	Abraham, first Hebrew patriarch
1290	Moses
1200	The Vedas begin to be composed
950	King Solomon builds first temple in Jerusalem
900	Homer writes the Iliad
700	Hesiod writes major work on Greek gods
600	Upanishads begin to be composed
563-483	The Buddha
527	Traditional date for the death of Mahavira, Jain leader
500	Confucius in China
428-348	Plato
384-322	Aristotle

was already culturally advanced as early as 6000 BCE, but we have little evidence relating to that period. However, in the 1920s, archaeological excavations of the ancient cities of Mohenjo-Daro and Harappa in northwest India and modern Pakistan revealed the existence of urban civilisation dating back to 2500 BCE. This is called the Indus Valley civilisation.

Evidence indicates it was extensive and with strong central government. Artefacts show its religion to be related to the forces of nature – for example, the worship of a mother goddess, sacred trees and fertility symbols. No temples have been found, indicating that religion was largely domestic. Many scholars believe that elements of this ancient religion continued uninterrupted, and that the roots of Hinduism lie here.

From around 1500 BCE new ideas were brought into India by Aryan invaders from what is now northern Iran and southern Russia. It seems this was a peaceful migration, but one which had a profound and long-lasting impact on the religion, language, society and political organisation of northern India. The Vedic culture of the Aryans was the other key root of Hinduism.

Vedic religion

The Aryans introduced the Vedic religion, based on a group of scriptures called the Vedas. 'Veda' is a Sanskrit word meaning 'knowledge'. The Vedas have no named human authors but were written down by ancient sages who, in certain intuitive states, 'heard' the truth of how things are. The truth of the Vedas is therefore considered to be a universal and timeless truth.

There is no one creator God but many different gods (and a small number of goddesses) related to natural forces. Central to the Vedic religion was the sacrifice of animals, carried out in public by priests in order to please the gods or ask them for favours such as children, prosperity, a good harvest and so on. The goals of this religion were often worldly, but fundamentally the priests were responsible for maintaining the good order of the world. In early times they would sometimes take the hallucinogenic drug *soma* to induce altered states of consciousness for their rituals.

Vedic language

The language of the Vedas is Sanskrit and this became the sacred language of India, equivalent to Latin in western Europe. The sacred texts of Hinduism, Buddhism and Jainism – the three native religions of India – are mostly in Sanskrit.

Vedic society

The Aryans brought with them a hierarchical social structure, the origins of which they traced to their oldest scripture, the *Rig Veda*. This means they believed their social structure to be part of the order of the universe, and not man-made. This is one reason the caste system that has since developed from it has been so resistant to change and still continues today in modern India.

In the Hymn of the Cosmic Man *(purusha shukta)*, the universe is said to have been created from a huge male figure compared to a cosmic man. Verse 12 says, "His mouth became the brahmin, his arms were made into the warrior, his thighs the people, and from his feet the servants were born." The cosmic man is equated with society, and society is seen as an organic whole. Each social ranking is symbolised by a part of the body of cosmic man, and a natural hierarchy of rankings is therefore evident. It follows that there were four main social classes or *varnas*. Beginning from the top they were:

- priests or *brahmins*
- warriors and kings, or *kshatriyas*
- farmers or *vaishyas*
- servants or *shudras.*

These were hereditary groups and there was no 'social mobility'. Each man's duty was to follow the profession suitable for his social class. It is relevant to note that India may be the only civilisation in the world ever to have placed religious priests unequivocally above kings.

Political organisation

Political organisation in Aryan culture was hierarchical and centralised. This usually took the form of monarchies. However, kingdoms could vary considerably in size, and 'kings' were sometimes no more than village rulers.

For many centuries up to and including the time of the Buddha, Indus Valley and Aryan influences co-existed side by side in northern India. So, for example, in the sixth to fourth centuries BCE there were both kingdoms and democratic republics in the region. These were not democratic in the modern sense but had leaders elected from, and by, a small group of elders. Scholars believe this was significant for the development of Buddhism since the Buddha chose a democratic model for his monks, with decisions made by consensus.

By this time social class and religion were intimately connected, and only the three higher classes were allowed to practise the Vedic religion. The servants or *shudras* were religious outcastes and considered morally impure; they were not allowed to participate in rituals and had to live in separate settlements at the edge of the village. Priests or brahmins, on the other hand, were so important and so powerful that the culture and religion are usually called *brahminical.*

The status of women is unclear. Socially, a woman's class would be determined by her birth, just as for men, and she would marry within her class. However, women did not directly wield political power, and it is possible that in the Buddha's time women did not have equal access to religious rites.

Society at the time of the Buddha

In the lifetime of the Buddha, economic developments had begun to destabilise the brahminical order. The introduction of iron plough shares and other tools produced agricultural surpluses which led to prosperity and strong trade. The period is characterized by the growth of large towns and the first use of money. One of the effects of these changes was the creation of new professions such as state officials and traders which had no place in the ancient class system. As Professor Gombrich writes in *Theravada Buddhism*, "in the Buddha's day the dominant strata of urban society were not catered for, not even recognized, by brahminism". It is therefore not surprising that the Buddha's message appealed especially to town dwellers and the new social classes.

Gombrich makes two further points about the impact of urban development on Buddhism. First, it is very possible that the high population densities of the new towns made illness and death seem more prevalent and widespread than they would be in a small village. This may explain why his teachings on suffering, illness and death in the Four Noble Truths became acceptable to people when they did.

Second, the large populations of towns and cities became crucial to the economic development of monastic communities. Monks and nuns depend on ordinary householders for their food and material needs, and small villages would not be capable of sustaining monastic groups of any size. It is therefore arguable that urban development was a pre-condition for the growth of Buddhist monasteries.

Not all scholars agree with Gombrich. Some argue, for example, that suffering, disease and death have always been present in human society and there is no good reason to suppose that economic conditions made the Buddha's teachings more relevant in his day than they would be in any other place and any other time. Some thinkers do not see the need to emphasize socio-economic factors to explain what are, they say, universally applicable truths.

In the Buddha's time, a relatively small population lived in the Ganges plain compared with today. Most people lived in small villages but a growing number of people were gathered in newly formed towns and cities. These settlements were surrounded by untouched forests in which wild animals such as tigers, monkeys and elephants lived.

Religion at the time of the Buddha

Scholars usually set the Vedic religion in the period between 1500 and 500 BCE. The Buddha therefore lived at the end of the Vedic period, at a time of enormous change. The three main religions of ancient India all took root between the seventh and fifth centuries BCE.

- Modern-day **Hinduism** was beginning to evolve from the Vedic religion, the indigenous folk religions and other ascetic trends. There are no precise dates for the beginning of Hinduism, partly because it is not a single unified religion, but many characteristic elements can be traced back to around 700-500 BCE.
- **Jainism** emerged at almost exactly the same time as Buddhism. The Buddha and Mahavira, the Jain leader, are known to have been contemporaries. Jainism developed from one of the most influential groups of ascetics who rejected the Vedic religion.
- **Buddhism** developed between the sixth and fourth centuries BCE, and involved a reinterpretation of asceticism and folk religions, and a rejection of the Vedic religion.

Figure 1.2 – Religious movements in India at the time of the Buddha

The following ascetics rejected Brahminism and developed their own teachings.

- Purana kassapa taught that there is no such thing as moral causation; whatever one does brings no virtue or sin.
- Makkhali Gosala taught a form of fatalism or predestination. Rebirth occurs again and again through destiny and nature, and nothing we can do will make any difference to our future.
- Ajita Kesakambali taught materialism: there is no life after death, humans are merely physical and their bodies return to nature at death. There is no merit in good deeds.
- Sanjaya Balatthaputta was a sceptic who taught that human knowledge of the ultimate, including what happens after death, is impossible.
- Vardhamana Mahavira, the twenty-fourth Enlightened Conqueror (Jina) taught what became Jainism.

In the last century or so of the Vedic period, a new set of scriptures began to be composed called the Upanishads, also known as Vedanta or 'conclusion of the Vedas'. Although based on the Vedas, these scriptures emphasize the personal rather than public dimension of religion, and replace the animal sacrifice with the inner sacrifice of ego and selfish emotions. The Upanishads speak of 'one God' called Brahman, the spirit of the universe, and the goal of the religion becomes union of one's soul or *atman* with the universal Brahman. The methods used to reach this union include meditation, contemplation of nature, yoga, reflective reasoning and dutiful action in society. The Upanishads also introduce the ideas of reincarnation and karma.

Hinduism as we know it today evolved from the later Vedic period, and is strongly influenced by the Upanishads. Animal sacrifice was gradually discontinued, and the religion was based on prayer and devotion to a pantheon of gods and goddesses. The social class system developed into a more elaborate system of castes, and the Vedas are still considered authoritative scriptures by Hindus. It is difficult to say whether the transition from the Vedic religion to Hinduism occurred before or after the Buddha; it is likely that the changes had already begun before the Buddha's birth and were continuing during his lifetime and beyond. A feature of developing Hinduism was a greater willingness to see the ultimate purpose of the universe in personal, rather than impersonal, terms. Scholars generally agree that from the time of the Buddha onwards there was mutual influence between Hindus and Buddhists. Just as Buddhism reinterpreted some key concepts found in the Upanishads, so later Hindus borrowed from Buddhist ideas. This dialogue continued for well over a thousand years.

The Buddha's period saw several movements away from orthodox Brahminism. Many adults (probably almost all men) chose to give up their jobs and families and live in solitude or in small groups in the forests to pursue their religious goals. These people, called *shramanas* or ascetics, developed a number of different sects following a range of approaches and methods. It is one such person that the Buddha met on his fourth trip out of the palace, and it was this ascetic life that he lived for six years (see Chapter 2).

The ascetics began as social drop-outs, but as Hinduism developed it included this individual pursuit of religious goals as an accepted part of the religion. The ascetics who are considered Hindus are those who follow the Vedas and the Upanishads. Still today, in India, one can see Hindu devotees living and meditating by the roadside. Generally, it is older people who adopt this life once their social obligations have been met.

Hinduism did not spread widely beyond India's borders but it did take root in parts of present-day Indonesia and in Sri Lanka where it is still practised today. In the 20th century it went to Britain and a few other countries through immigration. Today there are 900 million Hindus in the world, including 80% of the Indian population and 400,000 living in Britain.

Jainism

Mahavira, the Jain leader, lived further east than the Buddha in northern India. Although the two leaders never met there are a number of Buddhist scriptures that refer to conversations between the Buddha and some of Mahavira's disciples.

Jainism emphasizes austere asceticism, moral restraint and control as the way to free the transmigrating soul from the bonds of matter, reincarnation and suffering. Jains believe that everything, even material objects, is alive and has a *jiva* or life principle that is distinct and individual – unlike the *atman* of the Upanishads which is universal and which can merge completely with Brahman.

Mahavira also taught the law of moral causation or *karma* based entirely on actions, not intentions, so unintentionally killing an insect, for example, carries all the painful consequences of taking a life.

Today, strict moral values have led Jains to choose particular jobs for their livelihood, and many become doctors, lawyers or publishers. Both men and women are generally very well educated. Jainism did not spread beyond India until modern times when it went to Britain through immigration, but it is not a religion that seeks converts and remains self-contained. It is estimated there are 4 million Jains worldwide today, with 100,000 living outside of India.

Folk religions

Alongside these trends, the ancient folk religions of India continued, especially at village level. They involved beliefs in local nature spirits and demons. Folk religions had various magical practices such as fortune telling, palmistry, prophecies, charms and spells, propitiating spirits of various kinds and interpreting dreams. These practices were accessible to the ordinary people, and just before the Buddha's time some of them had begun to be appropriated by the brahmin priests and incorporated into the Vedic religion.

It was the ordinary village people following these religions who, probably around the time of the Buddha, began to portray Brahman as the one creator God who cares for us all. In the Upanishads written before the Buddha, Brahman is the supreme reality seen as impersonal. It is therefore possible that the idea of

Figure 1.3 – The Origins of Hinduism

The transition from the earlier religions to Hinduism was a continuing process during the Buddha's lifetime, and was therefore partly simultaneous with the emergence of Buddhism

VEDIC RELIGION
Vedic scriptures are authoritative – Sacrifice of animals – Social castes – Soma – Nature gods – Focus on this life

UPANISHADS
Vedic scriptures are authoritative – Inner sacrifice of ego – Meditation – Yoga – One God: Brahman – Human soul: atman – Religion unites the soul with God – Karma determines after-life

SHRAMANAS: FOREST DWELLERS
Reject social and material values – Asceticism – Meditation – Yoga – live in isolation – Some accept the Vedas, others do not

FOLK RELIGIONS
Local nature spirits – Rituals for the dead – Spells and charms – Divinations

→

HINDUISM
The Vedas and Upanishads are authoritative – Social castes – Nature gods – No sacrifice of animals – One God: Brahman – Human soul: atman – Meditation, yoga, devotion – Reincarnation – Karma – Seven stages of life: leaving society in old age to practise religion

Brahman, as it evolved in Hinduism, originated from pre-Aryan folk religion. The personal form of Brahman was given the name Brahma.

What did the Buddha reject? What did he adopt?

The teachings of the Buddha developed against a background of strong Vedic influence but possessed an equally strong rejection of it. In terms of the three religions of ancient India that survive today, Hinduism continued the Vedic tradition with substantial modifications, whereas Buddhism and Jainism rejected the Vedic scriptures, the social class system and many other elements of 'orthodox' religion. The Buddha, then, was not a lone dissenting voice. He belonged to a widespread movement that questioned the old values, systems and beliefs. This movement was one that attempted to establish a religion more adapted to society at that time and one that gave prime importance to personal religious freedom.

By identifying what the Buddha rejected from the society and religion of his time, and by considering what he adapted from them, we can see more clearly what was new and radical about his teaching.

Rejected Concepts

- The Buddha rejected the authority of the Vedic scriptures.
- He rejected animal sacrifice.
- He rejected the use of intoxicants like *soma* because they disturb our mental clarity and control.
- He refused to follow the class system. Although he was born into the kingly or *kshatriya* class, he decided to lead a religious life which was not the prescribed activity of his class. The story of Sunita also illustrates that he accepted the lowest social outcastes into his sangha (see Chapter 2). He argued that it is how a person thinks and behaves that really counts, not their social status.
- He rejected the hierarchical structures of Aryan society.
- He rejected extreme asceticism. After experiencing it first hand, he found it did not lead to spiritual liberation.
- He rejected any religion or philosophy that undermines morality. He taught that there is a law of moral causation, and good deeds do make a difference – we can change our future.
- He rejected materialism on the grounds that it renders life meaningless and morality pointless.

- He rejected scepticism. He called sceptics or doubters 'eel-wrigglers'. They sit on the fence and never follow their wisdom, which implies that they cannot act on decisions they have not taken. Their approach leads to an impasse.
- He rejected the solitary aspect of the life of an ascetic and advised his monks always to live in groups and communities. He found that living alone for long periods can sometimes have a detrimental effect on the mind.
- The Buddha rejected the ideas of Brahman and *atman* as found in the Upanishads, on the grounds that there is no empirical evidence or logical reason proving their existence.

Concepts the Buddha Accepted and Reinterpreted

- The Buddha accepted the idea that we are born again and again, which was introduced in the Upanishads and taught by various ascetic groups. However, his doctrine of rebirth is a complete reinterpretation of the idea and develops it in greater detail.
- The Buddha accepted the law of karma or moral causation, which was introduced in the Upanishads and also taught by some ascetics. But he was the only teacher to separate moral action and social duty, and to completely ethicise the concept. His explanation of how karma works was more detailed than in any other religion.
- The Buddha accepted the general Indian idea that suffering is related to ignorance, and the goal of religion is to free ourselves from both of these. This idea is also developed in the Upanishads and in Jainism.
- He accepted the Upanishadic move towards a personal religion, concerned with working on one's own mind and emotions.
- He tolerated folk religions but devalued their importance. Brahma, spirits and so on are seen to exist, but are not as powerful as folk religions would have us believe because they cannot help to liberate us from suffering. Monks were forbidden to engage in spells and charms but laypeople could do so if they wished. From its beginnings until today, Buddhism has happily coexisted with folk beliefs in every country to which it has spread.
- The Buddha was inspired by the democratic model of social organisation developed by the northern Indian republics and adapted this to his monastic communities.

Figure 1.4 – Religious Influences on the Buddha's Thinking

Influences		Buddhism
UPANISHADS Idea of personal, inner religion – Meditation – Karma – Rebirth – The ultimate truth is beyond words and expression **SHRAMANAS** Meditation – Yoga – Self-discipline – Value of abandoning social obligations **FOLK RELIGIONS** Nature spirits – Gods and goddesses – Divination – Rites for the dead	→	**BUDDHISM** • Emphasis on working on one's own mind • Karma determines rebirth • Ultimate truth is beyond words and expression • Meditation is key method: but Buddhism develops the method further • Self-discipline in everyday life, but moderation is encouraged • Monasticism reflects value of giving up social obligations • Buddhist monasticism is radically new: creation of communities • Tolerance of folk beliefs and rituals • Elaborate development of rites for the dead • Doctrine of no God and no soul

It is important to note that although the Buddha rejected many of the social and political values of his day (class, hierarchy and so on) he never took up a political position, nor did he advocate political opposition. He never sought confrontation. On the contrary, the Buddhist approach is to respect the laws of the country where one lives, and if any laws are considered wrong then one may oppose them non-violently.

Buddhism, Hinduism and Jainism

Buddhism shares a significant amount of common ground with the other two major religions of India, Hinduism and Jainism. Together, these three religions are the basis of Indian thought and Indian religion.

- All three value the principle of non-violence, *ahimsa,* the concern not to harm others or to take life.
- All three believe that we live again and again, and that our moral actions determine the outcome of each after-life.
- All three characterize life as one of suffering due to ignorance, and identify the goal of religion as liberation or emancipation from suffering and ignorance. Knowledge and wisdom therefore play an important part in the liberation process.
- All three religions have their own reasons for teaching tolerance of other religious beliefs and philosophies.

The common ground shared by Indian religions is clearly very different from that shared by Judaism, Christianity and Islam. If we are aware that the basic way of thinking in Indian religion is different and unfamiliar, we may be able to question the assumptions we have about religion in general, since current ideas in Western philosophy of religion are based on Judaism and Christianity. In his book *Being Different,* the Indian philosopher Rajiv Malhotra provides an illuminating comparison between Indian thinking and Western thinking that can help us understand the differences.

Personal reflection

Do you see parallels between the social and religious changes of the Buddha's time, and the world situation today?

Main points

- The Buddha lived in India during the Axial Age, a period of intellectual and religious change between 800 and 200 BCE.
- This age was a turning point in human civilisation. Religion became more personal, with more emphasis on morality and the after-life.
- The Aryans from central Asia peacefully introduced their Vedic culture to India from 1500 to 500 BCE.
- Vedic religion, based on scriptures called the Vedas, emphasised animal sacrifice to nature gods.
- Economic prosperity and urban development caused people in the Buddha's time to question Vedic values and to look for a religion that was more adapted to the times.
- India's three native religions emerged during this period: Hinduism, Buddhism and Jainism.
- The Buddha rejected some of the ideas of his time and adopted others while re-interpreting their meaning.

Chapter 2

GAUTAMA THE BUDDHA

This chapter presents the traditional accounts of the Buddha's life and some of the ways contemporary scholars evaluate those accounts. Buddhists are not concerned about the historical accuracy of the Buddha's life story; the main point for them is to learn from the events described and to apply the lessons to their own lives.

He is the conqueror who can never be conquered.
Dhammapada 179

The Ten Acts of the Buddha

The Buddha lived in northern India about 2,500 years ago. Scholars disagree about the exact dates of his life. It is generally acknowledged that he lived at some time between the sixth and fourth centuries BCE and the dates most commonly accepted are **563-483 BCE.**

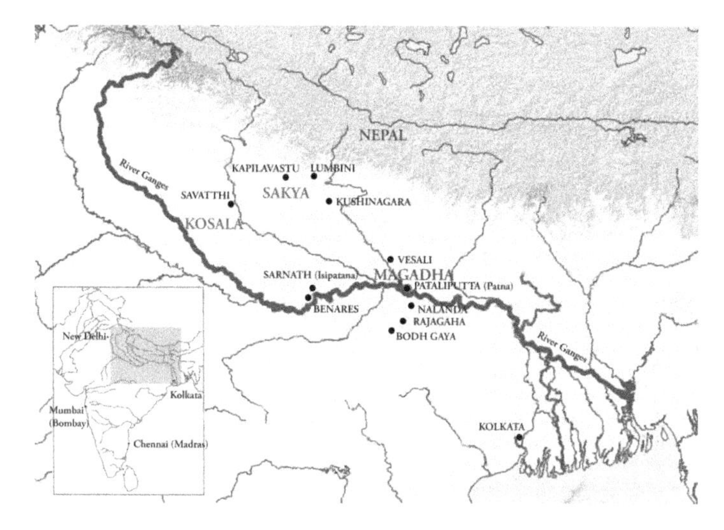

Figure 2.1 – Northern India in the time of the Buddha

The Buddha lived between the foothills of the Himalayan mountains to the north and the **Ganges River** basin to the south. He was born in **Lumbini,** in present-day Nepal, spent his childhood in **Kapilavastu** and attained enlightenment in present-day **Bodh Gaya.** He gave his first teaching in the Deer Park in **Sarnath,** where he spoke of the Four Noble Truths, and devoted the last forty-five years of his life to teaching people as he wandered through the villages and towns of the Ganges basin. He passed away in **Kusinagara.** (see map) The geographical area related to the Buddha's life is therefore relatively small and during his lifetime it is thought that his influence would have been quite localised.

Biographies of the Buddha only appeared many centuries after his death and by that time the story had become very elaborate and dramatised for the purpose of public story telling. The oldest sources of information about his life are found in the Buddhist scriptures called the **Pali Canon**, but there his life is not recounted chronologically and has to be pieced together. As a result, Buddhists have developed a narrative framework for the Buddha's lifestory so it is commonly recounted in terms of Ten Acts. A framework like this is useful for remembering the main points of his life. The value of the Buddha's life story for Buddhists stems from the fact that he was a human being like we are and therefore set an example that we can follow. From the academic point of view, however, his life story is a blend of historical events and legend and is problematic because it is so difficult to tell fact from fiction.

1. Conception

According to Buddhist tradition, the Buddha was born to Queen Mahamaya, wife of King Suddhodana who was leader of the clan of the Shakyas. Before he took birth as a human being he resided in the Tushita Heaven, or Heaven of the Contented, a pure non-physical dimension that is one of the many heavens included in the Buddhist view of the universe.

The Buddha's conception and birth are said to have been marked by miraculous events. As soon as his mind descended from that heavenly existence into his mother's womb, it is said that a tremendous light appeared in the world, and the event was marked by earthquakes. The queen dreamed that a splendid white elephant came down from the sky and entered her body. This is symbolic: the colour white represents purity, and the elephant represents supreme power and majesty. Her dream was later interpreted to mean that her son would be either a great king or a great religious teacher. There is no indication that this was a virgin birth. During her pregnancy the queen was naturally virtuous and felt no physical pain. Her pregnancy is said to have lasted ten months but these are lunar months, so they are equivalent to nine months in the modern calendar.

2. Physical birth

According to the custom at that time, women returned to their parents' home to give birth, so it was arranged for Queen Mahamaya to travel to the neighbouring kingdom of Koliya where her father was the king. On the way she and her party passed by a garden called Lumbini Park where the Queen ordered a halt. It was intended to be only a brief rest but as she relaxed in the shade of a tree she gave birth to her son.

The story of the Buddha's birth is very striking. It is said that Queen Mahamaya gave birth standing up, leaning gracefully against a Sala tree. The baby emerged not from her womb but from under her right armpit, with no blood or birth waters of any kind. Miraculously, two jets of water appeared from the sky, one cool and one warm, for bathing the buddha and his mother. And the earth trembled to mark the event.

As soon as he was born, the Buddha was able to stand up and took several steps in each of the four directions of the compass. This is seen as symbolising that his teachings would spread in all directions. At the same time, he declared that this would be his last birth and he was free from rebirth as a human being.

The child was named Siddhartha, meaning 'fulfilment of wishes'. One of the first visitors to the palace after his birth was a sage called Asita who was reputed for his wisdom and powers of clairvoyance. Asita predicted that the child would be out of the ordinary and could become either a great king or a spiritual leader. But since King Suddhodana hoped his son would be heir to the throne, he deliberately shielded the child from anything that might trigger his spiritual yearnings.

Figure 2.2 – Names of the Buddha

The Buddha has various names.

- **Siddhartha** is the name given to him at birth, meaning 'fulfilment of wishes'.
- **Gautama** (or **Gotama**) is his family name.
- **Shakyamuni** means 'sage of the Shakyas', a clan in northern India. He is called Buddha Shakyamuni to distinguish him from other buddhas.
- **The Buddha** is a title meaning 'the enlightened one' and in the Nikaya traditions is used only when referring to him after his enlightenment.

3. Accomplishment in worldly skills

The culture of India at that time was advanced and sophisticated. As a child the Buddha was educated along with children of other noble families. He excelled at everything he did. He was proficient in sports like wrestling and archery, and was schooled in mathematics, languages, music and so forth. He grew up to be tall, strong and handsome, and his good manners and kindness endeared him to everyone.

When he was seven, his father took him to the annual ploughing festival, and as he was only a child he was allowed to watch and rest under a rose-apple tree. As he was seated there his mind naturally fell into meditation and he attained an advanced mental state quite effortlessly. This was the first mystical experience recorded in his life. Time had stood still for him, and as if to illustrate this it is said that the shadow of the rose-apple tree had not moved from the time the attendants left him there to the time they came to collect him.

4. His youth: a life of pleasure and indulgence

All possible luxuries and comforts were provided for Siddhartha to ensure that he would be satisfied with his life as a prince. Three palaces were built for him, one for each season of the year (the hot season, the rains and the winter). He was surrounded with beautiful parks and gardens, music, attractive attendants and so on. He married the beautiful Yasodhara with much ceremony and rejoicing, and they gave birth to a baby boy named Rahula. The king thought that everything would turn out as he hoped.

5. *Leaving the palace*

But Siddhartha grew bored and restless. The story goes that one day he summoned his charioteer, Channa, to take him for a drive outside the palace grounds – apparently this was the first time he had ventured beyond the palace gates. On his first trip he came across a tired old man by the roadside with no teeth, white hair, bleary eyes and legs so weak he needed a stick. The sight astonished him and he asked Channa what it could be. Channa explained that old age comes to us all. Siddhartha was so upset he turned round and returned to the palace.

He made three other trips out of the palace. On the second trip he saw an ill person writhing with pain, his eyes bloodshot. Siddhartha was filled with compassion. On the third trip, he came across a funeral procession with mourners carrying a corpse to the river for its last rites. Siddhartha was stunned to realize that youth is not indefinite and every single one of us must die. Finally, on his fourth trip, he met a man with a shaven head, barefoot and wearing a simple robe, sitting quietly in meditation. He was an ascetic. There is a tradition in India – which still continues today – whereby some men choose to leave their life in society and take up a lifestyle of hardship and simplicity, staying in forests or on the roadside and begging for their food, as a way of seeking freedom from suffering. They are called *shramanas* or ascetics.

These four experiences were transformative and mark a turning point in the Buddha's life. They are known as the Four Signs or the Four Sights: old age, illness, death and the religious life. The experience of encountering them led him to decide to leave the palace and look for a solution to human suffering and this quest is what motivated the rest of his life.

It is unlikely that the Buddha actually witnessed the Four Signs in this literal way. This dramatisation of the story seems to have been a later embellishment of the narrative. It is hard to believe that he would have been as naïve as the story portrays him. It may be more useful to read this episode as his process of disenchantment with pleasure and luxury, and his growing realization that complacency cuts one off from the nature and meaning of life. He felt the need to explore life for himself.

Similarly, some people in modern societies can lead very sheltered childhoods, with their parents shielding them from the harsh realities of life. And even though we can be surrounded by images of poverty, old age, illness, death and other forms of suffering, they do not always touch our hearts or arouse our sympathy. And yet there are other times when human suffering suddenly becomes very real and can change our whole outlook on life, as when someone close to us is seriously ill or dies. The Four Signs can be understood as a moment when Siddhartha had a personal realization of the immensity of human suffering.

6. Life as an ascetic

Siddhartha renounced family life and left his palace at the age of 29. Tradition has it that he left at night in secret to avoid his family's pleas for him to stay. He spent the following six years as an ascetic. He followed a number of teachers in the forest and learned yoga and meditation from them. In addition, he practised mortification of the body: he fasted, for example, he held his breath for long periods until his head would seem to burst; he stayed out in the burning sun in summer and bathed in icy water in winter. He would stand on one leg for long periods or would squat for days without sitting down.

Long afterwards, the Buddha told his disciples that he learned a great deal from this experience. In particular, it developed his discipline and will power. However, in the end, he did not find the answers he was looking for and his mind grew weak from lack of food. One day a girl named Sujata found him in the forest and took pity on him. She offered him a bowl of milk rice which immediately restored his strength. After this Siddhartha abandoned asceticism and, remembering his childhood experience under the rose-apple tree, realized that only meditation could lead him to enlightenment.

This episode of the Buddha's life is taken to mean that extreme attitudes are unhelpful. Even if our goal is freedom, truth and happiness, if we try too hard to achieve it this can be counter-productive. Extremes of puritanism or austerity do not bring us closer to our goal – and neither do the other extremes of indulgence and hedonism. At this point in his life, Siddhartha discovered that a balanced approach is best.

7. Victory over Mara

Siddhartha then chose to sit under a large fig tree to meditate. At first he was confronted by worldly temptations depicted in the form of the demon Mara – a religious experience similar to the temptations of Jesus in the wilderness.

Mara symbolises the forces of desire and death. Mara is a deity who became powerful through previous good works, but who uses his power to entrap people in sensual desire and attachment so they stay within his realm of influence.

Mara wanted to prevent Siddhartha's enlightenment because it would make him free of death's clutches. According to the Mahayana account in the *Lalitavistara Sutra,* he began by sending his own sons to arouse anger in Siddhartha. The sons, dressed as warriors, approached menacingly and released their arrows to kill him, but Siddhartha remained unmoved and as the arrows came near they turned into flowers. Next, Mara sent his daughters to try to seduce Siddhartha. Some were fat, some were thin, some were young and others were old so Mara was confident that there was at least one the Buddha would find attractive. But the Buddha had overcome lustful desire so once again he remained unmoved, and the daughters eventually slunk away. Mara then tempted the Buddha's pride by offering him the whole of his kingdom provided he abandoned his quest for enlightenment, but the Buddha refused. He had overcome all hope for fame and glory so Mara's offer failed to tempt him.

Finally, Mara taunted the Buddha with the warning that nobody would ever believe him when he announced to the world that he had attained enlightenment. In response, the Buddha touched the earth with his right hand and called the earth goddess as his witness, whereupon the earth quaked in reply. Mara finally gave up and fled.

This story is a dramatisation of one of the Buddha's main religious experiences. It taught him that, before one can attain one's religious goal, it is necessary to overcome all desire, aggression, pride and other harmful emotions. The event is commemorated by many images and paintings, particularly by statues of Gautama cross-legged in meditation with his right hand touching the earth. This episode can be seen as victory over evil, but evil in Buddhism is not primarily an external force; rather it is the power of our own negative emotions.

8. Enlightenment

Siddhartha then experienced various stages of joy and ecstasy known in Pali as the four *jhanas* (or *dhyanas* in Sanskrit) of meditation. Gradually deepening his state of concentrated calm he reached the fourth *jhana*, a state of great even-mindedness, mental brightness and purity. Based on this state, at each of the three watches of the night he had three distinct insights in his meditation known together as the 'threefold knowledge': these insights are crucial, because they are the foundation of all his teachings.

- First, he saw countless numbers of his own previous lives: who he had been, his name, where he had lived, and so forth.
- Second, he understood the birth and death of all beings in the universe, and what causes them to be reborn into different situations.
- Third, he attained omniscience, the all-knowing quality of enlightenment. This means that he understood the true nature of all things.

The Buddha is sometimes depicted with his right hand touching the earth symbolising his victory over Mara. Photo: Seth Dye

With the third insight, at dawn, the Buddha attained enlightenment at the age of 35. This extraordinary event was marked by miracles: the earth shook and streams of flowers fell from the sky. Mahayana scriptures elaborate further and say that the gods rained down parasols, flower earrings, pearl necklaces, and garlands of moons and half-moons; and all the gods gathered together in the sky to praise the Buddha.

According to the Theravada tradition, the Buddha expressed his joy at liberation silently to himself in the following words:

> *I have gone round in vain the cycles of many lives, ever striving to find the builder of the house of life and death. How great is the sorrow of life that must die! But now I have seen you, housebuilder: never more shall you build this house. The rafters of sins are broken, the ridge-pole of ignorance is destroyed. The fever of craving is past: for my mortal mind is gone to the joy of the immortal nirvana.*[1]

By attaining enlightenment, the Buddha destroyed the 'house' of the ordinary mind, the structure and components of the ignorant self that wanders endlessly from life to life. He also exclaimed:

Victory is mine, knowledge is mine, and all purity, all surrender.
I want nothing. I am free. I found my way. Whom shall I call Teacher?[2]

According to the Mahayana tradition, the Buddha described enlightenment in terms of the nature of the mind, and spoke these words upon his enlightenment:

Profound and peaceful, free from complexity, uncompounded luminosity
I have found a nectar-like Dharma.
Yet if I were to teach it, no-one would understand,
So I shall remain silent here in the forest.[3]

The Sanskrit word for enlightenment is *bodhi* which means 'awakening', and someone who attains spiritual awakening is called a '*buddha*'. To become enlightened means to wake up from the sleep of ignorance, from all the misconceptions we have about ourselves and the world. An enlightened being understands things as they truly are. Enlightenment takes us beyond human limitations into a dimension that transcends such things as space and time. The unique feature of the Buddha's message is that such a transcendental state is achievable for human beings during their lifetimes and not only after death.

9. Spreading the teaching

At first, the Buddha remained silent in the forest because he thought nobody would be able to understand what enlightenment is. But the gods persuaded him that some people would be mature enough to hear his words, so he began to teach. The Buddha spent his last 45 years wandering throughout northeast India explaining how we can all attain enlightenment just as he did. He taught kings and poor people, men and women, old and young. Some of his disciples became monks and nuns, and others remained householders. On some occasions he drew audiences of several thousand people, a large number at that time. Even so, the Buddha's followers were a minority in the region, and lived alongside practitioners of India's other religions.

Westerners often judge the Buddha harshly for the way he abandoned his wife and son in pursuit of his religious goal. They think this is selfish and surely not an example for all to follow. The scriptures tell us, however, that during the period when the Buddha was teaching he went back to the region where he lived as a child and gave public teachings there. As a result, both his aunt and his son became monastics. Even the Buddha's father became reconciled to his son's life and respected him as a religious teacher.

All the Buddha's teachings were given during this period, and the scriptures were compiled on the basis of these teachings. During his lifetime, however, none of the Buddha's teachings were written down because writing was not common at that time.

10. Death or passing away

The Buddha was unwell for several months before he died, but he continued to wander on foot and teach. On his deathbed, in Kusinagara, he asked his monks whether they had any final questions for him. They remained silent. He then encouraged them not to hold back out of respect for him, but to ask any questions on their minds. Still they remained silent. He then spoke his last words: "All conditioned things are subject to decay. Attain perfection through diligence." His death was a final teaching on impermanence: all things come to an end, and one can never be complacent.

The Buddha passed away at the age of 80 as a result of eating tainted food. Recent research has indicated that the Buddha probably suffered from a stomach complaint for several years before he died and finally succombed after eating a dish of either pork or mushrooms. According to Theravada Buddhism, he passed into each of the *jhanas* of meditation one by one, then into the four 'formless' mystical states, and then into 'cessation of cognition and feeling'. He then gradually descended back into the first *jhana*, then back to the fourth, and attained *parinirvana* from there. For Buddhists he did not die in the ordinary sense, rather he attained the supreme nirvana *(parinirvana)* which is deathless.

He passed away lying on his right side, with his right hand under his head. In Sri Lanka there are many statues of the Buddha in this pose; they are used as reminders of the inevitability of impermanence and death.

His body was cremated. Some of his bones and teeth did not burn, and these were kept as sacred relics and placed inside eight stupas specially built to house them. These stupas became places of pilgrimage.

The Buddha did not appoint a successor. He told his followers that his legacy to them was his teachings, the Dharma, and this was the guide they should follow.

Figure 2.3 – Stupas are sacred monuments, housing the relics of the Buddha or a Buddhist saint, or copies of the scriptures. These are placed in the centre and become inaccessible because there is no door. Pilgrims walk round and round a stupa reciting prayers. Each country in Asia developed its own artistic style for building stupas. The stupa is an example of sacred architecture and symbolises the enlightened mind.

The stories of Angulimala, Sunita and Devadatta

There are several things we can learn from the stories about the Buddha's life as a teacher. First, they show us how the Buddha related to other people, how he got his message across, and how he was seen by others. Second, they contain elements of his teachings and illustrate his values and his understanding of life. Third, they tell us about the social context in which the Buddha lived: about the beliefs and prejudices of his day, and about the way the community of his followers developed. The following stories offer examples of conversion, the workings of karma, non-violence, and of the Buddha's rejection of certain social values of his time.

Angulimala

One day the Buddha found the village of Savatthi deserted. People were terrified because Angulimala, a mass-murderer, was in those parts. He had cut off a finger from each of his victims and wore 99 fingers around his neck – hence his name which means 'necklace of fingers' (some accounts claim that he wore 999 fingers in his necklace). Despite this the Buddha walked along the road as usual, and suddenly heard the sound of footsteps behind him.

Angulimala shouted out to him, "Stop, monk, stop!" The Buddha continued walking. When Angulimala had caught up with him he said, "I told you to stop, monk. Why don't you stop?"

"I stopped a long time ago. It is you who have not stopped," replied the Buddha.

Angulimala was startled by the Buddha's reply. He blocked his path and forced him to stop. The Buddha looked him straight in the eye like a friend or a brother. Angulimala had never met anyone who radiated such serenity and ease, and who did not run away from him in terror. His curiosity was aroused: why did this monk feel no fear? And what did he mean about stopping and not stopping?

The two men entered into conversation. The Buddha explained that what he had learned to do was to stop harming and causing suffering to others. Everyone is afraid of dying; the duty of a monk is to protect life, not destroy it. But Angulimala was cynical. "Human beings don't love each other. They are cruel and deceptive. Why should I love other people?"

"There may be cruel people in this world, but there are also many kind people. My path can transform cruelty into kindness," said the Buddha. "Right now you are on the path of hatred, but it is up to you: you can choose the path of love and forgiveness instead." Angulimala was thrown into confusion, but he could sense that the Buddha spoke from love and was worthy of respect. "It is a great pity I did not meet you sooner," he said. "I have gone too far, I can't turn back."

"No," urged the Buddha, "it is never too late."

Their discussion continued for some time, and in the end Angulimala knelt before the Buddha, vowed to change his evil ways and to follow him. He was ordained as a monk and tried very hard to practise meditation correctly and lead a disciplined life. Even the Buddha was amazed at the speed of his transformation. Just two weeks after becoming a monk he radiated serenity and stability and the other monks nicknamed him 'Ahimsaka' which means 'non-violent one'.[4]

Sunita

The Indian social order was based on a hierarchy of four classes: priests, warriors/kings, farmers and servants. 'Untouchables' were the lowest class of servant and were so-called because they were considered physically and morally tainted.

Sunita was just such a homeless 'untouchable' who survived by sweeping the streets. It was the custom for low-caste people like him to stand at a distance from anyone of high caste who might approach.

One day, as he was busy sweeping the road, he saw the Buddha approaching with a group of monks. He looked in vain for a place to hide from them, but the best he could do was to flatten himself against a wall and fold his hands in a gesture of respect. To his dismay the Buddha came straight up to him, and far from being angry, as Sunita had expected, he spoke in a friendly way. He asked Sunita whether he would like to give up his job as a sweeper and follow him instead.

Sunita was astonished and delighted. He was used to being ordered about. Nobody had ever spoken to him in a kind and respectful way before. He jumped at the chance and the Buddha ordained him there and then. In time, he became a respected and educated monk.

Devadatta

Devadatta was the Buddha's jealous cousin. They grew up together as children, and as an adult Devadatta became a monk and follower of the Buddha. But Devadatta was the archetypal troublemaker: he orchestrated three assassination attempts against the Buddha and also tried to create a split within the Buddhist community. In the long term, he failed. The stories about his adventures show that, for all the Buddha's greatness, he did not succeed in converting everyone around him. They also illustrate the Buddha's non-violent approach to solving problems.

Devadatta tried to kill the Buddha on three separate occasions. First, he hired assassins to kill him, but they were moved by the Buddha's persuasiveness and became converts instead. Second, Devadatta climbed to the top of a mountain called Vulture Peak and hurled a rock down on the Buddha as he was passing below. The rock narrowly missed him and wounded him slightly. Finally, Devadatta sent a wild elephant to attack him. The elephant charged down the road towards the Buddha, but as it neared him it unexpectedly slowed down and became quite tame. The Buddha used the power of love to subdue it.

Towards the end of his life, having failed to create a rival break-away group and after a long illness, Devadatta finally repented his behaviour and had himself carried on a litter into the Buddha's presence. He cried out, "I seek Refuge in the Buddha" and was received back into the community. The Buddha prophesied that he would eventually attain enlightenment.

Critical Evaluation

Modern academic scholarship makes a point of looking critically at these traditional accounts of the Buddha's life. As we have already seen, not all episodes need to be accepted literally even though they can still be seen as meaningful. The difficulty is knowing where to draw the line between legend and historical fact and it will probably never be known exactly what is fact and what is embellishment.

Among the points which scholars dispute is the question of whether Siddhartha was brought up in a kingdom or in a republic. There is no evidence to show that Shakya was a kingdom and many scholars now believe that it was a democratic republic relatively uninfluenced by the hierarchical values of the Brahmin priesthood (see Chapter 1). Buddhist writers may have felt it brought more prestige to say that the Buddha was a prince.

> *Everything in the scriptures has passed through several stages of transmission, and whatever the period of the actual discourses, the legends by which they are accompanied are in no case contemporary. Some of the scriptural legends, such as the descent from heaven, and the miracles of the birth and death, are just those which show most clearly the growth of apocryphal additions, as well as the development of a dogmatic system of belief about the person and function of Buddha. Another development is that which makes Buddha the son of a king, and the descendant of a line of ancestors going back to the first king of the present cycle... The only firm ground from which we can start is not history, but the fact that a legend in a definite form existed in the first and second centuries after the Buddha's death.*
>
> Edward J. Thomas, *The Life of Buddha*

Buddhists themselves are not troubled about the possibility of historical inaccuracies in the account; they feel that the point of the Buddha's life story is to learn lessons from it. As Karen Armstrong notes, "the people of North India were not interested in history in our sense: they were more concerned about the meaning of historical events."[5] Indeed, this perspective is not unique to Buddhism. Traditionally, Indians were never much concerned with historicity and, unlike the ancient Chinese, are not known to have kept systematic chronological records in early times. Modern interest in historical evidence is especially characteristic of Western culture and is not shared by the Buddhist tradition.[6]

How Buddhists see the Buddha

The significance of the Buddha for Buddhists is quite different from that of Jesus for Christians, or Mohammed for Muslims. Paul Williams explains:

> *The Buddha is thought by Buddhists to be one who has awakened fully to the final truth of things, and thus freed, liberated, himself once and for all from all form of suffering. He is also one who, out of supreme compassion, has taught others the way to attain liberation themselves. Buddhas are not born that way, and they are certainly not thought to be eternal gods (or God). Once (many lifetimes ago) they were just like you and me. They strove through their own efforts and became Buddhas. A Buddha is superior to the rest of us because he 'knows it as it is'. We, on the other hand, wallow in confusion, in ignorance. Thus we are unhappy and suffer.* [7]

Paul Williams makes the point that it is only convention that leads any book on Buddhism to begin with the life story of the Buddha. If it were necessary to begin that way, it would imply that the story of the Buddha's life is a crucial preliminary for understanding what follows. In some other religions it would indeed be the case that the story of their respective founders is an essential starting point, but this is not the case for Buddhism for the reasons set out below.

Was the Buddha the founder of a new religious teaching?

Buddhists do not consider that the Buddhist teachings were invented by Shakyamuni Buddha. Richard Gombrich presents the Buddhist view:

> *Outsiders see him as the founder of Buddhism; for Buddhists the matter is slightly more complicated. As they see it, the Truth is eternal, but not always realized. Time has no beginning or end but goes through vast cycles. Every now and again there arises in the world a religious genius, a Buddha, who has the infinite wisdom to comprehend the Truth and the infinite compassion to preach it to the suffering world, so that others too may attain Enlightenment. Gotama [Gautama Skt.] is the most recent teacher in the infinite series of Buddhas.*

The Dharma is considered an eternal truth that does not belong to anyone in particular. However, if we refer to Buddhism not as a teaching but as a historical development, then it is fair to say that the Buddha was the founder of the religion that began in India.

Buddha Shakyamuni is not the only buddha

The historical Buddha whose life we have described is one of many different buddhas who have come, and will come, to teach here on Earth. According to some Buddhist traditions there have been countless buddhas in aeons prior to our current human history, and there will be many more in the future. Some accounts say there will be 1,002 buddhas in this age. The next buddha will be called Maitreya, 'one who embodies loving kindness'. Like Shakyamuni before him, he currently resides in Tushita Heaven until the time comes for him to be born a human being.

Is the Buddha human or supernatural?

The Buddha declared he was neither divine nor a prophet yet his life story contains many instances of extraordinary powers and events. For Buddhists, these illustrate the qualities and powers that come from enlightenment or from being very close to enlightenment. They are powers that can be developed by anyone who becomes fully awakened.

The Buddha in the Mahayana tradition

There are a number of differences in the way the Buddha is understood in Nikaya and Mahayana, the two great traditions of Buddhism (see chapter 7). Most Mahayana accounts list twelve Acts of the Buddha, not ten. The extra two Acts are listed as the first and second and pertain to the idea that he was already enlightened before he took birth and was dwelling in the Tushita Heaven. During his human life he went through the motions of becoming enlightened, as it were, in order to show us the way.

1. Dwelling in the Tushita Heaven

According to the Buddhist view of the universe, the Tushita Heaven, or Heaven of the Contented, is a pure celestial realm inhabited by gods and bodhisattvas (advanced followers of the Mahayana path). It is from this realm that all buddhas take birth as humans. Having perfected selfless actions in his previous lives, the being who would become Buddha Shakyamuni took birth as a bodhisattva in the Tushita Heaven where he taught the Dharma to the gods. When the time was right, he resolved to take birth as a human being to teach the Dharma in the human world, and thus determined his birth in the Shakya clan in northern India.

2. Descent from the Tushita Heaven

When the time had come for the bodhisattva to take birth as a human, he gave his final teaching to the gods of the Tushita Heaven and placed his jewelled crown upon the head of the bodhisattva Maitreya. He appointed Maitreya to replace him as the main teacher in the Tushita Heaven and predicted that Maitreya would become the next perfectly enlightened buddha to take birth in the human world.

Another difference with the Nikaya view is the Mahayana principle of 'buddha nature' which is key to its understanding of the Buddha and of how human beings relate to the Buddha. The significance of the Buddha's life stems from the fact that he was a human being like ourselves, and we can therefore follow in his footsteps. His life story makes us realize that it is possible for us, too, to find liberation from suffering. It may take many lives but it *is* possible; indeed, it also took many lives for the Buddha himself to reach the point when he became a fully enlightened buddha. The important thing is that there is no unbridgeable gap between the Buddha and ourselves, and to this we can attribute the warm and relaxed spirit of Buddhism.

Mahayana Buddhism develops this point through the theory of 'buddha nature' or *tathagatagarbha,* the potential or seed for enlightenment that exists within every single being, both human and non-human. Just as we can never squeeze oil out of an ordinary stone, in the same way we would never be able to become enlightened if it were not for the fact that we have the seed of enlightenment within us already, and under the right conditions that seed can blossom into full buddhahood. That seed, or potential, is called buddha nature. This is a deeper way of understanding that there is no radical separation between the Buddha and ourselves.

Further points concerning the Mahayana understanding of the three *kayas* or 'bodies' of the Buddha are addressed in Chapter 7 on The Three Vehicles.

The life of the Buddha remembered in Buddhist culture

The memory of the Buddha's life is kept alive through an annual calendar of prayer festivals. At these times, the laypeople join with the monks of their local monasteries, and the entire community participates in the celebrations. Each Asian country developed slight variations in terms of the dating of festivals and the events celebrated. In particular, the birth, enlightenment and passing away of the Buddha are often commemorated together on the full moon day in the month of May or June. In Theravada this festival is called Vesak. The Table below summarises the main festivals.[8]

The more important national festivals in Mahayana (M), Theravada (Th) and Tibetan (T) Buddhism

February	15	Nehan-e	(M)	Buddha's passing away
March	Full Moon	Cho Trul Duchen	(T)	Display of miracles
March	21	Higan-e	(M)	Reminder of impermanence
April	8	Hanamatsuri	(M)	Buddha's birth
May	Full Moon	Vesak, Buddha Day	(Th)	Buddha's birth, Enlightenment and passing away
June	Full Moon	Saga Dawa	(T)	Buddha's birth, Enlightenment and passing away
July	Full Moon	Dhammacakka Day	(Th)	First teaching
July	Full Moon	Chor Khor Duchen	(T)	First teaching
September	21	Higan-e	(M)	Reminder of impermanence
October/ November	Full Moon	Kathina	(Th)	Offerings made to the Sangha
November	Full Moon	Lha Bab Duchen	(T)	The Buddha returns to Earth after teaching the Abhidharma in the Realm of gods to his mother
December	8	Jodo-e	(M)	Buddha's Enlightenment

Point for reflection

What elements of the Buddha's life story do you find useful in the sense that they exemplify principles you could apply to your own life?

Main points

- The most important scriptures with details of the Buddha's life are the Pali Canon in the Nikaya tradition, and the *Lalitavistara Sutra* and *Buddhacarita* in Mahayana Buddhism.

- The Buddha lived in northern India between the 6th and 4th centuries BCE, possibly between 563 and 483 BCE.

- The Ten Acts of the Buddha's life are:
  1. Conception
  2. Physical birth
  3. Accomplishment in worldly skills
  4. His youth: a life of pleasure and indulgence
  5. Leaving the palace
  6. Life as an ascetic
  7. Victory over Mara
  8. Enlightenment
  9. Spreading the teaching
  10. Death or passing away

- The Four Signs or Four Sights that marked a turning point in the Buddha's life are:
  - old age
  - illness
  - death
  - the spiritual life

- The Buddha's life is significant for Buddhists because it is an example they can learn from and follow.

Chapter 3

THE BUDDHA'S DISCIPLES

The lives and personalities of some of the most important disciples of the Buddha, both men and women, illustrate how the transmission of Dharma began.

Introduction

The power of Buddhism stems from the fact that Buddha Shakyamuni's teachings have been transmitted in an unbroken line, from generation to generation, until the present day. The deep personal connection between teachers and disciples over the centuries has ensured that the original meaning of the Buddha's message has not been lost, and that this message is still as vibrant and effective today as it was 2,500 years ago. It should therefore be noted that the development of Buddhism is primarily about the people who upheld its teachings and not about institution building. Buddhism has not developed over-arching hierarchical authority structures; there is no pan-Buddhist 'church'. In every country where Buddhism is practised, each monastery or community is led by its own elders.

The living lineages of Buddhism began with the Buddha's own direct disciples, so it is instructive to read about their lives, qualities and accomplishments. There are many stories and details scattered throughout the scriptures of Theravada Buddhism, as well as accounts in Sanskrit and Tibetan texts, that enable us to piece together biographies of his most important disciples.[9]

In many temples of southeast Asia one will find, on either side of the Buddha image, the statues of two monks. They are the Buddha's two chief disciples: Shariputra on the Buddha's right, and Maudgalyayana on the Buddha's left (Shariputta and Mogallana in Pali). To these two chief disciples one must add Ananda, another important figure who was the Buddha's personal attendant during his last twenty-five years. Although he seems rarely to have enjoyed official recognition according to the Theravada accounts, he nevertheless played a vital role in the history of the teachings.

The Buddha compared the leadership of the sangha to a state's administration. He spoke of Ananda as the treasurer of the Dharma because he could remember all the teachings perfectly and was instrumental in preserving them. He called Shariputra the marshal or general in command, and Maudgalyayana the minister of the interior. The Buddha and Ananda were both from the warrior caste, while Shariputra and Maudgalyayana were from the brahmin caste. These affinities showed in their lives because Ananda followed the Buddha like a shadow and they were always together, while Shariputra and Maudgalyayana had been childhood friends and, as monks, remained inseparable. As the Buddha grew older and more tired, these three disciples were the only ones whom he entrusted with teaching the Dharma on his behalf.

Both Shariputra and Maudgalyayana died a few months before the Buddha's parinirvana so their role is limited to the Buddha's own lifetime. When the great stupa at Sanchi was opened up in the middle of the 20th century, the relic chamber was found to contain two stone receptacles. The one to the north contained the bodily relics of Maudgalyayana, while the one to the south enclosed those of Shariputra. They had lain undisturbed for two and a half thousand years.

The Buddha did not appoint a successor but did entrust a small number of disciples with the future of the Dharma. The Theravada sources name these disciples as Upali and Mahakasyapa. The latter was greatly respected by the sangha as a figure of strength and authority, and he was chosen by the assembly of monks to preside over the First Buddhist Council after the Buddha had passed away. However, Mahayana sources emphasize that Ananda, too, played an important part and, on closer reading, one finds that the Theravada scriptures also mention that Ananda slowly became the chief elder of the sangha, particularly after the Buddha had passed away. He was a monk under the Buddha for forty years, and survived Shakyamuni by a further forty years, thus becoming one of the foremost *arhats* of that era. An arhat is someone who has attained nirvana.

The Buddha had thousands of other disciples who were from all walks of life, both monastic and lay. Amongst his lay disciples were kings such as his friend King Bimbisara and wealthy patrons such as Anathapindika who donated to the sangha the Jetavana monastery in Savasti. The Buddha also ordained many nuns and the scriptures contain details of some of the more remarkable stories of his women disciples.

Shariputra

Shariputra grew up in a village near Rajagaha, in a Brahmin family that was close friends with Maudgalyayana's family in a neighbouring village. The two boys were wealthy and well educated. One day, when they were youths, they both attended an annual festival and both felt disenchanted with the dances and shows, thinking how meaningless they were in the light of death. They both decided to go in search of a path that would free them from suffering and rebirth, and they became ascetics.

They began by studying under Sanjaya who was a sceptic and who taught that knowledge of the ultimate, and of what happens after death, is impossible for human beings. Shariputra and his friend mastered this teaching very quickly and realized that it did not go far enough, so they left to continue their search. They decided to separate so they would double their chances of meeting a true spiritual guide, and whoever found him first would inform the other.

One morning in Rajagaha, Shariputra noticed a monk on his alms round and was instantly struck by his air of dignity and peace. He asked him who his teacher was and what teaching he followed. The monk explained that he followed the Buddha, and summarised his teaching in this way:

Of those things that arise from a cause
The Buddha has explained the cause,
And also what their cessation is;
This is the teaching of the Great Shramana.

Upon hearing these lines, Shariputra realized their truth immediately and knew at once that this was the teaching he had been looking for. Before following the monk to the monastery where the Buddha was staying, he went to collect Maudgalyayana so they could go together. And before joining the Buddha, Shariputra took the initiative of going back with his friend to see Sanjaya and take leave of him respectfully, and also to persuade him to meet the Buddha, too. Sanjaya declined this offer but 250 of his disciples decided to accompany the two friends to see the Buddha.

Very soon the Buddha bestowed on each of them the rank of chief disciple, explaining that this honour was the result of aspirations they had had in many previous lives. He also said that all buddhas throughout the ages each have two chief disciples to support them. A chief disciple has three basic roles: to help the Buddha spread the teachings; to serve as a model for the other monks and supervise their training; and to help administer the sangha, especially when the Buddha is in retreat. The Buddha chose Shariputra for his excellence in wisdom, and one of his main contributions was to clarify and systematize the teachings, whereas he appointed Maudgalyayana on account of his range of spiritual powers which were directed to removing obstacles for the teachings and for the Buddha's followers.

Shariputra had many wonderful human qualities. It is said that he did not go out in the morning on his alms round as the other monks did, but instead remained in the monastery and went around sweeping, cleaning and tidying up wherever he saw a mess. He did this so that visitors would not speak of the monks with contempt. Also, whenever he travelled with the Buddha, he would not walk at the head of the procession to show his importance, but instead he would let young novices take his bowl and robes and go on ahead. He would stay back to attend to the old, the very young or the sick, and would leave later in the day together with them.

The scriptures show that Shariputra embodied a rare combination of keen intelligence and understanding on the one hand, and a warm, sympathetic interest in people on the other hand. He was both perfect teacher and perfect friend, often encouraged others, was tireless in answering their questions, and was quick to see the qualities in others. People would say that he had such great patience that even if someone abused him or hit him, he felt not a trace of anger. His humility was as great as his patience, and he would willingly and gratefully receive correction from anyone.

One of the greatest contributions that Shariputra made to the spread of the teachings was his codification of the Abhidharma (Buddhist philosophy and psychology). It is said that the Buddha first taught the Abhidharma to his deceased mother in the Heaven of the Thirty Three Gods. Each day during that three-month period, he would return briefly to the human realm to collect his alms food, and it was then that he would meet Shariputra and transmit to him the main points of the teachings he had just given. Shariputra continued these teachings, explaining them clearly, putting them in order, and developing numbered lists so that they were easier for the monks to memorise. For this reason, the Theravada tradition claims that the textual order of the points of Abhidharma originated with Shariputra.

In contrast to all the many friends that he made, Shariputra's mother remained a staunch Brahmin all her life and was hostile to the Buddha's teachings. Whenever Shariputra and his companions would go to her house for alms, they were met with verbal abuse. When Shariputra realized that his death would soon arrive, he asked the Buddha permission to die in his home town so that he could see his mother for the last time. The Buddha consented and they parted, and at that moment there was thunder and heavy rain.

Shariputra travelled to the village of Nalaka where his mother prepared the room in which he had been born. As soon as he arrived, Shariputra fell ill with severe pain and dysentery. His mother was worried because the news of his condition was not good, so she stood guard outside his door, leaning up against the wall. At that point the Four Divine Kings realized that one of the Buddha's chief disciples was about to pass away, and each one in turn came to attend to him. His mother was intuitive and she could see the coming and going of all these deities and wondered why they were paying homage to her son. She went into the room and asked Shariputra what was going on. He told her that the Divine Kings—who are all revered by Hindu brahmins—were attendants and protectors of the Buddha. She was impressed, both at the way they honoured her son and at what this must mean for the power of the Buddha himself. Rapture and joy arose in her, so Shariputra took the opportunity to say a few words of Dharma to her. She was converted immediately and, having finished his business in this life, Shariputra passed into nirvana. Some 250 years later, the Indian emperor Ashoka erected a memorial in Nalanda to commemorate the spot as the birthplace of Shariputra. After Ashoka, Nalanda became the site of one of the most famous Buddhist universities of ancient India.

Maudgalyayana

The childhood of Maudgalyayana (Mogallana in Pali) is inextricably linked with that of Shariputra. After the two friends reached the Buddha and received their first teaching from him, they each went into retreat to meditate. Shariputra took only a fortnight to eliminate all his defilements and become an *arhat*. By contrast, Maudgalyayana found the process very difficult. He tried to meditate but found that he fell asleep. Seeing this, the Buddha came to his aid and appeared in front of him through his psychic power. He taught him the methods to overcome drowsiness: focusing on the perception of light, walking up and down, arousing an inner vision of light, and if necessary, physical rest.

By applying these methods Maudgalyayana succeeded in overcoming his sleepiness, but then he found his mind was restless and prone to worry.

The Buddha again gave him advice, and after an intensive inner struggle Maudgalyayana became an *arhat* in only a week. In the end he achieved his goal quicker than Shariputra but only succeeded with the help of the Buddha, whereas Shariputra's progress had been smooth and unaided.

The Buddha once compared Shariputra to a mother and Maudgyalayana to a nurse. Shariputra was good at inspiring people to renounce the worldly life and start on the spiritual path, and once they were in the community Maudgalyayana's strength was to support them and nourish them on the rest of their path. The scriptures recount many stories about the way the two chief disciples worked in tandem. For example, they joined forces to induce the monks that had been led away by Devadatta to rejoin the Buddha's sangha. They would often share a cell in the monastery and would spend time together answering questions from the monks.

Maudgalyayana was known for the range and effectiveness of his psychic powers. Although the Buddha always stressed that such powers are neither requirements for, nor indications of, liberation many of his disciples did develop powers as secondary effects of their meditation practice. What distinguished Maudgalyayana from the others was the sheer range of his powers, for he had mastery of them all. There are six powers which are usually called the six 'superknowledges' in English; the first five are worldly and the sixth is transcendental. The first five are: mastery of psychic power, clairaudience, knowing the minds of others, recollection of past lives, clairvoyance, and understanding the death and rebirth of beings. The sixth is the knowledge that comes when all mental defilements are eliminated.

Through his clairaudience, Maudgalyayana was able to hear teachings from the Buddha even when the Buddha was physically very far away. He could also hear the voices of non-human beings and, for instance, was warned by a spirit that Devadatta would turn against the Buddha. His clairvoyance enabled him to see how the law of karma applied to particular individuals, and he often reported what he saw as examples of how karma works. Maudgalyayana was able to depart physically from the human realm and reappear in a celestial realm, and he used this ability for astral travel to teach the gods in the heavens. In addition, he had mastery over solid matter. On one occasion the Buddha saw that the monks in a particular monastery were becoming lazy and undisciplined, he therefore asked Maudgalyayana to use his supernormal powers to shake them up so they returned to their discipline. In response, Maudgalyayana pushed the building with his big toe and the entire monastery shook and trembled as if there were an earthquake. It had the desired effect.

Maudgalyayana passed away two weeks after Shariputra, and both died at the age of 84. But the death of Maudgalyayana was very different from that of the Buddha or his other main disciples because he suffered a violent end. The problem stemmed from a time when Maudgalyayana had reported on his travels in the celestial realms, where he had seen that the Buddha's followers had good rebirths whereas the followers of other ascetic teachers suffered in miserable, subhuman existences. On hearing this a certain group of ascetics was enraged at Maudgalyayana, and they blamed him for the massive number of people who had switched from their sect to the community of the Buddha's followers. They were determined to kill him.

While they were slightly hesitant about killing Maudgalyayana with their own hands, they had no qualms about paying a band of brigands to do their dirty work for them. At that time Maudgalyayana was staying alone in the forest. When he saw the brigands approaching he knew they wanted to kill him, so he used his powers to slip through the keyhole and the gangsters arrived at an empty hut. They searched everywhere but could not find him. They returned the next day, and this time he rose into the air and escaped through the roof. It is explained that Maudgalyayana did not react through fear of death but to protect his would-be assassins from the karmic consequences of their actions.

The brigands came back several times and eventually their persistence paid off. They entered his hut, knocked him down, and pounded his bones until they were as small as grains of rice. Then, thinking that he was dead, they threw his body behind some bushes and fled. The scriptures explain that his violent death came about as the final karmic result from a previous life when he had killed his own parents. But Maudgalyayana regained consciousness, and by the power of his meditation he soared up, flew through the air and arrived in the presence of the Buddha. He told him that he was about to die; the Buddha asked him to give a final teaching, which he did, and then he passed away.

Mahakasyapa

Mahakasyapa was born into a Brahmin family, and as he grew up his parents repeatedly begged him to marry. He himself would have preferred to become an ascetic but to please his parents he eventually married Bhadda. Fortunately,

Bhadda also wanted to live a spiritual life, so they agreed to remain married and, at the same time, maintain a life of celibacy. After Mahakasyapa's parents died, he and his wife became wandering ascetics and joined the Buddha's sangha. Bhadda was praised by the Buddha as being the nun with the best recollection of past lives. She was responsible for educating the young nuns.

The story of how Mahakasyapa first met the Buddha is a memorable one. When he and his wife separated on the road to find their spiritual teacher, it is said that there was an earthquake and, upon perceiving this, the Buddha knew it meant that an outstanding disciple was on the way to meet him. So the Buddha set out on the road alone and walked five miles in the direction of his future student. He stopped under a tree between Rajagaha and Nalanda, waiting for Mahasakyapa to arrive, and sat in glorious meditation emitting tremendous rays of light. When Mahakasyapa approached he could see his brilliance and immediately fell at his feet and asked to be his disciple. The Buddha accepted him as a monk.

As they walked along the road together towards Rajagaha, the Buddha stopped a while and Mahakasyapa spread out his robe for the Buddha to sit on. The Buddha commented how nice and soft his robe was, so immediately Mahakasyapa offered it to him. The Buddha then gave him his own worn out robe in exchange. This exchange of robes is seen as a great honour because it did not happen with any other disciple.

Seven days after he became a monk Mahakasyapa attained arhathood. He was known to be austere and very disciplined, and always satisfied with whatever food and lodgings he was given. Sometimes he was rather stern with others and, in fact, the scriptures mention that he had only few disciples. His greatest achievement was the power of his meditation, and the Buddha acknowledged that he could attain the highest levels of meditative realization, as well as the six superknowledges, at will, just like the Buddha himself.

Soon after the Buddha had passed away, Mahakasyapa overheard a very troubling conversation between a group of monks. Most of the monks were mourning the fact that the Buddha was no longer with them, but one monk named Subhadda said that he was relieved at the Buddha's death. So often, complained Subhadda, the Buddha had invented rules and regulations just to make life difficult, and now that he was gone the monks could do as they pleased and would not have to do what they didn't want. In response, Mahakasyapa decided to convene the Council of five hundred *arhats* to establish clearly the code of discipline and the sutras, so that there was no confusion as to what the

Buddha had and had not taught. After the Council, Mahakasyapa was treated as the leader of the community.

According to the Sanskrit texts, when he knew he was about to die Mahakasyapa walked to the top of a mountain and sat cross-legged in meditation in a cave. He prayed that his body should remain intact until the future Buddha Maitreya came to Earth because it was to Maitreya that he was to hand over the robe that the Buddha had given him at their first meeting. He then passed away. Soon afterwards Ananda and the king of the region went to the mountain to see Mahakasyapa, and the mountain partly opened to reveal him. Chinese Buddhist tradition locates this mountain in southwest China, and there are many Chinese legends of monks and pilgrims who have caught a glimpse of Mahakasyapa sitting in meditation waiting for Maitreya Buddha. Much later, in China, Mahakasyapa came to be regarded as the first patriarch of Ch'an Buddhism (see Chapter 18).

Ananda

Ananda is quite a unique disciple in many ways. According to tradition, he came to Earth, just like the Buddha, from the Tushita heaven, and was born on the very same day as the Buddha and in the same caste. His father was the brother of King Suddhodana which means the Buddha and Ananda were cousins. When he was 37 years old, Ananda became a monk.

When the Buddha and Ananda were both 55 years old, the Buddha called a meeting and announced that he was looking for a better attendant. He said that his previous attendants had all had a degree of wilfulness, and as he was getting older he needed someone who was completely trustworthy and reliable. All the monks immediately volunteered themselves, but the Buddha did not accept any of them. Then the monks turned to Ananda, who had held back out of modesty, and asked him to volunteer. When he was asked why he had not volunteered before, Ananda replied that the Buddha knew best who his attendant should be. He had so much confidence in the Buddha that it did not occur to him to express his own wishes. Then the Buddha declared that Ananda would be the best choice for the post.

The post of personal attendant could be seen by other monks as a very privileged position, so in order to avoid any jealousy or hatred from his fellow monks, Ananda accepted the role on condition that the Buddha grant him eight favours. These were that the Buddha should never pass on robes to him that had been donated personally to him; that he should never give him alms food that he himself had received; that he would never give Ananda a room that had been offered to him; and he should never include him in any personal invitations for a meal. The other four were formulated in a positive way: if Ananda were invited for a meal, he asked for the right to transfer the invitation to the Buddha; if people came from far away, he asked for the privilege to introduce them to the Buddha; if he had any doubts or questions about the Dharma, he asked for the right to have them cleared up at any time; and if he missed any of the Buddha's teachings, he asked for them to be repeated to him privately. The Buddha accepted all of these requests, and Ananda attended him for 25 years.

What is the job of an attendant? First, Ananda looked after the Buddha's physical wellbeing like a mother or a devoted wife: bringing him water to wash his face and wood to clean his teeth, arranging his seat, washing his feet, massaging his back, fanning him, sweeping his cell and mending his robes. He slept nearby at night and was constantly at hand. When the Buddha was sick he fetched medicine for him. Second, Ananda acted as his personal secretary and was a very important communication link between the Buddha and the rest of the *sangha* (the community of followers). Ananda was especially good at advising on relationship problems, clarifying doubts and negotiating arrangements.

Because of his close and constant connection with the Buddha, Ananda is seen in Mahayana Buddhism as the epitome of devotion. In the way that Ananda always put the needs of others before his own, and to the extent that he became an *arhat* very late in life, he can also be seen as a model *bodhisattva* who dedicated his entire life to the benefit of others.

Ananda was recognized as the disciple who excelled in five qualities of understanding the Dharma: he had heard all of the Buddha's teachings, he had a good memory, he mastered the logical structure of the teachings, he was diligent in his studies and he was personally close to the Buddha. These five qualities explain why Ananda had a special role as guardian of the Dharma. After the Buddha passed away, the assembly of monks requested Ananda to recite all the sutras from memory at the First Council. Every sutra begins "thus have I heard", and these words are Ananda speaking.

He had many personal qualities that endeared him to the community, and he was extremely popular and had no enemies. The Buddha praised him frequently. He said:

> *"His skill in dealing with people is admirable. If a company of monks goes to see Ananda, they become joyful on seeing him; and if he speaks to them on the Dharma, they are made joyful by his discourse; and when he falls silent, they are disappointed. And so it is also with the nuns, the laymen and the laywomen: each assembly taught by Ananda is always overjoyed and everyone wants to listen to him further. Ananda has such remarkable, extraordinary popularity, as one otherwise finds only in a world monarch."* [10]

Ananda was especially appreciated by women, although it must be said that there is no hint of misconduct on his part. He was charged by the Buddha to teach several groups of laywomen who requested the Dharma. It was also Ananda who was instrumental in creating the order of Buddhist nuns. The request for women to be ordained originally came from the Buddha's aunt, Mahapajapati Gotami, who asked the Buddha for this on three occasions and each time her request was refused. She was very upset at this, and one day Ananda found her with swollen feet, covered with dust and her face wet with tears. Out of compassion he decided to intervene and request the Buddha himself, and at last the Buddha gave his consent.

Ananda had been so busy for so many years that, even by the time the Buddha passed away, he had still not reached arhathood. The monks advised him to do retreat in the forest, but day and night even in the forest he found himself consoling the Buddha's disciples about the death of their master, and he was never alone. Finally, the monks gave him an ultimatum: unless he became an *arhat*, he would not be allowed to attend the First Council of elder monks when the scriptures would be established. Ananda applied himself and finally attained arhathood on the morning that the Council was due to open.

Mahakasyapa died soon after the Buddha, and from then on Ananda assumed the role of chief *arhat*. He continued teaching for a further forty years and led about ten thousand monks to the state of *arhat*. There are many accounts of the magical feats he performed to subdue non-Buddhist teachers during this period. Ananda lived so long that some of his direct disciples were making active contributions to the Dharma over a hundred years after the Buddha passed away. His disciple Madhyantika, for example, is credited with introducing Buddhism to Kashmir.

Ananda passed away when he was 120 years old. In order to spare people the trouble of organising his funeral, he summoned his supernatural powers, raised his body in the air and let it catch fire spontaneously. His relics were divided up and placed into stupas.

Women disciples of the Buddha

Just as the Buddha appointed two chief disciples from amongst his monks, he likewise named two women as his foremost disciples amongst the nuns. They were Uppalavanna and Khema, the first excelling in psychic powers and the second in wisdom. The Buddha held both of them up as models for all nuns to follow.

Khema was born into a royal family in Magadha and was extremely beautiful. As soon as she was of marriageable age she became one of the chief consorts of King Bimbisara who was a friend and disciple of the Buddha. Khema herself resisted meeting the Buddha or listening to his teachings because she was afraid that he would find fault with her beauty and preach to her about the vanity of worldly pleasures, to which she was rather attached. But one day the king succeeded in luring her to the place where the Buddha was teaching.

The Buddha had read her thoughts, and through his psychic powers he created the image of a young woman who was even more beautiful than Khema, who stood fanning him. Khema was enthralled. Then the Buddha made the image change gradually from youth to old age, until it had broken teeth, grey hair and wrinkled skin, and finally fell down lifeless. Only then did Khema realize how empty external beauty is, and how death would one day strike her, too. She listened to the Buddha's teaching and understood it immediately, becoming an *arhat* on the spot. With the king's permission she joined the order of nuns.

Khema became famous for her wisdom, deep insight, great learning and sharpness in debate. Through these qualities she made a deep impact on

King Pasenadi of Kosala. He was travelling through the countryside and sent his servant to find someone with whom he could discuss spiritual matters. The servant couldn't find any ascetic or monk who could do this, but people recommended that he approach Khema who was in those parts. So the king went to her, greeted her respectfully and asked her questions about what happens to a buddha after he has passed away. He wanted to know why the Buddha himself had refused to answer questions from others on this subject.

Khema asked the king whether he knew of a mathematician who could calculate the number of grains of sand contained in the River Ganges, and the king replied this was impossible. Then she asked him whether anyone could figure out how many gallons of water there are in the oceans, and the reply was that, too, is impossible. The Buddha is just like this, said Khema. He is deep and hard to fathom like the great ocean. Therefore, it's not appropriate to say whether or not he exists after death; none of the possible answers to this question can succeed in defining the indefinable. The king was satisfied.

The scriptures speak of another female disciple called Samavati who lived as a young girl in a region which was hit by the plague, so she fled to Kosambi with her parents. She would go out to obtain food, and the first day she asked for three portions, the second day for two portions, and the third day for only one portion. Mitta, who was distributing the food, could not resist asking her whether she had at last realized the capacity of her stomach. Very calmly, she told him that the first day her father had died of the plague, the second day her mother had also died of the plague, and now there was only herself. He felt ashamed of his sarcastic remark and offered to adopt her, which she accepted.

Samavati was very capable and she organised the distribution of food very efficiently and harmoniously. Ghosaka, the king's finance minister, heard of this and asked to meet her. He was so impressed with her elegance and dignity that he adopted her as his daughter, and Samavati became heiress to a vast estate and mixed with the highest nobles of the land. One day she was introduced to the king who fell in love with her at first sight. But the minister was very dependent on her and didn't want to let her go. The king was furious at this, sacked him and banned him from the kingdom. Samavati was so sad to see Ghosaka's suffering that out of compassion she accepted to marry the king, who restored Ghosaka to his former position. She thus became the king's third wife.

Samavati had great love for everyone. She always found peace in her own heart, whatever the circumstances, and did not judge others. She used to give one of her servants eight gold coins every day to buy flowers, but the servant kept back some of this money for herself. The servant then discovered the Buddha's teachings and this changed her life; she felt great regret at her stealing, so she went out and spent all that day's money on flowers. Samavati was surprised and asked her why all of a sudden there were so many flowers in the house. The servant confessed everything. As a result, Samavati was intrigued by the Buddha's teachings because they had had such an impact on her servant, so she ordered her to go and listen to them every day and come back and repeat them to her.

One day when the king told his beloved wife that she should have whatever she wished for, she asked that the Buddha be invited to the palace every day, given food and requested to teach. The Buddha declined the invitation and instead sent Ananda, and from then on Ananda would visit each day, and before long the whole of the women's quarters were following the Dharma.

However, the king's second wife, Magandiya, hated everything Buddhist. She was very beautiful, and when she was younger her father, who did not understand the discipline of a monk, had offered her in marriage to the Buddha. The Buddha had declined and Magandiya had taken this as a personal affront. Now that Samavati had become a Buddhist, Magandiya imagined her to be the Buddha's representative and turned against her. She thought up lots of tricks to turn the king against Samavati but they all failed and the king did not believe her stories. But at last one day, the king found a poisonous snake in his room, and all the evidence pointed to Samavati. In his fury he lost control and shot her with his bow and arrow. However, through the power of her loving kindness, the arrow rebounded from her and did her no harm. When the king saw this miracle he was deeply shaken and begged her forgiveness.

He became curious about the teaching that had so transformed his wife, and just about this time a monk visited the town. The king listened to his teachings and immediately took refuge in the Buddha and became a lay disciple.

But Magandiya was still plotting, and she came up with the idea of setting fire to the women's palace and making it look like an accident. She herself left beforehand so she was not suspected of anything. The fire destroyed the wooden palace completely, and all the women living there were killed, including Samavati.

When the Buddha was asked to explain why this happened, he said that they all died because of a joint murder they had all committed many lifetimes ago. He went on to say that one of the benefits of loving kindness is that it protects one from fire, poison and weapons. This means that while one is actually radiating loving kindness one cannot be hurt, but at other times one is vulnerable. Samavati had died and been reborn in a celestial heaven. Of all his female disciples he declared her to be supreme in loving kindness.

Through a cunning trick the king eventually discovered that it was Magandiya who had put fire to the women's palace. He had her burnt alive in public and then ordered all the ashes to be ploughed over so that nothing remained. Afterwards he regretted his cruel revenge. Yet the whole episode haunted him. Over and over again he would see Samavati's face in front of him, a face that was always full of love for all beings, and slowly he, too, began to practise the Buddhist teachings and learned to control his temper.

Concluding points

These portraits of the Buddha's earliest disciples communicate the flavour of all Buddhist lineages in general. Each follower has his or her strengths and weaknesses, qualities and skills. Each one develops organically to play a specific role in the community in line with these abilities. Independently of their spiritual attainments, some are more popular than others and some more friendly than others. Certain disciples, in the vein of Devadatta, struggle with deep-seated emotions and propensities that make the spiritual journey difficult for them and for those around them.

Becoming a Buddhist does not instantly turn anyone into a saint, or some idealised version of a perfect person. Karma and habits die hard. The story of Buddhism on the ground is a very human one. At the same time, it is an uplifting story of courage and transcendence.

Personal reflection

What role do a teacher's main disciples play in determining his legacy and the reach of his or her teaching?

Main points

- The Buddha had many disciples from all walks of life: priests, kings, traders and servants, men and women. Some became monastics, others lived in society.
- Shariputra was one of the Buddha's chief disciples, known for his wisdom and the clarity of his presentations of the Dharma.
- Maudgalyayana, a childhood friend of Shariputra, was the second chief disciple known for his psychic powers.
- Ananda attended the Buddha for the last 25 years of his life. He was known for his devotion and perfect memory.
- The Buddha did not appoint a leader to succeed him. Mahakasyapa was recognised as a leader by the sangha immediately after the Buddha passed away. After Mahakasyapa passed away Ananda was elected as head of the sangha. Ananda lived a further 40 years after the Buddha and died at the age of 120.

Chapter 4

A BRIEF HISTORY OF BUDDHISM

Buddhism did not long remain confined to northern India. Over the centuries it spread throughout Asia and is today considered a world religion. As it was introduced to different cultures, Buddhism proved very adaptable. It gave rise to art, architecture, music, festivals and universities, thus inspiring centuries of human civilisation. This historical overview falls into three main sections: a) Buddhism in India; b) the spread of Buddhism through Asia; and c) the spread of Buddhism to the West.

Buddhism is a vast and varied phenomenon: its history goes back over two and half millennia and its geography spans a large part of the globe. It has found expression in a score of languages and has stimulated a great variety of art styles. It has deeply shaped a great part of humanity past and present.

Klaus K. Klostermaier, *A Survey of Hinduism*

Introduction

Buddhism did not long remain confined to northern India, in the region where the Buddha lived and taught; from the time of emperor Ashoka onwards, the Buddha Dharma spread far and wide throughout Asia. There were periods in history when the entire civilised world east of Iran was predominantly Buddhist. In each new country Buddhist practices, culture and artistic styles adapted to the local conditions without compromising the Buddha's essential message of wisdom and compassion. And since Buddhism never developed an overall hierarchy of religious authority, or an institutionalised church, each country was free to develop its own religious structures.

The expansion of Buddhism occurred peacefully and conversion was never imposed. We could say that the spread of Buddhism happened in three ways.

- First, the Buddha himself set the example. He travelled from town to town and shared his knowledge with those who were receptive. He also asked his monks to go forth and share the Dharma with others. But the Buddha never demanded that people reject their ancient beliefs and convert to a 'new religion'. He was not seeking to establish a religion at all, but rather to help individuals find ways of overcoming their suffering.
- Second, Buddhism spread organically, especially when merchants visited and settled in different lands. This occurred in the cities along the Silk Route linking central Asia with China. The assimilation of new beliefs also happened when a country was conquered by others, as in the case of seventh century Tibet which conquered neighbouring Buddhist kingdoms to the west.
- And third, the spread of Buddhism was sometimes due to a powerful monarch who became Buddhist and who adopted policies that supported Buddhist beliefs and the construction of monasteries. This was the case with Emperor Ashoka in India, Prince Tissa of Sri Lanka, Prince Shotoku in Japan, King Trisongdetsen in Tibet and Altan Khan in Mongolia.

Buddhism became established in other Asian countries under Ashoka, from 268 BCE onwards. Today, each Asian country is associated with a particular tradition of Buddhism. This has had an impact in modern times, when Asian immigrants to the West have brought their religious traditions with them. Thus, Chinese, Japanese and Vietnamese immigrants have introduced Mahayana

Buddhism to the West, while immigrants from Sri Lanka, Thailand and Myanmar have introduced Theravada Buddhism, and Tibetan refugees have introduced Vajrayana Buddhism.

The three main traditions of Buddhism

There are three main traditions of Buddhism which are presented in detail in Chapter 7. For the sake of clarity as we address how Buddhism spread through Asia, these traditions are outlined very briefly here.

The three traditions are known as Hinayana, Mahayana and Vajrayana Buddhism. They developed gradually in India over the first thousand years after the Buddha and all are still practised today. Although they all share the same fundamental principles of the Buddha's teaching, such as the Four Noble Truths, there are many differences in emphasis and in interpretation between the traditions.

Hinayana Buddhism

'Hinayana' literally means 'lesser vehicle' or 'lower vehicle', but this term has been viewed as derogatory on account of its historical use by certain Mahayanists who were critical of this approach. 'Mahayana', by contrast, means 'great vehicle'. In view of the unfortunate value judgement associated with the term Hinayana many people these days regard it as unacceptable. A number of other terms are used to replace it: Nikaya Buddhism, for example, referring to the collections of scriptures called *nikayas*. We shall refer to Hinayana as Nikaya Buddhism.

The Nikaya traditions encompass the so-called eighteen 'schools' which developed in India from earliest times and of which only Theravada survives today. Theravada means 'the way of the elders'. It is often claimed that Theravada holds the original teachings and discipline laid down by the historical Buddha. The Theravada scriptures are generally acknowledged to be a record of the teachings collected together at the first Buddhist Council. For this reason, many Theravadins believe their tradition represents 'orthodox' Buddhism and that later traditions modified the Buddha's original teachings, swayed by the views of their various founders.

Mahayana Buddhism

Mahayana, 'the great vehicle', is an umbrella term which describes a number of different schools the earliest of which apparently emerged between first century BCE and first century CE. Mahayana is seen by modern scholars as a new movement which developed its own vast collection of scriptures between approximately the first and fifth centuries CE. It is characterized by interpretations of the Buddha's teachings that differ from those of the Nikaya schools, for example by its understanding of the nature of the Buddha and of enlightenment. Some Mahayana schools developed devotional worship which is unknown in Theravada.

Mahayana gave rise to two main philosophical schools in India: Madhyamaka and Yogacara. But over the centuries, as it spread to other countries, further schools developed which had not originally existed in India. This is especially the case for Ch'an (Zen) and Pure Land Buddhism, both of which developed in China and Japan, and both of which are still practised today.

Vajrayana Buddhism

In the sixth and seventh centuries CE, a new form of religion became widespread in India. This is called Tantra, which means 'thread' or 'continuity', and it influenced the development of both Buddhism and Hinduism. Tantric Buddhism, also known as Vajrayana Buddhism or the 'diamond vehicle', is associated with rituals and relies upon visualisation, the chanting of mantras (sacred formulae) and devotional practices. It has its own body of scriptures. It is very colourful and vibrant, and soon gained popular appeal.

Buddhism in India

From the moment that Buddha Shakyamuni began teaching, people were drawn to him and asked to become his disciples. The Buddhist *sangha*, or community of followers, grew steadily throughout the Buddha's lifetime and continued to grow and consolidate after he passed away. As monasteries were built and cultural practices were developed, what had started out as a series of simple and spontaneous encounters turned into what today we call Buddhism.

Western scholars analyse the development of Buddhism in India in various ways, and each identifies different historical periods for the phases of its development. Following Edward Conze[11], we can say that Indian Buddhism developed in four phases:

- 484-268 BCE: slow growth, localised in north India
- 268 BCE-250 CE: ascendancy and spread
- 250-500 CE: classical period, flourishing
- 500-1200 CE: gradual decline.

The first of these periods is relatively unknown because there is little or no historical evidence of events from that early time. Our knowledge is based largely on accounts in the scriptures which were only written down several hundred years later. From the accession of the Indian Emperor Ashoka (268 BCE) onwards, however, many events are documented through historical records and the picture is clearer and more precise.

The first 200 years after the Buddha (484-268 BCE)

According to the scriptures, the Buddha died confident that his teaching was firmly established. He had been teaching and advising his followers for 45 years, and there were hundreds of *arhats* who were able to guide the community after his death. He did not appoint a successor. Instead, he told his disciples that they should follow the Dharma as their guide, that is, the body of teachings that he left behind.

Universal Buddhist tradition claims that shortly after the Buddha's death there was an authoritative gathering of 500 *arhats* in Rajagaha, a village in the modern state of Bihar, northern India, who collected together orally all the authentic teachings of the Buddha. This is known as the first Buddhist Council.

Upali and Ananda, both senior monks, recited the teachings and the assembly memorised them. Upali recited the Vinaya or material on monastic discipline while Ananda recited the *suttas* or discourses on meditation and wisdom. The Dharma continued to be transmitted orally, from one generation to the next, for several centuries. It was not written down because writing was virtually unknown in India at that time, so the teachings were transmitted by communal chanting.

During the first centuries after the Buddha, Buddhism quietly established itself alongside India's other religions in the towns and villages of northern India. The monastic community was organised in small, self-contained units with no centralised authority. Monks would wander from village to village for alms but over the years they grouped themselves in monasteries so they developed a fixed place to live. This grouping had started in the Buddha's time, when the monks had no fixed home for most of the year but took shelter in one place during the monsoon in July, August and September when the violent rains make it difficult to travel. Gradually, after the Buddha, these shelters became permanent, were used year-round and were known as *viharas* or monasteries.

Given the lack of centralised authority it is not surprising that different schools of thought emerged over time. At first, the differences related only to points of monastic discipline, but later there were divergent interpretations of the suttas as well. Although modern descriptions of these developments use English terms such as 'disputes', 'schism' and 'sects', it is important to note that Buddhism as a whole was tolerant of these divergences and monks with different philosophical views could be found living side by side in the same monastery. Furthermore, the differences may well have been irrelevant to most lay Buddhists.

Most Buddhist sources agree that, in order to resolve differences in interpretation, a second Buddhist Council was held about 100 years after the Buddha, possibly in 350 BCE, in the city of Vesali. The result of this Council was a split between the School of Elders which was the forerunner of the Theravada school, and the Mahasanghikas or 'Great Assembly', a school regarded by some scholars as the forerunner of the Mahayana tradition.

Predictably perhaps, the Theravada account of the reasons for the Council is quite different from that of the Mahayana. Theravadins refer to points of discipline while the Mahayana tradition emphasizes differences in doctrine.

- Theravadins claim that the Second Council was called because many monks had become lax in their discipline. In particular, some monks were accepting money instead of food as alms, and some were eating after noon (both are forbidden in the Vinaya).
- Mahayana accounts claim the Second Council debated the nature of *arhats*. A monk named Mahadeva cast doubt on the perfection of those who claimed to be *arhats*. He said: 1) they had not fully conquered their passions because they still had wet dreams; 2) they were not omniscient because they often had to ask for directions; 3) they were still subject to doubts; 4) they had learned their knowledge from others and not from their own experience; and 5) they would exclaim out loud during meditation.

Further divisions occurred within each of these wings of Buddhism. Tradition has it that there were eighteen different groups or 'sects' in the first few centuries of Buddhism in India, of which only Theravada survives today. Some scholars have suggested the actual number of groups and subgroups could have been as high as thirty.

How reliable are the scriptural stories of these first centuries? Some modern scholars have doubts about the first Council because the details vary between the accounts of different Buddhist schools. Although Buddhist tradition accepts that the early scriptures were standardised at the first Council, subsequently there were changes and additions in the versions of the scriptures adopted by each school. Furthermore, some scholars consider that the memory required to recall the entire body of scriptures would be so extraordinary it is hard to believe such an exercise is possible.

However, other scholars are less sceptical. Variations in detail may be due to the very nature of oral communication but do not necessarily mean the first Council is a fabrication. And even after writing was introduced, memorisation and oral transmission remained sacred activities. Still today one encounters Buddhists in India who can recite entire volumes of scripture from memory.

Emperor Ashoka: Buddhism's ascendancy (250 BCE – 250 CE)

The reign of Ashoka marks a decisive turning point in the development of Buddhism. Ashoka came to power in 268 BCE probably by assassinating the claimants to the throne of Magadha, in northern India, including his own elder brothers. He expanded his empire through military conquest until it covered roughly the territory of modern India except for the extreme south. Ashoka is therefore famous in Indian history as the first ruler to unite almost the whole subcontinent in a single empire.

After a number of brutal campaigns Ashoka was sickened by violence and converted to the non-violent values of the Buddhist religion. He was instrumental in causing Buddhism to spread throughout India. He had hundreds of commemorative stupas built, especially in the holy places connected with the Buddha's life. He also erected a number of stone pillars on which he engraved decrees and edicts encouraging his people to lead a moral life; and he funded numerous Buddhist monasteries.

Ashoka transformed Buddhism overnight from one of the many non-Vedic groups in India to the 'state religion' of one of the greatest empires on earth. At the same time, he initiated a climate of religious tolerance, and supported not only Buddhist institutions but those of Hinduism and other religions as well. He encouraged religious freedom and innovation. In addition, Ashoka sent missions far and wide 'to conquer according to Dharma', and effectively turned

Buddhism into a world religion. Under Ashoka, Buddhism became firmly established in Sri Lanka and Kashmir, and missions also travelled west to Syria, Egypt and Macedonia.

According to Sri Lankan sources, Ashoka convened a third Buddhist Council in order to clarify certain doctrinal disputes. These Theravada sources claim that the third Council validated the conservative teaching of the Elders. There is no record of this Council in Mahayana sources.

Chapter 22 includes a detailed and critical presentation of Ashoka and his significance for the development of Buddhism.

The flourishing of Buddhism (250-500 CE)

Buddhism spread very rapidly throughout India. By the third century CE it was the major faith of India. Jainism, Vedic Brahmanism, and Hindu cults to Shiva and Vishnu, all existed more or less equally as secondary religions. It was not until the fourth century CE that Hinduism began its ascendancy.

There was an intense flourishing of scholarship, with new scriptures and philosophical treatises being composed. The flourishing of Buddhist culture is reflected by its great universities such as that of Nalanda which was established possibly as early as the second century CE. By the fifth century, Chinese pilgrims record that Nalanda housed several thousand monk-students and its library occupied a large three-storey building. It was like the Oxford or Cambridge of the time – or the Yale and Harvard. The ruins of Nalanda can be visited today in Bihar state.

It was during this period that many of the Buddhist scholars whose works are studied today composed their treatises. Madhyamaka scholars such as Buddhapalita and Bhavya were influential, as well as Yogacaras such as Asanga and Vasubandhu (see Chapter 21).

Many reasons have been given for the popularity of Buddhism in India.

- The Dharma is universally applicable and is not restricted to a particular tribal or cultural group.
- Buddhism was attractive to travellers and merchants who were detached from traditional beliefs and social structures, and who played an important role in spreading Buddhism on their travels.
- Buddhism was accessible to the masses, unlike Brahmanism which was restricted to a small class of initiates. Buddhist teachers used local languages

and not Sanskrit, which was the sacred language of India but understood only by the educated elite.

- The monastic community was well organised and provided a good example of a spiritual way of life.
- The teaching itself was attractive to intellectuals for its systematic analysis, and to ordinary people for its values of non-violence and compassion.
- There were many aspects of life that the Buddha did not pronounce upon, so people were free to continue with traditional customs if they wished. Buddhism was very flexible.

Decline and revival (500 to the present day)

Between about 400 and 1000 CE, Buddhism and Hinduism developed very closely together, with many points of mutual influence. Many eminent Buddhist scholars continued to emerge during this period. In the long run, however, there were some disadvantages to Buddhism becoming an established religion. In particular, the religious commitment of those wishing to become monks gradually became weaker. With extensive state patronage, monastic life became secure, comfortable and potentially appealing to the less fortunate, who sometimes might have become involved for material rather than religious reasons. In addition, the success and wealth of Buddhist monasteries attracted the envy and rivalry of non-Buddhist communities, especially the brahmin priests. These weaknesses were eventually to prove fatal for Indian Buddhism.

From 700 CE onwards, Buddhist monasteries in central Asia and northwest India were gradually destroyed by invasions of Muslims and Turks. Over the following centuries Buddhist monasteries, universities and libraries in all parts of India were destroyed by the progressive Muslim advance, and Buddhists were persecuted and massacred. The last great monastery to fall was that of Vikramashila.

> *At Vikramashila, the Muslims slaughtered the monks. The libraries burned for days. The attackers shattered the statues and stole the gold and jewels that adorned them. The army demolished every building, down to the last stone in the foundations of the dozens of temples that once towered in the morning mists; they uprooted them and threw them into the Ganges River. The destruction of Vikramashila was complete: the site has never been identified.*[12]

By the 12th century Buddhism survived in a handful of pockets in the extreme south, east and north of the subcontinent where Muslims were not dominant, but it subsequently disappeared from India altogether.

How can we account for the collapse of Buddhist institutions which a few centuries earlier had been so strong and vibrant? A number of reasons have been given for the decline of Buddhism in India.

- The flexibility of Buddhism can mean that it becomes almost indistinguishable from surrounding religions, and it has been argued that Buddhism became indistinguishable from Hinduism
- Buddhist values of peace and non-violence make it vulnerable to military force
- The monasteries' dependency on patrons and donors makes them economically vulnerable when those in power withdraw support
- Monasteries and robed monks are an easily identifiable target, and with their destruction Buddhism loses the core of its identity. The importance of the monastic community is such that when monastic life is disrupted, it can be difficult for Buddhism to survive.

In popular histories, the decline of Buddhism in India is often blamed solely on the Muslims but the Dalai Lama points out that nothing is ever caused by one factor alone. The decline of Buddhism in India, he suggests, was due to the combination of several causes. First, the patrons who had supported Buddhist monasteries gradually favoured Hindu institutions instead. Second, external forces like the Muslim invasions openly tried to destroy Buddhism. And third, some of the monasteries and monks had become very wealthy and there was corruption and a lack of monastic discipline so the public lost respect for the monks. The Dalai Lama therefore believes that Buddhists themselves share a measure of responsibility for the collapse of their religion.[13]

Buddhism had been so successfully eradicated from the Indian consciousness that when the British ruled India in the 19th century nobody was aware that the Buddha had been an actual historical figure; he had become a character of myth and legend. It was thanks to the efforts of colonial archaeologists that historical remains were found which substantiated the story of early Buddhism as we know it today: texts, stupas, Ashoka's pillars and stone edicts, the ruins of Nalanda, and the Mahabodhi temple in Bodh Gaya are some examples of what was uncovered.

Following the restoration of numerous sites and buildings connected with Buddhism, the religion experienced something of a revival in India through the 20th century. There are three main factors behind this change. The first is the role played by refugees from Tibet who brought their Buddhist faith with them when they fled into exile after the Chinese Communist occupation of their homeland in 1959. They have established refugee communities in India and neighbouring Nepal, practise Buddhism freely and visit the main pilgrimage sites. In Bodh Gaya, for example, Tibetans organise several prayer festivals each year where tens of thousands of Buddhists congregate.

A second factor is international religious tourism. Every year thousands of Buddhists from many other countries such as Japan, Sri Lanka, Thailand and Vietnam, and from Europe, North America and Australia, visit the land of the Buddha's birth on pilgrimage. This has helped to bring awareness of Buddhism back into the Indian consciousness.

A third factor is the influence of Dr. B.R. Ambedkar (1891-1956) from Maharashtra state who encouraged many members of the lowest 'untouchable' classes to convert from Hinduism to Buddhism. Ambedkar was himself an untouchable but gained a good education and became a lawyer. From the 1920s he worked for the emancipation of untouchables in India and became a minister in the first post-independence government. He was attracted to Buddhism because of its emphasis on love, equality, freedom and tolerance. Today there are around 4.5 million 'Ambedkar' Buddhists in India. After 'conversion' they report an improvement in self-esteem, a greater sense of dignity, and a determination to become well educated as a means for social advancement.

The Spread of Buddhism in Asia

Under Ashoka, the Nikaya schools were established in Sri Lanka, Kashmir and central Asia. There is evidence that Mahayana Buddhism also spread to central Asia possibly around the same time or a little later, and it was introduced to northern China by traders plying the Silk Route in the first century CE. As Buddhism spread throughout Asia, each country followed one or more specific tradition but only in India itself were all traditions present.

Sri Lanka and southeast Asia

Buddhism was introduced into Sri Lanka in approximately 250 BCE by a mission sent by Emperor Ashoka. Sri Lanka thus claims the most ancient verifiable continuous practice of Buddhism in the world. It is considered the homeland of Theravada Buddhism and has produced some of the most important historical chronicles of early Buddhism and several major commentaries on the Buddhist scriptures.

Ashoka's mission was led by his son, the monk Mahinda. It met with the royal prince Tissa who subsequently, through his alliance with Ashoka, was recognized as the first historical king of the whole island. Later Ashoka's daughter, the nun Sanghamitta, is said to have brought to Sri Lanka a cutting of the original tree under which the Buddha attained enlightenment. The tree that grew from this can still be seen today in Anuradhapura, and many other cuttings from this tree have since been planted all over Sri Lanka. Many of these trees have been turned into outdoor shrines decked with prayer flags.

Buddhism in Sri Lanka thus enjoyed state protection and financial support from the outset, and this relationship continues to the present day when prominent monks bear considerable political influence.

The ruins of impressively large monasteries bear witness to the flourishing and strength of Buddhism in Sri Lanka. However, political upheaval, sectarian rivalries and famine weakened Buddhism so much between 43-17 BCE that Sri Lankan monks decided to preserve the Buddhist scriptures in writing to ensure they would not be lost. This first systematic recording of the scriptures in writing was completed in around 17 BCE: it produced the Pali Canon. Pali is the sacred language of Theravada.

Further political disruptions and Hindu invasions from India meant that by around 1070 CE it was necessary to invite monks from Myanmar (Burma) to revive monastic ordination in Sri Lanka. The ceremony requires a minimum of ten ordained monks to be present together to give ordination to new candidates. It appears that the ordination of nuns had lapsed completely by that time and was only recently revived, in 1998, with the help of nuns from Korea and Taiwan. Later on, in 1741, when Sri Lanka was under Dutch rule, monks were invited again, this time from Thailand, to revive monastic ordination on the island. This shows how weakened Buddhism became at certain times in the island's history. Nevertheless, it survived persecution and reform from successive waves of Portuguese, Dutch and British colonialists and remains the majority religion of Sri Lanka today.

It is possible that Ashoka sent a mission to Myanmar but this has not been verified. The existing Theravada traditions in Thailand, Myanmar, Cambodia and Laos were established there from Sri Lanka in the second millennium. The earlier Mahayana influences in the region mostly gave way to Theravada except in Vietnam, where Mahayana flourished from the first century CE. In 580 CE Ch'an Buddhism was introduced to Vietnam from China by the monk Vinitaruci, and has remained strong there for centuries.

Laos became a state in 1353, and from that time until the present day it has followed Theravada Buddhism, introduced from Cambodia. Between the fifth and eleventh centuries CE, the Malay Peninsula, Sumatra, Java and Indonesia followed Mahayana Buddhism which they received from China and India. After the eleventh century, Buddhism was replaced as the dominant religion by either Hinduism or Islam.

In the 20th century some Buddhists played a supportive role in southeast Asia's Communist movements and, as a result, southeast Asian Communism has not been particularly anti-religious. In Vietnam, for example, Buddhism was part of the identity which Communist independence movements were trying to reassert. Buddhism continues to be practised and even to flourish throughout the region.

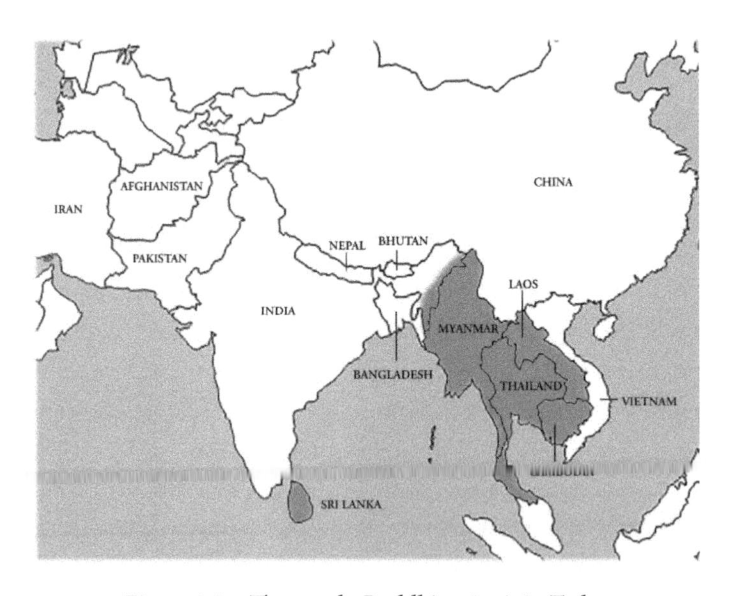

Figure 4.2 – Theravada Buddhism in Asia Today

Central Asia and the Far East

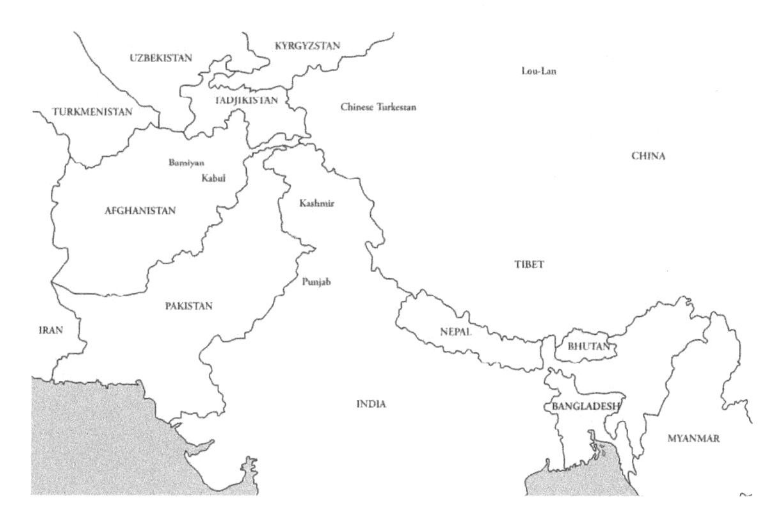

Figure 4.3 – The region of Central Asia

There is evidence that Buddhism was present in central Asia from at least the second century BCE. From east to west this region covers present-day Chinese Turkestan, Kashmir, Northern Pakistan, Tadjikistan and Afghanistan. It is not a unified area politically or geographically, but throughout this region Buddhism flourished for roughly a thousand years until Muslim conversions caused monasteries to be deserted. By around 1000 CE what was left of Buddhist culture in the area was buried under the desert sands, not to be rediscovered until the 19th century.

Buddhism spread to this region from northwest India, and also from China along the long trade route known as the Silk Road or Silk Route. Nikaya, Mahayana and Tantric Buddhism were all present in the region, making it particularly rich in Buddhist art, architecture and manuscripts. Among the most internationally known artistic expressions of Buddhist culture in central Asia are the monumental standing statues of the Buddha carved out of cliff faces in Bamiyan, Afghanistan. They briefly attracted media attention during troubles in that country, when the Taliban publicly defaced and destroyed all the statues.

Some important discoveries were made in Afghanistan after that event, when researchers found ancient Buddhist texts in some of the meditation caves that are carved out of the cliff face near Bamiyan. These texts include Mahayana scriptures, and they are among the oldest Buddhist manuscripts that have survived until today. One copy of the Prajñaparamita Sutra has been dated to the second century CE. Many of these texts are now preserved in the British Library and in the Schoyen Collection in Norway.

Buddhism was introduced into China through two separate routes. First, in the first century CE, it was spread from central Asia by foreign merchants plying the Silk Road and, second, in at least the third century CE, it entered China along the southern route from Sri Lanka through Indo-China, Canton and the lower Yangtse.

In China, Buddhism encountered an advanced and literate civilisation with highly developed religious, philosophical, social and political systems of its own. The story of Buddhism in China is therefore very different from its spread to most other countries. Buddhism never replaced these systems but grew alongside them.

The last Asian region to which Buddhism spread was the Himalayan region. It was established in Tibet in the seventh century CE under the patronage of King Trisongdetsen and spread to Bhutan in the same period. Despite a brief time of persecution confined to central Tibet in the ninth century, Buddhism remained the dominant religion of the country until the Chinese Communist take-over in 1959. Most Buddhist scriptures were translated from Sanskrit to Tibetan thus preserving many texts which are now lost in the original. Buddhism inspired the entire Tibetan culture for centuries, including art and architecture, music, scholarship and social organisation. From Tibet, Buddhism was introduced to Mongolia after the conversion of Kublai Khan in around 1250. Tibetan Buddhism is also practised in some areas of the former Soviet Union.

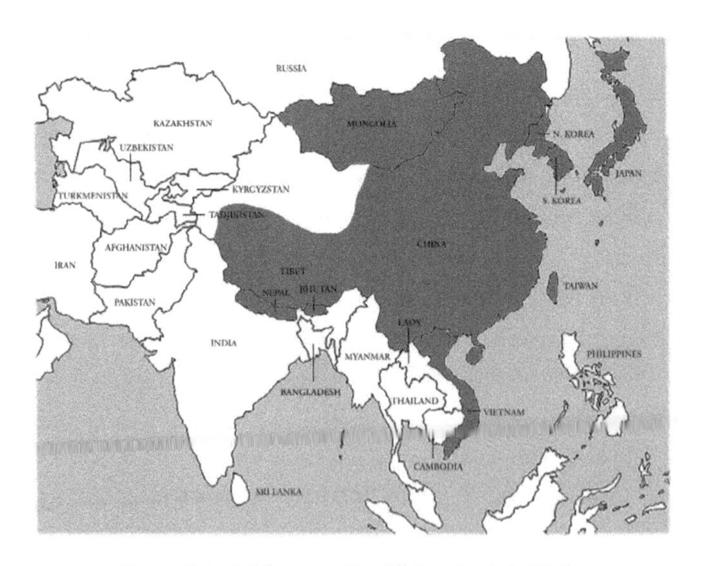

Figure 4.4 –Mahayana Buddhism in Asia Today

Contemporary Asia

Over the last 500 years or so, Buddhism in some Asian countries, Sri Lanka and Vietnam for example, has suffered at the hands of European colonialism and Christian missionary activity. More recently, Buddhism was persecuted by Communist regimes in China, Cambodia, North Korea, Tibet and Mongolia. By the end of the 20th century, however, Buddhism had begun to make a comeback in many of these countries although Christian missionaries remain very active in Sri Lanka, South Korea and Mongolia in particular. Buddhism remains strong in many parts of Asia especially in Japan, South Korea, Taiwan, Laos, Thailand, Myanmar, Cambodia, Sri Lanka, Nepal and Bhutan, and increasingly in mainland China.

Buddhism in the West

Although Buddhism spread to the West only recently, most people are unaware that contacts and cultural exchanges actually occurred between Europe and India from the earliest times. In 334 BCE, Alexander the Great marched into India but he only went as far as the Indus Valley and did not reach the Buddhist heartland. After that, there were constant diplomatic exchanges between Greece and India. The first documented exchange with Buddhism is that of Menander, one of the generals in the army of Demetrius who invaded India in 182 BCE. Menander became a Buddhist, and it is he who engages in dialogue with the monk Nagasena in the Theravada scripture *The Questions of King Milinda.*

The Indian Emperor Ashoka also sent missions westward to Syria, Egypt and Macedonia around 250 BCE, but we have no evidence they arrived in these countries.

After the time of Christ commerce between Asia and the Roman Empire was strong, and Buddhist ideas were well known in Europe. A small number of Indians, including Buddhist monks, settled in Athens and Alexandria and are mentioned in early Christian writings. There is considerable evidence of cross-cultural exchange: for example, many of the Jataka Tales (stories of the Buddha's previous lives) were retold as Aesop's Fables. And several early Christians such as Origen and Basilides believed in reincarnation and in freedom from suffering through knowledge, showing similarities with Buddhist ideas. However, with the fall of the Roman Empire contacts with Asia were lost and so was knowledge of Indian religions.

During the Middle Ages the popes sent several missionaries to Asia who came back with information on Buddhism and Hinduism. William of Rubruck and Marco Polo went to Mongolia in the 13th century. Their accounts were sympathetic but Christian institutions at that time were generally intolerant of all non-Christian religions.

European colonialism

European powers expanded into Asia between the 16th and 19th centuries. Portugal, for example, occupied Sri Lanka as early as 1505. As a result, Europeans came to know about Indian religions once again. In the 18th century, Europe was particularly receptive to new ideas and this led to a new academic discipline: the comparative study of religion. What brought about this new openness?

- The European Enlightenment brought a belief in reason and science which weakened the authority of revealed Christianity.
- Some people began to believe in 'natural religion', a fundamental truth that is common to all mankind and that is cross-cultural.
- Scientific evolution theory seriously weakened the Biblical account of creation.

By the end of the 19th century there was a vogue for Buddhism in Europe. People were attracted by its ideas of self-help instead of dependence on God or priests, its similarities with science in that it is based on experience, and its belief that the universe is ruled by laws and that humans are not radically distinct from other species. Buddhism was more than science; it also had mysticism, and paradoxically appeared to bring together both faith and reason.

In the 19th and early 20th centuries, therefore, interest in Buddhism was primarily intellectual and mainly touched the cultured elite. Scholars began to translate Buddhist scriptures. The German philosopher Schopenhauer (1788-1860) was strongly influenced by Buddhist ideas. And the editor of the London *Daily Telegraph*, Sir Edwin Arnold, wrote a life story of the Buddha in verse, published in 1879 as *The Light of Asia* while Herman Hesse wrote *Siddhartha* in 1922.

Spiritualism was also in vogue at this time, based on the belief that the spirits of the dead communicate with the living, especially through mediums. Madame Blavatsky and Colonel Olcott founded the Theosophical Society in New York in 1875, offering a mix of esoteric religions influenced more by Hinduism than by Buddhism. This movement spread to London and succeeded in introducing many key concepts to the British public, such as karma and rebirth. Then, in

1924, a British lawyer, Christmas Humphreys, founded a Buddhist Lodge in the Theosophical Society which in 1943 became an independent charity called The Buddhist Society. This society played an important role in introducing Buddhism to the upper classes, and now provides information on all Buddhist groups in the UK to the general public.

Many of the 19th and early 20th century writers and scholars of Buddhism have since been criticised for inventing their own version of Buddhism rather than studying the subject with Buddhists themselves. They have been accused of over-rationalising and over-romanticising Buddhism, and of creating an exotic image of it in the minds of the general public.

The role of migrant communities

At the same time as Westerners were travelling to Asia, Asian immigrants steadily settled in North America and Europe. Chinese immigration to the USA and Canada was strong by the 1860s and 1870s, and Japanese immigration began in 1868. These migrants took their Buddhist faith with them and built small temples in their communities. However, there was little or no spread of Buddhism from these Asian communities into society at large. There are a number of Chinese and Japanese Buddhist centres in North America, Brazil and Europe today, but most of their adherents are of Chinese or Japanese descent. Asian migrants also settled in Europe and, since 1975, they include refugees from Vietnam, Laos and Cambodia, but there is not much spread of Buddhism from these communities into the general population. In the UK, for example, although Buddhists of Asian origin account for well over 50% of all Buddhists in the country today, they remain very self-contained.

A change in this pattern came in the 1960s and 1970s with the arrival of Tibetan masters (*lamas*) and Japanese Zen masters (*roshis*) in Europe and North America. This was a time when young people belonging to the hippy counter-culture were interested in all things Eastern. They were attracted by the colourful rituals of Tibetan Buddhism and the simplicity and aesthetic of Zen. Many Westerners came to know about Buddhism when they went on the 'hippy trail', travelling overland to India and Nepal. In the UK and the USA, Theravada also attracted a significant number of followers during that period. The big differences between that period and the earlier interest in Buddhism were that Westerners wished to practise it themselves as a religion, not simply to learn about it from a distance; and that Asian masters were willing to take Western students seriously.

The present day

From the 1960s to the present day, numerous Buddhist centres have been established throughout Europe, North America, South America and Australasia, and the majority of their followers are Westerners. They come from all walks of life and include ordinary people, scholars, professionals and film stars. In the USA, UK and France alone there are now almost five million Buddhists.

Theravada, Mahayana and Tantric Buddhism are all now being practised in the West. The precise pattern of establishment was initially dependent upon colonial and diplomatic connections so in the UK, for example, there are Theravadins from Sri Lanka and Thailand whereas in France there are Mahayana followers from Vietnam and Cambodia. The forms of Buddhism that can be found relatively evenly throughout the Western world are Tibetan Buddhism, Zen and Theravada.

What is unique about the way Buddhism has expanded into the 'developed' world is that so many different traditions and schools of Buddhism have been introduced almost simultaneously and coexist side by side. Whereas in Asia Theravada and Zen, for instance, were geographically circumscribed and virtually unknown to each other, in the West a new pan-Buddhist understanding is emerging, together with a new appreciation of the value of each form of Buddhism in its own right.

Buddhist Population in the World Today

Source: World Population Review 2021

World	**487,091,090**
Asia	480,370,930
Europe	670,000
Russia	170,000
Africa	390,000
Middle East	600,160
North America	3,850,000
Latin America	370,000
Australasia	670,000

Main Points

The history of Buddhism in India can be divided into four phases:

1. **The historical Buddha until Ashoka (5th century to 250 BCE):**
   Monasteries were established, the scriptures were consolidated orally, and there were three great debates on discipline and the teachings

2. **From Emperor Ashoka to the Gupta dynasty (250 BCE to 250 CE):**
   Buddhism spread throughout India, and to central Asia and Sri Lanka. Under Ashoka Buddhism became a social and political ethic. Mahayana Buddhism emerged together with the writings of Nagarjuna and Madhyamaka philosophy.

3. **Classical Buddhism (250 CE to 500 CE):**
   Buddhist scholarship flourished; Nalanda university was established and grew; there were great debates between Buddhists and Hindus; both Madhyamaka and Yogacara philosophies were developed.

4. **Gradual decline (500 to 1200 CE):**
   Hinduism gradually became dominant; invasions by Muslims and Turks destroyed monasteries and their monastic communities; Buddhists fled India especially to the north, across the Himalayas.

Buddhism became extinct and unknown in its homeland from 1200 until British colonialists made archaeological discoveries in the 19th century.

There was a revival of Buddhism in India in the 20th century, partly from Dr. Ambedkar who converted many Hindu untouchables to Buddhism, and partly from the migration of Tibetan refugees.

Buddhism spread throughout Asia south, west, east and north and is still practised in many Asian countries today. It has now spread to Europe, the Americas and Australasia.

Chapter 5

BUDDHISM IN THE FAR EAST

This chapter gives a historical overview of the spread of Buddhism to China, Korea and Japan and the way it adapted to their respective cultures. For more detail on the traditions and teachings that became characteristic of the Far East (including Ch'an/Zen and Pure Land) see Chapters 18 and 19.

China

The Chinese context

Buddhism was introduced into China in the first century CE. According to the traditional story, the Han Emperor Ming, who ruled in 58–75 CE, dreamed of a divine being in the shape of a golden man. He was told this must be 'the foreign god called Buddha', and so he sent envoys to India who returned with one or two Indian Buddhist masters, a white horse, and a text of the *Sutra in Forty-Two Sections*. The Emperor later founded the Monastery of the White Horse near Lo-yang.

Modern scholars are more comfortable with accounts that attest to the introduction of Buddhism through two separate routes: first, in the first century CE, from central Asia by foreign merchants plying the Silk Road and, second, by at least the third century along the southern route from Sri Lanka to Indo-China, Canton and the lower Yangtse.

In China, Buddhism encountered an advanced and literate civilisation with highly developed religious, philosophical, social and political systems of its own. Buddhism never replaced these systems but grew alongside them. The two main influences on Chinese Buddhism were Confucianism and Taoism. We begin by reviewing the salient features of the cultural context into which Buddhism was introduced.

Confucianism

Confucius (551-479 BCE) established the main system of ethical behaviour in Chinese culture which continues to be followed by Chinese communities today. It consists of guidelines for the behaviour of individuals, of the family and of society as a whole. The fundamental virtues are considered to be respect for others, courtesy, hard work, social concern and honouring one's parents. Moral behaviour is motivated by a sense of genuine loving kindness towards others, and results in the best possible benefit for all. The Golden Rule of Confucianism is: 'Do not do to others what you would not like them to do to you', usually rendered in English as 'do as you would be done by'.

Confucianism is concerned with the best and most harmonious way of living this life and contains no speculation about an after-life. It is therefore called a 'this worldly' system, as opposed to an 'other worldly' system. Human beings are seen as one point in a triangle of forces: earth, man and an impersonal heaven. The emperor is the mediator of the three forces and so worthy of the greatest respect. This gives rise to a hierarchical social and political system where everyone knows their place, and each person must pay respect to their superiors for harmony to prevail.

Confucius did not mention any reward or punishment for moral behaviour in an after-life, so the benefits of morality seem to be the tangible benefits arising from a healthy and harmonious society. *T'ien* or heaven is where one can place one's trust when things go wrong on earth, but it is not for human beings to speculate about heavenly matters.

Confucians developed these ideas in a religious or humanistic way in the fourth and third centuries BCE. Well before the Common Era, Confucianism had developed the classic *I Ching* which is a manual for divination, now well known in the West, based on maintaining harmony between the two principles of yin and yang. Yin stands for darkness, passivity and femininity, while yang stands for light, activity and masculinity. The balancing of these principles can be applied to medicine, to diet and to *feng shui* (the art of positioning objects – graves, buildings, furniture – for a balanced, propitious flow of the *chi* energy of the environment and user).

Under the Sun dynasty (960-1279 CE) Confucianism became the official state cult. It became known as Neo-Confucianism because it was heavily influenced by Taoism and Buddhism. All government officials or civil servants had to take exams based on knowledge of the Confucian classics, so this system of thought remained the dominant influence on the ruling classes until the Communist take-over in 1949.

Taoism

Taoism (pronounced Dow-ism) is said to have been founded by Lao tzu in the sixth or fifth century BCE, but there is doubt about his historical existence. The ideas of Taoism are found in two foundational texts: the *Tao te Ching* and the *Chuang tzu*. They speak primarily of the unity that underlies all existence and that can be experienced in nature and through quiet contemplation. Taoism therefore tends to emphasize qualities and aspects of life that are quite different from those prized by Confucianism: natural and spontaneous behaviour rather than formal etiquette; the simplicity of nature rather than the sophistication of government or imperial courts; the value of the individual rather than that of society; the benefit of withdrawing from society, living close to nature and engaging in contemplation as opposed to active social and economic engagement. Taoism emphasizes peace and quiet and shuns the violence that often comes with politics. Its main virtues are humility, compassion and effortless naturalness. Many of the ideas of Taoism are embodied by Pooh Bear in A.A. Milne's stories for children, as pointed out in the popular book *The Tao of Pooh*.

Taoism was vague about life after death and simply considered life to be a dream, and death a natural change. By the second century CE it had combined with folk religions to form a Taoist religion with nature divinities, temples, rituals and priests. The emphasis of this religion was the quest for immortality, healing and the forgiveness of sins. In practice, the Chinese see Confucianism and Taoism as complementary, and they incorporate both Confucianist ethics and Taoist beliefs and attitudes into the way they view the world.

Socio-political context

The Chinese ruler was sanctified by the Mandate of Heaven and maintained the cosmic equilibrium of man, earth and heaven by performing perfectly his ritual, ethical and administrative duties. In principle, the authority of the emperor and of the imperial government was unlimited and all-inclusive. They had the power to rule over both public and private life.

Chinese society was highly structured and hierarchical. Its prevailing style was authoritarian and paternalistic. There was an immense difference between rich and poor, between the educated elite and the uneducated peasantry, and this gap was accepted as part of the social order. The basic social aims were pragmatic and secular: maintaining law and order, peace and harmony. The assumption was that the emperor and the government must maintain overall control for this to be possible.

Buddhism in China

The introduction of Buddhism to China brought about a clash of cultures. It was not immediately successful for several reasons. First, the Buddhist teaching was culturally difficult to accept.

- It was considered foreign and therefore inferior.
- It was seen as morbid, stressing suffering rather than happiness, and death rather than life.
- It was seen as selfish, because it did not follow the Confucian values of contributing to society through hard work.
- It introduced strange new beliefs unknown in China before this, such as rebirth.

Second, the Confucian-influenced state found Buddhist monasticism unacceptable and questioned its right to exist.

- Initially, monks would not bow to the emperor since, in India, the religious or priestly class had always been above the ruling class.
- Monks were organised independently — they had their own Vinaya rules and their own system for punishing monks who disobeyed those rules — and this was seen as a threat to social cohesion. Monks did not consider themselves liable to government supervision.
- The Chinese saw celibacy as an unnatural violation of the sacred laws governing family behaviour; it undermined the family as the basic social unit.

- Monasteries were economically autonomous — they were supported by believers and expected to be exempt from state taxes, as they had been in India. This was seen as politically unacceptable and potentially dangerous.
- Monks were accused of being economically unproductive and socially useless — twentieth-century Communists later called them 'social parasites'.
- Some monks had no fixed place to live and wandered from village to village begging for alms. The state disliked this way of life because it is impossible to control.

Despite all these factors, Buddhism gradually attracted growing numbers of Chinese. What was it that impressed them? No doubt a complex range of factors came into play. There is some evidence that the common people were drawn to Buddhism when they discovered how effective monks were in healing illnesses, for example, while members of the educated classes discovered in Buddhism a detailed and compelling discussion of topics that were not addressed elsewhere in Chinese thought. Between the second and third centuries CE the first Buddhist scriptures were translated into Chinese. The turning point came when the Han dynasty (206 BCE–220 CE) broke up, and in the turmoil that ensued, Buddhism filled the cultural vacuum. From that point its development is traced in terms of Buddhism in northern China and Buddhism in southern China.

In northern China, Buddhism was popular but was under the control of the ruler. This could mean patronage or it could mean persecution (Buddhism was persecuted in 446 and 574–577CE). Despite this fragile situation, ancient documents indicate that in the sixth century there were 30,000 Buddhist temples in northern China, indicating the tremendous popularity of the religion. Initially, it attracted small traders, clerks, copyists and people with limited education, but by the end of the fourth century it started to penetrate the upper classes.

Perhaps the greatest of all translators of the Buddhist scriptures into Chinese was named Kumarajiva (344-413 CE). He was from Kucha in central Asia, now known as Xinjiang in China. Kumarajiva was a child prodigy who became known from a very young age as a scholar of Buddhism. First, he studied Nikaya texts and later became a Mahayana specialist, with a great understanding of Madhyamaka philosophy. He studied in Kashmir, and his fame spread as he defeated eminent people in debate. He was ordained as a monk at the age of twenty.

The emperor of northern China heard of his talent and summoned him to his capital, Xi'an, but on the way there Kumarajiva was seized by a rebel warlord and imprisoned for seventeen years. He made the most of this period by learning excellent Chinese. Finally, the emperor sent an army to liberate him, and Kumarajiva arrived in Xi'an, possibly in 401. There he organised a translation team on a grand scale, working from Sanskrit to Chinese, with hundreds of editors, proof-readers and scribes. About one hundred translations are attributed to him including those of the *Diamond Sutra*, the *Amitabha Sutra*, the *Lotus Sutra*, and Nagarjuna's *Mula-madhyamika-karika*.

Although Kumarajiva is mainly recognized for his translation work, he is also acknowledged as the founder of the Chinese school of Madhyamaka philosophy (see Chapter 21). This is called the Three Treatises School, or San-lun school. He therefore played a leading role in the flourishing of Buddhism in northern China in his time.

In southern China, Buddhism was more intellectual from the start, appealing to the educated classes. It was independent of the political rulers and allied itself with Taoism.

The famous T'ien-t'ai school of Chinese Buddhism was known for its intensive twelve-year programme of scriptural study. Most of the great Chinese Buddhist scholars were educated in T'ien-t'ai academies. Tantric Buddhism was also transmitted to China and although Nikaya Buddhism never took hold in China as a living tradition, scriptures of all Buddhist traditions were translated into Chinese and all philosophies were well known.

The Golden Age of Buddhism in China was from the sixth to ninth centuries CE, under the Sui and T'ang dynasties. Buddhism was the dominant religion of the people, although rulers varied in their favours. It was the dynamic stimulus of intellectual and cultural life. It is said, for instance, that China invented wood-block printing in the eighth century in order to print Buddhist images and texts. This alone would mean that Buddhism made an enormous social contribution.

Some village temples were quite small, with just one or two monks who worked among the local people, while other monasteries grew large, enjoyed official patronage and, as a result, became powerful and wealthy. Peasant families and serfs were allocated to large monasteries to work in the temple fields, so monasteries had regular, tax-free incomes. Monasteries functioned as study centres and temples, hospitals, guest houses and banks. Many of them owned mills and oil presses, used by the local population for a fee. Monks helped to build roads, bridges and irrigation projects and to plant trees as a way of engaging in socially useful work and of being more accepted in Chinese culture.

From this brief description it can be seen that Chinese Buddhism made significant adaptations to the national culture. There were several important developments.

- Monks engaged in economic activities.
- Monks were given an 'ordination certificate' showing their 'spiritual genealogy', that is, who they received ordination from. This echoed Chinese respect for family lineage.
- Chinese ancestral worship was incorporated into Buddhism: ancestors could be cared for by transferring one's good karma to them.
- The Mahayana *bodhisattva* of compassion, depicted as a male in India, assumed a female form in China. She is called Kuan-Yin and symbolises the motherly qualities of compassion.
- Yama, the ruler of death and the hells, was depicted as a Chinese magistrate who decided on each person's rebirth by weighing up his or her good and bad deeds. This can be seen in some paintings of the Wheel of Life (see Chapter 11).

Hsuan Tsang

Hsuan Tsang (also written Xuan tsang) was a Chinese monk, scholar, traveller and translator. He was born in Luoyang in 602 into a Confucian family, but became a Buddhist monk at twenty and studied Buddhist scriptures in Chang-an. In order to pursue his studies, he asked the emperor's permission to travel to India, but the emperor refused because the regions he had to cross were at war. So Hsuan Tsang left China secretly in 629 travelling west along the Silk Road.

He journeyed for sixteen years all over central Asia and the Indian subcontinent and wrote down what he discovered during his travels. His report is priceless because it provides the first reliable information we have of life in these regions and of the state of Buddhism at that time. It has been translated into English and is published as *Buddhist Records of the Western World* by Samuel Beal. Hsuan Tsang travelled as far west as Tashkent and visited Samarkand (Turkestan), Taxla and Kashmir before going to northern India and staying for a while at Nalanda University. He then went to southern India and returned to China via Assam.

His travels were marked by numerous dramas. He survived a murder attempt and almost starved to death in the Takla Makan Desert. He was imprisoned on the Silk Road and only released after a hunger strike. On the positive side, he was a guest and personal friend of King Harsha (reigned 606-647), the last great Indian emperor who was also India's last great patron of Buddhism. And the king of Turfan became his disciple and gave him letters of introduction for the rest of his journey.

His book gives us a picture of Buddhism in decline. Throughout central Asia and central and southern India, monasteries and sacred sites were abandoned or neglected. He also says that the Nikaya schools were stronger than Mahayana in most of India and central Asia. He collected together an enormous number of Buddhist manuscripts which in those days were rare, and deposited some of these in the Tun Huang caves, north of Tibet, on his way back home. These texts were discovered intact in the 20th century. Many are preserved in the British Library and a project is underway to digitise them and translate them into English. Hsuan Tsang returned to China carrying 520 cases containing 657 different Buddhist scriptures. His fame preceded him, and he was given a hero's welcome by the apologetic emperor. With the emperor's support he established an important translation bureau. His particular contribution was the large number of texts he introduced from the Yogachara school of philosophy. He died in 664.

Decline of Buddhism in China

The decline of Buddhism in China came as a result of political jealousies and rivalries prompted by the wealth of the monasteries. In 715, the government confiscated all copper and bronze religious statues to turn them into cash. In the eighth century, civil war impoverished the state, so Emperor Wu-tzung (841–847) finally decided to break Buddhist dominance. In 845, there was a tremendous backlash against Buddhism. All Buddhist establishments were destroyed, monks and nuns were secularised, and all temple lands and property were confiscated. Monastic Buddhism was suppressed throughout the empire and never recovered its dominance.

Decline was steady and gradual. Most of the different schools of Chinese Buddhism disappeared, and intellectual life went back to Confucianism. Under the Ming dynasty (14th to 17th centuries), for example, state officials were forbidden to be Buddhists. This meant that the best minds in the country were no longer drawn to the Buddhist debating halls but to the Confucian classics required for state examinations.

The two main schools of Chinese Buddhism to survive were Ch'an and Pure Land. The approach of these schools meant that neither depended on large institutions or vast libraries of scriptures, and they therefore succeeded in continuing after the persecution despite the lack of political and economic support. Although monasteries were destroyed, Buddhism was still practised by lay people right up to the Cultural Revolution of 1949. It had become confined to being a popular religion rather than a religion of the educated elite. Buddhism was severely persecuted during the Cultural Revolution but, since the 1990s, it has seen a significant revival in mainland China, and monasteries have once again been established and statues renovated. In 2012, a Pew Research Centre survey estimated that Buddhists account for at least 20% of the population.

Korea

Korea is sometimes known as 'the hermit kingdom' and has played a significant role in the history of Asian Buddhism. It received Buddhism mainly from China and then transmitted it to Japan. Korea produced many outstanding Buddhist masters over the centuries who influenced the development of Buddhist thought in mainland China and in Tibet.

The year 372 CE is traditionally considered the year in which Buddhism was introduced into Korea although modern scholars have found evidence that it may have been introduced earlier. This occurred during the Three Kingdoms Period (c.200-668) when the peninsula was divided into three independent but warring kingdoms: Koguryo in the north, Paekche in the southwest, and Silla in the southeast. The Emperor of northern China, Fu Chien, sent a diplomatic delegation to Koguryo in that year, which included a Buddhist monk named Shun-tao bearing Buddhist scriptures and images as gifts. The Korean king offered him a lavish reception and is said to have built the Hunguk Monastery for him.

Buddhism was then introduced to the other two kingdoms separately: to Paekche in 384 by the Indian monk Malananda who travelled by sea from southern China, and lastly to Silla where it initially received a hostile reception. It is said that a court official named Ich'adon, under King Pophung (r.514-540), secretly approved the construction of a Buddhist monastery, and when the king discovered this Ich'adon was beheaded. According to tradition, at his execution Ich'adon's blood flowed as white as milk and his head flew through the air and landed on a mountain top. These miracles moved everyone to reconsider their opposition to Buddhism.

Indeed, it seems that Buddhism first became popular in Korea on account of its magical aspects, especially protection from disease and misfortune, long before particular philosophical teachings became known. In this early period, it was portrayed mainly as a sort of national shamanism and gained the role of protecting the Korean nation, a role it continued to play for centuries. *Hoguk pulgyo*, or 'state-protection Buddhism', is characteristic of Buddhism in Korea.

The Korean peninsula was unified under the Silla banner in 668, and between 668 and 935 several schools of Buddhism became clearly established there, in particular the Sarvastivada school of Nikaya Buddhism, the Madhyamaka and Yogachara schools of Mahayana Buddhism, the Chinese school of T'ien-t'ai and the school of Tantric Buddhism known as Zhen Yan in China. Korean monks would travel to China to receive Buddhist teachings there, and several became respected scholars in their own right. For example, a commentary by Wonch'uk (613-696) on the *Samdhinirmocana Sutra* influenced the early scholars of Buddhism in Tibet.

The Korean monk Pömnang (mid seventh century) is said to have studied in China under the fourth patriarch of Ch'an, and he introduced Ch'an to Korea where it is known as Sön. The Sön school continues to flourish in Korea to this day. It developed from the Lin-chi lineage (which became Rinzai in Japan).

Another influential Korean monk named Musang (or Moheyan), also known as Kim Ho-shang, was regarded as a patriarch of a subschool of Ch'an in the Szechuan region of China, and is famous in Tibetan history as one of the first Ch'an masters known to Tibetans. He is said to have engaged in a two-year public debate on Buddhist doctrine in 792-4 with the Indian master Kamalashila in Lhasa, and according to Tibetan accounts he lost the debate and was banished.

As in China, Korean monks enjoyed a privileged position in society since they were exempt from taxation, military service and conscripted labour. Monasteries were able to amass considerable wealth and political power, and by the eleventh century they had become a 'state within the state'. One of the most important achievements of the golden age of Korean Buddhism (roughly 918-1392) was the carving and woodblock printing of the first Korean canon in Chinese characters. It took forty years to produce some 6,000 volumes, and the project was completed in the reign of King Munjong (r. 1046-83). During this period, Korea also invented metal type, possibly the ancestor of the movable type developed by Gutenberg in 15th century Europe, and on account of this there was a flourishing of literature of all kinds.

As Buddhism evolved in Korea, a distinction grew between the 'scholarly' schools that emphasize study of the scriptures, and Sön which emphasizes meditation. Some masters tried to bring these two approaches together, creating a unified synthesis of Buddhist thought and practice. The most successful attempt was that of Chinul (1158-1210) who is widely seen as the most influential Buddhist in the history of Korea. He created the distinctly Korean school of Sön called Chogye-chong which is the predominant school today.

Between 1231 and 1258, six Mongol invasions put an end to this creative period and thoroughly destroyed all the artefacts of Korean culture. Then from 1392 to 1910, Korea was ruled by a Confucian dynasty which saw the closure of most Buddhist monasteries in the 15th century. After this Buddhism steadily declined. When Korea was annexed by Japan in 1910 some attempts were made at reviving the religion, but the results were mixed. After the Second World War in 1945, Korea was divided into two. The North surrendered to the Soviet Union which, after the Korean War (1950-53), was replaced by Communist China, and the South came under the influence of the United States.

From the limited information available it seems that Buddhists are a small minority in North Korea today. Buddhism is practised under the auspices of the Korea Buddhist Federation, an organ of the State which officially declares itself to be atheist. Buddhist monks are entirely dependent on State wages for their livelihood as well as State authorization to practise. There are only 60 Buddhist temples in the country, and they are viewed as cultural relics of the past rather than places of active worship. However, a limited revival of Buddhism is apparently taking place and includes the establishment of an academy for Buddhist studies and the publication of a twenty-five-volume translation of the Buddhist scriptures.

In South Korea the vitality of Buddhism is undeniable although it faces serious challenges. Results of national censuses in 2005 and 2015 show that between 15% and 20% of the population are self-declared Buddhists. However, the majority of young people claim to have 'no religion' and it is the older and rural populations that tend to be religious. Furthermore, since the 1980s, Buddhist temples and statues have been desecrated by Protestant Christians. Nevertheless, Korean culture remains strongly influenced by Buddhist values and attitudes.

Japan

Buddhism spread from China to Korea, and from Korea to Japan. It was introduced into Japan in the sixth century CE along with other elements of Chinese civilisation. At that time Japan had no strong institutions of its own so there was no opposition to Buddhism. In 538 or 539 a Korean ruler sent a deputation to make an alliance with a Japanese ruler, and the delegation included Buddhist monks, scriptures and Buddha statues. From that time some of the Japanese ruling class began to follow Buddhism, which was later supported by Prince Shotoku (574-621) who is considered the father of Japanese Buddhism. He was a generous patron, built monasteries and temples, and virtually made Buddhism a state religion.

Shinto

The main religion already present in Japan at that time was Shinto. Shinto is related to the forces of nature and is concerned with creating good circumstances here and now. It is based on the belief that the gods are immanent in nature and do not live somewhere else, in some transcendental sphere. The deities of Shinto are called *kamis* and they are the spirits of mountains, trees, waterfalls and other powerful forces in the world. There is no chief kami corresponding to the idea of God. The kamis are considered to have an influence on human life so this is why prayers and offerings are made to propitiate them. Shinto is practised mostly outdoors with local shrines in nature, although families may have a 'kami shelf' in their homes where symbols of the kami are kept.

When Buddhism arrived, Shinto had no written scriptures or strict doctrines so it did not present an intellectual challenge in the way Confucianism or Taoism had done in China. Furthermore, Shinto had no iconography – the kami were not represented by images but by symbols such as a mirror, sword or jewel. Over the centuries Shinto and Buddhism coexisted peacefully in Japan and mutually influenced each other. People still see them as complementary.

Buddhism in Japan

Japanese Buddhism is characterized by its extensive secularisation. It is not so concerned with escape from the endless cycle of life and death, or with transcendental states and realities; it focuses more on this-worldly questions – on the importance of finding oneself and realizing enlightenment here and now. This is reflected in the way Buddhism pervades cultural life: in painting, in gardening, in flower arranging, in calligraphy and in drama. Each of these arts was developed on the basis of Buddhist meditation and contemplation.

In addition, Japan developed a unique form of Buddhist clergy which is highly secularised. The largest sect, Jodo-shinshu or True Pure Land, abandoned monastic celibacy altogether in the 13th century and created what is usually called a priesthood where Buddhist priests can marry, can take ordinary paid jobs, and pass responsibility for their temples from father to son. As part of modernisation and Westernisation, in the late 19th century the emperor decreed that monks could marry.

There are three features that make Japanese Buddhism unique:

1. **Buddhism and authority:** Buddhism was first accepted by the ruling classes and was then disseminated throughout Japan from the top down. Buddhist faith is connected with absolute devotion to a leader – for example, to the founder of a sect. Furthermore, most sects developed a close connection with the central government of the time.
2. **Magic powers:** Buddhism is associated with magic powers and this is one reason why it was accepted by the authorities. Buddhist monks were requested to use their powers to prevent disease, maintain peace, bring rainfall and good harvests, and so forth. Buddhism was given the role of 'pacifying and protecting the state'.
3. **Buddhism and Shinto:** Buddhism did not attempt to replace Shinto but amalgamated with it. It recognized the Shinto gods as manifestations of the buddhas. From the 14th century onwards, the buddhas were often seen as manifestations of the kamis.

Between the seventh and tenth centuries several different schools of Chinese Buddhism became established in Japan. The most influential was the Tendai (T'ien-t'ai in Chinese) school which incorporated a twelve-year programme of study, meditation and monastic discipline with Tantric Buddhist practices. However, by the tenth century many of the monasteries had become decadent and a period of social, religious and political chaos ensued. Two far simpler forms of Buddhism emerged from this time, which continue to be strong today: Zen and Pure Land (see Chapters 18 and 19). They are more adapted to the common people.

Between the 12th and 16th centuries there were periods of military conflict between rival Buddhist monasteries. These battles were waged by hired troops or sometimes by armed monks. The True Pure Land sect developed fortified temples and was known to lead peasant uprisings. Another sect founded by Nichiren (1222-1283) set out to attack all other forms of Buddhism in Japan denouncing them as misguided and doomed, and caused considerable chaos. Two powerful warlords finally put an end to military monasteries in the 16th century, and Zen, Pure Land and Nichiren were the main forms of Buddhism that survived.

In the 19th century, Japanese nationalism reacted against European colonialism and Christian missionaries (Christianity was banned in Japan in the 17th century) and declared Shinto to be the state religion with Buddhism as the secondary religion. Most Japanese people today combine both religions.

Main Points

- Buddhism spread to China through two separate routes:
  - By the northern route in the first century CE, from central Asia by traders plying the Silk Route
  - By the southern route from the third century CE from Sri Lanka, Indo-China and Canton
- Its development in China was influenced by Confucianism and Taoism.
- Buddhism made significant adaptations to Chinese culture: e.g. monks engaged in economic activities and ancestral worship was incorporated into Buddhism
- Political jealousies and rivalries emerged with the prosperity of the monasteries and Buddhism was persecuted in 715 and in 845.
- The two schools to survive were Ch'an and Pure Land.
- Buddhism was introduced from China to Korea in 372 CE.
- It was given the role of 'protector of the State'.
- From Korea, Buddhism went to Japan in the sixth century where it was influenced by Shinto.
- Japanese Buddhism became highly secularised and many monasteries engaged in political conflicts between warlords.
- Four main schools survive: Pure Land, True Pure Land, Zen and Nichiren.

Chapter 6

BUDDHISM IN CENTRAL ASIA AND THE HIMALAYAS

Buddhism spread to central Asia soon after the Buddha passed away whereas the Himalayan region did not adopt Buddhism as its religion and way of life until over a thousand years later. Finally, in the 13th century, Mongolia was the last country in Asia to become predominantly Buddhist.

Central Asia

Central Asia is not a unified area, either politically or geographically. The only reason for treating it as one is because Buddhism flourished there for many centuries, despite tremendous changes and upheavals, so one can speak of a Buddhist-inspired culture that pervaded throughout the region. Although it is almost entirely Muslim today, central Asia was predominantly Buddhist for almost a thousand years, between the third century BCE and the fifth century CE.

Roughly speaking, central Asia covers the Karakoram, Hindu Kush and Pamir mountains of Kashmir, northern Pakistan and Afghanistan; Tadjikistan and Uzbekistan up to the Aral Sea; and then continues across the Tian Shan mountains to the Takla Makan Desert of far western China. Before modern times the region was divided into many different kingdoms and, in some periods, influential empires, all of which have now dissolved. These ancient kingdoms include Gilgit, Sogdiana, Bactria, Gandhara, Uddiyana and Zhang Zhung.

Central Asia was a centre of Buddhist scholarship and art that had tremendous influence on the development of Buddhism throughout Asia. In particular, central Asia played an important role in the early transmission of Buddhism from India to China in the first century CE, situated as it was on the ancient Silk Road. And later on, in the seventh and eighth centuries, it also played a vital role in the transmission of Buddhism to Tibet. There is textual evidence suggesting that Vajrayana Buddhism has its origins in central Asia. Padmasambhava, considered by many to be the founder of Tibetan Buddhism, is reputed to have brought Vajrayana and Dzogchen (Great Perfection) teachings from the kingdom of Uddiyana.

The date when Buddhism spread from India to central Asia is unclear. Inscriptions and ruins from the time of Emperor Ashoka have been discovered in Pakistan and Afghanistan, and we know that Ashoka helped to establish Buddhism in Kashmir during his reign. On the strength of this evidence, the histories of Buddhism written by Western scholars invariably associate the beginnings of Buddhism in central Asia with Ashoka's missions. However, the Buddhist tradition dates Buddhism in Kashmir to some two hundred years before Ashoka.

The Buddha predicted that one hundred years after his passing away, a monk named Madhyantika would introduce the Dharma into Kashmir, which the Buddha described as 'the best place for meditation that one could wish for'.[14] Tradition has it that this was indeed the case, and that an Indian monk named Madhyantika, who was a disciple of Ananda (see Chapter 3), travelled to Kashmir some fifty years after the Buddha's passing. He stayed there for the rest of his life and built five hundred monasteries, one for each of the five hundred arhats he invited to Kashmir to spread the Dharma. Later, Kashmir was conquered by Ashoka's grandfather and became part of the Indian empire, and when Ashoka was emperor he had more Buddhist monasteries built there and gave the whole country to the monks as a gift.

After Ashoka, the region was dominated by various waves of invaders including the Iranians and the Greeks, but Buddhism continued despite these upheavals. It flourished particularly under the Bactrian king Menander (c.155-130 BCE) and under Kanishka (c.78-123 CE) in the Kushan empire. It seems that stability and religious tolerance enabled Buddhism to grow alongside other cultural and religious influences at that time.

The Kushan empire embraced various peoples living side by side, especially Iranians, Greeks and Indians. Greeks had been living in Gandhara since the fourth century BCE, and it is generally agreed today that it was due to the influence of the Greeks that the style of Buddhist art known as Gandharan developed. The most important feature of this art is the depiction of the Buddha in human form, according to the idealised rules of artistic perfection developed by the Greeks. In the first centuries after the Buddha it had been felt that the Enlightened One was beyond artistic representation, and he was solely depicted by symbols such as the eight-spoked Wheel of the Dharma, or a stupa. Thus, the image of the Buddha that we are familiar with today has its roots in central Asia and in Greek art.

Kashmir (which in ancient times was larger than it is today) became a highly respected centre of education and philosophy. Kushan rule opened up the trade routes of central Asia and from Kashmir Buddhist monks spread their learning, travelling north to Khotan, east to the Takla Makan basin and to Tun Huang on the northern border between Tibet and China. Both Nikaya and Mahayana monasteries were established in the oasis cities along the Silk Road, and during this period many Buddhist scriptures were translated into central Asian languages. One of the most famous of the Kashmiri-educated translators was Kumarajiva (see Chapter 5).

Some of the very oldest Buddhist manuscripts in our possession today come from central Asia, possibly because the dry climate has preserved them well. For example, a Gandhari edition of the *Dhammapada* has been dated to the second century CE. From the same period we have found Mahayana manuscripts too, including translations of the long *Prajñaparamita Sutra*, the *Diamond Sutra* and the *Lotus Sutra* into the language of Khotan.

In the third century, Iranian invaders overthrew the Kushan empire. These same invaders were also present in northern India, and in both regions it seems that they tolerated and even encouraged the spread of Buddhism. Some of the most impressive Buddhist art in the region dates from the third to fifth centuries: the beautiful Jaulian stupa at Taxila in present-day Pakistan, and the monumental standing statues of the Buddha carved out of cliff faces in Bamiyan, present-day Afghanistan.

Then, in the sixth century, the White Huns invaded Kashmir and from there moved into Gandhara. At first they followed their own religion, which resembled Zoroastrianism, but soon became strong supporters of Buddhism. In 515, however, the White Hun king Mihirakula suppressed Buddhism under the influence of jealous non-Buddhist factions in his court. He destroyed many monasteries and killed hundreds of monks especially in northwestern India, Gandhara and Kashmir. By the seventh century, the Chinese pilgrim Hsuan-tsang reports that the destruction had been quite thorough: only a hundred active monasteries remained in Kashmir and another hundred in Khotan, but he found not a single monk left in Gandhara. This part of central Asia was subsequently invaded by Arab Muslims who were respectful of non-Muslim religions. Some rulers did persecute Buddhism in the eighth and ninth centuries, and caused monks to flee east to Khotan and Kashmir, but on the whole Buddhism was tolerated and continued to be practised. Buddhism was not seriously weakened until the destruction of monasteries by Mahmud Ghazni (r.998-1030) in Uddiyana, and by Muhammed Ghuri (r. 1173-?) in Punjab, Bihar and West Bengal. In 1200 he destroyed two of the greatest monasteries in India, Vikramashila and Odantapuri. Finally, the Mongol invasions, too, began by being tolerant and even supportive of Buddhism, but after 1321 conversions to Islam were systematic and Buddhism did not survive.

Uddiyana

Buddhist texts speak of Uddiyana (Orgyen in Tibetan) as a beautifully green and fertile kingdom, inhabited by gentle people often clothed in white, who had great respect for wisdom and learning. It was surrounded by high, rugged mountains, and in the broad valleys were towering white stupas and golden temple roofs. It seemed a paradise on earth and so was called 'the royal garden' from the Sanskrit *udyana*. Uddiyana was also known as 'the paradise of the dakinis', as it was reputed for its unique sisterhood of priestesses—ladies dedicated to wisdom and spiritual development. These priestesses were not nuns and lived in sanctuaries or forest chapels.

The central Asian kingdom of Uddiyana played an important role in the history of Buddhism, especially from the perspective of Tibetan Buddhism. It is believed to be the homeland of both the Vajrayana and Dzogchen (Great Perfection) teachings which some consider to be the highest, most esoteric teachings in Buddhism[15]. Uddiyana is said to be the land where Garab Dorje, Vairotsana, Padmasambhava and Tilopa, among others, received transmissions; they are all revered lineage masters in Tibetan Buddhism.

Most Tibetan texts simply explain that Uddiyana was a kingdom that lay to the west or northwest of India, and many Western scholars have identified it with the valley of Swat, in present-day northwestern Kashmir, in Pakistan. However, the master Patrul Rinpoche[16] gives a more precise indication of where Uddiyana was when he describes the birthplace of Garab Dorje as being close to Lake Kutra in the region of Dhanakosha. This corresponds to a region between Chitral, Gilgit and Swat. Archaeology and art history have failed to confirm that Uddiyana was restricted to Swat, and Patrul Rinpoche's description confirms the latest scholarly thinking which is that Uddiyana was much more extensive than the Swat valley itself. John Reynolds suggests that "perhaps Uddiyana is actually a name of a much wider geographical area than the Swat Valley alone, one embracing parts of Pakistan, Afghanistan, and even Western Tibet (Zhang zhung). The best approach is to remain open-minded and not restrict the name only to the Swat Valley."[17]

With regard to the origins of the Vajrayana teachings, the Tantric scriptures recount that it was King Dza of the kingdom of Zahor who first received the Tantras, which landed miraculously on his palace roof. Some scholars believe that Dza is another name for King Indrabodhi of Uddiyana. If this is the case, then the Tantras began to be disseminated in Uddiyana. There is indeed evidence to suggest that Tantric Buddhism was practised there very early, possibly even before it was practised in India. The Chinese pilgrim Hsuan-tsang travelled there in the seventh century and reported, with some distaste, that people were chanting 'superstitious spells', possibly indicating that he was unfamiliar with the tantric practice of *mantra*.

As for the origins of the Dzogchen teachings, according to Tibetan tradition the first human Dzogchen master was Garab Dorje, who was born near Lake Kutra in Uddiyana. His disciple, Manjushrimitra, was Indian and received the teachings in Bodh Gaya, but the next lineage holder, Shri Singha, came from the central Asian kingdom of Khotan which at that time was under the Chinese. It is said that another Dzogchen master, Vairotsana, met Shri Singha in Uddiyana near Lake Dhanakosha in order to receive transmission. And Padmasambhava, the tantric master who introduced Vajrayana and Dzogchen to Tibet according to the Tibetan histories, was miraculously born on Lake Dhanakosha and raised by the king of Uddiyana. We also know that many of the Dzogchen texts that were translated into Tibetan during the early period of transmission were translated from the language of Uddiyana.

The Himalayas and Mongolia

The last direction to which Buddhism spread in Asia was north: to the Himalayan region and the Mongolian steppe. Buddhism was introduced to Tibet in the 6th century and became firmly established there in the 8th century under the patronage of King Trisongdetsen. The Indian monk Shantarakshita and the yogi Padmasambhava worked together to introduce all three Vehicles of Buddhism at that time. They also visited Bhutan and established Buddhism there in the same period. Finally, the Buddha Dharma was introduced to Mongolia from Tibet after the conversion of the Mongol leader Kublai Khan in around 1250.

Tibet

According to Tibetan legends, the first appearance of Buddhism in Tibet occurred in the second century during the reign of King Totori Nyentsen (born in around 173 CE). One day a Buddhist text and relics consecrated to the buddha of compassion, Chenresig, fell miraculously from the sky and landed on the roof of the king's palace. The text was written in Sanskrit which nobody in Tibet could read, but the king had a dream indicating that in four generations a king would be able to read and understand the books. The exceptional significance of this event for Tibetans is reflected in the fact that before the Chinese takeover in 1959, Tibetan currency was dated in terms of years since that event, held to be the year 233 CE.

From the historical point of view, Buddhism first began to be transmitted in Tibet during the reign of Songtsen Gampo (618-650). He was the first of Tibet's three Dharma Kings and considered to be an incarnation of the buddha of compassion, Chenresig. During this period Tibet was expanding militarily, and since it was surrounded by states where Buddhism was dominant, it discovered Buddhist culture in the process. As a result of their travels Tibetans realized that their culture lagged behind that of their neighbours, and many associated social advancement with Buddhism. Therefore, just as in Japan, the introduction of Buddhism went hand in hand with the introduction of a more refined civilisation.

Another similarity between Tibet and Japan is the religious situation prevailing in both countries when Buddhism was introduced. Shamanistic religion was strong and linked with divine rule; in Japan this religion was Shinto, in Tibet it was called Bön. Throughout the period of the Dharma kings, there was fierce opposition to Buddhism from the followers of Bön who wielded magical power as well as political influence. Over the centuries, however, despite their differences, there was much mutual borrowing between the two religions.

King Songtsen Gampo is credited with having sent the scholar Thönmi Sambhota to Kashmir and India in order to develop a script and grammar for the Tibetan language. The king made this the standard throughout Tibet. The Tibetan language was tailor-made for the translation of Sanskrit, and its creation therefore laid the foundation for future translation of the Buddhist scriptures.

The next step in the development of Buddhism in Tibet came during the reign of the second Dharma King, King Trisongdetsen (742-798), who is considered an incarnation of Manjushri, the buddha of wisdom. It is under his patronage that the first monastery was built at Samye, the first Tibetans were ordained, and the task of translating the Buddhist scriptures began. The eminent Indian scholar Shantarakshita established the Vinaya and the Mahayana teachings, while Padmasambhava introduced Vajrayana and Dzogchen.

From Kamalashila to Langdarma

When Buddhist teachings were introduced into Tibet during this early period, Tibet was open to teachings and texts from anywhere in the Buddhist world. Buddhism was still flourishing from central Asia in the west to China in the east, and Tibet absorbed Buddhism from both these areas as well as directly from India. This inevitably meant that there were differences in views and methods between the various traditions. The histories recount a decisive debate that took place in Lhasa around the year 792 between the Indian scholar Kamalashila and the Korean Ch'an master Hvashang Mahayana. The purpose of the debate was to decide once and for all which approach was correct: the gradual bodhisattva path taught by Kamalashila, or what is called the sudden path of Ch'an that teaches that complete enlightenment can happen suddenly and spontaneously, in a flash, without years of gradual effort. Kamalashila emerged victorious and thereafter Ch'an teachings were banned from Tibet.

The third of Tibet's Dharma kings was Ralpachen who reigned from 815 to 836, and who is considered to be an incarnation of Vajrapani, the buddha of enlightened activity. Under Ralpachen, Tibet's influence in Asia had never been greater, but he seems to have neglected the affairs of state in favour of Dharma and to have been over-generous with the nation's wealth. He systematised the way scriptures were translated and established a glossary of Buddhist terms. He financed numerous monasteries and monks and Buddhist building projects. He supported visits by Indian scholars and trips by Tibetan scholars to India. He decreed that each monk should be supported by a group of seven households, irrespective of whether or not those households were sympathetic to Buddhism. By the end of his reign, Tibet's wealth and power had weakened, and the glory of the early kings was over.

In the end, too many pressures conspired against Ralpachen and, one day, two of his ministers strangled him as he sat resting. Langdarma then took the throne and during the four years of his reign (838-842) persecuted Buddhism and destroyed it in central Tibet. Monasteries were ransacked and monks were forced to disrobe. Langdarma himself was later assassinated. After this a period of chaos and instability ensued for almost 300 years, dominated by factionalism and regional rivalries, and a lack of centralised government. Tibet lost many of the areas it had annexed, and in 905 the Chinese T'ang dynasty also collapsed, increasing political instability throughout the region. Gradually the Mongol empire grew in strength and exercised power over both Tibet and China.

The second dissemination

Despite its destruction in central Tibet, Buddhism survived intact in the far west of Tibet (Guge) and in eastern Tibet (Kham and Amdo). It was transmitted mainly by householder yogis rather than monastics. Towards the end of the tenth century, the king of Guge in western Tibet decided to renounce the throne and become a monk. His ordination name was Yeshe Ö. Intending to revive the Dharma, he sent twenty-one promising Tibetan scholars to India and Kashmir to study, but all but two died there. The two survivors returned to Tibet in 978: they became the great translators Rinchen Zangpo and Lekpe Sherab.

The work of Rinchen Zangpo (958-1055) marks the beginning of a renaissance of Dharma in Tibet, and a second translation period. He visited Kashmir twice and India once, spending a total of seventeen years travelling from teacher to teacher receiving instruction, initiations and acquiring copies of texts, particularly authentic Indian Tantras. This new wave of translations forms the basis of the scriptures compiled in the 13th century by Butön that constitute the Tibetan Canon known today.

Atisha (982-1054)

The most important event in this period was the arrival in Tibet of the Indian scholar Atisha[18]. Atisha is remembered as the first great restorer of Buddhism throughout Tibet. In particular, he re-established the strict monastic rule. Atisha emphasized genuine realization and embodiment of the teachings rather than ritual or ceremony, and exposed many a pretentious monk and lama. For almost a thousand years, Tibetan Buddhism developed on the basis of his approach and, indeed, of his achievements.

Atisha arrived in western Tibet in about 1042, at the age of 60, and spent the last years of his life there, travelling widely and visiting Samye. It is said that he sent the vast sums of gold offered to him back to India, to help support the monastery of Vikramashila which no longer enjoyed the financial patronage of earlier times. His main disciple was Dromtön (1008-1064) who established the Kadampa school of Tibetan Buddhism, based on Atisha's strict approach to monastic discipline. Dromtön established Reting monastery in 1056 where monks were bound by four rules: abstinence from sex, intoxicants, travel and possessions.

The schools of Tibetan Buddhism

The last thousand years of Buddhism in Tibet can be characterized by the development of a number of different schools, each with its own emphasis and style. All schools follow Mahayana, especially the philosophy of Madhyamaka, in combination with Vajrayana. The key difference between them is that they follow distinct lineages and they have developed different interpretations on certain specific points.

The followers of Padmasambhava and the early transmission form the **Nyingma** or ancient school of Tibetan Buddhism. This school has a body of Tantric scriptures that are not recognized by other schools in Tibet and that were not included in Butön's scriptural compilation. Nyingmapas emphasize personal realization more than scholarship. Unlike other schools the Nyingmapas did not generally engage in politics. They have strong traditions of both monastics and householder yogis.

The **Sakya** school was the first to develop after the Kadampas. It derives its name from the *grey earth* around the monastery founded by Konchok Gyalpo of the Khön family in 1073. The lineage was transmitted by Drokmi and systematised by Kunga Nyingpo (1092-1158) who is known as the "Great Sakyapa" because of his tremendous learning. The Sakya school emphasizes scholarship as well as Vajrayana practice.

In 1249, the Mongol leader Godan summoned Sakya Pandita (1182-1251), the most eminent master of his day, with the intention of demanding the surrender of Tibet to Mongol control. Instead, however, Godan was so impressed that he converted to Buddhism, and the Sakya lamas were appointed spiritual advisors of the Mongol khans. This patron-priest relationship lasted intermittently for several centuries and ensured that Tibet was never conquered and laid waste by the Mongol armies. The relationship gave the Sakyapas political dominance in Tibet in the 12th century and this attracted the jealousy of another school, the Kagyüpas.

The first Tibetan master of the **Kagyü** school was Marpa (1012-1096) who travelled to India and studied under the great Tantric master Naropa (1016-1100). Marpa lived as a householder teaching several disciples and especially Milarepa (1040-1123) who is well known through his autobiography. Perhaps his most important disciple was Gampopa (1079-1153) who first formulated the Kagyü teachings in writing. One of Gampopa's disciples was the First Karmapa (1110-1193), who was the first to establish a reincarnating line of *tulkus* who are recognized as children, according to predictions and signs, to be the incarnation of a deceased master. In this way they continue their work from one life to the next. The tulku system is a uniquely Tibetan institution and is now followed by all Tibetan schools. The Kagyü school gives emphasis to practice and realization rather than scholarship and has strong traditions of both monastics and householder yogis.

Finally, the **Gelugpa** school was developed by the disciples of the great master Tsongkhapa (1357-1419). Tsongkhapa travelled widely throughout Tibet, receiving teachings from masters of all schools and traditions. He was unable to go to India, however, since by then Buddhism had been wiped out in its homeland. As a result, the Gelugpa school is the only Tibetan school that did not develop directly from an Indian lineage master.

Apparently disillusioned by the worldliness and political intrigue that characterized some of Tibetan Buddhism in his day, in 1409 he founded his own monastery known as Ganden, on an isolated mountain top 25 miles from Lhasa. Inspired by the Kadampas, he taught strict monastic discipline and withdrawal from worldly affairs. By the time he passed away in 1419, his disciples had established two more monasteries, Sera and Drepung, which over the centuries developed into the largest monasteries in the world, each housing up to ten thousand monks at a time. It was a later abbot of Ganden, Gedundrup (1391-1475), who was recognized as the first Dalai Lama of Tibet and who initiated his own incarnating line of tulkus.

The non-political position of the Gelugpas was dramatically transformed in the 16th century under the leadership of the third Dalai Lama, who travelled to Mongolia at the invitation of their chief Altan Khan. The two men revived the patron-priest relationship initiated by Sakya Pandita, and Altan Khan named him "Ta-le lama" usually rendered 'Dalai' Lama. *Ta-le* means 'ocean' in Mongolian. It thus came about that not only Mongolians but all Tibetans recognized the line of Dalai Lamas as the legitimate political and religious leaders of Tibet. Supported by this power and influence, the Gelugpa school grew quickly to become the dominant and largest school of Buddhism in Tibet.

Nepal

The present-day kingdom of Nepal was consolidated only in the 18th century by the Gurkhas, and until then 'Nepal' referred only to the Kathmandu valley. For the purposes of this account, therefore, we refer to Nepal as the entire area it covers today even when describing events many centuries before the country was constituted.

Thus defined, Nepal can claim to have the world's longest continuous history of Buddhism. Lumbini, the birthplace of Buddha Shakyamuni, is located in Nepal about 100 miles west of Kathmandu. Kapilavastu, where the Buddha spent his childhood and youth, is also in Nepal. We do not have many historical details of the development of Buddhism in Nepal after the Buddha, but it is likely that it has been practised there continuously since early times. It retained its Indian characteristics and Nepal has always been open to the cultural influence of India. Ashoka erected pillars there and, according to legend, his daughter married a Newari prince. From the 6th century CE onwards, Nepal became one of the main routes for travel between India and Tibet.

Although Nepal has been ruled by Hindu dynasties, Buddhism flourished there and coexisted alongside Hinduism, especially within the Newari community of the Kathmandu valley. When Buddhists began to flee India in the face of the Muslim invasions, many went to Nepal and this spawned a resurgence of Buddhism there in the 11th century. Nepal became a sanctuary for monks, scholars and artists. However, with the loss of support from its parent tradition in India, Buddhism in Nepal absorbed Hindu elements very quickly. The majority of Buddhists became lay householders, and only a small minority maintained the celibate monastic lifestyle. Many monasteries were transformed into living quarters for whole families. Vajrayana practices were heavily influenced by Shaiva Hindu Tantra, and Buddhists worshipped Hindu deities.

Another blow to Indian-style Buddhism came in the 18th century when the Gurkhas conquered the Kathmandu valley and controlled the trade routes. They attempted to impose Hindu culture on the entire country and

Buddhism was repressed. The Nepali Buddhism that survives, amongst the Newari people for example, is heavily mixed with Hinduism although the Sherpa people in the north of the country practise Tibetan Buddhism. There is currently a limited revival of Buddhism in Nepal due to the presence of Tibetan refugees and to the interest of international tourists in the ancient Buddhist sites.

Bhutan

Bhutan did not receive Buddhism directly from ancient India. Traditional sources state that the first two Buddhist temples built in Bhutan were the Kyerchu and Jampa temples, and that they were constructed by the Tibetan king Songtsen Gampo in the seventh century. Furthermore, according to tradition, both Padmasambhava and Shantarakshita visited Bhutan from Tibet in the eighth century and converted many people to Buddhism. Paro Taksang, in Bhutan, is one of the thirteen *taksang* or 'tiger's lairs' which are sacred caves blessed by Padmasambhava. There is historical evidence that Tibetan monks and others fleeing Langdarma's persecutions in the ninth century settled in Bhutan.

Once Buddhism was re-established in Tibet in the eleventh century, masters of all schools travelled freely to Bhutan. The Nyingma scholar Longchenpa

Figure 6.1 – Paro Taktsang, or 'the tiger's nest', is one of the oldest temples in Bhutan and a site where Padmasambhava did retreat.

established a monastery there. The other influential school in Bhutan is a subsect of the Kagyü school, the Drukpa Kagyü, which was decisively boosted by the arrival of the Zhab Drung from Tibet in the 17th century. The Zhab Drung (Ngawang Namgyal) was enthroned as head of the Drukpa Kagyü sect in Tibet and was widely believed to be the incarnation of Padma Karpo, one of the greatest scholars in Tibetan history. But a dispute involving a rival claimant to be this reincarnation led the Zhab Drung to flee to Bhutan in 1616. He became the undisputed religious and secular authority in Bhutan. He established both Nyingma and Drukpa Kagyü schools as the basis of Buddhist practice, and both are still vibrant today. His armies successfully repelled several attempted invasions by Tibetans and by Mongols; but internal conflicts and more invasions from Tibet meant that by the 19th century the incarnate line of Zhab Drungs ceased to have much authority. An alliance between Bhutan and Britain instituted the present monarchy in 1907.

The most famous Bhutanese scholar is Pema Lingpa (1450-1521), one of the great finders *(tertons)* of *treasure* teachings concealed in the eighth century by Padmasambhava. At the age of 26 he had a vision of Padmasambhava, and a year later discovered the first of his profound treasures, the *Dzogchen longsal gyi kornam*. Surrounded by a large crowd of people, he dived into Lake Mebar, near Naring Trak, holding a burning lamp in his hand. Miraculously, when he re-emerged, the lamp in his hand was still burning and under his arm he carried a treasure chest the size of a clay pot containing the treasure teaching. He went on to discover many more teachings and sacred objects.

One of the characteristics of Buddhism in Bhutan is the way the monasteries function as centres of administration. Buddhism is still flourishing there, with monasteries of up to 500 monks. It is the only independent country left in Asia that is guided by the Tibetan religion and culture, and where Buddhism continues to be taught and practised as it was in Tibet before the Chinese takeover.

Mongolia

The indigenous religion of Mongolia is a form of shamanism that relies on worship and magic rituals associated with the spirits of nature. Against this background, according to ancient Chinese texts, contacts between the Mongols and Buddhism occurred as early as the third or fourth centuries CE through Chinese monks in the border regions. By the seventh century, Buddhism was practised as far as the Yenisei region. In addition, Buddhism flourished amongst the Uighur tribes in the oasis states along the Silk Road, especially from the tenth century, and Buddhist scriptures were translated into Uighur. Historians have also discovered ruins of a Buddhist temple in Khara Baishing, near Ulan Bator, that date to the eleventh century. But the evidence for this early period is sparse and most histories of Buddhism in Mongolia begin much later, in the 13th century, when the Tibetan lama Sakya Pandita visited the Mongol chief Godan Khan in 1244. The two leaders initiated a priest-patron relationship between the two countries that was to last for centuries.

Although Godan Khan himself may have been converted to Buddhism through this encounter, the religion does not appear to have become widespread in Mongolia until the conversion of Kublai Khan (reigned 1260-1294) in about 1250 by the great Sakyapa scholar Phagpa (1235-1280). In 1269, Phagpa invented a script for the Mongolian language which allowed many Buddhist scriptures to be translated from Tibetan, and sometimes from Uighur, and printed with the block-print method. It seems that Buddhism spread mainly amongst the noble and ruling families and did not touch the population at large which continued to practise shamanism.

A second and more lasting wave of interest in Buddhism arose in the 16th century under Altan Khan (1507-1583), the most powerful leader of the southern Mongols, who met the third Dalai Lama of Tibet in 1576 and re-established the priest-patron relationship between the two countries. A year later, the leader of the northern Mongols, Abadai Khan, also embraced the Buddha Dharma. Virtually all the nobility converted to Buddhism at that time. The third Dalai Lama spent the last ten years of his life teaching in Mongolia. Shamanism was outlawed by Altan Khan, and the sacrifice of animals and humans was banned. Buddhism became the national religion for the next 300 years.

With the support of princes and regional leaders, the Dharma was able to flourish and spread. Numerous monasteries were built which became cradles of education in art, literature, philosophy and the ancient sciences. Mongolia produced a great many learned and realized masters. In particular, the incarnation of the fourth Dalai Lama was identified as a Mongolian, the great-grandson of Altan Khan, and this inspired the Mongolians to establish their own lines of incarnating lamas called *khutuktu*.

Buddhism in Mongolia was further boosted when the Chinese Ming dynasty was replaced in the 17th century by the Manchurian Ching dynasty. The Ming emperors had suppressed Tibetan-style Buddhism in China, but the Manchus were ethnically related to both the Tibetans and the Mongols and vigorously promoted Buddhism in Mongolia. It was under Manchu patronage that the complete Mongolian translation of the Tibetan Kangyur scriptures was published in 1718-20 and distributed throughout the country. Finally, in 1742-49, the Tengyur scriptures were also translated, printed and published in 226 volumes (see Chapter 8).

The most eminent reincarnating lama in Mongolia was known as the Jebtsundamba, who was ranked immediately after the Dalai Lama of Tibet. The first Jebtsundamba was identified as the incarnation of the Tibetan historian Taranatha (born in 1575). Lamas in this line are recognized as the political heads of the country as well as the heads of the Gelugpa school in Mongolia. When Mongolia declared independence in 1912, the eighth Jebtsundamba was the monarch until his death in 1924. Soon after, China took over what became Inner Mongolia and Russia ruled Outer Mongolia. Buddhism was firmly suppressed in both, but since the collapse of the Soviet Union there is an enthusiastic Buddhist revival in Outer Mongolia. The Dalai Lama was invited to teach there in 1979 and 1982 to crowds of many thousands.

The Communist dismissal of the effectiveness of religion was recently challenged in Russia when the remains of the previous Hambo lama were unearthed in newly independent Mongolia. The Hambo lamas are the heads of Buddhism in Russia. Lama Itigelov was a Buryat (a Mongolian people living around Lake Baikal, north of the Mongolian-Russian border) and was well-known in his lifetime and participated in social reforms initiated by the Tsar between 1913 and 1917. He also opened the first Buddhist temple in St Petersburg. Hambo Lama Itigelov died in 1927 at the age of 75, leaving a testament in which he asked his disciples to bury him upright in meditation posture in a specially-made cedar coffin, and also asked them to unearth him after several years. He was buried accordingly in a cemetery near Ulan Ude. Only after the fall of the Communist regime did monks in the region dare to unearth him as he had requested, and when they did so, on 10th September 2002, they were amazed to find that his body was preserved as though it had been mummified. Muscles and skin were soft and joints were mobile.

The lama's body was transferred to the home of the present Hambo lama, Ivolginsky Datsan, and examined by scientists. Their official statement was that the body was well preserved, without any signs of decay, with whole muscles, inner tissue, soft joints and skin. Two years passed while the body was kept in the open air, in contact with people and without any temperature or humidity regulation, and still it didn't decay. Scientists are unable to explain this phenomenon. It was reported in the Russian mass media and then worldwide; a video of the event is on the internet. This is one of the very few confirmed cases of an imperishable body known to the scientific community, where the body is preserved without embalming. Although there are accounts of such realization in Buddhist texts, the materialistic perspective shared by science and Communism leaves no room for the possibility of mind's mastery over the laws of physics.

Main Points

- Buddhism became established in central Asia under Ashoka (2nd century BCE).
- All Vehicles of Buddhism were taught and practised there.
- The region is known for its outstanding art, sculpture and scholarship, and its translations of Buddhist texts.
- Some Muslim invaders supported Buddhism and others persecuted it. Mahmud Ghazni (r.998-1030) and Muhammed Ghuri (r.1173) destroyed monasteries in central Asia and northern India, and Mongol invasions continued this trend.
- After 1321, Buddhism had been eliminated from the region.
- Buddhism spread to Tibet from the 6th century onwards. It was established as the state religion in the 8th century under King Trisongdetsen.
- The Vinaya and Sutra traditions were introduced from India by the abbot Shantarakshita, while Vajrayana and Dzogchen teachings were introduced from central Asia (Uddiyana) and China.
- Four schools of Tibetan Buddhism emerged: Nyingma, Kagyu, Sakya and Gelug.
- Tibetan Buddhism spread to Bhutan in the 8th century and to Mongolia in the 13th century. It is practised throughout the Himalayan region.

Chapter 7

THE THREE VEHICLES

There are three distinct approaches to the Buddhist path, and in each country to which Buddhism spread, one or other of these approaches became dominant.

Introduction

During his lifetime the Buddha taught for some forty five years and spoke to many different types of people: old and young, men and women, kings, peasants and untouchables, educated and uneducated. It is therefore not surprising that, as a good communicator, he found different ways of expressing the teaching according to the needs of his audiences. This is the logic behind the idea that the Buddha's teaching can be categorised into three different 'vehicles' or *yanas* because, like a vehicle, these approaches serve as means to help different kinds of people journey on the path to enlightenment. It is important to note, however, that these three sets of teachings are not to be considered as separate entities; it is one and the same subject presented in different ways and on different levels.

The three Vehicles are:

- **Hinayana** or the Lesser Vehicle;
- **Mahayana** or the Great Vehicle, and
- **Vajrayana** or the Diamond Vehicle, sometimes also known as Tantric Buddhism.

The term 'Hinayana' literally means 'lesser vehicle' and was sometimes used by Mahayanists as a derogatory term indicating that Mahayana is greater than the eighteen or so schools of Buddhism that emerged in the first few hundred years after the Buddha. These days, such bias is considered unacceptable so the term Nikaya Buddhism is preferred because it is neutral. The *nikayas* are literally the collections of scriptures that were considered authoritative by these schools.

Nikaya Buddhism has been flourishing ever since the Buddha passed away, so it is undoubtedly the oldest public tradition of Buddhism. In contrast, the origins of Mahayana Buddhism are unclear. It appears to have gradually emerged in India somewhat later, possibly as early as the second century BCE or between the first century BCE and the first century CE. Vajrayana emerged in India around the fifth century CE onwards. So, broadly speaking, there is a chronological order for the historical emergence of these Vehicles.

Theravada, the only surviving school of Nikaya Buddhism, is practised today in Sri Lanka, Cambodia, Thailand, Laos, Myanmar and Vietnam. Theravadins do not accept the model of the three Vehicles since they do not accept that the teachings of Mahayana and Vajrayana were given by the historical Buddha. They assert that these two Vehicles were taught by eminent Buddhist masters but not by the Buddha himself. The model of the three Vehicles is therefore a Mahayana and Vajrayana model.

The Mahayana and Vajrayana both generated several different schools or traditions of Buddhism, so they are umbrella terms which include all the various schools relating to each. Today, Mahayana Buddhism is present in Vietnam, China, Taiwan, Korea and Japan while Vajrayana Buddhism is practised notably in Tibet, Mongolia, Nepal, Bhutan, Japan and parts of the former Soviet Union, as well as within communities of Tibetan exiles in India. There are now followers of all three Vehicles in the West.

One way of characterizing the three Vehicles is to relate each one to a line of the summary that the Buddha made of his own teaching in the *Dhammapada*. The Buddha said:

To do no harm whatsoever;
To cultivate good to perfection;
To tame this mind of ours:
This is the teaching of all the buddhas.[19]

1. *To do no harm whatsoever* is the emphasis of Nikaya Buddhism: the principles of non-harming and non-violence *(ahimsa),* the ethics of refraining from harmful actions, and the practice of overcoming negative emotions through meditation and mindfulness.
2. *To cultivate good to perfection* is the emphasis of Mahayana Buddhism: perfecting virtuous actions so they become totally selfless (the *paramitas*), developing the positive qualities of one's 'buddha nature', devoting one's life to the altruistic benefit of others.
3. *To tame this mind of ours* is the strength of Vajrayana Buddhism: working with the mind and its perception of the world, and transforming confusion into enlightenment through meditation, mantra, visualisation and *guru yoga.*

It is important to note that all three aspects of the Buddha's summary are present in every Vehicle so the difference between them is only one of emphasis.

In examining the features of these three approaches we need to identify their similarities and differences. In this book we focus on a comparison between Theravada, representing Nikaya Buddhism, and the core doctrines of Mahayana, concentrating on the following themes:

1. Buddhology, or the study of what a buddha is
2. The goal of the Buddhist path
3. The main features of the Buddhist path
4. Other core principles.

A summary of these topics will be followed by a detailed explanation.

Theravada and Mahayana: a summary

Buddhology

Theravadins recognize only the historical person of the Buddha and the teachings believed to have been given by him during his lifetime. Mahayanists believe that the Buddha can also appear and teach great masters in visions and dreams, and that he can also communicate in *Sambhogakaya* form. The Sambhogakaya (literally 'body of joy') is a dimension of energy and light that is visible in special meditative states but intangible, like a rainbow. It is believed that buddhas can exist in this dimension. Theravada does not accept the Sambhogakaya.

The goal of the Buddhist path

In Theravada, the goal of the Buddhist path is *nibbana (nirvana)*: the extinction of the three mental poisons of ignorance, craving and aggression, freedom from karma and rebirth, and liberation from suffering. *Nibbana* brings liberation from *samsara*, the cycle of conditioned existence. It is considered that *nibbana* has no beginning and no end and is a state that is outside of time. When one attains *nibbana* one is called an *arhat*, someone who has conquered the mental poisons.

In Mahayana the goal of the Buddhist path is complete buddhahood. Nirvana is acknowledged to be freedom from samsara but is viewed as only a stepping stone on the way to complete enlightenment. The difference between nirvana and buddhahood is that there are some subtle mental veils remaining in nirvana that perpetuate a very subtle level of ignorance; these are removed by means of the Mahayana path, enabling the practitioner to attain the omniscience of full enlightenment. When one attains the goal of the Mahayana path one becomes a *buddha*, an enlightened one or awakened one. Anyone following the Mahayana path is called a *bodhisattva*.

The main features of the Buddhist path

In Theravada, the path is called the Noble Eightfold Path and is taught as the fourth of the Four Noble Truths. Its eight elements are as follows:

1. Right View
2. Right Attitude
3. Right Speech
4. Right Action
5. Right Livelihood
6. Right Effort
7. Right Mindfulness
8. Right Concentration

These eight elements can be grouped into what are called the Three Higher Trainings:

1. Moral discipline (3,4,5)
2. Meditation (6,7,8)
3. Wisdom (1,2)

All Nikaya Buddhists follow the Eightfold Path, whether they are monastics or laypeople, although different guidelines will apply to each group.

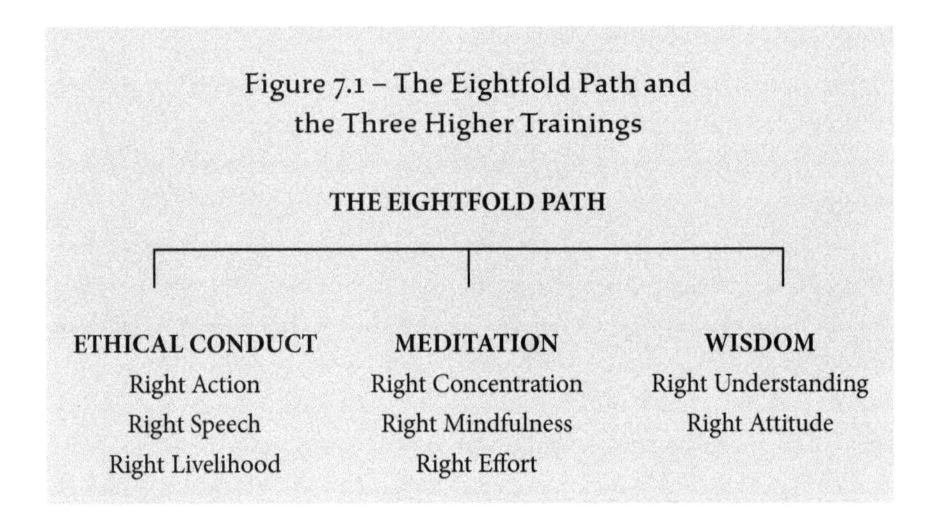

The Mahayana path is called the Bodhisattva Path and this is divided into ten stages or *bhumis* (literally 'grounds') on each of which specific qualities are perfected. These are called the ten *paramitas* or 'perfections':

1. Generosity
2. Moral discipline
3. Patience
4. Diligence
5. Concentration or meditation
6. Wisdom *(prajña)*
7. Skilful means
8. Strength/power
9. Aspiration
10. Primordial wisdom *(jñana)*.

After the tenth stage of the path one attains buddhahood. A *bodhisattva* is someone who follows the path in order to attain enlightenment both for themselves and for all other beings. The *bodhisattva* reaches his or her goal by arousing *bodhichitta,* the awakened mind, and taking the vows of a *bodhisattva.*

Other core principles

Of the other core principles of Mahayana that are not found in Theravada, the most salient are the following:

- The belief that every single being has the 'buddha nature' *(tathagatagarbha)* or potential for enlightenment within, so that enlightenment is not a matter of attaining a distant and inaccessible state but rather of discovering, uncovering, revealing and expressing who we truly are.
- The ethical principle of skilful means *(upaya):* see Chapter 15.
- The distinction between conventional truth and ultimate truth, known as the Two Truths. Conventional truth refers to what we accept as true in the everyday world, while ultimate truth refers to truths that are beyond words. Conventional truth is how things appear, ultimate truth is how they really are.

Theravada and Mahayana in detail

Buddhology

The key to understanding how the Buddha is seen according to the three Vehicles is the Buddhist doctrine of the Three Bodies of the Buddha, or Trikaya doctrine. The word 'body' as a translation of *kaya* does not mean a physical body; it does not mean that the Buddha had three separate 'bodies' in this sense. Rather it has the collective meaning the word sometimes has in English in expressions like 'a body of literature' or 'a body of knowledge'. In other words, 'body' here means a collection of qualities and characteristics. Hence the three *kayas* refer to three aspects of buddhahood, or three dimensions of the enlightened mind. These three aspects are:

1. *Dharmakaya:* the body of truth
2. *Sambhogakaya:* the body of joy or enjoyment
3. *Nirmanakaya:* the body of manifestation.

The Nirmanakaya refers to the physical manifestation of an enlightened being, and in the case of Shakyamuni it refers to the historical Buddha whose life story we learn. In Nikaya Buddhism, the Nirmanakaya may have referred originally to the doubles of himself that the Buddha 'magically' displayed in order to teach certain audiences.[20]

From the Mahayana perspective, the Buddha was already enlightened before he was born as Siddhartha, and his decision to take physical form was a voluntary one and not determined karmically as it is for ordinary beings. Buddhas have the power to manifest in any physical form they wish, in any part of the universe and even in several universes at once. This means that buddhas can manifest as animals to guide animals, as human beings to guide humans and so on, and they may also manifest as the religious teachers of other religions.

The Sambhogakaya refers to the dimension of energy and light and can be described in two ways. First, it refers to the experience of bliss and joy that comes from experiencing the Dharma for oneself; and, second, it refers to the magnificence of the buddhas and bodhisattvas that one is increasingly able to perceive as one advances on the path.

After they have passed away, buddhas and bodhisattvas may choose to abide in the dimension of energy and light out of compassion, in order to remain accessible to suffering beings. In their Sambhogakaya form, buddhas and advanced bodhisattvas are intangible but visible, like a rainbow. All the pure realms or heavens of the buddhas, such as the Sukhavati Pure Land of Buddha Amitabha, are Sambhogakaya realms, and the beings that dwell there are in the Sambhogakaya dimension. Only human beings at advanced meditative levels are able to see the Sambhogakaya with their mind's eye and to communicate with the buddhas and bodhisattvas. Visionary experiences are understood as perceptions of Sambhogakaya beings rendered possible by deep meditation.

Those who are not so advanced simply pray to these beings for support and guidance, with the confidence that they are present even though they cannot be seen. This conviction is what makes the path of devotion such a powerful one. The Vajrayana practice of visualisation is a method that refines ordinary perception so that one is able to see this dimension of reality for oneself in a stable, sustained and repeatable way.

The Sambhogakaya dimension of reality is not recognized in Theravada thought even though there are many examples of miracles related to the life story of the Buddha and his disciples in the Pali Canon.

The Dharmakaya seems to refer, in early Buddhism, to the collection of auspicious qualities of the Buddha: wisdom, compassion and mental power. The notion of the different bodies of a buddha was developed in relation to the Three Refuges. Since the physical body of the Buddha is subject to decay and death it is not a suitable object of Refuge; instead, one takes refuge in the group of enlightened qualities displayed by the Buddha.

Figure 7.2 – Green Tara. Tara embodies the feminine aspect of buddhahood and exemplifies a deity in Sambhogakaya form

In Mahayana the term evolved into a cosmic principle regarded as the true nature of a buddha, and the nature of the enlightened mind itself.[21] It is the nature of purified consciousness, totally free of all defilements, and beyond even the distinction between pure and impure. In fact, the Dharmakaya is beyond words and cannot be described in ordinary language. It is the source from which the worlds of light and physical matter manifest. It corresponds to the ultimate truth in Mahayana.

The three *kayas* are related to each other in that the Dharmakaya gives rise to the Sambhogakaya, and the Sambhogakaya gives rise to the Nirmanakaya. The Dharmakaya is the ultimate truth, and both Sambhogakaya and Nirmanakaya exist in relation to it on the level of conventional truth. One image used to evoke the Dharmakaya is that of a clear and cloudless sky, or infinite space. An image for the Sambhogakaya is that of the brilliant sun in a cloudless sky, and an image used for the Nirmanakaya is that of the warmth of the sun's rays, which touch everyone everywhere.

The *kayas* not only describe aspects of enlightenment, they are cosmic principles that describe the way mind transforms into light and energy, and how light and energy transform into matter. This principle can be used to explain how the universe arises. Some modern religious leaders have drawn parallels between the Trikaya doctrine and that of the Christian Trinity, with God the Father being similar to the Dharmakaya, the Holy Spirit to the Sambhogakaya, and God the Son to the Nirmanakaya.

Some scholars claim that the Sambhogakaya and Dharmakaya are not cognitive, in other words that they are concepts but not cognitively experienced and known. They say that the *kayas* reflect ideas we may have about reality, but there are no grounds for their validity in cognitive experience. Theravadins may assert this in relation to the Sambhogakaya, for example. Mahayana and Vajrayana Buddhists dispute this and argue that this is a misunderstanding. They speak of the Sambhogakaya and Dharmakaya precisely as a way of expressing meditative insights into these dimensions of reality, and the Buddhist path contains methods that are specifically designed to open the mind to these dimensions. In particular, visualisation practice opens the mind to the Sambhogakaya and silent meditation, as well as methods such as koans, open the mind to the Dharmakaya. All three kayas are considered to be fully cognitive because, in all traditions of Buddhism, meditational states are included along with the five senses as bases of valid knowledge.

The principle of the three kayas is important for the integrity of Buddhist thought because it enables us to understand many things that would otherwise be mysterious and inexplicable. In particular, energy and light transcend the laws that govern solid physical matter, and also transcend time and space. It is through that dimension of reality that enlightened beings like the Buddha can perform miracles because they are no longer subject to the laws of physics. The Sambhogakaya dimension also serves as a bridge that permits communication between human beings and the buddhas and bodhisattvas who abide on that level.

The goal of the Buddhist path

The Lotus Sutra is a Mahayana scripture that teaches the superiority of the Mahayana goal in relation to that of Nikaya Buddhism, and that also claims the Buddha really taught 'only one single vehicle' *(ekayana)*, not two or three, in the sense that all Vehicles of Buddhism ultimately lead to the same goal, which is buddhahood. According to this view, the teachings of Nikaya Buddhism are preliminary instructions for those with little spiritual maturity, and their goal of *nirvana (nibbana)*, although a very worthy one, is only a temporary resting place on the long road to buddhahood.

The principle of the *ekayana* is illustrated by the parable of the phantom city in the Lotus Sutra. A group of people are travelling along a road through a wild and deserted region to reach a place with many rare treasures. The road is long and the terrain is difficult so they become disheartened, frightened and exhausted. They feel like turning round and going back but their compassionate leader, who knows the road well, encourages them to carry on and describes a city which is not far ahead, an oasis of calm and rest. Everyone is overjoyed at the thought that the goal is not far off, and they soon reach the city. Once they are well rested the leader explains that the place they are in is only a phantom city that he created through the magical power of his mind; they need to go a little further to find the treasures, which eventually they accept they must do. In the same way, nirvana is a resting place, the thought of which inspires those who are weary of suffering to start out on the spiritual journey.

This view is based on the idea that the Buddha adapted his teachings to the needs of his audiences, so he chose to offer nirvana as a goal for those with intense suffering, whose deepest wish was to find a way to be free of suffering. The prospect of a mental state in which suffering and its causes are totally eliminated is effective in motivating such people to follow a spiritual path. However, for those whose suffering is less intense, whose karma is somewhat purified and who have already lived many virtuous lives, there is a greater goal which embraces not only the elimination of suffering for oneself but the ability to lead others to enlightenment. The *bodhisattva* following the Mahayana path is motivated by *bodhichitta,* the genuine and heartfelt aspiration to become enlightened for the sake of others.

The difference between nirvana and complete buddhahood is a subtle one. Nirvana is freedom from samsara and the cycle of rebirth. This attainment is based on the realization of *anatta (anatman)* or 'no self', the principle that there is no essence or inherent entity that constitutes personal identity; there is nothing that I can truly call 'me'. Mahayana extends this realization of *anatta (anatman)* and applies it not only to persons but to all phenomena, even at the level of the minutest particles and moments. This gives rise to the realization of *shunyata,* 'emptiness', the lack of inherent existence in all things without any exception. Realizing *shunyata* as the nature of all things brings the omniscience of buddhahood.

Figure 7.3 – The eight-spoked wheel symbolises the eightfold path and, more generally, Buddhism as a world religion.

The main features of the Buddhist path

The Eightfold Path

In Nikaya Buddhism, the path is described as the Eightfold Path and contains eight different elements, depicted on the Eight-spoked Wheel which symbolises the Buddhist religion. These elements are not sequential; they all work together and reinforce each other.

- **Right view** refers specifically to understanding the Four Noble Truths, and intuitively grasping their meaning. In other words, right view is a correct understanding of how things really are, the highest wisdom that sees ultimate reality. At a preliminary level, right view is explained as accepting the importance of generosity and moral actions, and accepting rebirth.
- **Right attitude** includes thoughts such as selfless renunciation, detachment, love and compassion for others, non-violence and equal-mindedness.
- **Right speech** is refraining from lying, backbiting, idle gossip and harsh words.
- **Right action** refers to honest actions that do not harm others.
- **Right livelihood** means abstaining from any work that involves harming others.
- **Right effort** is the energetic will, enthusiasm and diligence to prevent unwholesome states of mind and the actions that result, and to cultivate wholesome states of mind and virtuous actions.
- **Right mindfulness** is continual awareness of the activities of one's body, and to thoughts and feelings in the mind.
- **Right concentration** refers to the mental concentration developed especially by *shamatha* meditation and is an antidote to distraction.

It would be a mistake to take the word 'right' in English to mean the opposite of wrong. It is easy to interpret the Eightfold Path in this way, and to see it as a set of dogmatic instructions for leading a righteous life. Instead, 'right' should be understood as 'correct'. The meaning is that these eight elements of the path are ways of being spiritually 'noble' or worthy; by following them one lives in harmony with one's true self and with reality.

Moral discipline is motivated by right view and made possible by effort, mindfulness and concentration. Similarly, meditation is aided by moral discipline because if one leads an unruly or unvirtuous life one will not be able to meditate. Examples of this are trying to meditate with a hangover or failing to find peace of mind because one feels guilty about what one has done. In this way, all aspects of the Eightfold Path support each other and strengthen each other in a constant 'cycle of happiness'.

The Bodhisattva Path

The path followed by the bodhisattva in Mahayana is similar to the Eightfold Path in that it, too, includes the Three Higher Trainings of moral discipline, meditation and wisdom. The first four *paramitas* or perfections fall under moral discipline (generosity, moral discipline, patience and diligence); the fifth is meditation; and the last five relate to wisdom (wisdom, skilful means, power, aspiration and primordial wisdom). The main difference with the Eightfold Path is the motivation of *bodhichitta* which is the union of ultimate wisdom and limitless compassion.

Generating the motivation of *bodhichitta* is in itself a tremendous achievement which requires great merit and wisdom. Mahayana practitioners usually take a formal 'bodhisattva vow' to mark their conscious commitment to the Bodhisattva Path. The vow is taken in the presence of a Mahayana master or simply in the visualised presence of the buddhas and bodhisattvas. In contrast to monastic vows, which are taken only for the duration of the present life, the bodhisattva vow is taken with the aspiration that one will continuously follow it throughout present and future lives and until the point of reaching enlightenment. The vision of this path is therefore very vast. The great eighth century Indian poet-scholar Shantideva expresses the aspiration of a bodhisattva in these words:

For as long as space exists
And sentient beings endure,
May I too remain
To dispel the misery of the world.[22]

The Bodhisattva Path begins with a tremendous experience of joy arising from the glimpse one has of the ultimate truth. On this basis one gradually perfects each of the transcendental actions of the path one by one, with the wisdom of *shunyata*, emptiness, pervading all the *paramitas* at least to some degree. This is why perfected actions are not self-conscious and have no ulterior motive. In the case of generosity, for example, the bodhisattva realizes that neither the gift, nor the giver, nor the beneficiary, truly exist; all are empty of inherent existence. In practice, this safeguards against any pride, arrogance or smugness that might come from the thought of having performed a virtuous deed.

Once the bodhisattva has accomplished the sixth *paramita* of wisdom, he or she is free of rebirth caused by karma and is able to take rebirth deliberately in different realms to help suffering beings. All actions of body, speech and mind are so many skilful means to help others. At the eighth stage of the path the bodhisattva reaches the point of 'no return' meaning that he or she will no longer fall back into inferior births and is certain to progress to buddhahood. The ability to 'transfer merit' is fully mastered, so that if anyone prays to him or her the bodhisattva is able to transfer a store of tremendous *merit* – the result of good actions – to uplift that person and transform their situation. At the ninth stage, the bodhisattva has the power to teach all beings according to their needs, and at the tenth stage he or she reaches the Sambhogakaya level and dwells in the Tushita heaven, from where fully enlightened buddhas may manifest. Buddhahood is attained at the eleventh stage.

Figure 7.4 – The Bodhisattva Path

The bhumis or stages	*The paramitas or qualities perfected*
Complete Joy	Generosity
Without Stain	Moral discipline
Giving out light	Patience
Dazzling with light/radiant	Diligence
Difficult to overcome	Concentration
Advancing/Knowing clearly	Wisdom (prajña)
Gone Far	Skilful means
Immovable	Strength/power
Perfect intelligence	Aspiration
Cloud of Dharma	Primordial wisdom (jñana)
Buddhahood	

Other core principles

We have said that Mahayana is an umbrella term denoting a number of different schools. There were two main Mahayana schools of philosophy in India which have had a far-reaching impact: the Madhyamaka school and the Yogachara school. Their philosophical systems are considered in detail in Chapter 21 and summarised here.

Figure 7.5 – Nagarjuna

Madhyamaka philosophy was founded by the Indian scholar Nagarjuna in around the first century CE. Madhyamaka literally means 'the middle way', and specifically refers to a middle way between the extreme views of believing that things really exist and believing that nothing exists at all. Philosophically these extremist views are termed eternalism and nihilism. Nagarjuna argued that things do not exist inherently, but this does not imply that they do not exist in any way at all; they do appear to us and Buddhists do not deny the obvious fact of empirical experience; they acknowledge that things like pots and pans exist on a conventional level. Yet on an ultimate level, under analysis, the nature of things is seen to be 'empty' of true existence; things are entirely interdependent; nothing exists independently and permanently, not even the minutest particles from which objects are made. The ultimate truth of Madhyamaka is therefore emptiness *(shunyata)* or interdependence *(pratityasamutpada),* and the main framework of analysis is called the Two Truths: conventional and ultimate addressing respectively how things appear and how they are.

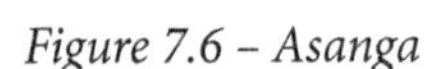

Figure 7.6 – Asanga

Figure 7.7 – Vasubandhu

Yogachara, the school of those who practise yoga, was founded in the fourth century CE by the brothers Asanga and Vasubandhu. This school holds that everything we perceive is a projection of the mind, and the way we see the world is dependent upon the characteristics and limitations of the human sense apparatus which does not give us an objective view of reality. For example, animals of different species each perceive the world differently. I see you as a human with a head, two arms and two legs, but a spider might perceive you as a vast undulating landscape that it could crawl around. Likewise, for humans, water is something to drink but for fish it is a home to live in. It would be arrogant on our part to imagine that the way human beings perceive the world must be the only objectively true way. The world of our experience is therefore a mental construct. Only through wisdom can we perceive how things truly are, the ultimate truth being the realization that subject and object are not two separate entities but one in nature.

Yogachara also embraced the theory of buddha nature or *tathagatagarbha*, the principle that all sentient beings in samsara, from the smallest insect to human beings, have the potential to become fully enlightened. Like gold buried in the earth, this potential is hidden from view on account of all our defilements, but once we have removed these it naturally shines. Most importantly, this buddha nature can never be spoiled by mental poisons or harmful actions which are only like dust collecting on a mirror. The mirror itself remains intact and clear, the dust is only superficial and, when wiped away, reveals the mirror to be what it has always been.

Figure 4 is a mindmap which presents the main features of Mahayana, including an outline of four Mahayana schools. Some points are explained in later chapters.

Figure 7.8 Mahayana Buddhism

ORIGINS

- Origins are unclear
- Separate Buddhist Council?
- Secret transmission in India?
- Mystical revelation of new scriptures?
- Rise of the laity?
- Emerges in India between 2nd century BCE and 1st century CE.

GEOGRAPHICAL SPREAD

- India until 12th century
- Pakistan, Afghanistan
- China, Korea, Japan
- Indonesia
- Tibet, Mongolia, Bhutan
- Europe, N.America, Australia in 20th century

CHARACTERISTICS

- The goal is full buddhahood, not merely nirvana
- Motivation to follow path is for oneself and others
- Enlightenment is omniscience and bodhichitta
- Those on the Mahayana path are bodhisattvas
- The path has ten stages *(bhumis)*
- Bodhisattvas develop six or ten paramitas
- Enlightenment is possible for monastics and laity, men and women
- Trikaya doctrine of the Buddha

MAHAYANA BUDDHISM

MAIN SCHOOLS

INDIA: Madhyamaka, Yogachara

CHINA, KOREA,

JAPAN: Zen, Pure Land

MADHYAMAKA

- Founder: Nagarjuna, 1st century CE
- Prajñaparamita Sutras (Heart Sutra)
- Two Truths: a) Conventional: things exist as accepted conventionally;
  b) Ultimate: emptiness *(shunyata)* is not non-existence: it means things have no essence, are not independent or unchanging
- Neither wholes nor parts exist ultimately

CH'AN OR ZEN

- Traced to Buddha, who holds up a flower; Kasyapa understands meaning without words
- Maybe secret transmission in India
- Founder in China: Bodhidharma (5th/6th century CE)
- In Japan, two schools develop:
  Rinzai (founder Eisai, 1141-1215), sudden enlightenment *(satori)*, use of koans, dramatic methods, martial arts
  Soto (founder Dogen, 1200-1253) *zazen* (meditation), simple life, discipline, gradual path
- Little study (mainly Lankavatara Sutra)

YOGACHARA

- Founders: Asanga & Vasubandhu, 4th century CE
- Lankavatara Sutra, Samdhinirmocana Sutra
- Criticise Madhyamaka, saying their interpretation of emptiness is nothingness
- Three natures: *parikalpita* (thought-constructed), *paratantra* (what we experience), *parinispanna* (reality as it is).
- Eight aspects of consciousness: 8th is *alaya,* which continues after death and stores karmic seeds
- *Tathagatagarbha*: buddha nature or potential in everyone

PURE LAND

- Traced back to Indian scripture; story of monk Dharmakara who upon his enlightenment becomes Amida Buddha (Buddha Amitabha) and vows to take his devotees to his heaven or pure land, Sukhavati
- Begins in China in 5th century, Japan in 10th century
- Two schools in Japan: Pure Land (Honen) and True Pure Land or Shin Buddhism (Shinran)
- Main practice: nembutsu and devotion to Amida
- Emphasises other-power for this degenerate age

The Vajrayana

The view of Vajrayana is based on Mahayana, including both Madhyamaka and Yogachara. The aspiration of *bodhichitta* is the same, and the goal of buddhahood is also the same.

The difference between Mahayana and Vajrayana lies in the methods used, which include visualisation and mantra recitation and, most importantly, devotion. The core practice of Vajrayana is known as 'guru yoga', merging one's mind with that of the spiritual master or *guru* in Sanskrit, until there is no difference between student and teacher. Devotion is considered fundamental to this process, and a skilful way of helping the student give up any sense of 'I' or ego.

Vajrayana requires that the practitioner has already reached a degree of spiritual maturity, so that he or she has strong trust in the Dharma and in the teacher, as well as a mind that is clear and focused enough to practise visualisation. It is said that the Vajrayana path is more powerful and more effective than those of the two previous Vehicles, and that it will enable the practitioner to reach enlightenment much faster. It is believed that the Vajrayana path is particularly appropriate in this morally degenerate age, when only the most powerful of methods are able to cut through the thick clouds of ignorance engulfing our minds. Its methods are seen to enable access to, and communication with, the Sambhogakaya dimension of reality. Today, Vajrayana is practised in Tibetan Buddhism and in Japanese Shingon.

Personal reflection

How do you view the idea that a teacher might choose to teach in different ways depending on the audience, and that in doing so his teaching does not necessarily lack coherence?

Main Points

- The Three Vehicles are a Mahayana framework presenting the three ways of expressing the same basic teaching according to the needs of different audiences.
- The Three Vehicles are Hinayana (or Nikaya Buddhism), Mahayana and Vajrayana.
- They differ in their understandings of the nature of the Buddha, the goal of the path and their description of the stages of the path.

Chapter 8

THE BUDDHIST SCRIPTURES

Buddhism has a vast corpus of scriptural texts that are classified into separate collections. These scriptures transmit the words of the Buddha or are based on his words. They are not 'revealed' scriptures in the Western sense. It follows that Buddhists have a unique way of understanding the authority of scripture and this topic is further addressed in Chapter 23. The present chapter gives an overview of the texts that are considered scriptural by each tradition and considers how Buddhists relate to scripture.

Those who recite many scriptures but fail to practise their teachings are like a cowherd counting someone else's cows.
Dhammapada 19

How Buddhists relate to their scriptures

The Buddha was wandering from town to town in the ancient kingdom of Kosala, in northern India, and one day arrived, together with a large group of monks, at

Kesaputta, a town of the Kalamas.[23] As they sat down with the Buddha, the Kalamas presented their problem to him. Lots of different religious teachers visited their town, one after the other, and each one glorified his own teaching and spoke with contempt about the teachings of everyone else. The Kalamas were confused and no longer knew what to believe. "How can we tell which teachers are really wise? How can we distinguish between a true teaching and a false one?", they asked.

The Buddha listened sympathetically. He began by explaining what we should *not* base our views on, so he advised them: "Don't go by reports, by legends, by traditions, by scripture, by logical conjecture, by inference, by analogies, by agreement through reflecting on views, by probability, or by the thought 'this contemplative is our teacher.'"

According to the Theravadin translator Thanissaro Bhikkhu, the Buddha meant that we should not follow traditions just because they are traditions; and we should not follow reports, such as historical accounts or news, simply because the source seems reliable. Furthermore, we should not follow our own preferences just because they seem logical or resonate with our feelings. We should not be convinced by one isolated persuasive example or accept something because it sounds likely to be true. Nor should we base our views on logic alone, or solely on trust, for example on the basis that since we have chosen a person as our teacher then anything he says must be true. All of these traps are very easy to fall into; most of us fall prey to them every day of our lives!

The Buddha continued by pointing out that what we should look at is a teacher's motivation in order to decide whether he is genuine or not. Whenever there is greed in a person, or aversion, or delusion of any kind, then these tendencies can only bring about harm and suffering, and they will not give rise to skilful actions that can lead us to liberation. So, the first step is to ask ourselves the question: do these negative qualities exist in this teacher? Our answer will depend on our own experience and wisdom, nothing else.

Then, of course, we can ask ourselves whether the opposite, positive qualities exist in his mind instead. In particular, is the person's mind free from greed, hostility and ill will, undefiled and pure, alert and resolute? If we find that it is, then these are positive indications that he is indeed an authentic teacher and worthy of praise and respect, and he should be followed.

The Buddha indicated to the Kalamas that this general advice should be applied not just to other teachers but to him, too. And in particular, the same guidelines apply to the Buddha's teachings as set down in the scriptures. Buddhists are not expected to believe in anything simply because it was said by the Buddha, or to believe in scriptures just because they are scripture. The Buddha encouraged everyone to reflect on his words in order to come to their own personal conviction about whether they are valid or not. The Buddha said to the Kalamas:

O monks and wise men,
Just as a goldsmith would test his gold
By burning, cutting and rubbing it,
So must you examine my words and accept them
But not merely out of reverence for me.[24]

Any view or belief must be tested by the results it brings when put into practice. And, to guard against the possibility of bias, or any limitations in one's understanding of those results, they must be further checked against the experience of people who are wise. This means that we need to develop the ability to question and test our beliefs in an appropriate way, as well as the ability to recognize and choose wise people as our advisors.

This is why some masters tell their students, with some humour, that when they study the Dharma, they should make sure they don't become like bookworms. A bookworm might devour a book from cover to cover, but at the end it won't remember anything and it won't have learned anything useful. The information will have gone in one end and come out the other—literally, in this case; or, as we say, gone in one ear and come out the other. In the end, the bookworm will just be fat and sleepy with indigestion! Instead, we need to study the Dharma by relating the ideas to ourselves, by reflecting on them in the light of our own experience and understanding, and by making the ideas our very own. This is how to gain spiritual knowledge that benefits and transforms the mind.

It follows from this that Buddhists have a unique way of understanding the nature, value and role of scripture. Other religions don't actively encourage their followers to question the scriptures in a constructive way, nor do most religions shift the emphasis from the words on the page to the wisdom within.

The Buddhist understanding of scripture

There are three other ways in which the Buddhist relationship to scripture is unique.

Scripture is not divinely revealed

First, Buddhism rejects the theistic idea of 'revealed scripture' because it doesn't teach belief in God. The scriptures contain the words of the Buddha, and these words have authority not because he is divine or in touch with the divine, but because he gained the supreme wisdom and compassion of enlightenment. So, for a Buddhist, the scriptures can only be called 'revealed' texts insofar as the Buddha 'revealed' to us truths that we were previously unaware of, due to our confusion and ignorance. The role of a buddha is to explain the truth to the unenlightened.

One of the most important consequences of the fact that the Buddhist scriptures are not divinely revealed is that it is possible for human beings to understand them. The scriptures do not contain unfathomable mysteries. If one applies the correct process of studying, reflecting and meditating on the texts, it is possible, in time, to come to the same realization of the truths they contain as the Buddha did himself.

Another consequence is that scriptural words do not have a special status for Buddhists as the qur'ans do for Muslims. For Buddhists, all words, even those of scripture, are conventional and part of human language. The highest truths can never be put into words. Scripture therefore has a value only insofar as it helps human beings transform themselves from ignorance to enlightenment, from suffering to freedom. Scriptures, like the spiritual path itself, do not have intrinsic value but instrumental value.[25]

The number of scriptural texts is very large

Second, Buddhism has the largest number of scriptures of all religions. Not only is the collection of scriptures enormous in terms of the number of titles it contains, but many of them are extremely long. If the Chinese scriptures were translated, it is estimated they would fill over half a million pages of print. So, when we speak of scripture in Buddhism, we are not talking about a single sacred book, like the Torah, the Bible or the Qur'an, but about a whole library of texts.

Buddhism has several distinct collections of scripture, not just one

And third, Buddhism is also unique in that it has not one but several separate collections of scriptures, each of which is considered authoritative. Such a collection of scriptures is called a canon. This situation arises from the way Buddhism developed in India without any centralised authority and therefore without any institution which could claim that some scriptures were 'orthodox' while others were not. These various collections exist side by side.

The Buddhist canons today exist in four main languages: Pali, Sanskrit, Chinese and Tibetan; as well as in Korean, Japanese and Mongolian. Most of the Pali Canon has now been translated into English, but the majority of the Sanskrit, Chinese and Tibetan texts have not yet been translated into Western languages. In 2010, the '84,000' project began the process of translating the Mahayana sutras from Sanskrit and Tibetan into English while the 'Kumarajiva Project' is translating scriptures from and into Chinese. Both are under the auspices of the Khyentse Foundation.

Knowledge of scripture

Given their sheer volume, it may not be surprising that ordinary Buddhists would never be expected to read and study all these books. They rely on monks to tell them the essence of the main scriptures in an accessible way. Even amongst the monks, only the most scholarly study the scriptures in a comprehensive manner.

But there are some stories and sayings from the scriptures that every Buddhist would know. For example, stories of the life of the Buddha found in the Pali Canon are part of Buddhist culture. The advice on meditation is still followed today. And some passages from the scriptures would be recited either every day or on festival days as part of the morning and evening chanting in monasteries. In other words, the most well-known parts of the scriptures are a living part of the Buddhist tradition.

Copies of the scriptures are treated with great respect. In ancient times, when each text was copied by hand, the scriptures would be rare and hard to find. Pilgrims would travel many thousands of miles to find a text they wished to study. Indeed, it is claimed that the Chinese invented printing in the eighth century in order to reproduce Buddhist scriptures more easily. Their rarity is one reason for the respect shown to the scriptures. Religious texts are placed high up off the floor and sometimes on a Buddhist shrine. Scriptures are also occasionally placed inside stupas. The meaning behind this respect is that the scriptures represent not only the Dharma, the Buddha's teachings, but also, more universally, they represent wisdom and truth.

The Pali Canon

The Pali Canon contains the scriptures accepted by the Theravada tradition. Pali was a language spoken in the Buddha's time, and was probably very similar to the main language he would have known himself called Old Magadhi. Buddhists believe that the Buddha spoke many different local dialects and not just one language, and Theravadins believe that the Buddha spoke Pali. Their scriptures are therefore said to contain the original words of the Buddha.

Modern scholars accept that the Pali Canon contains some of the oldest texts of all the Buddhist scriptures, and is probably very close to the teachings originally recited in the first Buddhist Council. Having been transmitted orally for generations, by communal chanting, the Canon was first written down in Sri Lanka in the first century BCE.

The Pali Canon is divided into three sections or 'baskets' known as the *Tipitaka* (Pali) or *Tripitaka* (Sanskrit). They are called 'baskets' because the early scriptures were written on palm leaves which were stored in baskets; baskets formed their ancient filing system. The three sections are Vinaya, Sutta and Abhidhamma.

- The **Vinaya** consists of the code of discipline for monks and nuns. The Theravada Vinaya contains a total of 227 rules for monks. But it is far more than a list of rules; the Vinaya contains stories about the situations that prompted the Buddha to make each rule. For example, the rules for helping the sick were made when the community neglected to care for a sick monk. Likewise, the monastic rule of celibacy arose as Buddha's response to an occasion when a particular monk visited his ex-wife because she wanted a son. The purpose of the Vinaya is to maintain harmony within the community. It also acts as an aid to a disciplined and mindful lifestyle, free from the distractions of lay life, where energies can be focused on spiritual development. Monastics learn the Vinaya by heart and recite it together as a group once a fortnight.
- The **Suttas** (Sanskrit **sutras**) are the 'discourses' of the Buddha, that is, the talks and teachings he gave over a period of 45 years. Each sutta states the village or town in which the teaching was given and the names of the individuals involved, but there is no dating. The suttas contain all the central teachings of Buddhism and they run into the hundreds. They make up the five collections of the Pali Canon.
- The **Abhidhamma** (Sanskrit **Abhidharma**) texts contain philosophical analysis of the Buddha's teaching. The underlying doctrinal principles presented in the suttas are organized into a systematic framework. These texts address topics such as human psychology and the relationship

between mind and matter. Some Buddhists believe that the Buddha himself explained this analysis, while others assert the Abhidhamma was composed by later Buddhist scholars. For the former the Abhidhamma is authoritative but for the latter it may not be.

We can relate these three categories of scripture to the three Higher Trainings of the Buddhist path as follows:

- the Vinaya teaches moral discipline
- the Suttas teach meditation
- the Abhidhamma teaches wisdom.

According to the 19th century Tibetan scholar Mipham, each category of teaching brings a particular benefit. Through the Vinaya we overcome negative conduct; through the Suttas we overcome doubt; and through Abhidhamma we overcome faulty views.

Two Theravada scriptures are particularly popular: the *Dhammapada*, which contains a series of brief verses summarising the main principles of the Buddha's teaching, and parts of which can be easily memorised; and *The Questions of King Milinda,* a dialogue between the Buddhist monk Nagasena and the Greco-Bactrian King Menander, setting out key Buddhist arguments on a number of topics. This dialogue took place in the second century BCE when Greek armies had crossed central Asia and reached India. Both texts are available in English translation.

The Mahayana scriptures

The origin of the Mahayana scriptures

Modern scholars believe that the Mahayana scriptures were not simply written down but actually composed between the first century BCE and the fifth century CE in India. They say there is no evidence to support the idea that these texts derive from an oral tradition that had continued from the time of the Buddha. According to this view then, unlike the Pali Canon, the Mahayana scriptures were first written and not oral. However, one can also argue that the earliest Mahayana manuscripts in our possession are just as ancient as the earliest existing Theravada manuscripts (see Chapter 6), so it can also be said that there is no evidence to suggest that the origin of the Mahayana scriptures is different from that of the Theravada ones.

The origin of the Mahayana scriptures is, in fact, a much debated topic and there are a number of differing views, both among Buddhists and among Western scholars.

- Some claim that because they emerged so many centuries after the Buddha, with no evidence of their existence beforehand, the Mahayana scriptures can only have been written by later Buddhist scholars, giving their interpretation of the Buddha's teachings. They do not represent the teaching of the Buddha himself. This view is held by most Theravadins.
- Some followers of Mahayana claim that there was another Buddhist Council held in parallel to the first Buddhist Council, at which the Mahayana teachings were recited. These teachings were then transmitted orally for generations until they were written down. It is explained that the lack of evidence for this claim is due to the secrecy with which Mahayana was guarded, because it was considered a very advanced teaching and not communicated widely or publicly.
- Others explain that although the historical Buddha did teach Mahayana during his lifetime, it was too advanced for people; they did not fully understand or appreciate it. So teachings such as the *Prajñaparamita Sutras* were magically hidden and given to mythical sea serpents called *nagas* for safe-keeping until human beings were ready for them. (*Nagas* are sometimes depicted rather like mermaids.) Several centuries after the Buddha, the Mahayana teachings were mystically re-discovered by Buddhist masters such as Nagarjuna (first century CE) and written down by them during states of religious inspiration.

Theravadins do not consider the Mahayana scriptures to be authoritative but Mahayana followers do. They consider that their scriptures represent enlightened wisdom, albeit the words heard by Buddhist masters in special states of meditation and not the words of the historical Buddha himself.

The Mahayana scriptures do not fall into the three baskets in the same way as the Pali Canon. In Theravada Buddhism, each text falls into one or other of these categories. This means that the Vinaya is one set of scriptures, the Sutras are another, and the Abhidharma is yet another separate collection of scriptures. But in Mahayana, the Tripitaka relates more to the content of a scripture rather than to separate texts. One scripture may include different passages on each topic. For example, statements on the vows correspond to the Vinaya; explanations of the stages of meditation correspond to the category of Sutras; and teachings on emptiness deal with wisdom and correspond to Abhidharma. The same approach applies to the Vajrayana scriptures.

We should also note the following differences:

- There is no Mahayana Vinaya. Mahayana (and Vajrayana) monks and nuns follow one or other of the Vinaya codes of discipline belonging to the Nikaya traditions.
- Most of the Mahayana scriptures are sutras. Some of these sutras present the words of a disciple of the Buddha – not the Buddha himself – who speaks in the Buddha's presence and is inspired by him. At the end of the disciple's discourse the Buddha confirms that what he said was correct and true. We should note that Mahayana extends the authority of the Buddha beyond that of the historical Buddha to include any Buddhist with enlightened insight.
- Some Mahayana works contain Abhidharma analysis. For example, some texts explain the psychological process of meditation, or the different qualities and powers of enlightenment. Many of these texts are believed to be inspired not by Buddha Shakyamuni but by Buddha Maitreya, the next buddha who is due to come down to the human world and teach the Dharma in the future.

While the Theravada scriptures were written in Pali, the majority of the Mahayana scriptures were originally written in Sanskrit. Many of these Sanskrit texts are now lost and survive only in translation. Original Sanskrit texts from India were translated into Chinese and Tibetan, and subsequently the Chinese Canon was translated into Japanese and the Tibetan Canon into Mongolian. The Chinese and Tibetan Canons include texts of Nikaya Buddhism as well as the Mahayana corpus.

A number of Mahayana sutras became especially popular or important in Asia.

- The **Prajñaparamita Sutras,** or Discourses on the Perfection of Wisdom, set out the Mahayana understanding of *shunyata* or 'emptiness', the idea that nothing in the universe exists independently, permanently and inherently.

The shortest of this series is called the **Heart Sutra** and is often recited today in Japanese, Chinese and Tibetan monasteries. These sutras are the foundation of the Madhyamaka school of philosophy.

- The **Lankavatara Sutra** sets out the theory of buddha nature or *tathagatagarbha*, the idea that we all have a seed of enlightenment within us which simply needs nurturing and developing for us to become buddhas ourselves. This sutra is important in the Yogachara school of philosophy and in the Ch'an/Zen tradition.
- The **Lotus Sutra** is seen by some schools of Buddhism in the Far East as the expression of the Buddha's definitive teaching. It is therefore regarded as the most important sutra of all and some schools, such as Nichiren in Japan, have developed a ritual cult around it. The Lotus Sutra emphasizes the idea that Mahayana is superior to Nikaya Buddhism; it illustrates the *bodhisattva* ideal, the idea of skilful means and the principle of *ekayana*.

How do Mahayana followers relate to their scriptures?

Mahayana schools vary significantly in the importance they give to the Buddhist scriptures.

- Some schools refer to one or more sutras as the foundational texts of their philosophy or religious practice. This applies to the Prajñaparamita sutras for Madhyamaka and the Lankavatara Sutra for Yogachara. But, at the same time, followers of these schools read and respect all the other scriptures too.
- Some schools focus entirely on a single scripture which they consider supreme, and do not place value on the study of other scriptures. This applies to the Lotus Sutra for Nichiren Buddhism in Japan and the Sukhavati Sutras for Amida Buddhism (Pure Land).
- Other Mahayana schools discourage the study of all scriptures on the basis that meditation practice is far more effective for attaining enlightenment than intellectual study. This is the case in some schools of Ch'an (Zen) Buddhism. In practice, however, Zen teachers do study some scriptures, especially the Lankavatara Sutra, the Diamond Sutra and the Heart Sutra.

The Tantric scriptures

Vajrayana Buddhism follows all the Mahayana scriptures outlined above and, in addition, has its own distinctive collection of scriptures called Tantras. The earlier tantric texts appeared in India and other regions of Asia around the sixth century CE. They describe various rituals and visualisation practices, and present teachings on the nature of the mind and on the various world systems.

The Tantras are written in cryptic language which is extremely difficult to understand for the uninitiated. Vajrayana generally lays particular emphasis on the importance of following a master or guru, and in the case of scriptural study this is vital because without individual tuition students would be unable to understand the Tantras on their own. The Tantras are found in both the Chinese and Tibetan canons, as well as in the Japanese and Mongolian canons. Today they are especially influential in Tibetan and Japanese Buddhism.

Summary

There is no set way in which all Buddhists relate to their scriptures. To begin with, followers of each school or tradition will each regard a different set of texts as the authentic body of scripture they consider authoritative. In other words, the scriptures that Buddhists refer to vary from one tradition to another. Second, there is a broad range of approaches in terms of the respect felt for scripture. Attitudes vary from the extreme of honouring one single text (Lotus Sutra, Nichiren) to the other extreme of according little value to the study of any scriptures at all (Zen). Most Buddhist schools follow a more relaxed path between these extremes: people with scholarly inclinations study a broad range of scriptures while those who are not able to do this simply learn the main points and try to apply them in their lives.

Many of the key points we have seen in connection with the Buddhist scriptures stem from the basic idea that they are not divinely revealed. Because of this, scriptural words do not have a special status for Buddhists; words, even those of scripture, are merely conventional and part of human language. Scripture has value only insofar as it helps human beings transform themselves from ignorance to enlightenment, from suffering to freedom. Scripture does not have intrinsic value, only instrumental value. Ultimately, the highest truths cannot be put into words.

Personal reflection

If scripture is not divinely revealed, what is its value?

Main Points

- The Buddha encouraged his disciples to examine his words and come to a personal conviction in their truth, not to accept his teaching blindly on trust.
- The Pali Canon is the set of scriptures of the Theravada school in the ancient Pali language. It contains some of the oldest Buddhist texts.
- The Pali scriptures are arranged in three categories or baskets, the Tripitaka:
    - the Vinaya is on discipline
    - the Sutras are on meditation
    - the Abhidharma is on wisdom.
- Most Mahayana scriptures were composed in Sanskrit. Some contain the words of Buddha Shakyamuni, others contain the words of Buddha Maitreya or those of Buddha Shakyamuni's foremost disciples.
- The Mahayana and Vajrayana scriptures exist today in Sanskrit, Chinese, Japanese, Korean, Tibetan and Mongolian.

Chapter 9

THE FOUR NOBLE TRUTHS

The first teaching given by the Buddha after his enlightenment is called the Four Noble Truths. They form a framework for the entirety of his subsequent teachings and are therefore key to understanding what Buddhism is about.

The man wounded with a poisoned arrow

We usually expect religions to give us answers to the big questions of life, such as how the universe began, why we are here, and whether our souls survive after death. The Buddha was not so concerned with these questions, however. He considered these matters to be vain metaphysical speculation because they are questions that can never be satisfactorily answered. He insisted that religious teaching must be practical. It should not aim to satisfy intellectual curiosity but, instead, it should lead to complete freedom from suffering. If a religious teaching does not do this then he considered it of little value. The Buddha did not begin with big philosophical questions; his starting point was everyday experience.

Some of the Buddha's disciples did not appreciate his approach, and there is a well-known story of one disciple, named Malunkyaputta, who complained that the Buddha had not given him the answers he was looking for.[26] He accused the Buddha of failing to answer his questions simply because he did not in fact know the answers to them. The ten questions on which the Buddha was silent are:

1. Is the universe eternal?
2. Is the universe not eternal?
3. Is the universe finite?
4. Is the universe infinite?
5. Is the soul the same as the body?
6. Are the soul and the body two separate things?
7. Does the Buddha continue to exist after death?
8. Does the Buddha no longer exist after death?
9. Does the Buddha both exist and not exist after death?
10. Is the Buddha both non-existent and not non-existent after death?

Malunkyaputta challenged the Buddha to answer the questions if he knew the answers, and said that if he did not know them then he should be honest enough to admit that. He then threatened that he would stop being his disciple if the Buddha did not respond to his satisfaction.

The Buddha replied by pointing out that he had never promised answers to such questions to any of his disciples, and therefore he could not be accused of misleading them. He then went on to tell the story of the man who is wounded with a poisoned arrow. The wounded man's relatives take him to a surgeon, but he insists that he does not want the arrow to be removed until he has established who shot it, what social background the assailant came from, his name and what he looks like. And on top of this, he insists he needs to know what sort of bow was used, what sort of arrow and what wood the arrow was made of. Only then will he accept treatment. In such a situation, said the Buddha, the man would surely die before all this information could be gathered. Likewise, one might well die before understanding the answers to these ten metaphysical questions. Malunkyaputta was convinced by this and remained a monk.

According to the Buddha, one does not need to depend on such answers in order to lead a religious life. Whatever opinions we may have about the beginning of the universe, the nature of the soul and eternity, they will not help us to understand our suffering nor will they help us to overcome it. From the

Indian point of view at least, the whole point of religion is to eliminate suffering. This is why the Buddha taught the Four Noble Truths, because they are useful and practical in this precise respect.

Another way we can understand the Buddha's silence on these questions is from the point of view of logic. If we take question 5 as an example: the way it is phrased means that neither a 'yes' answer nor a 'no' answer would be satisfactory from the Buddha's point of view. This is because the question rests on the assumption that there exists something called a soul that we can talk about and define in relation to the body. However, for the Buddha, the very existence of the soul is an assumption that needs to be questioned, and this makes question 5 unanswerable as it stands. Each of Malunkyaputta's questions rests on a similar type of assumption.

A framework for all teachings of Buddhism

The theme of the very first teaching the Buddha gave after his enlightenment is known as the Four Noble Truths. On that occasion he spoke in a place known as the Deer Park in Isipatana (modern-day Sarnath) near Benares, to five ascetics who had previously been his companions in the forest. After that he taught on the Four Noble Truths again and again for many years, and we find presentations of them in many different suttas in the Pali Canon.

The Four Noble Truths are the foundation and the heart of all the different teachings the Buddha gave over his 45-year ministry. They offer a framework into which everything fits. They are taught in every tradition and school of Buddhism in the world, either explicitly or implicitly, even though there can be variations in emphasis and interpretation.

The Four Noble Truths are:

1. The truth of suffering or dissatisfaction
2. The truth of the causes of suffering
3. The truth of the cessation (or end) of suffering
4. The truth of the path leading to the cessation of suffering.

Why are these truths called 'noble'? This is an awkward translation into the English language because the meaning is not that the truths themselves are noble. Rather, they are the truths that are realized by the 'noble ones' meaning those on the path who have direct, intuitive, non-conceptual insight into the true nature of things. A better translation would therefore be 'The Four Truths of the Noble Ones'. But that could be misunderstood as meaning that they are true only for noble beings and not for anyone else. The Four Noble Truths are taught as being universal truths that apply to everyone, but only noble beings recognize their truth.

The word 'truth' in this context means 'reality', the way things are; it does not refer to a philosophical or theological propositional statement with which one is free to agree or disagree. Suffering, for example, is a universal fact of life that applies to everyone, whether Buddhist or non-Buddhist. Whether you believe in suffering or not, you will experience it anyway. Yet the Buddha was not saying that there are four 'realities' out there we should know about. Rather, these Truths are realizations about the nature of things, they are insights that arise through hard experience. The Four Noble Truths should therefore not be seen as a set of dogmatic truths in which all Buddhists must believe. In this sense, they are not the equivalent of the Christian Creed or the Five Pillars of Islam.

Briefly, the Buddha teaches that:

1. Suffering is universal and is experienced by every living being, yet nobody wants suffering and we all long to find happiness.
2. The root causes of suffering lie within our own minds. They are craving, aggression and ignorance – known as the Three Mental Poisons. Motivated by these poisons we engage in actions which, through the laws of *karma* or action, cause harm to others as well as ourselves, and the suffering we experience only prompts us to react even more aggressively or blindly to the next situation.
3. It is possible to put an end to suffering by putting an end to the causes of suffering. If we transform our actions and our minds and become selfless we can find true and lasting happiness known as nirvana *(nibbana)* or enlightenment.
4. The way to free oneself from suffering is to follow the Buddhist path of moral discipline, meditation and wisdom.

Many teachings in Buddhism are preserved as numbered formulae: the Four Noble Truths, the Three Marks of Existence, the Six Paramitas and so on.

These should be seen simply as convenient ways of memorising the Dharma, especially in a context where followers retain teachings by heart. Buddhists do not view the Four Noble Truths in a rigid way, as though there were precisely four 'truths' out there to understand, but rather they see them as a tool to help cultivate a truer vision of the world. The Buddha said that no words or formulae can really capture the truth and experience he was trying to share, because the ultimate is beyond words.

The logic of the Four Noble Truths

The Buddha began his teaching life by addressing the universal problem of suffering. Everyone suffers in life. Although each of us longs to be happy, somehow we rarely find the lasting happiness we seek. And when we look beyond our own situation and see just how many people in the world are going through far greater suffering than we are, the weight of human misery can feel overwhelming. Nowadays we only have to switch on the television to see this: wars, natural disasters, starvation, disease, violence, divorce, betrayal, poverty, death. Suffering feels endless and nobody is spared.

When the Buddha left his father's palace he set out to find a solution to suffering, and this teaching is the fruit of his search. In the Four Noble Truths he describes the problem, explains what is causing the problem, finds that the problem can be solved, and sets out the method for solving it. One image often used to illustrate this teaching is that of a wise doctor tending a patient. Suffering is the patient's condition; the causes of suffering are the doctor's diagnosis of that condition; the cessation of suffering is the good news that the complaint is curable; and the path is the treatment prescribed by the doctor to bring about a cure. In this analogy, the Buddha is the doctor and each one of us is a patient.

Some doctors can exaggerate the seriousness of an illness while others might lack the experience to know just how serious it is. But the Buddha is a wise doctor, whose analysis of the situation is objective and accurate. This is why Buddhists believe that the Buddha's teaching is neither pessimistic nor optimistic; instead, it offers a realistic appraisal of the human condition. It shows us who we are, what our world is, and what actions are effective in bringing about change.

The logic of the Four Noble Truths can be analysed in different ways depending on one's point of view. For example, if we take them purely theoretically they can be seen as two sets of pairs. Each pair consists of a cause and an effect as in the diagram below.

First pair:	suffering	effect
	causes of suffering	cause
Second pair:	cessation of suffering	effect
	path	cause

If we follow this logic we could present them in a different order, taking the second truth first, then the first truth; and taking the fourth truth next, then the third. This is because we usually think that causes come before their effects. This pairing of the Four Noble Truths highlights the contrast between them: the first pair describes how our lives are at the moment and what lies at the root of the suffering we experience. The second pair describes how things could be if we changed: how, by following the path of moral discipline, meditation and wisdom, we can turn things around and create the causes of nirvana where suffering ceases altogether. So the first pair describes samsara and the second pair is related to nirvana.

On the other hand, we can approach the Four Noble Truths from the point of view of personal experience and take them in the order they are usually given. Our experience of suffering is the starting point. If we did not suffer at all, then we would have no wish to follow a spiritual path to change the situation. When we do undergo painful experiences, we naturally ask ourselves why. Why is this happening to me? Why do I have to go through this? Why did things go wrong? We instinctively look for an explanation of the reasons for our predicament. If we find an explanation, it usually entails some understanding of how to end our suffering in the short or long term. Finally, we have to make the necessary changes to put an end to our suffering.

The Middle Way

The Buddha characterized his approach to the religious life, as set out in the Four Noble Truths, as 'the middle way'. This expression is now commonly used to describe the Buddhist approach in general. The Buddha distinguished his middle way from other approaches which promote extreme positions. Such approaches need not only be religious ones – they can include any vision or method for finding happiness, however that is defined.

For example, one extreme pointed out by the Buddha is 'devotion to the indulgence of sense pleasures, which is low, common, the way of ordinary people, unworthy and unprofitable'. He had had first-hand experience of this way of life from his years of luxurious indulgence in the royal palace. Clearly, 'ordinary people' does not simply refer to the poor but rather to anyone, of whatever social or educational background, who is satisfied with the everyday pleasures of this life and does not yearn for higher things. Such a hedonistic outlook is associated with materialism because it leaves no room for spiritual goals and values, and it denies any form of after-life.

Another extreme mentioned by the Buddha is that of self-mortification. This is the opposite of indulgence in sense pleasures: deliberately subjecting one's body to extreme pain and discomfort with a view to freeing the spirit from the shackles of the body and finding lasting peace and happiness. Once again, the Buddha had experienced this approach at first hand when he lived as an ascetic in the forest. He describes self-mortification as 'painful, unworthy and unprofitable'; it causes one to suffer, to lose one's dignity, and does not lead to the desired goal.

The Buddha said that it is by avoiding both these extremes that he realized a middle path which 'gives vision, gives knowledge, and leads to calm, to insight, to enlightenment, to nibbana (nirvana).' The Buddha assures us that this path of moderation and balance really does lead to the happiness we seek. It is this 'middle way' approach that gives rise to the qualities of non-violence, tolerance and compassion for which Buddhism is known.

Concluding points

In Nikaya Buddhism, the entire path is about coming to the deepest and most complete understanding of the Four Noble Truths. They are not simply the framework of the teaching, they are the core of the teaching. Analytical meditation, or vipassana, takes themes from the Four Noble Truths as points of focus for deep reflection.

In Mahayana, the emphasis is on the Four Noble Truths as encapsulating the structure of the Buddha's teachings as a whole. Even though suffering, its causes, enlightenment and the path are all interpreted differently from the Nikaya approach, this four-point structure remains the same.

When any Buddhist engages with the Four Noble Truths in practice, each truth is applied in a different way.

- The first Noble Truth, suffering, has to be understood
- The second Noble Truth, the causes of suffering, has to be abandoned
- The third Noble Truth, the cessation of suffering, is that which is to be realized
- And the fourth Noble Truth, the path, needs to be followed.

Mere knowledge of the Four Noble Truths is not enough to attain nirvana. It is vital to apply that knowledge by changing attitudes and behaviour, and by adopting a wholesome way of life. Like other religions, Buddhism is not simply about holding certain beliefs but about adopting particular practices in life. The Thai master Ajahn Chah explains how we pass from knowledge to action:

> *What is this going beyond suffering all about? What should we do to escape from suffering? It's necessary for us to do some study; we need to study the thinking and feeling in our hearts. Just that. It is something we are presently unable to change. We can be free of all suffering and unsatisfactoriness in life by changing this one point, our habitual world view, our way of thinking and feeling. The authentic Dharma of the Buddha is not something pointing far away. It teaches self.*[27]

The Four Noble Truths help us to understand ourselves and how we can change. More elaborately, the benefits of studying the Four Noble Truths for a Buddhist are explained in three points.[28]

- The minimum benefit is that one will gain some confidence that problems and difficulties in life can be stopped, and that one is able to make them stop.
- The medium benefit is that one establishes the Three Refuges (see Chapter 14). One decides to follow the Buddhist path in order to transform one's difficulties, so one is closer to seeing the meaning of Dharma and, by being with those who are practising the Dharma, one begins to experience the meaning of Sangha.
- The highest benefit is seeing cause and effect and the real nature of suffering for oneself. One sees how one has fallen into tricky situations, and how other people do the same. By putting the fourth Noble Truth into practice with that understanding, one is able to benefit both oneself and others.

Each one of the Truths will be explained in detail in the following chapters.

Personal reflection

By addressing our experience of life in terms of causes and effects, the Buddha presents a logical and systematic approach to the pursuit of true happiness. How effective do you think this presentation will be for someone who is (a) suffering intensely or (b) living a prosperous and comfortable life?

Main Points

- The Four Noble Truths are the core teaching of Buddhism and a framework for the Buddha's entire teaching.
- The Four Noble Truths are:
  - the truth of suffering or unsatisfactoriness
  - the truth of the causes of suffering
  - the truth of the cessation of suffering
  - the truth of the path leading to the cessation of suffering.
- An analogy is used to illustrate the Four Noble Truths: that of a wise doctor diagnosing the causes of illness in his patient, informing him that the disease is curable and prescribing a cure. The doctor represents the Buddha, the patient ourselves, the disease refers to suffering, and the cure to nirvana.
- The Four Noble Truths exemplify the Middle Way of Buddhism, a path of moderation free of extreme views and extreme lifestyles.

Chapter 10

THE THREE MARKS OF EXISTENCE

The Buddhist view of the world can be summarized in terms of Three Marks or Characteristics of Existence. They tell us that everything is: a) impermanent and constantly changing; b) a cause of suffering and unsatisfactoriness; and c) devoid of inherent existence. This chapter presents all three of these important Buddhist insights which are the bedrock of Buddhist thinking.

Introduction

The Three Marks (or 'characteristics') of Existence encapsulate the basic Buddhist world view. In a nutshell, everything that exists in our ordinary world is conditioned, impermanent, causes suffering and is interdependent with everything else. The reason Buddhists hold the three Marks of Existence to be so important is because ordinary people do not usually think this way, and it is this basic ignorance or unawareness that is the root cause of their suffering. To attain enlightenment and realize the unconditioned, we need to dismantle the false ideas we have of our world so we understand how things really are. And we have to see through the mistaken images we have of ourselves and connect with who we truly are. The entire Buddhist path is about freeing oneself from a distorted view of reality and the suffering it brings.

The Three Marks of Existence are:

1. Impermanence (*anicca* in Pali, *anitya* in Sanskrit)
2. Suffering (*dukkha* in Pali, *duhkha* in Sanskrit)
3. 'No self' (*anatta* in Pali, *anatman* in Sanskrit)

The Buddhist teachings present these Three Marks in a detailed and systematic way. Since they are so fundamental to Buddhist thought, we examine them in order.

The impermanence of all things

The Buddha found that everything in the world is impermanent and changing, which implies that there is nothing whatsoever that is permanent. We could say that change is a fact of life. This truth might sound banal, but the Buddhist view is a very radical one because it does not allow for any exceptions. It covers everything from the book in your hand to the solar system and more. In the moment a book begins to exist, its impermanence is assured. This is because it is composed of many different parts. If a thing is compound it only begins to exist when certain factors come together; and at some point in time those factors naturally separate and disperse and then the compound thing will cease to exist. All compound things therefore have a beginning, middle and end.

Although we all know that things change, in practice most of us believe there are some things in life that are permanent and lasting, or at least we behave as though they are. For example, there may be some values we believe are universal and eternal: justice, peace, truth or beauty for instance. Those who follow a religion other than Buddhism might believe there is an eternal God, an everlasting soul and an eternal heaven. Even in terms of everyday life, when we have a crush on someone we think it will last for ever. We also relate to ourselves as permanent; for instance, we make plans as though we were always going to be healthy and young. When death approaches we regard it as a failure, a shock or a surprise.

The Buddha examined everything people regard as permanent and came to the conclusion that there is nothing at all that is not subject to change. He explained that change or impermanence operates on two levels, the gross and the subtle. On the gross level, impermanence is defined as that which arises, abides and ceases, while on the subtle level it is defined as that which does not abide for a second moment.

The gross level is the obvious physical level of change: changes we experience like the weather, the seasons, the way things decay or get broken, the way people grow up and age and die. This gross level also applies to historical change, social change, geographical change and so on. This is what we commonly call change – a phenomenon we can usually observe with our own eyes and that does not require special scientific or philosophical analysis to be discovered. Buddhists consider that change in this sense is undeniable.

The subtle level of change is sometimes called 'momentary change': it means that everything is in a perpetual process of flux, from moment to moment. Although objects like tables and chairs look the same today as they did yesterday, in fact they are continually changing in each moment. If we use a microscope we will see that the atoms and molecules that objects are made of are in perpetual motion and are continually changing their configurations. So, even though at the gross level objects appear to remain the same for a certain length of time before they are broken or decay or are destroyed, nevertheless at the subtle level they are subject to the change process all the time. It is on account of this subtle level of change that things eventually change visibly at the gross level: we don't suddenly grow old on a certain day or even in a certain year; it's a gradual process. So visible changes like ageing or the change of the seasons do not just happen as one special event but result from the culmination of millions of smaller changes.

Momentary change cannot be observed by the naked eye: that is why it is called subtle. Nowadays we can relate to the idea by referring to modern science and the use of microscopes but the Buddha, of course, did not have any microscopes nor did the Buddhist scholars who wrote the philosophical treatises of the Abhidharma. They made their observations of momentary change through the special insight they developed in meditation.

You might think that radical impermanence makes no sense because things don't change all the time and there *is* some continuity. If we could not recognize our friends from one day to the next because of change, life would be chaotic. Clearly, this is not the case: we do recognize people from one day to the next, even from one decade to the next, so does this mean that Buddhists have got it wrong?

All philosophers, East and West, grapple with the problem of the relationship between continuity and change. The way Buddhists account for this relationship is by explaining that momentary change happens as a continuum of linked moments. Each moment is so short that we don't notice it (a moment is sometimes defined as one sixty-fifth of a finger snap). That is why we have the impression that life is continuous. It is rather like the frames of a movie that go through the projector at just the right speed to give us the illusion of a continuous sequence. But, if we check the film reel, we see that each frame is separate.

This continuum of moments does not happen haphazardly. I cannot be a human being in one moment and an elephant in the next. The continuum happens in an orderly fashion because one moment produces the next, and a moment can only produce another moment that is similar to it because there are causal connections between each of the factors that make up a situation. For instance, if we imagine change in slow motion the process is rather like looking at a dancer in a night club under stroboscopic light. Each time the light flashes we see one dance pose, and although we cannot see what happens between the flashes we know that a dance pose is produced by the previous one. There is a causal connection between the situations we see in each flash of light.

Finally, even if we agree that impermanence affects all inanimate and animate objects in the world, what of our abstract ideas of permanent things? What about beauty, truth and God? Why does the Buddha deny that these things are permanent? The very definition of all these terms includes the notion of permanence: God would not be God if he were not eternal.

Here, Buddhists make a distinction between the ideas we have about things and the reality to which our ideas refer. They say that the mere fact we have an idea that something exists is no proof that it exists in actuality. It is clear we can have quite convincing ideas and images of the existence of things or people that do not actually exist: unicorns are the classic example of this, but we could add modern examples such as hobbits or pokemon. The Buddhist view is that none of our *abstract* concepts actually corresponds to something that objectively exists; they are only human ways of interpreting experience. Beauty, truth, justice, God and enlightenment are all instances of human beings creating an idea in order to understand and communicate experience, but they are not reals. The same goes for the idea of permanence itself. The first Mark of

Existence is telling us that there is no such thing as a permanent existent. To say that anything exists permanently is a contradiction in terms.

It is one thing to agree with the philosophical reasoning on impermanence, but it is quite another to accept it in practice because we are so habituated to our own views. This is why change is one of the first themes on which a Buddhist will meditate. Flowers are often used as a focus of meditation because their beauty does not last long and they therefore readily symbolise impermanence. The other image that is often used is that of the Buddha lying on his right side passing into *parinirvana* because this is a reminder that everything, even the people we value the most, are subject to death. By contemplating and reflecting on impermanence we may come to a deeper acceptance of the truth of change.

Figure 10.1 – Statues of the Buddha passing away are used as reminders of impermanence and death. This statue is in Polonnaruwa, Sri Lanka. Photo: Detlef Hansen.

This reflection also makes us realize that change is not always a reason to be sad. On the positive side, it is because we change that we are able to learn and make progress. It is because we are subject to impermanence that it is possible to change a negative situation into a positive one, or transform a negative emotion into a positive one. The main benefit of reflecting on change is that it loosens our attachment to things. If we realize deeply that things come and go, that everything in our experience will eventually come to a natural end, this helps us to stop hanging on to things. We will grasp at things less and it will be easier to let go when the time comes. We will have less resistance to change, and accepting change as a natural part of life will make us happier because we can then 'go with the flow'. The Buddha taught that much of our suffering is caused by grasping at things or craving for things or desiring things that are not, ultimately, real.

Dukkha: the nature of things is suffering

The end of desire is the end of sorrow.
Dhammapada 354

All too often we resist going with the flow; we don't want certain things to change. We cannot let go of our desire and craving. We fail to see the transitory nature of the things and people we are attached to most, and when they change we experience pain and suffering. *Dukkha* (Sanskrit *duhkha*) is the first Noble Truth as well as one of the three Marks of Existence; it is usually translated as 'suffering' in English but this word does not fully convey the meaning of what Buddhists mean by *dukkha*. Walpola Rahula explains:

> *It is true that the Pali word dukkha (or Sanskrit duhkha) in ordinary usage means 'suffering', 'pain', 'sorrow' or 'misery', as opposed to the word sukha meaning 'happiness', 'comfort' or 'ease'. But the term dukkha as the first Noble Truth, which represents the Buddha's view of life and the world, has a deeper philosophical meaning and connotes enormously wider senses. It is admitted that the term dukkha in the first Noble Truth contains, quite obviously, the ordinary meaning of 'suffering', but in addition it also includes deeper ideas such as 'imperfection', 'impermanence', 'emptiness', 'insubstantiality'. It is difficult therefore to find one word to embrace the whole conception of the term.*[29]

Buddhists distinguish three broad types of *dukkha*.

Ordinary suffering

The first type of suffering includes experiences that human beings universally identify as obvious forms of suffering, regardless of whether they follow a religion or not: experiences such as giving birth and being born, illness and disease, old age and dying. The quality these experiences have in common is that they are all painful. This type of suffering also includes the grief of being separated from those we love or from places where we feel at home; the distress of not getting what we want; and the pain of witnessing the suffering of people we love.

The suffering of change

The second type of suffering includes the many types of distress, anxiety and stress that result from changes in our life situation. As the first Mark of Existence showed, everything in the world is impermanent and because either we don't realize this fact or don't want to accept it, we suffer when things change beyond our control. Happy feelings or happy situations do not last for ever, even though we wish they would, so when they change they bring about suffering and disappointment. Examples of this are marriage break-ups and divorce; bereavement; losing one's job; having to move house or leave one's country.

Sometimes it is we who change rather than our circumstances: for instance, the music you love at one time you might later find rather boring, and then you look for something new to bring you pleasure in an endless cycle of frustration and lack of contentment. Consumerism and advertising are successful because of the impermanence of our likes and dislikes, and indeed they feed the cycle. One reason why people who seem to have everything can still feel bored and unhappy is that their feelings about things fluctuate.

The suffering of conditioned existence

The suffering of conditioned existence, or conditioned states, refers to the background dissatisfaction we have with life, a latent anguish or *angst* which arises from a sense of insecurity. It is the frustration we feel at our own limitations and at our powerlessness to control our life and our world. We often find we don't fully understand why things are the way they are, we don't know where our actions will lead or what the future holds in store. And when we consider that whatever we achieve it all ends with our death anyway, life itself can feel pointless. This is not a dramatic form of suffering or one that is sparked by any event in particular, rather it is a more fundamental and more subtle background feeling of unease.

This third type of suffering may be more difficult to relate to than the first two because it is based on analysis. While the first two types are self-evident, the third type is unique to the Buddhist understanding of *dukkha.* According to Buddhism, everything and everyone in the world exists only in dependence on other things, which means that there is absolutely nothing that has independent and permanent existence. It is for this reason that we sometimes feel that things are insubstantial, that life is like a dream, and that even the things we value most – like love for example – are not ultimately real. More to the point, perhaps, is the fact that we ourselves are constantly changing, and the identities we create for ourselves are not who we really are. This line of reflection and analysis leads to a big question: is there anything at all in the world that *is* real?

One Buddhist answer to this question is that none of the things or people of our everyday experience is ultimately real. To understand what is meant by this we need to look at the other two Marks of Existence, the other two factors that describe what our world is actually like.

In brief, *dukkha* covers pain, suffering, grief, frustration, dissatisfaction, unease and anguish. This characteristic of existence implies that everything can at some point become a cause of suffering. Even happiness is seen as a cause of suffering because when it comes to an end it will bring pain and misery. However, this does not mean that Buddhism is gloomy and pessimistic, or that the Buddha did not value life and the pleasures it can bring. Sometimes Buddhism is misunderstood as a religion that sees 'all life as suffering'. The Buddha acknowledged that there are both material and spiritual forms of happiness. For example, in one Theravada sutta he lists several types of happiness such as that of family life and that of monastic life; the happiness of sense pleasures and that of renouncing sense pleasures; the happiness of being attached to what you love and that of being detached; and physical happiness and mental happiness. It is important to note that all such states of happiness are included in *dukkha* from the Buddhist point of view. Even very high states of meditation are included in *dukkha*. This is simply because they are all subject to change and, as the Buddha said, 'whatever is impermanent is *dukkha*'.[30]

This view is not pessimistic since the Buddha went on to tell us that there is an alternative to the life of suffering. He said that true happiness – the lasting happiness we are all looking for – is *nibbana (nirvana)* or enlightenment, a state free of suffering and the causes of suffering. It is a state that is not conditioned by anything else and that is therefore beyond change since it is beyond time. Until we reach this state, however, our experience will invariably be marked by suffering, change and the insubstantiality of things.

Anatta: no-self or interdependence

The Buddhist notion of impermanence is developed philosophically as *anatta* (Sanskrit *anatman*) or 'no-self', sometimes translated as 'non-self'. This is a difficult principle to understand and it is one which is unique to Buddhism. Whatever common ground we can find between all world religions, this is one point on which Buddhism differs from the rest.

Radical impermanence implies that nothing has an unchanging essence or 'self'. Buddhist thought makes no distinction between the core or essence of a thing, which is unchanging and has ontological existence, and its secondary qualities which may change and have only contingent existence. Instead, everything is process, and things are simply made up of lots of constantly changing parts and particles. Rupert Gethin puts it this way:

> *Buddhist thought understands change not in terms of a primary substantial essence remaining constant while its secondary qualities change, but solely in terms of the causal connectedness of different qualities. There is no primary substance to remain constant.*[31]

This is radically different from Plato's theory of Forms, for example, where the perfect Form of each thing exists unchanged in a separate dimension from that of empirical experience.

If we believe that things have an unchanging essence, and that change only affects their secondary qualities, then even if we chop a large branch off a healthy tree we would still consider that it remains a tree. It does not lose its 'treeness'. Its existence as a tree does not depend on the continued existence of all its parts. Likewise, in the case of a human being, if, through learning biology, I realize that hundreds of cells in my body have died compared with a moment ago, and hundreds of new cells have replaced them, I could consider that such a level of cellular change has no effect on who I really am. I continue to be me, with or without my cells; my identity has not changed; the true me is not dependent on the existence or non-existence of cells.

There are problems with this view for both Buddhist and non-Buddhist philosophers. If we take the example of the tree again, how much of a tree can you chop down before it ceases to be a tree? Two branches, three, all the branches, the trunk? And how much change and destruction can my body undergo before you might say that my identity has changed? It is very hard to know where to draw the line.

The 'no self' of inanimate objects

Anatta means 'no essence' or 'no inherent existence'. This idea is linked to the Buddhist understanding of causality, the principle that everything in the universe – and the universe itself – comes into existence through the power of certain causes and conditions. A causes B, X causes Y, and so on; also, A causes B and B causes C, and so on. This is what is meant by *conditioned existence*: everything arises from causes and conditions. The implication of conditioned existence is that everything must therefore be impermanent. If there is a chain of causes and effects this logically means that causes must exist before their effects; and, if this is so, it means that effects begin to exist from a particular point in time, and before that point they do not exist.

We can illustrate this in a simple chart, where T is a moment in time, and A, B and C are objects.

$A \Rightarrow$	B	$B \Rightarrow$	C
T_1	T_2	T_3	T_4
Cause	effect	cause	effect

B does not exist at T_1, nor does it exist at T_4, so the existence of B has a clear beginning and end. It exists from the moment it is caused by something else until such moment as it produces its own effect. This model can be applied to a particular situation. 'A' could be a cherry seed; once planted, watered and fertilised, A produces B, a young sapling. Later, when all the growing conditions have been good, B produces C, a cherry tree. When the tree is fully grown the seed and sapling no longer exist. And at T_1 when only the seed exists, the sapling and the tree do not yet exist. This example shows how, if things are caused by other things, they have to have a beginning and an end and are therefore impermanent. In other words, conditioned things are necessarily subject to time.

The Buddhist analysis goes one step further. Impermanence, in itself, is not enough to prove non-inherent existence because it could be argued that change only applies to a thing's secondary qualities and not to its essence. Buddhists must show why they do not think there are essences. They do this through reductionist analysis, that is, by logically breaking things down and reducing them to their parts, and by reaching the conclusion that things are merely the sum of their parts. Buddhists argue that the existence of a thing can be fully accounted for by its parts without the need for positing an unchanging essence.

They point out that an essence is something one cannot perceive and of which we have no experience, so its existence cannot be validated either logically or empirically.

Example of the chariot

The classic example of this principle is found in *The Questions of King Milinda*. The monk Nagasena asks King Milinda what mode of transport he used to come and meet him, and his answer is 'a chariot'. He asks the king what a chariot is. Is it the axle, the wheels, the wooden frame, the yoke or the reins? Naturally, the answer is that none of these things on their own constitute a chariot. But if none of the parts are the chariot, where is the real chariot? The king replies:

> *"It is in dependence on the pole, the axle, the wheels, the framework, the flagstaff, etc., that there takes place this denomination 'chariot', this designation, this conceptual term, a current appellation and a mere name."*

Nagasena agrees with the king. He is saying that what we conventionally call a chariot only exists in dependence upon all the parts that make it up; if some or all of those parts were missing, there would be no chariot there. A chariot is not something that exists over and above the sum of its parts: it is simply a concept, a word that we apply when all the parts are assembled and function together in a particular way. One can go even further and conclude that there is nothing called 'chariot' that exists in actuality; 'chariot' is simply a term used to designate a particular association of pieces of wood and metal. The corollary of this is also true: if we take all the pieces apart, or destroy them, then the 'chariot' no longer exists. Therefore, chariots only have conditioned existence: they exist in dependence on certain causes and conditions coming together in a particular way, and once those causes and conditions change chariots cease to exist.

A modern example of this would be a car. What is a car? Clearly it is not simply the tyres or the engine or the steering wheel, and so on, on their own. A car exists when all its parts are assembled in a particular way so that it functions like a car. So once the car gets old and we take it to the car breakers, can we still call it a car when it has no wheels, or no windows, or no engine, or no steering wheel? At what point does a car cease being a car when we start taking it to pieces? And once we have disassembled the entire car and there is nothing left but spare parts, is there still an 'essence of car' that exists? And if so where, how, and how do you know?

The principle put forward by Buddhist philosophy here is called dependent origination, dependent arising, conditioned arising or interdependence (*paticcasamuppada* in Pali, *pratityasamutpada* in Sanskrit). All these terms mean that things arise or originate in dependence on causes. Nothing exists without a cause. One of the classic formulations of this idea in the scriptures is the following:

When this exists, that exists;
From the arising of this, that arises;
When this does not exist, that does not exist;
From the cessation of this, that ceases. [32]

Nothing is unitary – nothing is just one single thing – everything is made up of numerous parts, so the existence of an object depends on the coming together of all its parts. This analysis makes us realize that the objects of our everyday world do not exist in the way we think they do, as substantially distinct entities. This is just how they appear to us, how we perceive them. This philosophical analysis enables us to make a distinction between the way things appear and the way they truly are. By reflecting and meditating on this, we mentally break down the phenomena that make up our world until we realize that they are as insubstantial as a dream, a mirage or a rainbow.

The philosophical analysis used in Nikaya Buddhism reduces the objects of our world to their parts, and so on down to the tiniest particles that things are made of. The conclusion of this reasoning is that there are only two types of reals: the infinitely small particles that join together to produce material things, and the infinitely small moments of consciousness that produce our stream of consciousness. Particles and moments of consciousness are therefore the building blocks of reality; they are the starting point of the causal chain. Logically they are considered necessary because otherwise, if things were reduced to their parts and those parts further reduced to their parts, and so on, endlessly, the argument would fall into infinite regress. There never would be a starting point to causation. These two types of reals therefore make this theory of causation tenable.

Another modern example of interdependence is provided by chemistry. As we know, water is H_20; it is made of hydrogen and oxygen. There is no such thing as 'water' that exists apart from hydrogen and oxygen. When its chemical parts come together in this particular way it has its own characteristic function

– it flows, for example, and has a certain temperature – but likewise, if through a chemical experiment one separates the hydrogen from the oxygen, there will be no water there. If one extends this analysis further, one can see that water is not a distinct, substantial entity that is entirely different from, say, the air or the earth. Chemical analysis demonstrates that the elements that make up water (atoms and molecules of hydrogen and oxygen) are also present in the air and the earth, but in combination with other elements. It follows that everything in the world is interconnected; nothing is completely separate from anything else even though that is not how we usually perceive things.

Figure 10.2 – Interdependence

The Vietnamese Zen master Thich Nhat Hanh has coined a new English word to describe interdependence: he calls it 'interbeing'. Things inter-are. In this passage he conveys the meaning of interdependence poetically.

If you are a poet, you will see clearly that there is a cloud floating in this sheet of paper. Without a cloud, there will be no rain; without rain, the trees cannot grow; and without trees, we cannot make paper. The cloud is essential for the paper to exist. If the cloud is not here, the sheet of paper cannot be here either. So we can say that the cloud and the paper inter-are.

If we look into this sheet of paper even more deeply, we can see the sunshine in it. If the sunshine is not there, the forest cannot grow. In fact, nothing can grow. Even we cannot grow without sunshine. And so, we know that the sunshine is also in this sheet of paper. The paper and the sunshine inter-are. And if we continue to look, we can see the logger who cut the tree and brought it to the mill to be transformed into paper. And we see the wheat. We know that the logger cannot exist without his daily bread, and therefore the wheat that became his bread is also in this sheet of paper. And the logger's father and mother are in it too. When we look in this way, we see that without all of these things, this sheet of paper cannot exist.

Thich Nhat Hanh, *The Heart of Understanding*

The Buddhist theory of persons

The chariot example applies the reductionist analysis to inanimate objects, but Nagasena extends the example to cover animate objects as well, namely human beings or persons.

> *"Your Majesty has spoken well about the chariot. It is just so with me. In dependence on the thirty-two parts of the body and the five skandhas there takes place this denomination 'Nagasena', this designation, this conceptual term, a current appellation and a mere name. In reality, however, this person cannot be apprehended."*

In this passage, Nagasena outlines the Buddhist concept of a person. Persons have no unchanging, permanent, inherent essence or soul, they have no intrinsic identity, instead they are entirely dependent on the various parts that make them up. In fact, our names (Nagasena, Harry, Sue and so forth) do not refer to any separate reality but merely to the sum of these parts functioning in a particular way. There isn't really any particular entity that can be called Dominique Side; the fact that I think there is, in Buddhist terms, is my delusion and one of the main reasons that I am not already enlightened! We do not exist in the way we think we do, and gaining an experiential understanding of the 'no self' of persons is perhaps the most important single attainment on the path to enlightenment.

What we call an individual or person, according to Buddhist philosophy, is a combination of ever-changing physical and mental energies, which can be divided into five groups technically called 'aggregates' or *khandhas (skandhas).* **The five aggregates are form, feeling-tone, perception, mental formations and consciousness.** Together they constitute the person: the body and mind of a human being.

The Buddha has said that 'in short, these five aggregates of attachment are *dukkha*', and again, 'What is *dukkha*? It should be said that it is the five aggregates of attachment.' He clearly identifies *dukkha* with the aggregates, so suffering and these five aggregates are not two separate things. This is because each aggregate is a focus or object of our grasping and attachment, and according to Buddhism grasping is one of the main causes of suffering. The way they function, then, is that each one of us grasps at one or other of the aggregates, or all the aggregates combined, and mistakenly identifies with that as 'me', 'I' or 'mine'. It is therefore helpful to examine the aggregates in some detail.

Form or Matter

The first aggregate is translated as form or matter, and it refers to our body as well as the physical world. It includes our bodies, our sense organs, and the objects we perceive in the external world. This aggregate is itself composed of the physical elements (earth, water, fire, and air).

Feeling-tone

The second aggregate refers to all the sensations that are experienced through the contact of the sense organs with the external world. We should note that this aggregate refers to the feeling-tone of each experience and not feelings in the sense of emotions. Feeling-tones can be either pleasant, unpleasant or neutral. In Buddhist psychology, there are six senses and not five as in Western thought. The six senses include the usual five – eyes, ears, nose, tongue and body – plus the mind considered as a sense in its own right. Each sense organ apprehends only sense objects related to it so, for example, the eyes can see form but they cannot hear sound. The objects apprehended by the mind are thoughts and feelings.

Perceptions

Like sensations, perceptions are produced through the contact of the sense organs with the external world, but perceptions recognize objects. Perception is the faculty of identifying objects as mental or physical, as a table rather than a chair, and so on, and involves an initial process of conceptualising and categorizing sense data. Perceptions recognize, identify and classify, and play the important role of putting sensory experience into words.

Mental formations

This aggregate groups together different mental factors. The most significant cover volitional activity, that is, any activity that involves will power, intention or determination. Crucially, mental formations concern *kamma (karma)* because, in Buddhism, the moral effects of action are determined primarily by the intentions behind those actions (see Chapter 12). The aggregate of mental formations thus covers the mental conditioning that results from karma accumulated in previous lives as well as earlier in this life; this colours the way we understand and react to situations, and it shapes our personality and character. At the same time, this aggregate includes mental activity that produces new karmic effects – activity such as attention, determination, confidence, concentration, desire, hatred and pride: these are all examples of 'mental formations'. They are called 'mental formations' because they condition us and 'shape' (or give form to) our lives.

Consciousness

In this context, consciousness refers to a mental reaction or response that has one of the six sense faculties as its basis. For example, visual consciousness has the eye faculty as its basis and a visible form as its object. The aggregate of consciousness is connected with each one of the sense faculties. It does not recognize objects, it is more of an awareness of the presence of an object. So, when the eye comes into contact with a blue object, for example, visual consciousness is the awareness of the presence of a colour but it does not recognize that it is blue. It is perception, the third aggregate, that recognizes it as blue. Seeing is not the same as recognizing.

In addition, the aggregate of consciousness plays a coordinating role between the sense channels so that in any given situation we perceive sights, sounds, smells and so on in an integrated picture and not separately with no connection between them. Consciousness is therefore the faculty of making overall sense of what we perceive, in collaboration with the other aggregates, and the way we do this constitutes our mentality or mind set.

How the aggregates function

There are many different ways of explaining how the aggregates work. The main point is that we don't realize how these different factors function and instead we think we are a self that is permanent and separate from everything else. This is a big mistake and it creates tremendous anxiety and insecurity. How often do we feel lonely and isolated, lost and depressed? Such feelings come from a belief that we are separate from the world, and they lead to an experience of life that is fraught with fear.

As a result, we can become over-sensitive and take life very personally. One way this works is that the aggregates become objects of our attachment. We might identify with only our body and think that our body is all we are. Or we might attach to, and identify with, ideas that other people have given us about life and who we are: for example, we might believe we are worthless or we are good, better than others or worse. Because we believe we are 'something' we hang on to these labels as a way of describing ourselves, and sometimes we can get stuck into believing in a particular self-image for a lifetime. Alternatively, we might identify with a particular experience in our past, either a happy one or a painful one, in a way that colours and distorts our ability to relate to situations in the present or future.

Identifying with the fourth aggregate of mental formations might take the form of accepting certain personality traits or habits and tendencies as being who we are. 'I'm like that, I can't help it.' With regard to the fifth aggregate, it may be tempting for scholars or academics, for example, to identify with the consciousness or mind. Indeed, the caricature of a professor who cannot tie his shoe laces depicts someone who is out of touch with the aggregate of form (his body) and whose sense of identity is based entirely on his mental life.

Reflecting on each of the five aggregates in turn, and seeing how one relates to them, is one of the themes used in Buddhist meditation, especially in *vipassana (vipasyana)* or insight meditation. The first benefit this brings is that we learn to understand ourselves better; we can distinguish between views and biases that come from our conditioning and our habits, and insights that are pure and unattached. The second benefit is that a shift gradually takes place deep within, and rather than identifying with the 'person' we imagine we are, we identify with our pure awareness or wisdom self. Ajahn Sumedho, an American-born Theravadin monk, expresses the process like this:

> *If we allow our personality, with its views and biases, to be the subject of our consciousness, we experience reality in terms of that personality. Because the personality can take any form, we can be elated or depressed – we can feel successful or feel like a failure. We live in a culture that very much emphasizes personality as being oneself. (…) If we are feeling good we are happy, if we are not feeling good, we are unhappy. That's the personality view. Any success that comes to this being is personal, and any failure is personal. But when pleasure and pain, praise and blame, are seen from the viewpoint of the subject who is aware – rather than the viewpoint of a person – this is the awakened mind. When we contemplate more and more, we are making pure awareness the subject of our consciousness.*[33]

By meditating on the aggregates and on *anatta*, one starts to correct one's self-image and to balance and harmonise the various factors of personality. This leads to the realization that one is not, in fact, a unitary 'person'; one is made of many interacting parts each of which is constantly changing. This then leads to a personal conviction in 'no self' *(anatta)*. The Buddha acknowledged that philosophical analysis alone is not sufficient to establish conviction in the truth of *anatta*, so strong is the attachment to our own unitary existence. That is why analysis needs to be complemented by meditation. Without meditation on the five aggregates, *anatta* will only be an interesting idea, at best; it will never transform our understanding.

The Mahayana perspective

The Mahayana schools of Buddhism accept the three Marks of Existence but generally present them slightly differently, in terms of what are called the Four Seals. The Four Seals are impermanence, suffering, no-self and nirvana. They are regarded as the four key points that distinguish the Buddhist perspective from non-Buddhist perspectives.

Mahayana scholars have their own characteristic interpretation of the meaning of the Three Marks of Existence. In particular, the Madhyamaka analysis of causation is far more radical, and this leads to a more subtle understanding of no self. In addition, Mahayana applies the paradigm of the Two Truths to suffering and therefore asserts that suffering only exists on the conventional level but does not exist in ultimate truth.

The Madhyamaka analysis of causation

To put it simply, Madhyamika scholars argue that the usual explanation of causation, where a cause at T_1 produces an effect at T_2, must be mistaken. It makes no sense to say that at T_1 the cause exists but not the effect, and later at T_2 the effect exists but not the cause. If this were the case, then the cause and the effect would never meet and the action of production could never take place. It follows that effects must exist simultaneously with their causes if they are to relate to each other; and, if this is the case, then our whole notion of production occurring in linear time has to be revised.

For Nikaya Buddhism, however, interdependence based on production through causes and conditions is one of the cornerstones of Buddhist thought. As we have seen, it underpins the Buddhist understanding of impermanence *(anicca)* as well as the idea of no self *(anatta)*, and it is the cause of the third type of *dukkha*, the suffering of conditioned existence. In other words, one could say that it is the basis for all three Marks of Existence. Madhyamaka does not in fact reject causation, it just understands it differently. Interdependence plays the same role within Madhyamaka thought as causation does in the thought of the Nikaya schools.

According to Nagarjuna, the great Indian scholar of Madhyamaka (first to second century CE), interdependence means *shunyata* or 'emptiness'. Things are 'empty' of inherent, independent and permanent existence; they have no intrinsic essence; everything is constantly subject to a process of change. And this 'empty' quality applies to absolutely everything, even the parts and particles that make up the objects of our experience. This radical view of 'no self' means that there is nothing that exists that can be called a cause, and nothing that exists that can be called an effect, because no unitary entities exist at all. Even atoms and particles and moments of consciousness – the unitary reals of Nikaya Abhidharma – are themselves made of parts and are constantly changing, so when one looks for causes one can never pinpoint a definite starting point for the analysis.

How are things produced then? The Buddha said that if anyone is able to answer this question fully they are already enlightened. One way of trying to understand it is to say that things come together in each moment through the mysterious interplay of dynamic energies and forces. The convergence of a particular set of factors in a particular moment gives rise to the situations and objects of our experience; and these will change from moment to moment as some energies fade and new energies and forces come into play. The process is not linear and chronological, but synchronic.

The concept of emptiness *(shunyata)*, just like that of no self *(anatta)*, allows for the impermanence of things, on both gross and subtle levels, and also accounts for the suffering we experience when we try to grasp and hold on to objects, situations, emotions and so on, which are actually insubstantial and ungraspable. There is really nothing there to hold on to, either physically or conceptually. At the same time, if we realize the emptiness of all things we can enjoy life to the full because we will have overcome all the cravings and misunderstandings that hinder and limit our freedom to connect with the way things truly are. Far from being a desperate state of nothingness, enlightenment is full of joy and love and wisdom and understanding.

Nagarjuna goes on to warn us of the temptation of holding on to the idea of emptiness itself as the answer. Madhyamaka does not replace the existence of ordinary things with the existence of emptiness. 'Emptiness' *(shunyata)* is a concept like any other, and like all concepts is simply an interpretation or intellectual fabrication; the concept 'emptiness' is itself empty. What the concept is pointing to is interdependence; that although things appear they are insubstantial, and although they are insubstantial nevertheless they do appear to us. Although an object appears as one thing, it includes many things within it, indeed it includes the whole universe. These statements are not contradictions.

The Mahayana approach to suffering

Mahayana distinguishes between conventional and ultimate truth (the Two Truths). Conventional truth refers to what is true in the world of empirical experience, while ultimate truth refers to the way things really are. We could also say that conventional truth appears true to those with deluded understanding while ultimate truth appears true to those who have enlightened insight.

From the Mahayana point of view, *duhkha* is real only to deluded beings so it can only be accepted as a truth conventionally. It cannot be an ultimate truth because it is possible to bring about the complete cessation of *duhkha*. By definition, an ultimate truth must be true all the time; it is not something that is true only under certain circumstances. The Four Noble Truths present the fact that *duhkha* is produced by causes and is therefore impermanent; and that it is brought to an end completely when *nirvana* is attained. For someone who has reached nirvana there is no suffering. *Duhkha* is therefore a conventional truth.

Let's take the example of a child who makes a fantastic sandcastle and plays with it for hours. But then the tide comes in and flattens the whole building and the dream. The child cries and is very upset but the parents are not. The suffering of losing one's sandcastle is not real for the parents because they know from experience that sandcastles don't last and destruction is always what happens to them. If one has a true understanding of how things are then one does not have attachment to them and does not experience the suffering that attachment entails.

One of the key Mahayana texts teaching emptiness is called the Heart Sutra. When the sutra says: "*There is no... suffering, no origin of suffering*" this does not mean that Mahayana totally rejects the Four Noble Truths of Nikaya Buddhism, nor that what Mahayana upholds contradicts the Four Noble Truths. Rather, the Heart Sutra is pointing out that suffering and the causes of suffering, and the rest, do not exist *ultimately*. The entire sutra is written from the perspective of ultimate truth.

THE HEART SUTRA

Thus have I heard. Once the Blessed One was dwelling in Rajagriha at Vulture Peak mountain, together with a great gathering of the sangha of monks and a great gathering of the sangha of bodhisattvas. At that time the Blessed One entered the samadhi that expresses the dharma called 'profound illumination', and at the same time noble Avalokitesvara, the bodhisattva mahasattva, while practising the profound prajñaparamita, saw in this way: he saw the five skandhas to be empty of nature. Then, through the power of the Buddha, venerable Shariputra said to noble Avalokitesvara, the bodhisattva mahasattva, "How should a son or daughter of noble family train, who wishes to practise the profound prajñaparamita?"

Addressed in this way, noble Avalokitesvara, the bodhisttva mahasattva, said to venerable Shariputra, "O Shariputra, a son or daughter of noble family who wishes to practise the profound prajñaparamita should see in this way: seeing the five skandhas to be empty of nature. Form is emptiness, emptiness also is form, emptiness is no other than form, form is no other than emptiness. In the same way, feeling, perception, formation, and consciousness are emptiness. Thus Shariputra, all dharmas are emptiness. There are no characteristics, there is no birth and no cessation, there is no impurity and no purity. There is no decrease and no increase. Therefore, Shariputra, in emptiness, there is no form, no feeling, no perception, no formation, no consciousness; no eye, no ear, no nose, no tongue, no body, no mind; no appearance, no sound, no smell, no taste, no touch, no dharmas; no eye dhatu up to no mind dhatu; no dhatu of dharmas and no mind consciousness dhatu. No ignorance, no end of ignorance up to no old age and death, no end of old age and death; no suffering, no origin of suffering, no cessation of suffering, no path, no wisdom, no attainment, and no non-attainment.

Therefore, Shariputra, since the bodhisattvas have no attainment they abide by means of prajñaparamita. Since there is no obscuration of mind, there is no fear. They transcend falsity and attain complete nirvana. All the buddhas of the three times, by means of prajñaparamita, fully awaken to unsurpassable, true, complete enlightenment. Therefore, the great mantra of prajñaparamita, the mantra of great insight, the unsurpassed mantra, the unequalled mantra, the mantra that calms all suffering, should be known as truth, since there is no deception. The prajñaparamita mantra is said in this way: TEYATHA OM GATE GATE PARAGATE PARASAMGATE BODHI SOHA (Gone, gone, gone beyond, completely exposed, awake, so be it.) Thus, Shariputra, the bodhisattva mahasattva should train in the profound prajñaparamita."

Then the Blessed One arose from that samadhi and praised noble Avalokitesvara, the bodhisattva mahasattva, saying, "Good, good, O son of noble family; thus it is, O son of noble family, thus it is. One should practise the profound prajñaparamita just as you have taught and all the tathagatas will rejoice." When the Blessed One had said this, venerable Shariputra and noble Avalokitesvara, the bodhisattva mahasattva, that whole assembly and the world with its gods, humans, asuras and gandharvas, rejoiced and praised the words of the Blessed One. Thus concludes the Sutra of the heart of transcendent knowledge.

Translated by the Nalanda Translation Committee
and reproduced with permission

Critical evaluation

Religious arguments

When the Buddha developed his theory of no-self he consciously did so as a counter to the Hindu theory of atman. *Atman* is often translated as 'soul' but it does not have any of the meanings that souls are given in Western thinking. According to different philosophers from the ancient Greeks onwards, 'soul' can refer to the intellect, to the capacity for moral judgement, simply to the mind, or again to a personal, individual essence that continues after death. The characteristic of *atman*, however, is that it is an instance of the impersonal God *Brahman* and, at the moment of liberation, the *atman* merges completely with Brahman and becomes indistinguishable from it. There are other Sanskrit terms that are used for intellect and mind (*chitta, manas* and so on), so the meaning of *atman* is quite specific in Hinduism.

It is important to bear the Hindu context in mind when evaluating the idea of *anatta* or *anatman* because it sheds light on exactly what the Buddha was rejecting. When he taught no-self, he did not mean that human beings don't exist at all, or that we don't have minds, or that we don't have an intellect, or that we don't have the capacity to make moral judgments. He was specifically denying the existence of an unchanging, impersonal essence or reality, a principle that is explained by Hindus as *atman* and *Brahman*.

The implication of the three Marks of Existence is that Buddhism also rejects the Christian idea of the soul. Naturally, the Buddha did not reject this explicitly because Christianity did not exist in his day, but by applying the Marks of Existence to the Christian soul we can see that it is not logically acceptable for Buddhists. The Buddha denied the *ultimate* existence of the person or individual by showing that we are merely the sum of the five aggregates. This does not mean we do not exist at all – we do of course exist as individuals in conventional reality, as Mary and Sue, Peter and Paul. It means there is no over-arching personal identity that continues independently of the aggregates, either during life or after death. It follows that there would be no *personal* soul that continues after death.

Scientific arguments

The Dalai Lama, the Tibetan Buddhist leader who has engaged in many dialogues with scientists, believes that science is very close to Buddhist thinking in terms of the radical impermanence of things:

> *The Buddhist view of phenomena as dynamic and of momentary nature – which emerges as a consequence of the principle of universal impermanence – is quite close to the view of a dynamic, ever-changing physical universe as presented by modern physics.*

Nagarjuna's view of *shunyata* and interdependence as a dynamic and synchronic emergence of things, persons and situations is often compared to the view of quantum physics where everything exists contingently, and where even the object of an experiment depends on the person carrying out the experiment. By contrast, the view of traditional physics based on linear causality is similar to the Abhidharmic analysis of Nikaya Buddhism.

For scientists in general, reality is that which can be perceived and experienced, so any truths that relate to ideas that have no empirical basis are regarded as scientifically invalid. That is the case for the existence of souls, for example, or for the metaphysical idea of essences. The Buddhist approach is very similar to this in that abstract ideas like essences and souls, which have no basis in experience, are not accepted as true even on the conventional level. If nobody has ever seen a soul, or can describe one, or has had insight of one through meditation, or can explain its existence rationally, then it is not valid to claim that a soul has objective existence.

There is perhaps room for some discussion on this point since certain Christian mystics like Hildergaard of Bingen claim to have had visions of souls. The Buddha, however, claimed not to have had any such visions. It is possible that more clarification is needed around what is meant by 'soul' in each case.

One of the most interesting scientific models that can help us evaluate the Buddhist theory of the aggregates is the recent research in neurobiology of the brain. In his ground-breaking book *Emotional Intelligence*, Daniel Goleman reports that research by LeDoux and Damasio shows that sense data from eyes, ears and so forth travel first in the brain to the thalamus, and then to the amygdala which is the main brain area for emotion; then a second signal goes from the thalamus to the neocortex which is the thinking brain. Thirdly, the prefrontal lobes function as a coordinator of data and are able to plan and organise actions towards a goal. This three-step process echoes the function of the aggregates: feeling-tone (the second aggregate), the conceptualising intellect (the third aggregate), and the capacity to act or react (the fourth and fifth aggregates). These stages in brain activity are measured in thousandths of a second so we are not aware of them in everyday life. We may wonder how Buddhists ever devised such a scheme without modern laboratories.

Conclusion

The Three Marks or characteristics of Existence are impermanence, suffering and no-self. Although they are listed as three distinct factors, they overlap a good deal and as soon as one begins to explain one of them, one is automatically drawn into referring to the other two. They are inextricably linked together and are like three different ways of approaching the same truth. For example, the Buddha said that impermanence is suffering, and also said that the aggregates of the person are suffering. And conversely, amongst the three types of suffering we find the suffering of change and the suffering of conditioned existence.

All three Marks of Existence, then, point to dissatisfaction with our world of experience. Reflecting on them might motivate us to try to break free from this and to find something more real, more lasting and more meaningful.

Personal reflection

How does the sense of dissatisfaction (dukkha) manifest for you? Does it motivate you to look for 'a better life'? Examine what these words mean for you personally.

Main Points

- The Three Marks or Characteristics of Existence are a set of axioms that are common to all Buddhist schools and traditions, and that distinguish Buddhism from other religions and philosophies.
- The Three Marks are:

  1. All compounded things are impermanent and subject to change
  2. Conditioned existence is characterised by suffering or unsatisfactoriness
  3. Nothing has permanent, independent or inherent existence.

- Impermanence refers to the gross, visible level of change and to the subtle level of momentary change, and it applies to all objects and living beings. Accepting the fact of impermanence reduces attachment and grasping.
- When we think, feel or act on the basis that things are lasting and permanent and really exist, then we suffer because this is a delusion.
- Everything and everyone exist only in dependence on other things. The nature of all things is such that they are empty of inherent existence.

Chapter 11

THE CYCLE OF BIRTH AND DEATH

The ancient wisdom of India conceives of time as circular, not linear. Cyclical processes in nature – like day and night, and the seasons – illustrate the continuous movement from growth to decay and to another growth. This principle applies not only to the natural world but to the life and death of all the beings who inhabit that world. This chapter presents the Buddhist account of rebirth and examines the evidence for it.

In the Buddhist approach, life and death are seen as one whole, where death is the beginning of another chapter of life. Death is a mirror in which the entire meaning of life is reflected.
Sogyal Rinpoche, *The Tibetan Book of Living and Dying*

The Buddhist understanding of rebirth

In the first watch of the night, when Gautama sat under the bodhi tree in meditation, he saw with his mind's eye all the previous lives he had had over thousands of years. This insight, based on meditation experience, was the basis for his teaching on rebirth, the idea that all beings are caught in a continuous cycle of life and death. Death is not the end, it is the gateway to a new beginning.

Indian religions – Buddhism, Hinduism and Jainism – all hold that we have a series of lives, and that death marks the end of one life and the beginning of a new one. This continuous cycle of life and death is called *samsara*. It is characterized by suffering. Nobody wishes to die but the fact is that death spares no-one. Indian religions link together the principles of karma and rebirth, with the idea that every moral action must be accounted for in this or future lives, and that the experiences of the present lifetime are the consequences of past actions performed either earlier in our present life or in previous lives. The ultimate goal of every religion that is indigenous to India is freedom from the cycle of rebirth or reincarnation. Karma and rebirth are profoundly connected in the sense that if one is free from the law of karma one will also be free from automatic rebirth. While all three Indian religions share these points in common, each has a distinct way of explaining them, so there is a need to refine the understanding of rebirth that is specific to Buddhism.

Rebirth in Buddhism is not the same as reincarnation in Hinduism. The Hindu idea of reincarnation is that the essence of our self *(atman)* survives without our body, continues after death and joins another body to live a new life. This process happens for an unimaginably long period of time until we reach liberation *(moksha)*. There is therefore personal continuity from one life to the next; we can say that it is 'me' or the 'essence of me' that is literally re-incarnated into another body. 'I' am therefore identified not with my body but with my mental self and life force.

The word 'reincarnation' is not used in Buddhism; instead the term is 'rebirth' or 'rebecoming'. Buddhism teaches that there is no essential self so that means there is no 'self' or soul that journeys from one life to another. That is why rebirth is a complex process and why Buddhists have developed elaborate theories to explain exactly what it is that continues after death if we have no essence or soul.

Rebirth should not be confused with the Christian concept of resurrection. Resurrection is a theory that assures believers that they will be 'born again' when the Christ returns to Earth at the final Judgment. This idea entails not only spiritual continuity but physical continuity and is the reason why Christians are buried and not cremated. It is believed that the physical body will come back to life and will be re-animated by the soul. In Buddhism, as in Hinduism, the physical body is subject to death, by definition; it is impermanent and after death all the elements that make it up disintegrate and scatter. This is seen as a natural process, and neither rebirth nor reincarnation ever entail the *physical* continuity of a person in another life.

What continues?

Buddhism does not have just one single answer to the question about what continues after death, rather there are a number of answers that vary according to each philosophical tradition. However, the basic principle is common to all schools of Buddhist thought, and we will establish that first.

If there is no personal, individual self that continues from life to life, how can one explain the principle that there *is* continuity from one life to the next? Some form of continuity is essential because, without it, one would have to say that the future life involves a *different* person from the one I am now, and so *I* would not be reborn. Nagasena gives a classic formulation of this problem in *The Questions of King Milinda*. When asked by the king whether the person who is reborn is the same as the one who died, Nagasena replies, 'Neither the same nor different'. He illustrates the principle of continuity within change through analogies.

- First, if we compare ourselves as a baby with the way we are today there is obviously a big difference between the two; in fact, physically you might be unrecognisable yet at the same time you consider you are 'the same person'.
- Second, if we light a big candle in the evening and let it burn throughout the night, is it true to say that the candle flame is the same at the end of the night as it was at the beginning? Again, the flame will change physically, beginning small and gradually getting bigger and hotter, yet we generally consider it is the same candle and the same flame.
- Third, he uses the example of the way milk turns into butter. Fresh milk is left to ferment so it separates into whey and curds; the curds (the solid part) are then churned into fresh butter and the butter is then melted for cooking and (in India) is called ghee. Are the milk, the curds, the butter and the ghee all the same thing, or are they different?

It is incorrect to say that all these different stages of a thing or person are exactly the same as each other, but each has been produced by the preceding one. There is therefore a collection of successive moments of existence that are linked by causal connections. There is no 'one thing' only a series of successive moments, and it is the causal series that provides continuity without identity. There is no substance, either material or spiritual, only process.

King Milinda is not fully satisfied with this explanation so he pursues the problem of continuity after death. If the person who is reborn is neither the same nor different from the person who has died, is there not a loophole in Buddhist thinking which makes moral responsibility impossible for actions in a past life? If the person who is reborn is not identical then how can he/she be held responsible for the moral consequences of someone else's past actions? In other words, the Buddhist theory of rebirth appears to undermine the Buddhist theory of karma. The Buddha's teachings are flawed by internal contradiction.

Nagasena explains that exactly the same applies from life to life as applies from moment to moment within a single life: that is, there is nothing other than a series of causally linked moments. At death, the physical series continues as an impersonal physical process (the process of disintegration of the body) and it ceases to have a connection with the mental series. Death marks the separation of mind and body but it does not necessarily entail total discontinuity of the mind. The mental series continues after death independent of the body.

It is helpful to mention the Buddhist understanding of conception at this point so all the causal links in the life and death cycle are clear. Just as death is the separation of the mind and the body, conception is the coming together of the consciousness with a fertilised egg. The reason why a particular consciousness joins with the fertilised egg of particular parents would be primarily karmic. The parents provide the basis of the physical body – the genes and so on – but not the basic characteristics of mentality, which will result from the stream of consciousness of previous lives together with the karmic imprints embedded in that consciousness. Incidentally, it follows that for Buddhists there is a person present from conception and not only later, at the moment of birth, because conception is defined as the coming together of a consciousness with the physical basis of an embryo. Abortions are therefore seriously discouraged.

In order to answer the question about what continues after death, then, Buddhists need to define the nature of the mind that continues after death. Three Buddhist theories on this matter are considered below: the Theravada response, the Mahayana response of the Yogachara school, and the Vajrayana response of Tibetan Buddhism.

Theravada view

In its analysis of the mind, Theravada asserts the existence of a subtle type of consciousness called the *bhavanga* consciousness. *Bhavanga* is the state of mind we are born in and the state of our mind in deep, dreamless sleep. It is also the state to which our minds return in the gaps between moments of consciousness. More significantly, perhaps, it is the state of mind that arises at the moment of conception in the womb, so it forms the link between the consciousness of the past life and the consciousness of the next life. The characteristics of the *bhavanga* consciousness are unique to each individual and reproduce themselves throughout a person's life, thus defining him or her as an individual.

In Theravada philosophy, rebirth is considered to take place in the moment immediately following the moment of death. The final moment of consciousness in one life is the immediate causal link to the first moment of consciousness in the next life. The gap between two lives is similar to the gap that exists between any two moments of consciousness in life. There is no intermediate state between one life and the next; the transition is instantaneous.

Yogachara view

Yogachara scholars developed a model of eight types of consciousness. It does not mean that people have eight minds each, rather it is a way of describing eight different functions of any given consciousness. The first six types of consciousness are the same as those already presented in relation to the person and accepted in Theravada: each is related to one of the six senses. To these six Yogacharas add two more types that are not accepted by other schools. The seventh consciousness is the one that discriminates and judges according to its conditioning and prejudices, but this consciousness is also the one that can be transformed through spiritual practices such as meditation so that it thinks positively and selflessly rather than divisively and selfishly. The eighth consciousness is called the *alaya* consciousness, sometimes translated as 'storehouse consciousness' because it is the storehouse for karmic seeds. According to this model, it is the *alaya* consciousness that survives without the body and that continues, along with its store of karmic seeds, from one life to the next. The *alaya* consciousness therefore denotes the most subtle level of consciousness which exists independently of the body and it should be distinguished from the other types of consciousness which depend upon, and interact with, the physical body. At death, any aspect of consciousness that depends upon the body will naturally cease while the aspect of consciousness that does not depend on the body will continue.

We should note that the *alaya* consciousness is not an entity, and it has not been smuggled in by Yogacharas as a surrogate soul. It is a stream of consciousness that changes from moment to moment.

The Vajrayana view

The Vajrayana understanding of life, death and the dying process is presented in great detail in *The Tibetan Book of the Dead*. According to the Tibetan tradition associated with that book, the mind is generally categorised into two: the pure, pristine, primordial mind that has no beginning and no end *(rigpa)*, and the conditioned, conceptual mind which is the mind that is deluded *(sem)*. The primordial mind is the nature of the mind itself; it is never stained by negative thoughts and emotions and always remains pure. The deluded mind is that aspect of mind that does not recognize its own nature and gets lost in its own thoughts, emotions and projections.

For a brief instant at death the deluded mind dissolves, and what continues is the primordial mind that is universal and not specific to any individual. If one recognizes the primordial mind for what it is, one is instantly enlightened. However, unless one has learned to control the mind through spiritual practice, this moment will not last very long and karmic patterns will arise again and sweep one along in a strong current of thoughts and emotions. That chain of deluded thoughts and emotions is the causal link to the next rebirth.

Figure 11.1 – Vajrasattva: a Sambhogakaya buddha embodying the principle of purity and purification, who appears to us soon after death, according to the Tibetan tradition

According to the Tibetan tradition rebirth is not immediate, rather it occurs after an intermediate period called *bardo*. 'Bardo' means 'interval' and here it refers to the interval between one life and the next. This interval varies in length from a few days up to 49 days, depending on karma and the deceased's state of mind, and Buddhists will generally conduct prayer ceremonies for the deceased for 49 days. In the *bardo* state, the consciousness experiences various visions that present themselves in several phases, and the way one reacts to these visions (for example, whether they provoke fear or anger or longing) is critical in determining the kind of rebirth one takes. The purpose of meditation is not only to gain peace and clarity of mind in this life but to strengthen the mind in such a way that one is better able to cope in the *bardo* after death. This is because meditation is the only systematic way of developing familiarity with the pure nature of our minds. In this sense, Buddhist practice can be seen, quite literally, as a preparation for death.

The arguments for rebirth

Hundreds of millions of Buddhists, Hindus and Jains believe in rebirth or reincarnation, and a Gallup poll in the USA at the turn of this century showed that 23% of Americans believe in it, too. But where is the proof? How can we decide whether rebirth is valid or not? Is it possible for rebirth ever to be scientifically proven? In this section we consider the arguments for rebirth, first from modern perspectives and second from the point of view of the Buddhist tradition itself.

A small number of modern academics have engaged in discussion or carried out research in an effort to determine whether or not rebirth is a tenable principle in the context of contemporary knowledge. We consider the most significant avenues of inquiry: firstly in philosophy, with scepticism, and secondly in the sciences with research on children's testimonies, birthmarks, regression therapy and near-death experiences.

The sceptic's position

Many people in the modern world will react to rebirth incredulously, pointing out that it is impossible for anyone to really know what happens after death. Ironically, this argument has also been used to *support* the idea of rebirth. Since we cannot know for sure what happens after death, the theory of rebirth is no less plausible than the Christian theory of Heaven and Hell, or the materialist theory that death is annihilation. This line of thinking generally leads to a sceptical position: not only do we not know, but we can't know. From this standpoint, anything we say either for or against existence after death is mere speculation.

The sceptical view is based on two key assumptions:

1. That for any statement to be valid it must be based on empirical and verifiable evidence, and the absence of such evidence renders the statement either untrue or inconclusive
2. That scriptural authority is not an accepted source of authority, and for it to become acceptable its statements must be corroborated by science and reasoning.

This is not the place for a general discussion about scepticism, but the interesting point is that the after-life is a topic that does not fit comfortably with either of these assumptions. Even if one accepts the first assumption as a truth criterion that applies in general, how can it be valid to require verifiable evidence of what happens after death? Aren't after-death states beyond the limitations of scientific investigation by their very nature? What sort of events could count as forms of evidence? How could such experiments be conducted?

The second assumption depends on the first, insofar as reason is given primacy over 'faith' with respect to truth claims. This means that one would not believe what the scriptures say simply because it is the Buddha who said so. Furthermore, no notion of scriptural authority is acceptable beyond the bounds of a particular religion (that is, scriptures have no authority for those who do not follow that religion) so dialogue between religions cannot be based on scripture; it needs to favour logic and reason. But it could be argued against the sceptics that life after death is precisely one topic that lies specifically within the domain of religion rather than that of reason and science, because knowledge of after-death states is knowledge of a dimension that is beyond human knowledge. However, this argument itself assumes that religion is a valid field of knowledge in its own right, and that is what the sceptic questions.

Another theoretical difficulty for research into this area is the belief that what continues is a soul or spirit defined as independent from matter. The problem is that science cannot prove that something spiritual like a soul continues after death because this spiritual essence is beyond the bounds of the physical world and therefore beyond experimentation. Faced with this dilemma, the scientist would have to say she didn't know and was unable to find out.

Can rebirth be proved by logical reasoning?

Buddhists consider that rebirth can be validated by logical reasoning, but only to a point. The argument is as follows: everything in the universe is produced by causes, and those causes must be related to their effects according to the law that like produces like. Physical phenomena are produced by physical causes, so our body is produced by a sperm and egg, together with associated physical conditions such as food, drink, temperature and so forth. Similarly, our mind is produced by mental causes, specifically the previous moments of our past consciousness. Buddhist philosophers do not accept that the mind is reducible to matter, or that the mind can be produced by, or from, matter. Mind is not simply the epi-phenomenon of a complex nervous system, for example. It follows that mind can only be produced by a previous moment of the same continuum of consciousness.

Most scientists usually consider that thoughts are caused by chemical changes in the brain, and they in turn create physiological changes in the body. But their working assumption is that mind depends on the body/brain. Until very recently, little research had been carried out on the basis of the opposite assumption: that pure thought can give rise to chemical changes in the brain. This field of research is evolving very rapidly and recent work on the effects of meditation, mindfulness and compassion practice on the brain goes some way to indicate that the trained mind can indeed effect chemical and physiological changes in the brain and nervous system. The philosophical implications of such findings have yet to be fully determined. If one accepts the body/mind model of Buddhism, where mind is a distinct principle in its own right, then rebirth becomes logically possible and even probable.

Buddhists redefine the debate

Buddhist scholars also take the debate further and redefine its parameters. The American scholar Robert Thurman writes:

> *The inner science of Buddhism is based on a thorough and comprehensive knowledge of reality, on an already assessed, depth understanding of self and environment, that is to say, on the complete enlightenment of the Buddha.*[34]

Buddhism is an 'inner science', a science of the 'inner world', a science of the mind. The Buddha and the Buddhist masters who followed him, came to their conclusions about the mind, and about life and death, after meticulous study and experiential exploration. The knowledge gained through enlightenment is just this: complete and thorough knowledge of the nature of the mind and the universe. And the source of the Buddhist teachings on death and rebirth is the enlightened mind itself. As *The Tibetan Book of Living and Dying* explains:

> *(This) answer may seem initially difficult to understand for many readers, because the notion of the mind the West now has is an extremely narrow one. Despite the major breakthroughs of recent years, especially in mind/body science and transpersonal psychology, the great majority of scientists continue to reduce the mind to no more than physical processes in the brain, which goes against the testimony of thousands of years of experience of mystics and meditators of all religions.*[35]

Enlightenment and the possibility for a human being to become a buddha mean that Buddhism redefines the boundaries of what it is possible for humans to know. The Buddhist teachings on rebirth, and on the cycle of life and death, are based on insight and knowledge gained through enlightened meditation states and mystical states, and this knowledge is accessible to any human engaging in the appropriate religious practices. That is why one can argue that this knowledge is valid because it is replicable; anyone engaging in such meditations will have the same knowledge as the Buddha had. Indeed, this is exactly what the tradition claims: that subsequent meditators and mystics shared the same insights as the Buddha. Buddhists, certainly from the Mahayana and Vajrayana traditions, therefore believe in the authority of mystical knowledge that is replicable and verifiable against another's experience, and that does not contradict reason. This is the basis of their theory of rebirth.

Links with quantum physics

The philosophy of science related to quantum physics prompts us to redefine some of the usual categories of our thinking, or at least to question whether these categories correspond to any objective reality. As Albert Einstein said, 'Time and space are modes by which we think and not conditions in which we live'. Religious descriptions of death often speak of a movement towards 'the Light', and many of those who have near-death experiences (NDEs) also report meeting a figure of light or being one with the light. In terms of quantum physics, continuing existence after death might be explained by the nature of light. All matter is reducible to electromagnetic radiation which includes light; time ceases to exist at the speed of light, and the energy of light is infinite. If, after death, our existence continued in the dimension of light this could account for some of the mystical descriptions of the after-death process.

Children's testimony about past lives

The most respected researcher of children's testimonies of their past lives is Dr Ian Stevenson, now retired from the Division of Personality Studies at the University of Virginia, USA. He has documented hundreds of cases of very young children who report memories of past lives including names, locations, the specific way they died in their previous life, and intimate details about people that they could not possibly have known in any other way. His methods are scientific and unemotional, and it is hard to ignore the large amount of data he has collected. The evidence is difficult to understand on any other grounds than those of reincarnation or rebirth.

One case concerns a five-year old Indian boy named Parmod Sharma who remembered specific details about a man named Parmanand, including street directions in Parmanand's city. He visited the factory Parmanand owned and despite being only five, gave directions for repairing complicated machinery.

Some sceptics are critical of this type of research because most cases occur in countries with a belief in reincarnation, so children might be predisposed to make up stories involving past lives. Nevertheless, there are documented cases of past life memories in children in the USA and Europe as well, in families with no belief in past lives.

Birthmark matches

Several researchers have studied birthmarks as a possible source of evidence of past life connections. The size and location of a child's birthmark has been found in many cases to correspond to injuries sustained in a past life. Where this evidence is strong, medical records including x-rays have confirmed the location and type of injury sustained. In the case of one Sri Lankan girl who remembered being hit and killed by a bus, the birthmark on her chest corresponded to the drawing of the injuries in the medical records of the deceased.

It has been argued that it is statistically improbable that such birthmarks are coincidences given the precision of location and patterns. Birthmarks are also convincing because they do not depend on any cultural beliefs in the family or on a child's imagination: they have an objective value. Nevertheless, sceptics maintain that such birthmarks are just a matter of chance.

Adult regression therapy

Some believe that memories that surface during hypnotherapy may offer evidence of a person's past life. Under hypnosis, adults have recounted details about past lives in other historical periods: as a foot soldier in the Middle Ages, or a Middle Eastern warrior, or a European peasant and so forth. In one famous case, a woman from Colorado, USA remembered her life as a 19th century woman from Cork in Ireland, and under hypnosis she talked in an Irish dialect, sang Irish songs and remembered kissing the Blarney stone.

Some psychiatrists find the level of detail in these accounts very persuasive while critics claim that most of these so-called memories are merely self-fulfilling prophecies. This type of evidence has not been researched as rigorously as children's memories and birthmarks, and since the former lives in question have usually taken place in the distant past the statements made under hypnosis cannot be verified as accurate. The evidential value of adult regression is therefore thin.

Near-death experiences

Near-death experiences (NDEs) are the most convincing type of evidence of all, particularly for those who actually have the experience. An NDE occurs when a person has, to all intents and purposes, died and is later medically resuscitated. Such experiences occur relatively frequently these days as a result of road accidents or complex medical interventions. In one survey in Connecticut, USA, in 1993 as many as 70% of people who had had an NDE subsequently believed in reincarnation, even though many had no previous religious beliefs at all. Experiences range from floating out of the body, travelling down a tunnel and emerging in a world of light, meeting a radiant figure of light, and meeting people who are dead. Dr Kenneth Ring is a pioneer in this research field and one experiencer told him:

> *"My whole life went before me of things I have done and haven't done, but not just of this one lifetime, but of all the lifetimes. I know for a fact there is reincarnation. This is an absolute. I was shown all those lives and how I had overcome some of the things I had done in other lives. There were still some things to be corrected."* [36]

Raymond Moody, another NDE researcher, reports another testimony in his book *Life After Life:*

> *"Now, my entire life through, I am thoroughly convinced that there is life after death, without a shadow of a doubt, and I am not afraid to die. I am not. Some people I have known are so afraid, so scared. I always smile to myself when I hear people doubt there is an afterlife, or say, 'When you're dead, you're gone'. I think to myself, 'They really don't know'."*

Many experiencers say that the main purpose of rebirth is spiritual learning or enlightenment. For example:

> *"We progress at our own rate to reach the light. If you do things that take you away from the light, then you are perpetuating your time here."*[37]

Such descriptions mean that NDEs can be classified as a religious experience, and in particular as a noetic experience giving certainty and new knowledge. The new knowledge derived from NDEs specifically concerns certainty in rebirth.

In evaluating the evidence for rebirth provided by NDEs, although the subjects' accounts are persuasive most scientific attempts at validation are inconclusive. For example, scientists have tried to demonstrate that there is *something* that leaves the body and that explains out-of-body experiences, but the problem is the impossibility of measuring the non-physical. Some critics claim that NDEs are an instance of dreaming, or a hallucination caused by lack of oxygen to the brain. But Dr Michael Sabom has been successful in carefully documenting reports from patients who suffered cardiac arrest and who accurately observed readings on medical machines which were out of their line of vision, thereby pointing to the possibility of visualisation far geographically removed from the body. This research is verifiable and potentially reproducible; certain readings, for instance, can be timed and shown to have occurred when the patient was clinically dead or brain dead. So, although there is no scientific consensus on the status of NDEs at present, their religious significance cannot be discounted.

Arguments from the Buddhist tradition

Rebirth is an important part of the Buddhist view of the world and, together with the laws of karma, accounts for the different realms and types of existence in the universe. It also plays a key role in Buddhist ethics since many Buddhists are motivated to act ethically because of the promise this holds for better future lives. Buddhist philosophers put forward a number of logical explanations of rebirth covering topics such as the nature of what continues after death, the events that take place between one life and another, and the philosophical reasons justifying rebirth based on the nature of the mind.

Buddhist scholars have not relegated rebirth to the domain of blind faith and unreasoned belief. On the contrary, they have addressed the questions and challenges it raises in some detail. Certain contemporary thinkers charge Buddhism with the fault of accepting rebirth on the basis of faith alone, thereby attempting to weaken its validity, but given the lengthy debates on the subject in the scriptures that charge appears to be unfair and unfounded.

One well-known discussion on rebirth is found in the works of the 7th century Indian master Dharmakirti.[38] Dharmakirti is concerned about establishing the validity of the Buddhist teachings using logical reasoning – not relying exclusively on the authority of the scriptures themselves. He ascribes the validity traditionally accorded the scriptures to the qualities of the person who taught them, namely the Buddha. This leads to the question of what it is that renders the Buddha authoritative, and this is presented in four points.

Dharmakirti identifies two perfect causes for the Buddha's spiritual authority: his perfect intention, which is the great compassion to benefit beings, and his perfect training, following the path and teaching it to others. He then identifies the two results that ensue from those causes, which are the benefit for oneself – the complete abandonment of all mental defilements and the realization of ultimate wisdom – and the benefit for others, crystallised in the teaching of the Four Noble Truths.

It is in his discussion of the first of these factors, the great compassionate motivation of the Buddha, that the question of rebirth is addressed. The point Dharmakirti makes is that in order to have great compassion, one must train repeatedly in cultivating compassion over the span of many lifetimes. The commentary states:

> *The perfect cause that is the means to achieve the state of an authoritative being is the cultivation repeatedly over many lifetimes of the great compassion that wishes to liberate all wandering beings forever from the great ocean of suffering. One achieves the state of an authoritative being from that, so that is the cause by which one achieves that state.*[39]

In other words, if we each had only one single lifespan, then it would be virtually impossible for an ordinary being ever to attain enlightenment. Enlightenment, whether in terms of nirvana or in terms of buddhahood, requires diligent and repeated application on the spiritual path over numerous lifetimes. This is therefore a crucial reason for accepting rebirth, since if the cycle of life and death were to be rejected this would put the entire Buddhist path in jeopardy. Within the confines of a single life one could, of course, lead an ethical life and reap certain immediate forms of happiness, but Buddhism is not primarily concerned with such a mundane goal. Within a single lifetime the transcendental goal of enlightenment would not be feasible. This shows that the principle of rebirth is integral to Buddhist thought, and that Buddhism as a perspective and as a path cannot do without it.

Buddha Shakyamuni himself is no exception to the rule. The *Jataka Tales* recount stories from hundreds of the Buddha's previous lives, some virtuous and some unvirtuous. Over the course of these existences he learns lessons, perfects his qualities and skills, and gains understanding of life. The lifestory of Buddha Shakyamuni is seen as the culmination of all these previous existences; it is the point at which his ignorance is overcome and all his compassion, wisdom and skills mature so he is able to attain buddhahood. All beings, even buddhas, are therefore understood to have honed their spiritual accomplishments over many lives.

In the end, understanding rebirth may well be similar to understanding no-self in the sense that logical explanations alone are usually not enough to convince us of such unfamiliar truths. Religious experience appears to be the main factor that brings complete personal conviction about rebirth: experiences such as NDEs, past life memories or insights in meditation.

Personal reflections

Does the idea of rebirth ring true to you?
On what basis would you decide whether or not to accept rebirth?

Main Points

- *Samsara* is the endless cycle of life and death, where beings wander from life to life driven by their karma. It is known as 'conditioned existence' and is characterised by suffering.
- More fundamentally, samsara is the way we live life under the influence of ignorance. Enlightenment is liberation from the cycle of life and death propelled by karma.
- In Hinduism, 'reincarnation' involves the essence of the person taking birth in another body again and again until liberation (moksha).
- In Buddhism, 'rebirth' is part of the continuity of the mind stream which takes successive births determined by karma. No essence or soul is involved.
- Each Buddhist tradition explains the details of the rebirth process slightly differently.
- Modern research has attempted to find evidence for this phenomenon by studying children's testimonies, birthmarks and near-death experiences (NDEs).

Chapter 12

KARMA AND THE CAUSES OF SUFFERING

One of the hallmarks of the Buddha's teaching is its emphasis on causation as a fundamental law governing all things in the universe, both physical and mental. In the Four Noble Truths the causes of suffering are identified as the mental afflictions and actions motivated by those afflictions. This chapter looks at the causal laws governing such actions, known as the laws of karma, and explains how they work.

If you want to know your past life, look into your present condition;
if you want to know your future life, look at your present actions.
Padmasambhava

The causes of suffering

It was in the second watch of the night, as he was meditating under the bodhi tree, that the Buddha fully realized the laws that determine why each one of us has the life situation we have and how the process of rebirth occurs. A very detailed and elaborate explanation of the laws of karma was developed on the basis of this insight.

Fundamentally, everyone wants to be happy and Buddhism sees nothing wrong here. On the contrary, it is quite natural that not only human beings but also animals have a strong wish to be happy. But if we are looking for happiness, why is that we suffer instead? This is the question addressed by the second Noble Truth, the truth of the causes of suffering. The Buddha explains that our problem comes from the fact that we do not understand what happiness really is. We go for small happinesses – fleeting pleasures, momentary gratification – and so never find the lasting happiness that we seek deep down.

The Buddhist approach to this topic is quite different from the way most modern people are brought up to think, whether they follow a religion or not. In Buddhism, the root causes of all our suffering are not in anything or anyone that is external to us, but in our own minds. These causes are called the Three Poisons of craving, aggression and ignorance. They distort our understanding of true happiness and our ability to go about searching for happiness in an effective way. They cause us to act selfishly for our own benefit but unfortunately this selfishness backfires. As the Dalai Lama puts it, if we want to be happy we should at least be 'wisely selfish' and realize that happiness really comes from altruism – thinking of others and being compassionate and kind. Since we are all connected with each other, it is impossible to be happy if we are surrounded by others who are suffering. The Indian poet Shantideva wrote:

All the joy the world contains
Has come through wishing happiness for others.
All the misery the world contains
Has come through wanting pleasure for oneself.[40]

The point of the Buddhist path is to train the mind so we are less selfish and more compassionate. At the moment our minds are dominated by the Three Poisons which influence our motivation to act, and as a result our actions will be either good or bad. The Buddhist definition of 'good' and 'bad' is very precise. Bad actions are unskilful actions; they are actions that will produce suffering, either immediately or in the long term, and either for oneself only or for others as well. Good actions are skilful actions which bring spiritual benefit both to oneself and to others. Good and bad are not absolutes in the Buddhist view.

Three poisons ⇒ Intentions ⇒ Unskilful actions ⇒ Suffering

The Three Poisons

Craving

The Pali word *tanha* literally means 'thirst' but is usually translated as 'craving' or 'desire'. The suggestion is that deep within our minds there is a strong greed or desire that manifests as an unquenchable thirst, and this is the driving force behind our suffering. The Buddha identifies three types of craving:

- the craving for objects of sense desire
- the craving for existence
- the craving for non-existence.

We are all familiar with *craving for sense objects*: certain things give us pleasure and our attachment to the experience of pleasure means we are never satisfied with just one experience but are constantly looking for more. Examples are chocolate, alcohol, drugs, music and sexual partners. The problem here is that all sense objects are an unreliable source of pleasure (or of happiness defined as pleasure) because the experience doesn't last and needs to be repeated endlessly. In fact, desire for sense objects tends to increase the more we follow it, so we are never satisfied and look for experiences that are more and more intense. Also, the sense objects themselves are unreliable; they can be taken away from us and are subject to change. It is a tragic irony that craving for sense objects leads to suffering, because by following this craving we imagine it will bring us the opposite – pleasure and contentment.

Craving for existence refers to the desire to be someone. Nowadays this could simply take the form of wanting to be seen to exist on Instagram. Some of us desire to be a particular kind of person with a particular image or a particular profession. Some people crave to be famous; in the Far East many people crave immortality. We therefore do things to bring about our goal, but even if we succeed we find that the result is not what we imagined. Once you are famous, for example, you find you have a new set of problems you didn't have before – the press, fanatical admirers, people who want your money, and so on. Even if we do become the person we crave to be that will not last for ever, we will grow old, things will move on and what we have achieved may become meaningless.

Craving for non-existence means the opposite: wanting to be a nobody. We may experience this when we are very depressed. As the sayings go, 'we wish we were dead'; 'we wish we had never been born'. We wish that we could somehow disappear so we would not have to interact with the world. We close up and hide in our shell. At an extreme we may even consider committing suicide because we think that death is annihilation. Acting upon our craving for non-existence will probably produce many harmful actions that will make us suffer far more.

Aggression

The poison of aggression includes many types of emotion such as anger, jealousy, thirst for revenge and so on. Aggression can manifest as either 'hot' or 'cold': hot aggression could take the form of physically assaulting someone while cold aggression might be ignoring them. It is generally accepted in our society that aggressive actions do lead to suffering and tragedy. If we act on anger we will automatically set out to harm the other person either verbally or physically, and the effects of this will rebound on us in the form of retaliation or arrest or feelings of guilt. Medical research has also found that repeated anger and aggression have a harmful effect on health, increasing the blood pressure for example.

The fundamental mistake we make by being aggressive is that we are putting the blame for our situation on someone else. Instead, Buddhism teaches that we should look inside ourselves, not outside. It's as though we think that aggression will relieve us of our pain, and somehow if we can lay the blame at someone else's door our suffering will go away. From a Buddhist point of view, this is faulty logic.

Ignorance

The term 'ignorance' has a specific meaning in Buddhism. It does not mean that we don't know anything at all, or that we are very stupid. Rather the Pali word *avijja* (Sanskrit *avidya*) is often translated as 'delusion' or 'confusion' because it refers to not knowing how things really are. We do not know the true nature of things so we construct ideas of what we *think* their nature is and superimpose these on to what we perceive. Believing in our own ideas, and taking them seriously, is called delusion.

Ignorance is the root of the other two poisons of craving and aggression. For example, it is because we don't know what true happiness is that we follow our cravings. We don't understand what the true causes of suffering are and become aggressive to others. But the key element of our delusion from the Buddhist point of view is the belief in the existence of a self. It is because we believe that we exist as a permanent personality that we defend ourselves through aggression or seek to gratify ourselves through pleasure. All three poisons working together produce self-centred thinking and selfish actions. When we are motivated by craving and aggression we only care about how *we* feel and don't stop to ask ourselves about the effects of our behaviour on others. This, then, is the mechanism that leads to suffering. When craving, aggression or ignorance produce the motivation to act, the moral result of our actions will rebound on us like a boomerang and cause us pain and suffering.

Karma and the law of karma

The Indian word *karma* is now in the Oxford English dictionary which defines it as 'karma: (in Buddhism and Hinduism) the sum of a person's actions in one of his or her successive existences, thought to decide his or her fate for the next'. This is generally what Westerners understand by karma; that it is about the moral consequences of our actions, and that it determines our future. Although this is basically correct it refers primarily to the Hindu understanding, so this chapter aims to clarify the understanding of karma that is specific to Buddhism. In Buddhism, for instance, karma does not entail any idea of fate.

Literally, the Pali word *kamma* and the Sanskrit word *karma* both mean 'action', 'doing'. (We will use the Sanskrit word in this chapter because that is the term that has current usage in English.) In the Buddhist theory of karma, the word is given a more specific meaning and refers only to 'volitional action' or 'intentional action', in other words an action that is deliberately willed. This means that Buddhists distinguish between actions that are carried out with no clear intention – like getting out of bed, brushing your teeth, walking down the street and so forth – and actions that are motivated by the wish to achieve a goal. Only volitional actions carry a moral consequence; other actions are morally neutral.

Many of us use the word 'karma' quite loosely to refer not just to actions but to the results of action. If someone is in a difficult situation, a friend might turn to him and say, 'it must be your karma'. In fact, this is a mistake and in Buddhism karma does not technically refer to the effect of our actions which is known as the 'fruit' *(phala)* or 'result' of karma.

In addition to using the word karma for volitional action Buddhism also speaks of 'the law of karma', and indeed it is the law of karma that this chapter is really about. We can define this as follows:

The law of karma is the moral law of cause and effect related to intentional action.

There are a number of points to note in this definition. First, we are dealing with the *moral* nature of action and the moral consequences of action, not all consequences. For example, if I throw your favourite cup on the floor the physical consequence of my action is that it breaks into pieces, but the moral consequence is something quite different. It might be that I acted out of anger or spite, that I was deliberately trying to upset you, so according to Buddhism the karmic result will come according to these intentions. You might fly into a rage and hit me, for example.

A second point to note is that the law of karma is a law of causation, a law that says that certain types of causes (actions) will bring about certain types of effects (karmic consequences). Here we are talking specifically about the laws of causation that govern moral actions, not about causation in general. Theravada philosophers identify five laws governing causation called the five *niyamas* or 'natural laws'.

1. physical laws operating in the natural environment such as those that govern the weather, the way plants grow, gravity
2. genetic laws governing heredity, described as 'as the seed so the fruit'
3. laws governing the workings of the mind, the process of perception and knowledge, and the way we react to things
4. moral laws governing intentional actions (the laws of karma)
5. the generic law governing the causal relationships between all things, the law that determines how everything arises, exists and then ceases.[41]

The five *niyamas* make it clear that we cannot ascribe everything that happens to the law of karma in a simplistic way. At the same time, several different types of law can operate together in any given situation. So, for instance, if we go out in winter without a coat and catch a chill, we can explain this by reference to physical laws that mean our bodies are affected by outside temperatures; we could explain it in terms of genetic laws, because we happen to have inherited from our mother a chronic weakness of the chest; and we could also ascribe it to our own mindlessness, acting thoughtlessly without taking care of ourselves, which means we acted out of ignorance. Any or all of these possibilities can be present.

Volitional actions are classified as good and bad, and the general rule is that good actions produce good results and bad actions produce bad results. The big question is what do Buddhists consider a 'good' action and what do they consider to be a 'bad' action? Ideas about good and evil run deep in modern cultures so it is important to be clear on this point.

What makes an action good or bad?

There are two factors that determine whether an action is good or bad. The first is the intention behind it, and the second is the type of result it produces. Intention is always the main factor in the Buddhist theory of karma, since even the result produced also depends on intention. The Buddha said:

> *"It is will (cetana), O monks, that I call karma; having willed, one acts through body, speech and mind."* [42]

Bhikkhu Bodhi explains that this means volition is a necessary factor in creating karma, but not necessarily the only one. The Buddha's emphasis on intentionality thus demarcates his view from that of the Jains for whom even unintentional actions create karma.

It follows that we need to distinguish between the act of killing and the intention to kill. Even if you kill someone by accident this will not be considered a good action, but the moral consequences of the action will not be as serious as if you had deliberately set out to murder. A traditional example of this is the story about cutting a pumpkin. One day you are in the kitchen with your mother and you are making pumpkin pie. As you probably know, pumpkins can be rather enormous things, so you need a large knife to cut it into segments. Unfortunately, things get out of control and your knife slips. Your mother happens to be standing right there and the knife goes into her stomach accidentally and kills her. What is the karmic consequence of such a tragedy? The basic principle is that you will not get the full karmic result of the act of killing because it was not your intention to kill; you would nevertheless suffer from the karmic result of your mindless action.

A modern example that can affect us all is the case of a car accident. You approach a crossroads and it's foggy and you can't see very clearly. On top of this you are tired and haven't been concentrating very well on the road. Suddenly, out of the blue you find yourself in a collision and discover that you have killed the driver of the other car. What do you think are the moral consequences of this?

If the law of karma is about intentions, what makes intentions good or bad? The Buddhist answer is that it depends on whether, and to what extent, a person's intention is governed by one or more of the Three Poisons of craving, aggression and ignorance. The more one's mind is subject to these, the more morally harmful one's actions will be, and similarly the less one's mind is governed by these poisons, the more one will be able to act in a way that is beneficial for others as well as oneself. From this we can see just how important meditation is for ethical behaviour because meditation is a way of taming negative emotions so it leads to ethical action.

When we consider an action's effects, a good action is called *kusala* meaning 'skilful' or 'wholesome', while a harmful action is called *akusala* meaning 'unskilful' or 'unwholesome'. Skilful actions uplift the mental state of the doer, others involved, or both. Unskilful actions, on the other hand, go against intuitive wisdom, cause distress and are detrimental to the actor's spiritual progress. Generally speaking, the harm caused by unskilful actions refers to spiritual harm rather than physical harm.

One of the implications of the Buddhist approach to moral action is that actions are never black or white, they are different shades of grey. We all have some negative emotions and some positive emotions, so neither our motivations nor our actions will ever be absolutely good or absolutely bad. Goodness and badness are relative to our minds and to our situations. The law of karma is therefore flexible, it functions in accordance with all these various factors and is not some rigid law of fate.

This ties in, of course, with the fact that Buddhism does not accept the existence of God or the Devil personifying absolute Good and absolute Evil. Buddhists do not believe in the ontological existence of moral absolutes. This is why Buddhists would not use the term 'evil' at all because it has a connotation of being absolutely and irredeemably bad. The goodness and badness of people is a function of their craving and aggression, their misunderstanding of how things work and of who they really are, and the conditioning that has shaped their lives. Nobody is intrinsically evil. If all these factors can be changed and eventually eliminated then we would attain nirvana where we would be free from karma altogether, both from the effects of previous actions and from producing more karmic results for the future.

How the law of karma works

Three stages of an action

Each one of the three parts of an action, the intention, action and result, has the power to produce its own associated karmic effects. The most powerful effect will therefore be generated if we have the intention to do something, we actually do it, and we achieve the result we wanted. However, the karmic consequences of an action, whether good or bad, will be less powerful if only one or two of these factors come into play.

Imagine the case of someone who wants to rob your house. Scenario 1 is that the person intends to rob, is very experienced and skilled in doing so and actually manages to break and enter and steal your things, and then he succeeds in running off without getting caught. He or she feels really pleased that they pulled it off. This would produce the maximum karmic effect for an act of stealing. But in scenario 2, the person intends to rob you but something goes wrong. They can't manage to break the window or get through the door so the mission is aborted and they go home disappointed and empty handed. In this case they produce the karmic results of the intention to steal, and also the results of being disappointed that they didn't manage to steal, but they will not have produced the karmic effect of stealing itself. In scenario 3, the person intends to rob you and succeeds in doing so, but once they get back home and go through their loot they have a strong sense of guilt and regret. In this case, they would not have the karmic effect produced by satisfaction in accomplishing the action.

What form do karmic effects take?

How do karmic results affect us? Buddhists claim that they affect us either mentally or physically or both. In the case of a bad action, for instance:

a. Mentally, we might experience certain life situations as painful and difficult and full of suffering. This could explain why some people find situations such as poverty, illness or rejection very hard to take, while other people don't have the same reaction.
b. We might develop bad mental habits and tendencies. For example, if we succeed in stealing once it is easier to steal a second time, and this can lead us to develop a propensity to steal.
c. Physically we might experience our external environment as difficult, or our body might be prone to illness for example.

We can relate these points to the fourth aggregate of personality called mental formations which, as explained in Chapter 10, includes karma. The principle of this fourth aggregate is that the karmic consequences of our actions shape our character and mindset, and thereby become causes of future karmic actions in an endless chain of cause and effect. Karmic effects colour the way we experience the world as well as the way we relate to ourselves.

According to the Buddhist scriptures, certain results are associated with particular actions. For instance, stinginess leads to being poor, injuring others leads to frequent or chronic illness, and anger leads to being ugly. On the positive side, patience leads to being attractive, generosity leads to prosperity, and saving lives leads to having a long life. The Tibetan tradition[43] identifies four types of karmic effect:

1. **The fully ripened effect** or maximum effect of a negative action. For example, an action motivated by hatred can cause rebirth in the hells.
2. **The effect similar to the cause.** For example, if we are often criticised, belittled or lied to by others, this is the result of having lied in the past. If we have spoken harsh words in the past, everything that is said to us seems offensive or insulting, and whatever we say provokes an argument.
3. **The conditioning effect** acts on our environment. For instance, stealing causes rebirth in areas stricken by famine.
4. **The proliferation effect** refers to the way that whatever action we did before we will tend to repeat again and again. This accounts for habits and propensities, both virtuous and non-virtuous.

The time frame for karmic results

The time that elapses between an action and its karmic effects can vary considerably. In Buddhism, it is considered that karmic effects can come either in this present life or in the next life or in later future lives. The Buddha uses an analogy to make this point: *"Bad karma is like freshly squeezed milk... it takes time to sour."* [44] For this reason it is almost impossible for us to know what the karmic effects of our actions will be; if they occur much later on when the original action is all but forgotten, we will not know how to make the link back to their cause. Sceptics argue that this seriously weakens the Buddhist theory of karma because there is no clear proof that actions produce moral consequences at all. But such an absence of clear proof does not in itself disprove the theory of karma.

The idea that karmic effects do not necessarily follow on straightaway from the actions that produce them creates a philosophical problem: how can we account for the causal link between two very distant events? How can we explain the connection between an action carried out in, say, 1990 and its moral consequence which does not happen until 2020? The reason this is problematic is because, in Buddhist logic, a cause must *immediately* precede its effect; a cause occurs by definition in the very moment preceding the existence of its effect in a long chain of causal moments. So how do Buddhists solve this problem?

Their solution is to explain that the immediate karmic consequence of an action is to plant a 'karmic seed' *(bija)* or imprint in the mind of the actor. This imprint can either ripen very quickly and bear its fruit soon afterwards, or it can lay dormant for an indeterminate period of time until circumstances create the right opportunity for it to ripen and bear its effects. These karmic imprints are present in the mind in a continuous chain of moments and, crucially, they are carried by the subtle consciousness after death from one life to the next. This then accounts for the way karmic results can occur many lifetimes after the event.

Reward and punishment, fairness and justice

The law of karma is seen as a natural law inherent in the nature of things, just like physical laws, genetic laws and so on. From the Buddhist point of view, karma is not operated by God or any other supreme being because natural laws do not require any supernatural intervention in order to function. Do you consider that God has to intervene every time an apple falls to the ground? Most of us accept that the law of gravity operates as a natural part of the physical world. For Buddhists karma is just the same; good actions produce good results and bad actions produce bad results naturally, without any extra intervention.

This means that the results of karma are not described by Buddhists as forms of reward or punishment, because the idea of reward and punishment depends on a belief in a supreme power sitting in judgment and meting out good and bad situations in accordance with that judgment. In Buddhism, there is nobody to judge us, there is nobody to decide our future. We ourselves determine our future by the way we act and the way we think. In other words, we have nobody to blame but ourselves for any unfortunate karmic results that we may suffer. The first two verses of the *Dhammapada* express this clearly.

> *Our life is shaped by our mind; we become what we think. Suffering follows an evil thought as the wheels of a cart follow the oxen that draw it.*
> *Our life is shaped by our mind; we become what we think. Joy follows a pure thought like a shadow that never leaves.*[45]

Many people react against the Buddhist understanding of karma because they feel it is unfair and unjust. A few years ago, Glen Hoddle, a former England football manager, let slip to the press his belief that physical disability might be the result of negative actions in a past life. This idea was considered politically unacceptable and was strongly rejected in the media. Most people feel it is unfair to blame the disabled for their condition; they assume that, whatever their predicament, disabled people are innocent victims of life and cannot be held responsible for their situation. This is, of course, very different from the Buddhist approach which teaches that each one of us has a measure of responsibility for our life situation. The five *niyamas* are a way of saying that no situation can be explained solely in terms of physical or genetic factors – which presumably is the way that disability would be explained by general consensus these days – and there may also be moral factors at work.

For a Buddhist, whatever karmic results catch up with someone, this cannot be seen as unfair or unjust. The results of karma appear because of certain laws and none of us can change those laws. When an apple falls to the ground because of gravity and gets bruised, do we consider it unfair that the apple gets bruised? No; that's just how it is. Likewise, if I suffer because I have harmed someone deliberately, that is just how it is. There is nobody I can complain to. The Dharma is there to point out what actions should be avoided so we don't have to suffer. At the same time, the Buddhist response to another person's suffering is not a gloating 'they deserved it', but a compassionate 'unfortunately this is the result of a harmful action'.

It is also important to understand that karma is considered a universal law that applies to every human being, whether or not they are Buddhist. Karmic results do not depend on which religion we follow or even on whether we follow a religion at all. Nor do karmic results depend on whether or not we believe in the law of karma. Karma works whether we believe in it or not, according to our motivations, and anybody of any faith can have good intentions or bad intentions. From a Buddhist point of view, all the world religions encourage their followers to cultivate virtuous behaviour. If one does a good deed as a Christian, for example, the karmic effect will be no different for an identical motivation and deed on the part of a Buddhist.

Fate and freedom

The other common misunderstanding about karma, which is indeed part of the Oxford English dictionary definition, is that the law of karma is basically a law of fate. This is not the case in Buddhism. The idea of fate implies determinism: the idea that the future is determined by the past in a rigid way that allows for no changes or exceptions or freedom. In a theistic religion the idea of fate might also refer to a decision that God takes about your future, and which you are powerless to influence. As we saw in Chapter 1, the Buddha rejected fatalism because it does not allow for individual freedom and therefore undermines the very possibility of ethics. The law of karma is never presented as deterministic.

It is true that a particular karmic action will inevitably produce its associated karmic consequence if left unchecked. But the crucial point is that there are ways we can intervene and change the course of our future. As Buddhist masters put it, 'the future is in our hands'. We can divide the methods used into three groups: a) methods to purify past harmful actions before their effects fully ripen; b) methods to create a wholesome future by changing our behaviour now and acting ethically; and c) prayers when a loved one dies that are especially directed at purifying their karma.

a. **Methods to purify past harmful actions before their effects fully ripen.** Buddhism offers a number of ways to purify past karma, and each Buddhist tradition lays special emphasis on one or another of these ways. The practice of meditation and mindfulness helps us to become aware of our thoughts and mental habits, and in that process they can dissolve. The practice of loving kindness and compassion enables us to transform judgmental, aggressive or jealous thoughts into wholesome ones. The practice of confession (usually to peers) is also a way of coming to terms with past misdeeds. Regret and the resolve not to act in a harmful way again are also considered important for purifying karma. Finally, Vajrayana Buddhism employs visualisation and mantra as a powerful practice of healing and transforming negativity.
b. **Methods to create a wholesome future by changing our behaviour now and acting ethically.** Ethical conduct outlined in the Eightfold Path and the

Bodhisattva Path provides the guidelines for moral behaviour. By following these guidelines one accumulates virtue or 'merit' *(puñña)*, that is, the positive energy that will give rise to favourable circumstances in the future. Sometimes Buddhists will engage in deliberate acts of charity or kindness (generously giving to monks, for instance, or freeing animals being sent for slaughter) so these acts serve as an antidote to negative actions committed in the past.

c. **Prayers when a loved one dies that are especially directed at purifying their karma.** The moment of death is critical for a Buddhist, because it is at that juncture that one's rebirth will be determined by one's past karma. Buddhist rites for the dead involve directing the power of prayer to transferring one's own merit to the deceased person to enable a more favourable rebirth. When a parent dies, some Buddhists will do a short retreat or go on pilgrimage as a conscious way of accumulating merit that is then directed to the deceased through prayer.

There are also very striking examples in the scriptures of individuals of doubtful moral character who regret their bad actions and completely change. One such story is that of Angulimala, the mass murderer converted by the Buddha (Chapter 2); another is the conversion of the emperor Ashoka (Chapter 4). These stories illustrate that we are not necessarily a slave to our past; it is possible to change the course of our future if our wish to do so is strong enough. They show that nobody should ever be judged on their actions alone because each of us has the ability to change.

> *One who previously made bad karma but who reforms and creates good karma brightens the world like the moon appearing from behind a cloud.*[46]

This discussion implies that if Buddhism seeks to defend the possibility of moral action, it must believe in some form of freedom. However, it is difficult to say that Buddhism accepts free will in the sense that this is understood in Western ethics. If we take free will to mean an inherent freedom of the mind to make moral judgments, then Buddhism does not accept this because it considers the mind to be conditioned. Just like everything else in the world, my mind is produced by causes and conditions, and in particular is conditioned by society, education, life experience, past karma and so forth as well as the functioning of my body. I would be deluding myself if I imagined that I was really free to make all the choices that present themselves to me in life. From a Buddhist point of view mental freedom is certainly possible but it is difficult to achieve. As Walpola Rahula reminds us, "Mind is only a faculty or organ like the eye or the ear. It can be controlled and developed like any other faculty".[47]

This is arguably the key to understanding the entire theory of karma. If the mind functions just like the sense organs, and is dependent on numerous factors to exist and to operate, then the intentions it produces are subject to natural laws just like other senses are subject to natural laws. And surely it is because many other philosophies and religions consider mind (or spirit) to be an ontological principle radically opposed to matter, and irreducible to matter, that they address morality quite differently. Non-Buddhists might hold, for example, that laws of causation apply only to matter and that the mind, being of a radically different nature, is not subject to them; this is one definition of freedom. Materialists might hold that there is no such thing as mind defined as a different entity from matter, and then mental freedom and morality are impossible to explain. The ontologies of other religions and some other philosophies allow for the God-given existence of moral values which human beings simply need to know and follow; what is good and bad is already laid down for us. This, too, is quite different from Buddhism where no absolute values exist as such in a metaphysical dimension.

In Buddhism, freedom of mind is present only when one is free of the Three Poisons; that is what 'liberation' means. Until then, thoughts and emotions are entirely at the mercy of the Poisons. The point of attaining nirvana is to liberate ourselves from suffering by freeing ourselves from the causes of suffering. Until we have reached nirvana, freedom is only ever relative and occasional; different people have different degrees of freedom according to the extent to which they are able to tame their minds. Within the human world moral freedom is not absolute but relative. Only a buddha is totally free.

Is karma a matter of faith?

The Buddhist theory of karma is hard to accept because it lays such tremendous responsibility on our own shoulders. It is up to us to work on ourselves, transform our minds and improve our behaviour so that we create favourable conditions for ourselves and others, and so that, ultimately, we become free of the cycle of suffering altogether. The Buddha is not like a catapult that can miraculously propel us to a heavenly realm or to enlightenment; we have to do the hard work ourselves.

Buddhism is doubly hard to accept if we consider that we might be suffering today from the results of an action we did in a past life of which we are not aware. Whether or not this is the case, Buddhism encourages an attitude of acceptance and patience in the face of adversity, not in a weak or passive way but in a constructive way, because the manner in which we react to each situation will in itself generate new karmic consequences, and we may as well do our best to ensure they are good ones. For example, if I blame you for the trouble I am in and then decide to take it out on you, whether or not you played a part in the situation my negative reaction will only bring about more suffering for me in the future. The Buddhist approach is therefore not sympathetic to a 'compensation culture'. Buddhists take the long-term view.

If we find the law of karma hard to swallow we will want to have some evidence for it. Why should we believe in karma? What proof is there for karma? Surely everyone gets away with bad actions some of the time. There are many nasty people who seem to have quite a comfortable life and who might even be popular; it does not seem *they* are suffering from the consequences of their actions. And similarly, there are many good and kind people who have a hard time, things go wrong for them, they have accidents, get ill and seem to be innocent victims of circumstance. Can we not argue that life situations tend to disprove the theory of karma rather than the reverse?

Buddhists would have to accept these observations and would justify the theory of karma by stating that the consequences of actions occur over time, and sometimes over several lives. Although your nasty neighbour seems to be successful right now, from a Buddhist point of view he/she is bound to suffer for his actions sometime in the future. The problem with this logic, of course, is that none of us knows what our future will be and therefore we have no evidence that this is true, but as we get older we can perhaps look back on life and see that people's fortunes do change. Rich people can end up poor, poor people can become rich, presidents can be deposed and cast out as beggars. As the Buddha said:

> *A fool is happy until his mischief turns against him.*
> *And a good man may suffer until his goodness flowers.*[48]

The Buddha only understood the law of karma immediately before he attained full enlightenment. He acknowledged that only an enlightened buddha truly realizes how karma works. So, although we can all grasp the law of karma theoretically, we can only understand it fully when we reach enlightenment. Until then karma is partly a matter of faith.

We should note that Buddhists maintain that karma is not just a matter of faith because it can be defended through logical reasoning. Isn't it reasonable to explain certain situations with reference to karma, especially when they involve the suffering of apparently innocent and good-hearted people? Such situations are impossible to explain rationally in any other way; religious explanations defer to the Will of God which cannot be fathomed by human beings, so this is not a reasoned response. One can therefore argue that karma is the best logical explanation of suffering that we have. Furthermore, we do sometimes experience the moral consequences of our actions for ourselves – when we feel guilty about something we have done, for example, this takes away our peace of mind. So even within the limits of our present life it is possible to validate the general idea of moral consequences through personal experience. The Buddhist view is therefore that the principle of karmic causation is valid and reasonable because it is supported by both reasoning and experience, not only by faith.

Personal reflection

How do you understand the reasons behind the diversity of personalities and life experiences?

Main Points

- According to Buddhist thought, everything is subject to the natural law of cause and effect.
- The law of karma is the law of cause and effect that applies to the moral consequences of actions (the Sanskrit word 'karma' means 'action').
- The most powerful factor determining the karmic result of an action is the intention not the action itself.
- Harmful actions are those motivated by craving, aggression or delusion—the Three Poisons—and they cause our own suffering as well as that of others.
- The law of karma means that we are ultimately responsible for our own suffering and our own circumstances. There is nobody and nothing else to blame.
- The theory of karma is not fatalistic or a form of determinism. It is possible to purify bad karma before its effects have ripened. Every Buddhist tradition teaches methods for purification.

Chapter 13

SAMSARA AND NIRVANA

Samsara and nirvana form the axis of the Buddhist path. Samsara refers to conditioned existence tainted by the experience of suffering while nirvana is an unconditioned state that is free of all suffering and its causes. Buddhists try to free themselves from samsara to attain nirvana. These key pillars of the Buddhist view are illustrated through reference to the Wheel of Life. This chapter presents the perspectives of both Nikaya and Mahayana traditions.

Religions always point to the relationship of the mortal, or the conditioned, with the unconditioned. That is, if you strip any religion down to its very basic essence, you will find that it is pointing to where the mortal – the conditioned and time-bound – ceases. In that cessation is the realization and the understanding of the unconditioned.

Ajahn Sumedho, *The Mind and the Way*

The Buddhist worldview

Buddhists see the world very differently. The world most of us consider to be real is the world of sense experience – what we can see, hear, smell, taste and touch either directly or through the use of scientific instruments such as telescopes or microscopes. If we can't perceive something in such a way then either we infer it must exist for logical reasons, or we conclude that it is non-existent. It must simply stem from the imagination, from hallucination or from delusion.

The worldview of all Indian religions is vaster than this because it is not centred around human beings and what human beings know or don't know. It presents us with a much bigger picture of an infinite cosmos containing countless world systems, each containing many different forms of life. This means that, for Buddhists, the world is not limited to the type of beings we are familiar with, such as human beings and animals, but also contains forms of life that we cannot perceive with our normal senses. Buddhists believe that some types of being exist without a physical body, for example.

Buddhists do not merely describe this immense universe and all its inhabitants, they also explain why different beings are born in a particular realm and have particular characteristics. This explanation is possible because of a correlation between our mental state and the world we live in. Rupert Gethin[49] calls this "the principle of the equivalence of cosmology and psychology". The universe is not just a map of different realms of existence but also of every type of possible experience. Karma and rebirth enable this to function, so each being is reborn into a particular situation according to his/her karma and its corresponding mental disposition.

The Buddhist worldview recognizes a spiritual dimension to the universe which manifests as two distinct types of existence called *samsara* and *nirvana*. Samsara refers to 'the cycle of conditioned existence' also called 'the round of rebirth', where all beings are subject to birth and death, and where life is characterized by suffering. Nirvana is the opposite of this; it is unconditioned. It is a form of existence where suffering is completely eliminated, and which is characterized by peace. For Buddhists, there are enlightened beings in the world who are not subject to conditioned existence; they include buddhas and bodhisattvas.

When the Buddha taught the first Noble Truth he was making people aware of the nature of *samsara*, and of the fact that suffering exists. When the Buddha taught the third Noble Truth (cessation) he explained that this suffering can be brought to an end, and that true peace and happiness are possible. The whole purpose of Buddhism is to free us from samsara and enable us to attain nirvana. This is what Buddhism is all about: indeed, a buddha is someone who has gone beyond the cycle of life and death, and who is free from suffering.

This last point is crucial to understand the way Buddhists have developed their worldview. It is only because the Buddha became enlightened and was free of samsara that he was able fully to comprehend it. When we are immersed in samsara we are unable to see it for what it is because we are part of the problem. It is only when we are outside the cycle of life and death that we have sufficient perspective to be able to see samsara as a whole. So the Buddhist framework of samsara and nirvana arises directly from the enlightened understanding of the Buddha, and cannot be fathomed completely by the ordinary human mind. The cosmos taken as a whole is beyond the limitations of human understanding; if we don't know certain things about it this could be because we actually *can't* know them as long as we are limited by our senses and our defiled human mind. Buddhists, therefore, would not always say that if we can't perceive something with our senses it doesn't exist; instead, they might say that the limitations of the human mind prevent us from being able to say for certain whether something that is imperceptible exists or not. The only way out of this impasse is to transform our minds and deepen our understanding. Knowledge is determined by the kind of mind that knows.

In this chapter we review how samsara and nirvana are described in the Buddhist scriptures, and how they are understood in relation to each other. First, we present the basic Buddhist understanding that is common to all Buddhist traditions and, second, we indicate the points on which Mahayana Buddhists have a different view.

Samsara

One image that is often used to illustrate samsara is that of an ocean: many Buddhist scriptures and prayers talk about 'the ocean of samsara' or 'the ocean of suffering'. The process of freeing ourselves from this is often called 'crossing the ocean of existence' which means crossing over from the near shore (of samsara) which is fraught with dangers of all kinds, and reaching the far shore (of nirvana) which is safe and free from danger.

Literally, the Sanskrit word *samsara* means 'wandering on', which conveys the idea of a process that is long and aimless. We 'wander' endlessly from life to life, and from rebirth to rebirth, trying to find a permanent home where we can feel at ease and secure; and trying to find a lasting experience of happiness. However, because we are all bound to die sooner or later, whatever kind of existence we have it will not bring us the security we are looking for, and we will then be reborn somewhere else.

The idea of samsara also relates to the quality of experience we have when we feel that life is pointless. Sometimes we just see our life as a routine, we might feel like cogs in a wheel or trapped on an endless treadmill. We think that life is meaningless, that all our efforts are like running on the same spot getting nowhere. We want to break out of our situation, or of our own personality even, yet we don't know how. At such times we experience the nature of samsaric existence and have a taste of the third type of suffering presented in the first Noble Truth, the suffering of conditioned existence.

The Buddha taught that as long as we remain in samsara our search for happiness is futile because we have not understood why we suffer and what happiness depends upon. In the second Noble Truth he explained that the factors that produce suffering are mental defilements like ignorance, craving and aggression, while the factors that bring about happiness are the opposites of these, that is, positive emotions based on love and compassion leading to virtuous actions. So rather than looking for happiness in external life situations we should look at our own minds and transform our harmful tendencies.

The six realms of rebirth

> *There are people who do not understand suffering. They do not know where it comes from, where it totally ceases, or how to get to where it totally ceases. So without a chance to free the mind or achieve liberation through knowledge, they cannot bring suffering to an end. They can only go on and on, being born and getting old.*
>
> The Buddha, *Sutta Nipata*

Although many people in the West do not reject the general idea of rebirth out of hand, some find it more difficult to accept the Buddhist theory that there are six different realms of existence into which beings are reborn and that, according to our karma, we can be reborn into any one of them at any given time. The reason this is hard to accept is because it means that we will not necessarily 'come back' as a human being; we might be reborn as a cow, or a slug, or a god, or even in very unfortunate circumstances as a being in the hells. This is not a pleasant thought, nor is it something we can readily imagine.

The six realms of conditioned existence are **the realms of the gods, the demi-gods, human beings, animals, hungry ghosts and the hells**. Each has unique characteristics and our rebirth there results from particularly strong karmic actions. So, for example, anger and aggression are the main cause of rebirth in the hell realm while desire is the main cause of being born a human being.

Figure 13.1 – The Six Realms Of Conditioned Existence

REALM	CHARACTERISTICS	DOMINANT KARMIC CAUSE
Gods	Beautiful palaces and gardens, music, silks, perfumes and beautiful goddesses; the gods are absorbed in bliss, have very long lives but suffer tremendously when their life comes to an end.	Pride
Demi-gods or titans (asuras)	They constantly wage war on the gods. The tree of immortality has its roots in this realm but its branches and fruit are in the god realm; the demi-gods constantly fight to obtain the fruit they think should be theirs. It's a losing battle.	Jealousy, envy
Humans	Eight forms of misery: birth, illness, old age, death, separation from loved ones, meeting those we don't like, not having what we covet, fear of losing our possessions. Despite this, the human realm is the most fortunate of all realms because wisdom and compassion can be developed and enlightenment is possible.	Desire
Animals	Four categories: with many legs (insects), four legs (mammals), two legs (apes and birds) and no legs (snakes). Most animals live in the ocean. They suffer from hunger and thirst, heat and cold, human abuse and hunting, destruction of their habitat and being eaten by carnivores.	Ignorance, confusion
Hungry ghosts or pretas	Some pretas have long thin necks and swollen bellies and are unable to swallow their food; some breathe, excrete and urinate streams of fire. Food and water turn to pus and vomit. They live in a barren landscape and suffer constantly from hunger, thirst, heat, cold and seeing mirages.	Greed, insatiable craving, miserliness; stealing from charities
Hells	There are 8 hot hells, 8 cold hells, and 2 auxiliary hells. They are said to be located deep inside the Earth. Beings are tortured by extreme heat or cold, by fire, molten iron or by having their bodies sawn, crushed, impaled or devoured, and so on.	Aggression, anger, hatred

a. **Human realm:** The dominant karmic cause of being reborn as a human is desire. The suffering that characterizes the human realm is of eight kinds: birth, old age, illness, death, association with unpleasant people or conditions, separation from loved ones or from pleasant conditions, not getting what one desires, and grief or distress.
b. **The god realms:** these heavenly realms are characterized by all things pleasant, beautiful and satisfying: beautiful landscapes, music, luxurious clothes, perfumes and so on. The main experience of the gods is that of bliss. Their lives are long but eventually they will die and be reborn in another realm of samsara. The dominant karmic cause of being reborn in the god realm is pride.
c. **Realm of the demi-gods or** asuras: the dominant cause of being reborn in this realm is jealousy. The demi-gods are prone to conflict and fighting, they are never satisfied and always want what they can see the gods have. This is illustrated by a fruit tree the roots and trunk of which are in the demi-god realm, but the branches and fruit are in the god realm. The demi-gods consider the fruit is rightfully theirs and fight for it.
d. **Realm of animals:** the dominant cause for being reborn as an animal is ignorance and stupidity. Animals live in constant fear of their lives. Some are also subject to the suffering of being used as draught animals by human beings.
e. **Realm of hungry ghosts or** pretas: Hungry ghosts are depicted with large heads, tiny necks and bulging stomachs. They are never satisfied, but when they try to eat they have difficulty swallowing their food on account of their narrow throats. When their food does reach the stomach it produces a burning sensation and turns to vomit. They live in a desolate and barren landscape with no vegetation. The dominant karmic cause for being reborn in this realm is greed.
f. **The hell realms** are where suffering is at its most intense and relentless. The dominant karmic cause for being reborn there is anger, hatred and aggression. There are several types of hells, some characterized by extreme heat and others by extreme cold. Beings here suffer many different types of physical, emotional and mental torture and never have a moment of respite. However, beings in the hells will eventually be reborn elsewhere in the samsaric cycle when their bad karma is exhausted.

How are the six realms to be understood? There are two different approaches in the scriptures.

a. They are understood literally as different places. We could imagine that the six realms can be found on different planets, in different solar systems and different universes. They might also be different dimensions of existence, so that the beings in certain realms may not have tangible bodies, and even if they were present on Earth we would not see them.
b. The six realms are understood as states of mind and therefore as psychological worlds. A human being could live in any one of these psychological realms and in fact might go through several realms in the course of a lifetime. The gods might correspond to people who have everything to make them happy and who live in a 'perfect' bubble; hungry ghosts might be people who are never satisfied, who have a strong sense of lack and, at an extreme, those suffering from famine or malnutrition. And some people's lives seem to be a series of catastrophes entailing intense physical and emotional pain, and they will say that 'life is hell'.

Seeing the six realms as psychological states rather than physical places does not make them any less real. The Buddhist understanding is that our mental states largely determine how we see any given situation, and they therefore determine how we experience life. As the *Dhammapada* says, "Our life is shaped by our mind, we become what we think."[50] Buddhism does not claim that our minds literally create our physical world, but rather that they create the world of our experience, and whatever our experience is it will feel completely real to us.

If the six realms can be mental states, it is easier to understand how we are reborn into one of them according to our thoughts and actions in previous lives. The link between one life and the next is a mental one, so it is logical to say that when we are reborn our particular psychological outlook is produced from mental tendencies in previous lives. This is how Buddhists understand the functioning of the Wheel of Life.

Life in some realms is said to be extraordinarily long, so for instance one day in certain god realms is equivalent to fifty human years. But we are not speaking of some objective measure of time but rather of how long things feel subjectively; the more intense our experiences the longer they seem to last. It is important to note that none of these six realms is eternal, not even the heavens and the hells. Beings transmigrate according to their karma until such time as they have freed themselves from karma altogether. Even the gods are still trapped within the cycle of life and death.

Contrary to the Jewish, Christian and Muslim beliefs in Heaven and Hell, the heavens and hells understood by Buddhism are not everlasting. It is also important not to confuse the gods living in the god realm with the idea of God in monotheism. Buddhism accepts the existence of many gods but not the one Creator God. The gods are beings who have practised advanced meditation in previous lives and therefore have considerable mental power; some can therefore influence circumstances in the human world. But, according to Buddhism, the gods have not transcended life and death, cause and effect, and the law of karma; when the karma for life in the god realm is exhausted they are then reborn into one of the other six realms.

The realms of heaven and hell in Buddhism are not associated with any absolutes such as God or the Devil; they are simply forms of existence and types of experience which result from our actions and our states of mind. It is the law of karma that determines rebirth into one or another of these six realms, there is neither a judge nor a judgment process.

The Wheel of Life

Samsara is depicted as a large wheel called the Wheel of Life (see illustration). This diagram appears to have originated with the Buddha but is transmitted today only within the Tibetan tradition. It is entirely symbolic and brings together all the different factors that define and characterize the cycle of conditioned existence and that are taught by all Nikaya and Mahayana schools. The explanation below begins at the centre of the wheel and moves outwards.

- **The hub of the wheel** At the centre of the wheel are three animals representing the Three Poisons that perpetuate existence in samsara. The pig symbolises ignorance; the cock symbolises craving and desire; and the snake symbolises aggression. They lie at the heart of the mechanism that makes the cycle of rebirth go round and round.
- **The first circle** The first circle shows various ghost-like beings feeling their way towards their next rebirth. The idea is that, depending on past karma, beings accordingly find their way to an appropriate rebirth. The beings in this circle are in the *bardo* state between one life and the next in accordance with the views of Tibetan Buddhism (see Chapter 11).
- **The second and widest circle: the six realms of samsara** This circle depicts the six realms into which beings in samsara may be reborn. There are three higher realms (gods, humans, demi-gods) in which suffering is less intense, and three lower realms (hells, animals, hungry ghosts) where suffering is very intense and a major hindrance to spiritual progress.

Figure 13.2 – The Wheel of Life

Figure 13.3 – The Twelve Links Of Dependent Arising

Each link leads to the next in a cycle

	LINK (NIDANA)	SYMBOL IN WHEEL OF LIFE
1.	Ignorance (of the nature of life as analysed in the Four Noble Truths)	Blind man
2.	Karma-formations i.e. impulses or tendencies resulting from actions or thoughts	Potter
3.	Consciousness (which continues from one life to the next)	Monkey in a tree
4.	Name and form (the five skandhas including the consciousness of the present life)	Boat and four passengers
5.	The six senses (sight, hearing, touch, smell, taste and mind)	House with six openings
6.	Contact (with the objects of the senses)	Man and woman embracing
7.	Feeling (pleasant, unpleasant or neutral)	Man with arrow in his eye
8.	Craving (for experience, for life, or for oblivion)	Man takes drink from woman
9.	Grasping (at life, sense pleasures etc)	Man picking fruit
10.	Becoming (process of creating situations and then living them)	Pregnant woman
11.	Rebirth	Childbirth
12.	Suffering, decay and death	Corpse

The outer rim of the wheel: Around the rim of the wheel we find the twelve *nidanas,* known as the Twelve Links or the Twelve Links of Dependent Origination. These are a pictorial way of presenting the chain of causes and effects through which samsara is created. They can be interpreted in three ways:

a. as the chain of causes which link one life to the next. In this case the first two links relate to the past life; links 3 to 9 relate to the present life; and links 10-12 relate to the future life.

b. as the chain of causes which operates in every moment of our life, linking our intentions, our actions and their results.
c. as the chain of links within one life, from birth to death

The Twelve Links can either be shown as a circle or as a list, but the important point is that they operate as an endless cycle, with the twelfth link leading to the first one so the cycle starts all over again. There is no First Cause in this cycle: the first link (ignorance) is not a metaphysical first cause which sets the wheel in motion because ignorance itself is produced from causes. It is therefore clearer to depict the links in a circle.

The Twelve Links illustrate the vicious cycle of samsara, where nothing happens by random chance but everything comes about from one or several causes. In practice this means that when our existence is entirely determined by these causes we have little or no freedom. Our choices will be determined by karmic tendencies, cravings and so on, and will not be made freely. How can we ever break out of the circle? There are two weak links in the chain, namely craving and ignorance. By tackling one or both of them we will weaken these links still further and break the chain. Meditation is a primary method for eliminating craving while cultivating wisdom through study is effective against ignorance. The effect of longterm spiritual practice is to break this chain completely.

Yama, the lord of death: the whole Wheel of Life sits in the arms of a monster called Yama, who symbolises the lord of death. This represents the fact that all the beings who exist within the wheel are subject to death.

How does the Wheel of Life work in practice? It means that any being can be reborn in any one of the six realms, depending on karma. This means that we will not necessarily be reborn as human beings again next time. Maybe we will take birth as a horse or a mosquito – or as a hungry ghost or demi-god. Of all these six realms the human realm is considered the most fortunate because it is the one in which one can attain enlightenment. It is even more fortunate than the god realm because humans have just the right amount of suffering not to be overwhelmed by it, and just enough to be motivated to want to find a way out. The gods, on the other hand, have little or no suffering and can easily be trapped within their experience of bliss, feeling completely content and impervious to the sufferings of others. This is why Buddhism strongly encourages people not to waste their lives in meaningless activity but to make every effort to progress spiritually while they have the opportunity to do so.

Nirvana

What is nirvana? "The extinction of desire, the extinction of hatred, the extinction of illusion", said Buddha's disciple Shariputra.[51]

Literally, nirvana (*nibbana* in Pali) means 'blowing out, extinguishing', and here it refers to the extinguishing of the fires of desire, hatred and ignorance that rage inside us. These are, of course, the fundamental causes of suffering which implies that as soon as they have been extinguished then automatically one ceases to suffer. If the causes of suffering do not exist then suffering cannot be produced. It follows that nirvana is taken to mean the end of suffering, or the cessation *(nirodha)* of suffering, and so it is defined as the opposite of samsara.

The logic of this process entails that as soon as the causes of suffering have been extinguished one's actions no longer create karmic consequences. This is due to the fact that karmic results depend primarily on motivation, and once the Three Poisons have been eliminated from the mindstream then motivation (or intention) is free from both good and bad thoughts. This situation, in turn, means that one will not be bringing about a karmic rebirth after death, and that is why nirvana is also said to be freedom from rebirth. Once one has attained nirvana one is free of the cycle of birth and death, and no longer bound to be reborn within samsara.

It is important to remember that nirvana is not 'a thing': it is not something that one can get by following the Buddhist path, and neither is nirvana a place, like a heaven, where one will go as a result, or as a reward, for practising Buddhism. Nirvana is a realization, a way of seeing things. When one understands deeply the nature of things according to the Four Noble Truths, and when one is able to sustain that understanding continuously, one is said to have attained nirvana.

What is nirvana like?

The question most people ask is 'so what is the experience of nirvana like?' The only possible reply is that it cannot be put into words. Nirvana is beyond words, because words cannot convey the true nature even of ordinary things let alone of enlightenment. Imagine trying to describe the taste of a tomato to someone who has never seen or tasted a tomato before; or trying to describe to a young child what the experience of falling in love is like. Language is inadequate at communicating the quality of experience, and likewise it falls short as a means of expressing ultimate truth.

As a result, nirvana is spoken of in two ways. It is sometimes described positively in the form of metaphors, but more often it is described in negative terms as what it is not. This second way is similar to the *via negativa* in Christian and Sufi mysticism. The Buddhist scriptures use a number of classical images for nirvana and the list below is taken from *The Questions of King Milinda*.

Positive images of nirvana

- like cool water that relieves fever, nirvana relieves the fever of the passions
- like medicine that puts an end to illness, nirvana puts an end to all sufferings
- like an unshakeable mountain peak, nirvana is unshakeable
- like the wind that you cannot actually see, nirvana is there but you cannot point to it.

Negative expressions of nirvana

- it is not something that is produced, nor is it unproduced
- it is not past, or future, or present
- it cannot be perceived by the senses
- it is unborn and unconditioned
- it is extinction or absence of craving, hatred and ignorance
- it is freedom from suffering/absence of suffering
- it is freedom from rebirth.

Some non-Buddhists have interpreted the negative expressions of nirvana as meaning that nirvana is a negative state, a state of 'nothingness' or blankness or self-annihilation. This is a misunderstanding. Nirvana is freedom from suffering, from the causes of suffering and from rebirth, and freedom from these things can surely not be construed as negative. When it is said that nirvana is beyond time and space, and beyond human perception, this is not intended to convey a depressingly inaccessible state but rather to inspire the idea of a transcendent state. Other people are horrified at the prospect that one would no longer have any passions or emotions left, and they imagine that enlightenment would turn us all into boring, lifeless vegetables. This hardly seems like an attractive religious goal. But nothing is further from the truth, and the experience of nirvana is associated in the scriptures with joy, happiness, serenity, gentleness, compassion, kindness, tolerance and understanding. These are said to be the qualities of someone who has attained nirvana.

The experience of nirvana

- **Nirvana can be experienced in life.** Buddhism is quite different from other religions in that its religious goal can be experienced in life and not only after death. The lifestory of the Buddha exemplifies this.
- **Nirvana and parinirvana.** When nirvana is experienced in life it is called 'nirvana with remainder' because one still has one's body, which is something of a limitation. When it is experienced at death it is called *parinirvana* or complete nirvana or 'nirvana without remainder' because then one is free of the body so rebirth, or the reconstituting of the five aggregates, will not occur.
- **Nirvana and pain.** After nirvana has been attained in life, the person appears to think and function much the same as everyone else, but the difference is that his/her mind is quite different. For example, the body can still become ill or injured and one can still feel pain, but the pain will not affect one's mental state.
- **The arhat.** Whoever attains nirvana is called an *arhat*, meaning someone who has conquered their mind and the 'enemy' of the Three Poisons. This is the goal of Theravada Buddhism.

Nirvana cannot be produced

Although in one sense nirvana is seen as the result of many years or many lifetimes of virtuous effort, in another sense nirvana is not the result of anything. If it were the result of something this would mean that it was produced, and then it would be conditioned and therefore impermanent. But nirvana is permanent in the sense that it is beyond time, and the truth of nirvana is always there whether we realize it or not. Buddhists have to tread carefully between saying that nirvana is unconditioned on the one hand, and saying that one attains enlightenment by following the Buddhist path, on the other hand.

Are these two statements contradictory? Possibly not because nirvana does not automatically occur as the result of any particular action. There is no guarantee that if you meditate for x hours or behave virtuously for x years, you will automatically attain nirvana. It is more elusive than this and cannot be brought about through an A plus B equals C sort of approach. Like all mystical states it is beyond our control. *The Questions of King Milinda* illustrates this point with an image: it says that a path does not cause a mountain, it just leads there.

The Mahayana understanding of samsara and nirvana

The Mahayana master Nagarjuna made the startling statement that samsara is no different from nirvana. What could he mean? Does this not contradict all the Buddha's teachings on the subject? Was he not inventing a renegade belief of his own? Nagarjuna wrote:

> *There is no distinction whatever between nirvana and samsara. The limit of nirvana is the limit of samsara. There is not the slightest difference between the two.*[52]

Mahayana Buddhists understand samsara and nirvana within the framework of the Two Truths, that is, ultimate and conventional truth. According to Madhyamaka philosophy, the ultimate truth of all things is that they are empty of inherent existence, which means that they do not exist independently, permanently or as a single entity. Nagarjuna believed that some scholars of the Nikaya schools treated nirvana as though it were an exception to this rule: they regarded it as a permanent state, something that was unproduced and that existed independently of anything else, and as a result they treated it like an ultimate reality that actually exists. Nagarjuna argued that this is a serious mistake for a Buddhist to make, and that there should be no exceptions whatsoever to the principle that the ultimate nature of everything is emptiness *(shunyata)*.

It follows from this that both samsara and nirvana are ultimately empty in nature. Since they both have the same nature, one can therefore say that they are the same as each other in ultimate truth. On the conventional level, of course, they are very different and indeed are defined in relation to each other as opposites. So Nagarjuna's statement must be seen as referring specifically to the ultimate state of things as distinct from the way they appear to us conventionally.

The other major difference between the Mahayana and Nikaya views of this topic is that nirvana is not the ultimate goal of Mahayana Buddhism. As we saw in Chapter 7, Mahayana distinguishes nirvana from complete buddhahood and considers nirvana to be a provisional goal. Mahayana Buddhists believe that the experience of nirvana eventually comes to an end with a fortunate rebirth, and the individual then continues on the path to full buddhahood. It is said that an arhat still has the subtlest veil of ignorance remaining, and this must be eliminated for complete buddhahood to be attained.

Finally, the doctrine of buddha nature or *tathagatagarbha* explains why Mahayana emphasizes that nirvana is not something that we lack and are trying to attain, but rather it is something that is there all the time and that we realize once we have purified our ignorance and confusion. In other words, what we need to do is get rid of our ignorance, not gain a new wisdom that we lack. Following the Buddhist path is useful because it helps us to do just this. The path is seen as a process of abandoning not a process of acquiring. The buddha nature is with us always, we simply have to uncover it and realize it, so Mahayana carries a sense that enlightenment is immanent and fundamentally accessible.

Personal reflection

Reflect on how the six realms of existence can be experienced by humans as different psychological states, paying attention to the qualities of suffering in each realm.

Main Points

- The Buddhist worldview includes different dimensions of existence and different types of beings; it is not anthropocentric.
- There is a correlation between cosmology and psychology. Beings are reborn into circumstances that reflect their karma and mindset.
- There are six realms of samsara: those of the gods, the demi-gods, human beings, animals, 'hungry ghosts' and the hells.
- The process of rebirth in the six realms is depicted in the Wheel of Life.
- Karma helps to perpetuate our rebirth in the Wheel of Life:

    - Pride leads to rebirth in the god realm
    - Jealousy leads to rebirth in the demi-god realm
    - Desire leads to rebirth in the human realm
    - Confusion leads to rebirth in the animal realm
    - Greed leads to rebirth in the hungry ghost realm
    - Aggression and hatred lead to rebirth in the hells.

- Nirvana is beyond words so is described either through analogies or through negatives. It is unconditioned and understood as the end of suffering and its causes.

Chapter 14
THE THREE REFUGES

One becomes a Buddhist by committing to take refuge in the Buddha as teacher, the Dharma as guide, and the Sangha as the community of companions on the path. Buddha, Dharma and Sangha are known as the Three Jewels. This chapter unpacks the meaning of the Refuges.

Driven by fear, people run for security to mountains and forests, to sacred spots and shrines. But none of these can be a safe refuge, because they cannot free the mind from fear.
Dhammapada 188-9

The meaning of the Refuges

The notion of 'refuge' is fundamental in Buddhism. Buddhists take Refuge in the Buddha, the Dharma and the Sangha. Buddha, Dharma and Sangha are called the 'Three Jewels' because Buddhists consider them to be so precious and valuable. Other English terms for the Three Refuges include the Threefold Refuge and the Triple Refuge — they all mean exactly the same. To put it very simply, a Buddhist commits him or herself to: following the Buddha as teacher;

taking what he taught, the Dharma, as guidance; and respecting the community of fellow practitioners, the Sangha, as companions through life.

There are two ways we can talk about the Three Refuges. One way is to describe what each of them is according to common Buddhist practice and according to the scriptures; and another way is to explain what the meaning is behind the Refuges. With the first approach, we examine Buddhism as an outsider looking in, and with the second approach we try to understand what the Refuges mean from the point of view of a Buddhist. We shall take the second approach first.

What meaning does the Refuge have for a Buddhist? The concept of 'refuge' is fundamental in Buddhism and is connected with something that also applies within every spiritual tradition and even to every individual person: the need to find purpose in our lives. What is it that I really want? What is the highest goal that I want to realize? What is my ultimate dream? Asking ourselves these kinds of questions can enable us to identify our purpose, whatever it is that we want most to achieve, that would benefit ourselves and others. Taking Refuge is an answer to these questions.

The meaning of the Refuge can thus be stated in two main points:

- First, by taking refuge a Buddhist is consciously identifying nirvana or enlightenment as his or her ultimate aim. This means accepting the Buddha's analysis of what true happiness is, and therefore committing oneself to finding happiness not in anything external like a good job, money, love, friends, music, sport and so forth, the way many people do; but through inner development and transformation.
- Second, the basic meaning of taking refuge is that an individual is making a personal commitment to follow the Buddha's teachings and put them into practice. This includes following the external manifestations of the Buddhist religion – the scriptures, the practices, the festivals and so forth. In other words, taking refuge is deciding on Buddhism as the religious path one chooses to follow in order to attain one's aim in life.

The notion of a 'refuge' here does not mean a place to hide or a place to escape to. Taking refuge in the Buddha, for example, does not mean that one is pleading or praying to the Buddha as a saviour. Rather, taking refuge is more like making a decision based on the conviction that we all have the potential to attain nirvana or enlightenment. It is as though Buddhists see themselves as 'refugees' from *samsara,* the endless cycle of suffering, and by taking refuge they are trying to make their new home in *nirvana* and find a life of peace that is totally free from all suffering.

The Dalai Lama relates the Refuges to the Four Noble Truths to show how important intelligent understanding is to refuge in Buddhism.

> *"If your understanding of the Four Noble Truths arises from deep reflection, then you will gain a profound admiration for the Dharma, which is the true Refuge, and you will also develop a conviction in the possibility of actualizing the Dharma within yourself. On the basis of such a conviction you will be able to develop genuine devotion in the Buddha, the master who showed you the path, and you will also have a deep respect for the Sangha members who are your spiritual companions on the path.*
>
> *If your understanding of the Three Jewels is based on a realization of the Four Noble Truths that is as profound as this, then whenever you think of Buddha, Dharma and Sangha they will come alive for you with renewed freshness. This is what is meant by Going for Refuge."*[53]

While taking refuge in the Buddha, Dharma and Sangha is a way of placing one's reliance on these three principles, at the same time the deeper level of understanding is that one is ultimately placing one's reliance and trust in one's own enlightenment potential. This is called 'buddha nature' in Mahayana. Refuge is not so much a relationship of dependence on external principles, it is a way of taking responsibility for one's enlightenment. From the Buddhist point of view, supreme happiness is not to be found in anything outside of us, but deep within. As the Buddha said: "You are the master, you are the Refuge."[54]

He advised his disciples to be 'a refuge unto themselves' because dependence on anyone else is always unsatisfactory in the end. Each person needs to work with him or herself in order to attain nirvana. The Buddha, the Dharma and members of the Sangha can all help to show the way to follow, but each person has to tread the path himself or herself. Going for Refuge therefore gives Buddhists a sense of direction and meaning in life. It offers them the goal of ultimate happiness as well as the practical means through which they can find that happiness.

In terms of how Buddhists lead their everyday lives, the most important commitment entailed by taking Refuge is not to cause harm. This means making every effort not to harm others or oneself in any way.

Why Buddhists take refuge

There are three different motivations for taking refuge in the Three Jewels which correspond to the Three Vehicles.

- First, one might take refuge in the hope of better rebirth. One fears being trapped in the lower realms of *samsara,* the endless cycle of suffering and rebirth, where suffering is at its most intense. The Buddha offers a way out of such a terrible existence. This motivation is based on a sophisticated understanding of life and death, whereby one's distaste for suffering is so acute that one has no hesitation in doing everything one can to be free of it. This motivation also applies to the wish to be free of suffering in the present life, too.
- Second, one's motivation could be based not only on fear of suffering in the next life but also on the fear of getting stuck in happiness. As one master put it, "human beings can endure a lot of suffering but very little happiness".[55] Once we achieve the happiness of the higher realms of samsara, it is easy to become attached to blissful states and then they become another limitation. To avoid this, Mahayana Buddhists are especially keen to be free of samsara altogether – both fortunate and unfortunate states – and to attain enlightenment.
- Mahayana Buddhists can also take refuge because they are motivated by the 'vast attitude of *bodhichitta*', meaning that they aspire to attain complete enlightenment both for their own sake and for the sake of all beings. The sight of so many beings plunged in the depths of suffering is unbearable, and they spontaneously wish to liberate every single one.
- From a Vajrayana perspective, one takes refuge out of fear of distorted or 'impure' perception. The understanding is that the root of our suffering lies in our inability to see things as they really are, and from this ignorance arise all the negative emotions and harmful actions that produce suffering.

How Buddhists take refuge

There are two main ways in which Buddhists take refuge. The first takes place in a Refuge Ceremony. Generally, such ceremonies are held in a local monastery in the presence of several monks who serve as witnesses. In Buddhist countries, children generally take refuge in this way when they are around seven years old. This ceremony is the formal occasion when one commits to following the Buddhist path, that is, to becoming a Buddhist.

During the Refuge Ceremony, a lock of hair is cut symbolising that one is giving up vanity and worldly values to prioritise spiritual values. The individual is also given a refuge name, in much the same way as Catholics are given a name at Confirmation. The intention to participate in a Refuge Ceremony is to follow Buddhism until one has reached enlightenment. However, if later in life one decides to abandon Buddhism for another religion, or for no religion at all, one is free to do so and there are no sanctions against this.

During the Refuge Ceremony one recites the Three Refuges three times each:

"I take refuge in the Buddha,
I take refuge in the Dharma,
I take refuge in the Sangha".

This 'Refuge formula' was developed by the Buddha and in its ancient Pali form the words are:

Buddham saranam gacchami
Dhammam saranam gacchami
Sangham saranam gacchami

The second way in which Buddhists take Refuge is by reciting the Refuge formula each day as a reminder of their original commitment. For example, morning and evening prayer ceremonies in monasteries usually begin with three recitations of the Refuge formula.

The Buddha

Theravada understanding

When Theravadins take refuge in the Buddha, they acknowledge his historical role in communicating the Dharma, and express their respect and gratitude to him. They are also recognizing him as their ultimate teacher and guide, and recalling that his life serves as an example that all Buddhists can follow. This Refuge does not entail worshipping the Buddha in any way. The Buddha is seen as a human being and is respected because he succeeded in attaining enlightenment and showed us the way to do so ourselves.

Theravada emphasizes taking refuge in the historical Buddha Shakyamuni. In other words, the Buddha in Theravada refers to the person who founded Buddhism in human history. However, to a certain extent this tradition also understands Refuge in terms of past and future buddhas as well, and in terms of the principle of enlightenment. In this sense, taking refuge in the Buddha also points to honouring the principle of wisdom and enlightenment within each one of us, a principle that is understood to be supremely embodied by the Buddha.

Mahayana understanding

The Mahayana understanding of the Buddha is based on its 'three body' or *Trikaya* doctrine (see Chapter 7). According to this doctrine, one takes refuge not only in the Buddha Shakyamuni but in other Nirmanakaya buddhas of the past and the future and, most significantly, in Sambhogakaya buddhas as well.

Mahayana is an umbrella term for many different schools and certain Mahayana schools have unique ways of understanding refuge in the Buddha. For example, the Pure Land schools of China and Japan emphasize primarily or exclusively taking refuge in Buddha Amitabha rather than Buddha Shakyamuni. In Ch'an or Zen, the emphasis is on taking Refuge in the buddha nature *(tathagatagarbha)* within rather than in Buddha as an external figure.

Vajrayana understanding

The Vajrayana schools share the same understanding of this Refuge as the Mahayana schools. In addition, Vajrayana practitioners take refuge in their spiritual master. This is because the master is seen as a living embodiment of the qualities of the enlightened mind and of all Three Refuges. The master represents the Buddha since he is one's guide and teacher; his words express the truth of the Dharma; and, as a human being, he is also one's closest spiritual friend in life. In this way he or she embodies all three Refuges.

In the Tibetan tradition it is said that the master or *lama* is even kinder than the Buddha himself because he is physically here to train and guide us according to our individual needs. He also has the ability to make the Dharma accessible to us, so we know how to apply it to our own situation and to our own mind. Without a living master, enlightenment would be virtually impossible to achieve. So, in Vajrayana, one first takes Refuge in the master, then in the Buddha, Dharma and Sangha.

The statue of the Buddha

Buddha statue

The statue of the Buddha has become a familiar image in our world. He is usually depicted sitting in meditation, but one also finds statues of him teaching, standing up or lying down on his right side at the moment of his passing away. This classic portrayal of the Buddha dates back to around 250 BCE when Greek art had an influence upon central Asian and Indian art. Before then the Buddha was never portrayed in human form. His enlightenment was represented symbolically, mainly by stupas. The Greek-inspired image of the Buddha is not seen as a realistic depiction of what he actually looked like as a human being, rather it, too, is entirely symbolic – symbolic of the wisdom and compassion and peace and perfection of enlightenment.

When Buddhists express devotion in front of statues of the Buddha in their temples and on their shrines, they do not believe they are worshipping him either as an idol or as a human being. Rather, the statue is there as a reminder of the qualities and virtues of enlightenment that Buddhists seek to attain. Furthermore, many statues are so beautiful it is believed that they may inspire those qualities and virtues in those who see them. Buddhists express their devotion to the Buddha in various ways. They may offer candles or incense; and they may bow three times. All these practices can be understood within the context of what it means for a Buddhist to take Refuge in the Buddha.

Vajrayana has a special understanding of the value of Buddha statues. It is believed that great Buddhist masters can infuse a statue with transformational blessings so that the statue becomes a 'live' presence. These blessings can then benefit devotees.

The Dharma

Some meanings of the term 'Dharma'

The word *dharma* (Sanskrit) or *dhamma* (Pali) has many different meanings.

The following meanings are relevant to the Buddhist Refuge.

1. Dharma denotes the universal truth, the laws or order inherent in nature. This truth or order has no beginning or end. It exists whether human beings are aware of it or not. All Indian religions share a belief in universal truth and cosmic order.
2. Dharma specifically denotes the teachings of Buddha Shakyamuni and, in particular, the record of those teachings contained in the various collections of scriptures. The Buddhist understanding is that what the Buddha taught was no other than the universal truth.
3. Dharma is a term used for the path that one follows when one applies and practises the teachings of the Buddha. This meaning is especially emphasized in the Refuges, so that taking refuge in the Dharma means, above all, following the Buddhist path.
4. Dharma also refers to the personal realization of the truths of Buddhism attained through learning the teachings, reflecting on them and meditating on them.
5. In English, Dharma is commonly used as a generic word meaning 'Buddhism'. Sometimes the expression 'Buddha Dharma' is used.

When one takes refuge in the Dharma, then, the understanding is that the Buddha's teachings are there to be heard and read, studied and understood, practised in formal sessions as well as in everyday life, and finally they are to be fully realized so that the practitioner comes to embody them him or herself.

It is possible to argue that the Dharma is the most important of the three Refuges, especially since the scriptures quote the Buddha as saying:

He who sees the Dharma sees me; he who sees me sees the Dharma.[56]

To understand the nature and significance of the Buddha is to understand his teaching, and by understanding his teaching we come to understand who the Buddha really is. The key that opens the meaning of all Three Refuges is therefore an understanding of the Dharma.

The Mahayana understanding

All schools and traditions of Buddhism share a common understanding of the meaning of this refuge. The main point that differs from one tradition to another is the precise composition of what is accepted as the body of scriptures (see Chapter 8). However, in Mahayana there is an emphasis on taking Refuge in Dharma as truth, that is, as the universal truth, and not necessarily restricting oneself to the words of the Buddhist scriptures or those of Buddha Shakyamuni. Dharma as universal truth is the meaning behind the words. Since the ultimate truth is beyond words, the use of words to express it can become a hindrance rather than a help to understanding. In this context, refuge in the Dharma will emphasize Dharma in the sense of practice and realization of the teaching (meaning 4) rather than the scriptures themselves (meaning 2).

The Three Higher Trainings

When the Dharma is spoken of as a path it is often presented in terms of what are called the Three Higher Trainings, namely moral discipline, meditation and wisdom. Taken together the Three Trainings comprise the complete path to enlightenment, and all three are necessary to reach the goal. Nikaya Buddhism and Mahayana Buddhism describe their respective paths in different ways, but both the Eightfold path of Nikaya Buddhism and the Bodhisattva Path of Mahayana share the same basic structure of the Three Trainings. They are therefore a very useful framework for understanding the Buddhist approach to enlightenment.

Respect for the Dharma

What does 'taking Refuge' in the Dharma mean precisely? While Refuge in the Buddha primarily means feeling gratitude, appreciation and respect for what the Buddha achieved and gave us, in the case of the Dharma, Refuge is a matter of developing a fundamental trust in the teachings and a personal commitment to understanding them and practising them.

Buddhists are not required to have uncritical trust in the Buddha's teachings or to develop blind faith in the truth of what he said. On the contrary, they are very much encouraged to use their intelligence to think through the arguments for themselves, and to put the teachings to the test by reflecting and meditating on them. In this way, every individual personally experiences for themselves how true these truths are. Taking refuge in the Dharma therefore includes a commitment to engaging in this process of discovery.

Taking refuge in the Dharma is therefore not a form of escapism. The Buddhist approach is not to surrender one's intelligence or one's ability to reason, and to fall into blind belief in dogmatic truths. Refuge in the Dharma entails personal effort and discipline, and a willingness to learn and to change. It is an active process, not a way of avoiding responsibility.

The Sangha

The fourfold sangha

In the West, our image of Buddhist monks tends to be that they sit in meditation virtually all day long. Many people think that monks remain within the monastery walls and have little or no contact with the rest of the community. Since they do not take ordinary jobs and earn money we imagine there is nothing for them to do but meditate! In addition, many people in the West imagine that all Buddhists are monks. It is surprising how many people believe that to be a Buddhist means you have to give up your possessions and all your attachments to life – which means, becoming a monk. Some even think that becoming a Buddhist means having to give up sex entirely. All these views are mistaken.

Sangha is the word for the community of those who follow the Buddhist path. Very often, sangha refers to the monastic community – the monks and nuns who have abandoned worldly life to lead an exemplary life of virtue. But these days the term refers to laymen and laywomen as well. Laypeople are ordinary people who follow a religion but who have jobs, families and other social responsibilities. This is known as **the fourfold sangha: monks, nuns, laymen and laywomen.** In almost every country where Buddhism is practised, a follower has the choice of either being a householder or taking the special commitment of becoming a monastic. Buddhists include both monastics and laypeople.

The role of monastics in Theravada

Monks and nuns play an extremely important role in Buddhist societies. The practice of ordaining people into monastic life was initiated by the Buddha himself, and the rules they follow were set out by the Buddha in what later became the Vinaya scriptures. The authority of monasticism as an institution is therefore linked to its antiquity and to the authority of the Buddha.

First and foremost, monastics maintain Buddhism as a living religion. They study the scriptures, practise meditation every day, teach Buddhism to others, perform ceremonies and rituals, and offer advice according to Buddhist values. Furthermore, in their personal lives they are expected to uphold the ethical values of Buddhism and manifest the qualities that are to be developed on the path. In other words, monks and nuns are living examples of the religion. Buddhists usually consider that without them, their religion would simply be reduced to a collection of words in books. It follows that by taking Refuge in the Sangha, a layperson is acknowledging the vital role that monastics play, not only for the continuation of the religion as a whole but for the welfare of the community.

Being of exemplary conduct, members of the Sangha are worthy of respect and of gifts. Indeed, they are thought of as an excellent 'field of merit'. The idea is that, generally speaking, one gains merit or virtue by any act of generosity, but just as a seed planted in better ground yields better fruit, so a gift made to a virtuous person brings greater merit. Buddhists take Refuge in the Sangha because they appreciate the way monastics benefit the world by offering this special opportunity to gain abundant and purifying merit.

On a practical level, laypeople take refuge in the monastic sangha by honouring them with respectful behaviour, by supporting them with gifts of food, clothing and medicines, and by relying on them for advice and encouragement.

The Mahayana understanding

Refuge in the sangha is understood and practised quite differently in Mahayana, and there is variation in practice from one Mahayana school to another. Mahayana generally accepts the classification of the fourfold sangha, and the distinction is made between monastics and laypeople. Even though Mahayana is said to place more emphasis than Nikaya Buddhism on the status of laypeople, in practice monastics have tended to be more highly respected than laypeople in Mahayana communities.

The big difference in Mahayana concerns the nature of monasticism: the role of monks, their way of life, the discipline they follow and their relation to the larger community. In China and especially in Japan, the Vinaya evolved and changed as Buddhism became established. In Japan some Buddhist schools such as True Pure Land have no monks at all and instead have priests who are allowed to marry and have families, have jobs and earn money. They live as householders and perform their priestly duties on certain occasions only. They are therefore integrated into the community in quite a different way to a Theravadin monk. In Soto Zen, however, monks may live a communal life of poverty and simplicity akin to the lifestyle of Theravadin monastics, but in both Soto and Rinzai Zen Buddhist teachers also have the option to marry.

The other key difference in the Mahayana understanding of Refuge in the Sangha is that bodhisattvas are included within the idea of sangha. This refers to Sambhogakaya buddhas and bodhisattvas in whom one can take refuge. In doing so, the practitioner aspires to emulate them and become like them by developing their particular enlightened qualities, and he or she also prays to them for help and protection. So in Mahayana, the idea of sangha or spiritual community extends to those who no longer live on this Earth.

Conclusion

The question is often asked as to which of the Three Refuges is the most important. One answer to this is that all three are equally important. None of the Refuges are optional; a Buddhist takes Refuge in all three. However, the relationship between Buddha, Dharma and Sangha can be analysed in different ways to establish arguments that show that one or other of the Three Jewels has primacy over the others.

According to one argument, the Buddha must be the most important refuge because if it were not for him neither the Dharma nor the Sangha would exist at all. This logic establishes the Buddha's importance on the basis of the historical development of Buddhism. Another argument points out that in terms of someone's experience of the Buddhist religion, the Dharma is the most important Refuge. The Buddha himself has passed away and the core of the religion is now his teaching. The Sangha are those who follow that teaching. This reasoning is made from the point of view of a person encountering Buddhism now and whose conviction will be based on what they see as the truth of the teaching and the good example of those who follow it.

There is no single correct answer to this question from the Buddhist point of view, and it is very much up to each one of us to choose the reasoning we prefer.

Personal reflections

In times of difficulty and challenge, what do you usually turn to as your refuge?
What motivates anyone to take refuge in a spiritual path?

Main Points

- Buddhists express commitment to their religion by taking refuge in the Buddha, Dharma and Sangha — the Three Jewels.
- The three motivations for taking refuge are:

    1. fear of the suffering of the lower realms of samsara;
    2. fear of both the suffering and happiness of samsara;
    3. fear of one's own ignorance and negative emotions which are the causes of all one's suffering.

- Taking refuge in the Buddha means expressing gratitude and respect for his enlightened teaching.
- Taking refuge in the Dharma is an undertaking to study, practise and fully embody the Buddha's teaching.
- Taking refuge in the Sangha means honouring the role and authority of monastics, and in Mahayana extends to honouring Sambhogakaya buddhas and bodhisattvas, too.
- Taking refuge entails a commitment not to harm oneself or others.
- In Mahayana, the inner meaning of taking refuge is a commitment to developing one's inner strength and potential for enlightenment and to develop trust in the truth wherever one finds it, whether within oneself or in the world.

Chapter 15

BUDDHIST ETHICS

The topic of ethics touches on Buddhism as a way of life. We examine ethics in Theravada Buddhism in terms of the Eightfold Path, and in Mahayana Buddhism in terms of the Bodhisattva Path. This chapter also explores questions around the application of Buddhist ethics in the modern world.

With gentleness overcome anger.
With generosity overcome meanness.
With truth overcome deceit.
Speak the truth; give whatever you can; never be angry.
Dhammapada 223

The thorny question of moral discipline

As soon as Buddhists talk about moral guidelines and precepts, we might feel that Buddhism is just another way of oppressing people and limiting their freedom. Maybe we think moral guidelines of any kind are old-fashioned; they might have suited our parents and grandparents, but they don't apply to the modern world. Alternatively, we might fear that we can never meet the high standards of behaviour taught by the Buddha, and that Buddhism is so demanding that it must be for saints and not for ordinary people.

In Buddhism, the main point about moral discipline seems to be that rules by themselves are not enough; it is essential to have some understanding of *why* they are there and what benefits they bring. The Buddha went to great lengths to explain exactly this sort of detail so people could understand that moral discipline is about reducing negative karma and cultivating positive karma. The guidelines are there to help people, not to give them a hard time. What is interesting is that Buddhist ethics have an unexpected flavour: rules are not rigid, perfection is not required, and there is no Supreme Being to judge and to punish. Moral discipline is not a burden to carry, it is something positive. As the Buddha said:

> *Set your heart on doing good. Do it over and over again, and you will be filled with joy.*[57]

The word for moral discipline in Sanskrit is *shila* which literally means 'cooling'. The prospect of cooling may not appeal to people living in the Himalayas, in Canada or the north of Scotland where the climate is sometimes cold enough already, but it is appealing for people in India where the heat can be suffocating. Indian poetry often speaks of pain as being firey and hot, and pleasure as being sweet and cool. In the same way, ethics are meant to bring peace and ease.

They help to cool the fires of the Three Poisons that burn inside us; they bring a sense of relief. "Having knowledge of the precepts is like removing the darkness from the room so that you can see things clearly".[58]

The Buddhist teachings set out the moral guidance to follow yet Buddhism is far from being a moralistic religion, prescribing a set of commandments or laws that all true Buddhists must adhere to. The guidelines are never dogmatic. That is why the Tibetan word for ethics, *tsultrim,* can be translated as 'appropriate action'. In the Mahayana approach, actions are appropriate or inappropriate according to the situation and circumstances, so virtue isn't simply about following rules but about behaving in harmony with the Dharma on each occasion.

Paradoxically, the purpose of moral discipline is to make us happier and more free. Since our actions are so powerful in determining whether we are happy or unhappy, we all need a certain spiritual education to learn which actions are to be avoided and which actions are to be cultivated. And if we are to confess and regret any harmful actions we have done in the past, in order to purify them, we need to understand which actions need confessing. This is not simply a matter of learning what's right and what's wrong; it's about learning to see life from a spiritual perspective. If we have that spiritual understanding then everything flows from that, and everything hangs together.

The Principles of Buddhist Ethics

In Nikaya Buddhism, the fourth Noble Truth is the Eightfold Path and it sets out the main characteristics of the Buddhist way of life. The Buddha presented this path as the Middle Way, a way of life that does not fall into extreme views, or extremes of behaviour, but which cultivates balance and moderation. Unlike hedonism and utilitarianism, Buddhist ethics are not based on the pursuit of pleasure, whether sensual or otherwise, nor do they encourage extremes of deprivation, poverty or self-sacrifice, unlike asceticism. In the spirit of the 'middle way' approach, all the various moral guidelines in Buddhism should therefore be taken responsibly but with a light touch.

Ethics is about how we behave and how we act in everyday life. An ethical system, whether or not it is based on religion, offers a basic set of moral values and then suggests or prescribes the types of action that are encouraged and the types of action that are discouraged. Walpola Rahula emphasizes that the key values underlying all ethical conduct in Buddhism are those of love and compassion.

> *Ethical conduct (shila) is built on the vast conception of universal love and compassion for all living beings, on which the Buddha's teaching is based. It is regrettable that many scholars forget this great ideal of the Buddha's teaching, and indulge in only dry philosophical and metaphysical divagations when they talk and write about Buddhism. The Buddha gave his teaching "for the good of the many, for the happiness of the many, out of compassion for the world".*[59]

The Buddha emphasizes this when he says: "In this world hate never yet dispelled hate. Only love dispels hate."[60] Love and compassion are the prime motivators of ethical conduct in Buddhism.

Chapter 12 explains what types of action are thought of as good and what are considered bad: the main criterion is related to intention, and the determining factor is whether or not one is acting out of selfish desire and craving, out of anger or hatred, or out of mindlessness or confusion. Any actions that are motivated by these three Mental Poisons will, in the end, cause suffering to oneself and to others. On the other hand, if actions are motivated by love and compassion they bring well-being and happiness to oneself and to others.

In Buddhism, ethical behaviour depends ultimately on the mind and not on the body yet the Buddha did give specific advice about which actions are generally harmful and should be avoided. On the basis of this advice, Buddhism has developed various types of ethical guidance that Buddhists do their best to follow. It is important to note, however, that in Buddhism ethical rules are never rigid. It is accepted that everyone will do their best and there is a general atmosphere of moral tolerance.

The ethical disciplines of Buddhism can be divided into two: the guidelines for laypeople and the guidelines for ordained monks and nuns.

Lay morality

When one becomes a Buddhist, one begins by taking the Three Refuges: Refuge in the Buddha, Dharma and Sangha. The main commitment this entails in terms of behaviour is that one refrains from harming others and adopts the approach of **non-violence** (ahimsa). Non-violence can be said to be another of the most basic, fundamental principles of Buddhist ethics.

Lay people can take one or several of the **Five Precepts**, which are five basic vows that underpin the Buddhist way of life. The Five Precepts are:

- **I vow to refrain from killing**
  Killing refers not only to human beings but to all living beings, even mosquitos, spiders and cockroaches.

- **I vow to refrain from taking what is not freely given**
  'Taking what is not freely given' means stealing in any of its forms, not just stealing possessions but, for example, wasting your employer's time or infringing copyright. Stealing can happen openly or through deceit, for example through cheating.

- **I vow to refrain from misusing sexuality**
  Misusing sexuality is generally interpreted as using sexual relationships in a way that causes harm to someone else. This is very broad and can include adultery, incest, rape, paedophilia and so forth.

- **I vow to refrain from harmful speech**
  False or harmful speech includes lying, slander, harsh words and idle gossip.

- **I vow to refrain from taking intoxicants**
  The reason that intoxicants are discouraged is because they cloud the mind and weaken the judgement and, as a result, one might perform actions that one will later regret. Intoxicants include alcohol, leisure drugs, the misuse of prescription drugs and other substances (like glue), and some modern teachers also include tobacco because it is considered harmful to both body and mind. Lay Buddhists may drink alcohol socially but they refrain from drinking to excess.

Buddhism also encourages positive attitudes and actions. Love and compassion for all beings, tolerance, patience, forgiveness and contentment are all cultivated by Buddhists. In his advice to a young man called Sigala, found in the Pali Canon[61], the Buddha explained how this positive approach can be applied in daily life within the framework of **Six Relationships**.

1. **Take care of your family.** Respect, listen to and obey your parents, and look after them when they are old. Look after your children, see they are well educated, find appropriate work and marry well.
2. **Take care of your marriage.** Be loving and faithful to your partner and work hard at your side of the partnership. Husbands and wives should be fair to each other, trust each other and not squander joint money. They should also enjoy themselves together, and the Buddha even suggests that a husband should buy his wife presents and jewellery.
3. **Keep good company** and choose the right friends. Keep away from those who will have a bad influence on you. Be kind to your friends, keep promises, help them in times of trouble.
4. **Develop good relationships between teachers and students.** Respect your teachers, appreciate their help, be polite to them and work hard. Teachers, in turn, should respect their pupils and give them the best education possible.

5. **Develop good relationships between employers and employees,** or workers and management. Employers should take care of their workers, give them decent wages and fair work conditions. Employees should respect their employer, work hard and not waste time. Both should work harmoniously together and not complain about each other but praise each other.
6. **Choose a good career** and earn money in a wholesome way. To have money is not bad or immoral in itself, but it should be used wisely to help family, friends and community. This guideline relates to Right Livelihood in the Eightfold Path: choosing a job that does not harm or exploit others, and that does not require one to break the Five Precepts.

The Buddha's advice was very practical, and he often gave the reasons behind his guidance so people would be convinced. For example, he said that drinking alcohol is harmful because it wastes money, leads to quarrels, impairs your health, gives you a bad reputation, leads you to do immoral things you will later regret, and weakens the brain. As for gambling, he said it's harmful because when you lose, you lose money, and when you win you make enemies; in addition, nobody will trust you, friends despise you and nobody will want to be married to you.

In the framework of the Eightfold Path, ethical conduct includes three factors which overlap with the Five Precepts and Six Relationships:

1. **Right Action** encourages honourable and honest conduct. In particular, it holds we should not kill, steal, misuse sexuality or take intoxicants. In addition, we should not engage in activities that are considered dishonest, such as gambling.
2. **Right Speech** means refraining from:
    a. telling lies
    b. backbiting and slander, and any talk that brings about disunity, disharmony or hatred between people
    c. harsh, rude, impolite words, or speech that is malicious and deliberately sets out to hurt someone
    d. idle gossip and useless chatter which waste time and misuse the power of speech.
3. **Right Livelihood** means choosing a profession or a job that does not harm others, and that does not oblige one to break any of the Five Precepts. The

type of jobs one might wish to avoid include: trading in weapons or drugs, selling alcohol, killing animals (e.g. working in a slaughter house or as a fisherman); and being a lawyer, politician, journalist or salesman if this involves lying.

Lay morality rests on the principle that lay people aim to minimise their bad actions and maximise their good actions so they can have a better rebirth. Most lay people do not expect to attain enlightenment in this life, mainly because they are so busy with worldly responsibilities. Their goal is to gain a better rebirth and morality is indispensable for this. In summary, lay Buddhists who follow the Precepts and guidelines will be responsible citizens, responsible family members, and will try to be kind, respectful and appreciative of everyone they relate to. They will lead a life of moderation and try to cultivate tolerance and a non-violent attitude. Buddhist moral conduct aims to bring about harmony and happiness both for the individual and for society. If everyone lived like this maybe society would be more harmonious and peaceful.

Monastic morality

In most traditional Buddhist societies, Buddhists have the option to become a monastic and if they decide to take this step they follow a strict lifestyle. Like laypeople, monastics take the Three Refuges and all Five Precepts. As soon as they ordain as a novice they take an additional five precepts:

- To abstain from food after midday
- To abstain from a luxurious bed (i.e. high off the floor – a sign of wealth)
- To abstain from entertainment (music, dancing, shows, TV)
- To abstain from personal adornments (i.e. jewellery, perfume)
- To abstain from handling gold or silver (i.e. money).

This means that, if they follow the Vinaya faithfully, Buddhist monastics do not eat after midday, but they are allowed to drink. One reason given for this rule is that if one over-eats, or eats before going to sleep, this makes the mind sleepy and is not conducive to meditation. Monastics take no alcohol at all. They avoid places of entertainment, partly because they waste precious time and partly because they can lead to sexual temptation. The sexual misconduct precept is interpreted as celibacy, so they take a vow to refrain from any type of sexual relationship.

As we can see from the list above, some of the monastic rules are culture-bound, in other words they relate to the social conditions of ancient India and may be difficult to follow today. For example, in the Buddha's day money was not common and communities mostly traded by barter; and in village communities it was the custom to sleep at floor level and not in a bed on legs. As a result, a few monastic rules have been adapted so they apply to modern conditions.

A fully ordained monk in the Theravada tradition takes 227 vows altogether. They are found in the Vinaya. Some of these relate to the practicalities of everyday life in a community: taking care of sick monks, wearing soft shoes, not preaching to a woman alone. Others relate to genuinely moral actions. The rules are recited once a fortnight by the whole community at a ceremony called the *Uposatha*, and if any monk has infringed a rule he is expected to make a confession publicly to the community. Senior monks will give punishments according to rules that are laid down, and only in very serious cases can a monk be expelled from the monastery and asked to disrobe and become a layperson again. There are four actions that lead to expulsion: sexual intercourse, serious theft, murder (or encouraging someone to commit suicide) and making false claims about having supernatural powers. Another group of less serious actions leads to temporary expulsion, while for lesser offences monks forfeit certain rights.

In Buddhism there is no equivalent to the ex-communication possible in Christianity, where certain actions lead to the culprit's being forced out of the religion altogether. A Buddhist monk can only be expelled from the monastic order, not from being a Buddhist practitioner, and he could continue following his religion as a householder or layman.

Women had inferior social and religious status in the Buddha's day, and the Buddha was in fact very radical in accepting women as monastics at all. As a result, however, nuns have more rules than monks and some of the additional rules reflect the fact that all monks, however young and new, had higher status than a nun. The nuns' rules may have been the only acceptable way of dealing with the social beliefs of the time, but they remain the same today. Nevertheless, many monastic communities have significantly improved conditions for nuns over recent years.

In general, Buddhist monastics do their best to follow all their vows and rules strictly, not only for their own spiritual training but also because they have a duty to provide an example to the wider community. If their discipline becomes lax then laypeople will no longer respect them and may withhold their material support, so the system has built-in safeguards against moral laziness and corruption.

Mahayana ethics

The principles of Mahayana ethics are basically the same as for Theravada and other schools of Nikaya Buddhism. The key difference is *bodhichitta*: the realization of ultimate wisdom and limitless compassion which gives rise to the altruistic path of the bodhisattva. Ultimate wisdom means the realization of emptiness *(shunyata)*, and the limitless compassion of the bodhisattva encompasses the wish to bring all beings to enlightenment as well as the commitment to do everything in one's power to ensure this happens. It is because all actions are motivated by *bodhichitta* that they are selfless and are therefore called 'transcendental actions' or 'perfected actions' *(paramitas)*.

Ethical actions in Mahayana are those that are free of any notion of someone who is acting and someone else who is benefiting, and a virtuous action linking the two. Ethical actions transcend this subject/object thinking altogether; they arise from the pure motivation that is possible only when one has realized no self *(anatman)*.

From the Mahayana point of view, it is the motivation of *bodhichitta* that demarcates an action as ethical. The six *paramitas* of generosity, moral discipline, patience, diligence, meditation and wisdom are all expressions of *bodhichitta* in action.

Skilful means (upaya)

Characteristic of Mahayana and Vajrayana ethics is the use of skilful means or *upaya*, which depends upon the ability of the bodhisattva always to know the right action to take in order to help beings towards liberation in any given circumstance. Skilful means is only possible when it is based on both compassion and wisdom together, not only on the wish to help but on the wisdom to know how best to help. We might say that *bodhichitta* is what is meant by skilful means in Mahayana; any action truly motivated by *bodhichitta* will naturally be of spiritual benefit to others.

The most important implication of the idea of skilful means for Buddhist ethics is that the bodhisattva is free to perform *any* action that will achieve the goal of liberating others. The morality of an action is therefore determined by its ultimate outcome and not be the nature of the action itself. This means that the bodhisattva is not constrained by the ethical guidelines of Buddhism that were set out above. Even actions that in any other circumstance would be considered harmful – such as lying, stealing and even killing – could be used as skilful means in a particular situation provided they were motivated by *bodhichitta*. Buddhist teachers caution that the circumstances that might require someone to go against conventional morality and apply skilful means are very rare. Conventional methods should always be tried first. Nevertheless, the principle of skilful means explains why Mahayana Buddhism tends to be more flexible than Theravada in adapting traditional guidelines to modern situations.

A contemporary example can be used to illustrate the principle of skilful means. Suppose an advanced bodhisattva with tremendous compassion and wisdom had been alive in Hitler's day and could foresee that Hitler would cause great suffering and death to many people. It is conceivable that such a bodhisattva might have applied skilful means in order to prevent Hitler from doing this – thereby saving millions of people from suffering, and also saving Hitler from the bad karmic consequences of his own actions. We might imagine that skilful means might involve killing Hitler himself, which in any other situation would be a harmful thing to do, but in this case could be seen as a moral action according to Mahayana ethics. Such pre-emptive action, though, is only moral if it is genuinely motivated by the highest and most selfless compassion and wisdom, totally free of any hint of self-interest or aggression.

The story of the burning house

There is a well-known story illustrating skilful means in the *Lotus Sutra*. The story goes that there once lived an old man who was weak in health and strength but quite rich and well-to-do. He had a large house, but the house was old and in a state of disrepair, with a thatched roof and only one door. One day a fire suddenly breaks out inside the house and the building begins to burn from all sides. The old man manages to get out but then realizes that his young sons are still inside busy playing with their toys. He is beside himself with fear. He knows that they are too young to understand what fire is and what danger they are in, and this is why they continue to play unawares.

So the old man cries out to his sons. "Come here, my boys, come out of the house! It is burning fiercely. If you don't come out soon you will all be burned." But the children take no notice of him, they are neither alarmed nor terrified and carry on playing. Next the old man thinks of a plan to lure them out, and he calls out to them to come out quickly because he has lots of beautiful new toys for them – in particular bullock carts, goat carts and deer carts. When they hear their father's words all the children rush out of the house to see their toys. And as soon as he is assured they are safe and sound, the father takes them down to the village and buys them the best toys money can buy – ox carts!

What should we learn from this story? Was the old man wrong to lie to his boys, and tell them he had lots of toys for them when this was not the case? The Buddha says in the Sutra that he was not wrong, because he had tried conventional means and they didn't work, and this was the only way he could save their lives.

Furthermore, this story is seen as symbolic. The burning house represents samsara, the fire represents the fire of the passions or mental poisons, the only door out of the house is the Buddhist path to liberation. The children's unawareness in the face of danger represents our ignorance of the causes of suffering. The old man is like the Buddha who inspires us to renounce samsara and certain death.[62]

Both the Theravada and Mahayana models of ethics place ethical conduct firmly within the framework of a graduated spiritual path. However, some Mahayana schools place little emphasis on the gradual approach and express ethics differently. Two of these schools are Zen Buddhism and Pure Land Buddhism.

Ethics in Zen Buddhism

Dogen (1200-1253) established the Soto school of Zen in Japan, and he emphasized a strict and simple life of monastic discipline. After many centuries during which Buddhist monasteries had become rather prosperous and comfortable, he advocated a monastic life of poverty and simplicity where the focus was on spiritual practice and the effort to be of benefit to others. This was part of a return to the true Buddhism taught by the Buddha in ancient India.

Soto Zen sees both *zazen* meditation and ethics as ways to make manifest one's inherent buddha nature. If people already have the buddha nature *(tathagatagarbha)* then why do they need to exert themselves to attain buddhahood? Ethical conduct and meditation are not methods to attain enlightenment but are themselves enlightenment; they are ways of expressing the buddha nature that is inherent in us.

The Rinzai school of Zen, founded in Japan by Eisai (1141-1215), combines the principles of skilful means *(upaya)* and buddha nature *(tathagatagarbha)* into a distinctively dramatic form of Buddhism. Rinzai masters emphasize daily discipline and *zazen* or sitting meditation and, in addition, the meeting of teacher and student achieved through *koan* practice. Students are given *koans* which are questions that cannot be answered through normal logical thinking; for example, 'What is the sound of one hand clapping?'. Rinzai Zen also fosters healing on a deep level through the practice of the arts and the use of the body in daily work *(samu)*. Students may also be asked to engage in intense exercises that might stretch them to their limits. All these are the skilful methods characteristic of Rinzai, based on the belief that peaceful meditation alone is not powerful enough to lead deluded beings to enlightenment. Rinzai methods are intended to induce sudden insights into enlightenment (*satori)* which are possible at any time because the buddha nature is always present within.

Ethics in True Pure Land Buddhism

Shinran (1173-1263), the founder of the school of True Pure Land also known as Shin Buddhism, was extremely sceptical about the Buddhist teachings on ethical conduct. He felt that human beings are helplessly full of passion and depravity, and they are ignorant of what is truly good and bad. Even in the case of those who try to follow a path of virtue, ethical action only becomes a source of pride and self-righteousness, and a cause for loss of faith in Amida Buddha. The only way to make spiritual progress is to put one's total reliance on the power and blessing of Amida Buddha.

Shinran criticised the Buddhist attitude of trying to earn merit or virtue by following moral guidelines. He even said: 'even a good man will be received in Buddha's land, how much more a bad man' emphasizing the mercy of Amida Buddha. Reliance on Amida Buddha helps followers to remain humble in the thought that they themselves don't have the power to effect the personal transformation necessary to attain enlightenment.

In Shin Buddhism, there is no monastic celibacy. A small number of married clergy perform certain rituals and ceremonies but they do not follow traditional monastic ethics based on the Vinaya. Discipline in Pure Land Buddhism is not expressed in terms of action, speech and livelihood but refers to the mental discipline of remembering the presence of Amida Buddha throughout one's everyday life. Although this sounds quite simple, it is not, because maintaining genuine devotion to Amida all day and every day requires tremendous mental effort and diligence.

Applied ethics

To illustrate how a Buddhist might approach some of the ethical problems of today, we will take the questions of abortion, vegetarianism and cloning as examples of how one can think things through from a Buddhist perspective. It is important to remember that Buddhist ethics vary considerably in emphasis from one tradition to another, so there is no single 'Buddhist' approach to any of these questions. All we can do is outline a range of possible approaches. Each situation is unique, so the points listed below are those that would be taken into account in coming to a decision.

Abortion

- A foetus is considered to be a living being in the sense that it is endowed with both a body and a mind. The karmic consequences of killing another being therefore apply to abortion.
- Motivation is important: if I abort my unborn baby for selfish reasons – the timing is inconvenient, I don't want to give up my career, I think I don't have the right circumstances to bring it up and so on – then this is an unethical act.
- There may be mitigating circumstances, such as when the mother's life is threatened by her pregnancy for medical reasons. This is a difficult case, since choosing abortion is tantamount to saying that the mother's life is more important than the life of the child and in Buddhism all lives are equally precious.
- If an abortion is carried out reluctantly for medical reasons, there are purification practices in Buddhism to counteract its karmic effects.

Vegetarianism

There are many different views on vegetarianism, which make it the subject of lively debate within Buddhism. As a monk, Buddha Shakyamuni would accept whatever food he was offered as alms and did not prescribe a vegetarian diet for his monks. It is interesting to note that Asian countries that are traditionally Buddhist are not culturally vegetarian.

- The Pure Land school in Japan does not consider ethical action to be as important as devotional practice to Amida Buddha, so it rapidly became very popular with fishermen. The Japanese eat a lot of fish because the geography of their country supports little agriculture.

- Theravadins are generally not vegetarians, and Tibetans live in a climate where vegetarianism is impractical.
- Buddhists consider that the karmic effects of eating meat and fish are quite different from the effects of slaughtering animals and fish for market. It is easy to eat a hamburger but how easy would you find it to slit the throat of a cow?
- Nevertheless, eating meat and fish is a way of participating in the chain of activities that cause animals to be killed for food, so there is some degree of karmic responsibility involved.
- Many Buddhists believe that vegetarianism is the only option if they are to be true to the principles of not killing and non-violence.
- Some Buddhists argue that modern methods used to raise and slaughter farm animals are highly insensitive to their physical and mental wellbeing, so they cause tremendous suffering to the animals and also produce unhealthy meat. They argue that vegetarianism is the only ethical option.
- Other Buddhists point out that vegetarianism is not an ethical solution because of the enormous number of insects killed through the use of pesticides on vegetable and fruit crops. Whatever one eats therefore entails some form of taking life. In Buddhism, insects are treated the same as animals: they are beings with minds, and one refrains from killing any animate being.
- The Dalai Lama has said he supports vegetarianism but occasionally eats meat on the medical advice of his doctors.

Cloning

There are two types of genetic cloning:

- **therapeutic cloning** is intended to produce an embryo that can be used to generate stem cells for medical purposes. Such embryos are not allowed to develop beyond 14 days which is the point at which scientists believe the ability to feel pain is formed.
- **reproductive cloning** is intended to produce a foetus that will grow into an individual animal or human.

How would a Buddhist decide whether or not cloning is a moral activity?

- Buddhists do not have problems with the idea that we are 'playing God' by creating life since they do not believe in a creator God. Cloning and other genetic engineering techniques are therefore not sacrilegious in the way they might be to followers of other faiths.

- Motivation will be the determining factor. In the case of reproductive cloning, if one chooses to clone a child to satisfy one's own selfish desire to have a child, then that would be unethical; whereas if one chooses cloning because it is a way of bearing children without passing on hereditary diseases such as cystic fibrosis, one could be acting out of compassion and the action would be ethical.
- In the case of therapeutic cloning, the question for Buddhists is whether or not an embryo can be considered a person or animal for the first 14 days of its life. Technically, this would depend on whether a consciousness has joined with the embryo or not, and it seems that the point in time when this occurs varies from case to case and is obviously difficult to determine. Some Buddhist masters say that it is possible that, in the first few days, an embryo is not a complete being with body and mind and that therefore this form of cloning may be ethical. If this were not the case, however, Buddhists would not wish to sacrifice the life of a foetus to aid the medical treatment of someone else since all lives are equally precious.

Classifying the Buddhist ethical system

Buddhist ethics can be considered an instance of **virtue ethics**, centred on the idea that the basis of morality is the development of good character traits or virtues which, in Aristotle's system for example, include intelligence, wisdom and the ability to discern between good and bad. Acting ethically is not merely a question of 'what should I do?' but more importantly a question of 'how should I be?' The Buddha did not place the emphasis on the idea of doing one's duty but rather on becoming a kind, compassionate and wise person, and then acting accordingly.

Peter Harvey[63] has argued that the Mahayana idea of skilful means *(upaya)* is similar to Christian **situation ethics** because it allows ethical principles to be overridden in certain situations in the name of wisdom and bodhichitta. Situation ethics was developed by Joseph Fletcher in 1966 in his book of that name and has become a prevalent view within the Protestant churches. Fletcher claims it offers a middle way between the extremes of legalism or divine command theory on the one hand, for which there can be no exceptions to the rule, and antinomianism on the other hand where there is no foundation at all with which we can evaluate our morality.

Situation ethics does not propose rules but rather suggests a guiding principle to decision making: that principle is love. Acting morally means acting in the most loving way in any given situation. Rather like the approach of *upaya* in Mahayana, situation ethics does not ignore or reject traditional values but is not bound by them. The difference is that, in Buddhism, only very advanced bodhisattvas are permitted to break with the traditional values, while situation ethics can be applied by anyone with a loving heart.

Another possible way of classifying Buddhist ethics in Western terms is by relating it to **soft determinism.** Soft determinists tread a middle path between the hard determinism of philosophers such as Hobbes, Hume and John Stuart Mill, who assert that the law of cause and effect is universal and for whom, therefore, moral freedom is not really possible, and the libertarians who hold that uncaused, unconditional choices are possible and that free will exists. Immanuel Kant, for example, believed that free will was essential for morality. To resolve this debate, A.J. Ayer advocates a type of soft determinism which accepts that everything has a cause, but which defines particular actions as free volitions. An action is considered to be a free volition provided that: (a) if you had had the volition not to do the action, you would not have done it and (b) nobody compelled you to do it. For Ayer, we have responsibility for our volitional actions.

In order to explain the difference between phenomena that are caused and free volitions, some soft determinists distinguish between the internal and external causes of an action, for instance between its circumstantial and psychological causes. It can be argued that, while the external causes are determined, the psychological causes are not always so. This is similar to the view of Nikaya Buddhism which states that physical objects and circumstances are always determined through causes and conditions, that some mental decisions are determined both by physical and physiological causes and by psychological ones, and that certain mental thoughts or decisions are free to the extent that one has conquered one's own mind.

Personal reflection

How do you think the principle of non-violence can be applied in the modern world? Will it always be doomed to failure?

Main Points

- The Sanskrit word *shila* is translated as 'moral discipline' or 'appropriate action'. It is not so much about obeying rules but about behaving in harmony with the Dharma in every situation.
- There are various sets of guidelines in Buddhism to help practitioners maintain moral discipline on the path. None are taken in a rigid, dogmatic way.
- The Refuge vows involve the commitment not to harm, and to respect all representations of the Buddha, the Dharma and the Sangha.
- **Nikaya Buddhism:** Laypeople follow the five precepts (not killing, stealing, lying, and avoiding intoxicants and sexual misconduct); they follow the six relationships (taking care of family and of marriage, keeping good company, cultivating respect between teachers and students, and between employers and staff, and supporting the monastic sangha).
- **Mahayana:** practitioners take the bodhisattva vow, taking responsibility to bring happiness and enlightenment to all beings, and dedicating their present and future lives to doing this. They vow to maintain enthusiasm for bodhichitta, strengthen it each day, never give up on a single sentient being, and continually accumulate merit and wisdom.
- **Vajrayana:** the heart of all Tantric commitments is *samaya,* or the sacred bond between master and student. Practitioners avoid the fourteen root downfalls (including disrespecting the vajra master, contradicting the Buddha's words, despising other students of your lama, abandoning bodhichitta, and causing someone else to lose faith). Vajrayana practitioners follow the precepts and vows of Nikaya and Mahayana Buddhism as well.

Chapter 16

SOCIETY AND THE BUDDHIST WAY OF LIFE

This chapter offers a brief overview of the Buddhist way of life in Theravada communities today, which is no doubt very close to how life was lived in the Buddha's time. The relationship between monastic and lay communities is addressed, and their respective roles clarified.

Always remember, Dhamma is not an escape. It is an art of living: living in peace and harmony with oneself and also with all others.
S.N. Goenka, *Words of Dhamma*

Buddhism in Sri Lanka and Thailand

As it spread across Asia, Buddhism adapted to each new society especially on the level of social customs. This means that the social aspects of the Buddhist religion are culturally specific. We will focus on Sri Lanka and Thailand where the basic way of life of the Buddhist community today is very close to the way it would have been in India in the Buddha's day.

The main feature of Buddhist society in these countries is that it can be divided into two distinct groups of people: laypeople or householders who have families, jobs, property and so on; and monastics, mainly monks, who give up the householder life to live in a monastic community.

There are three widespread misunderstandings of this situation that need to be addressed.

- First, not all Buddhists are monks. Many Westerners imagine that to be a Buddhist *means* becoming a monk or nun, but this is not the case. It is a matter of personal choice.
- Second, monastics do not live completely isolated from the community, in seclusion behind the monastery walls. There is no Buddhist equivalent to the cloistered monasteries and nunneries found in Roman Catholicism and Orthodox Christianity. Monks and nuns interact with laypeople.
- And third, monks do not spend the whole day in meditation. This is often the image we have of Buddhist monks. They do have meditation sessions, but much of the day is taken up doing practical duties around the monastery, advising laypeople who come for help, performing rituals and working as teachers. Young monks spend most of the day doing their studies. Only hermits in forest monasteries spend their days in meditation.

Becoming a monastic

A child can be admitted to a monastery *(vihara)* around the age of seven years. At that age he would become a novice *(samanera)* and receive a good education. Only around the age of twenty-one does he need to decide whether or not he wishes to commit himself to being ordained as a monk *(bhikkhu)* for the rest of his life. At that point he is free to leave the monastery if he wishes and can become a householder. On the other hand, he could choose to take the 227 vows of a fully ordained monk, and most novices decide to do this.

The ordination ceremony follows instructions laid down in the time of the Buddha. First, the candidate's hair and beard are shaved off completely as a symbol of impermanence and of abandoning attachment to worldly values and any idea that we are physically attractive to the opposite sex. He is bathed in water as a symbol of purification, and then gathers the objects that are required for monastic life: an alms bowl, robe, sandals and umbrella (also used as a sun shade). These will be the monk's only possessions and are usually donated by his family. If the ordination is to full monkhood the candidate will be questioned on his knowledge of the Dharma. The ordination ceremony requires the presence of ten monks of good standing and takes place within the monastery grounds. The candidate wears the white robes of a layman and carries his yellow robes as he approaches and kneels in front of the presiding monk. He asks permission to wear the yellow robe and become ordained. The monk ties the sash of the robe around his neck and the candidate then puts on the robe while reciting prayers. He then asks forgiveness for any faults he may have committed and asks to take the Three Refuges and Ten Precepts of a novice or 227 vows of a *bhikkhu*.

When a Buddhist becomes a monk or nun, the intention is to remain so all their life. However, if circumstances change and they later decide they wish to give it up, they are free to do so without any shame. They go through a simple ceremony and hand back their robes. In Thailand there is also a custom that every adult spends a few months of his life as a monk in a monastery. This is done especially after a bereavement, when it is socially accepted that the person may wish to do a retreat as a monk for a few months before returning to their family and job.

Monasteries are run on democratic lines and the position of abbot is an elected one. Respect is shown for seniority, so those who have been monks the longest are shown the most respect. Many decisions are taken by the community as a whole and one of the guiding rules on such occasions is that 'silence means consent'.

The typical day of a monk might include the following:

Figure 16 – Theravadin novice monk

- Rising early
- Two meals, breakfast and lunch
- Periods for meditation
- Periods for study
- Periods for services to lay people
- Free time.

The situation for nuns is unfortunate since the ordination line in Theravada died out in the eleventh century. As ordination ceremonies require the presence of at least five ordained monks or nuns, when Buddhism has been under pressure this requirement proved difficult to meet and so ordination was impossible. Once the ordination line is broken it has gone for ever. Nevertheless, there are women who shave their heads and wear robes and keep the precepts of a novice nun. They are technically called lay sisters *(upasikas)* and have lower status than monks. They find it harder to get economic support and some even have to do their own shopping and cooking. This situation is being reviewed in the light of modern social changes. In recent years, the ordination of nuns has been revived in Sri Lanka and Thailand by ordained nuns from the Chinese and Korean traditions where the line had not died out.

The relationship between monastics and the lay community

Monasteries, or *viharas*, are of three main kinds. There are large monasteries in the big cities, where there will be considerable interaction between the monks and the local community. There are small monasteries in villages, which play a similar role but on a much smaller scale and with fewer resources. And there is a 'forest tradition', where monks live in isolated areas in the forest away from society. The relationship between monastics and laypeople will therefore vary according to each type of monastery. In the case of forest monks, their role within the community will be negligible.

In general, the relationship between monastics and lay people in Theravada countries is one of mutual benefit and mutual dependence. Each group plays a specific role in the life of the religion, and both groups are necessary for Buddhism to survive. This relationship has probably changed very little from the situation that prevailed in India in the first centuries after the Buddha.

The special role played by monastics is to uphold the traditions and practices of the Buddhist religion. They put these to the practical benefit of the community in two basic ways. First, they play an **educational role.** In centuries past, before Europeans introduced secular schooling, monasteries provided the only source of education and literacy in the community just as Christian monasteries did in Europe many centuries ago. Now they offer an alternative educational route alongside secular schools. Whether or not a child goes to secular school, monasteries continue to play a crucial role in educating all children in the basics of Buddhism. For example, Sri Lanka, influenced by colonialism, has introduced 'Sunday school' classes in Buddhism for children.

The second role of the monks, which is highly valued by the community, is the task of saying **prayers for the dead, conducting funerals and supporting the bereaved.** Death is perhaps the most important moment in a Buddhist's life. Since Buddhists believe in rebirth, for them death marks the gateway to another life. The way we live and the way we die, and the genuine prayers of loved ones, affect the type of rebirth that we may have. For these reasons, monks are very much appreciated for helping ease the passage to a better rebirth. They receive alms on behalf of the dead so that merit can be transferred to them.

In modern times there are also many examples of monks in Sri Lanka and Thailand **assisting in the economic and social development** of their villages. After a monastic education, which naturally means they can read and write, they are in a privileged position to help poor local communities better themselves. They can fill in forms for grants and help with the administration of development projects for the benefit of all. Some monks in Sri Lanka have also championed environmental projects, applying Buddhist values of non-violence and non-harming to the process of economic development.

For their part, the lay community supports the monastic community with material gifts. Above all it provides **food, clothing, medicines and shelter**. Monks are forbidden by the Vinaya to have any possessions other than the basic necessities, and this acts as a safeguard so the lay community's generosity is not abused. By providing the economic basis for monasticism, lay people ensure that those who wish can engage full-time in study and service. The Vinaya also forbids monks to earn money and to engage in agriculture, so if monks are to follow these rules they are materially dependent on others for their survival. People from the local community also support their monastery by volunteering to clean, cook, do the gardening, go shopping and carry out building maintenance. Monks do not usually have to engage in such routine tasks and can focus on their specific duties.

Both laypeople and monastics come together to celebrate **festival days.** It is at those times that they can all be seen to belong to one community. The most important festival celebrates the Buddha's birth, enlightenment and *parinirvana* on the full moon day in May; this is called **Vesakha or Wesak**. In addition, each Buddhist country has its own national festivals (see Chapter 2).

The monastic year is marked by the *vassa* or rainy season retreat during which all monks restrict their movements and remain as much as possible within the monastery boundary. During that time (which lasts for three months) they intensify their meditation and Dharma study. Throughout southeast Asia many laymen temporarily ordain for this period. For a month after the end of the retreat, Kathina ceremonies take place when the whole lay community goes to the monastery bringing gifts of food, flowers and new robes, and everyone joins together to eat, drink and exchange news.

This system relies on a shared belief that the pursuit of religious and spiritual goals is worthwhile and even supreme. It has continued uninterrupted in southeast Asia since Buddhism was first introduced there in the third century BCE, but other regions of Asia have been more troubled. Over the last hundred years the dominance of materialist views, and particularly Communism, has challenged this system to breaking point. If one dismisses the value of religion, then one may well look upon Buddhist monks as 'social parasites' on the grounds that they make no economic contribution to society. In country after country across Asia, political regimes have tried to eradicate Buddhism by destroying the monasteries and either killing the monks or forcing them to disrobe and become householders. This struggle has taken place in China, Cambodia, Korea, Tibet and Mongolia. After decades of suppression, there are now signs in the 21st century of a Buddhist revival in all these countries.

Personal reflection

How do you view the role and value of monasticism in the present day?

Main Points

- In southeast Asia, a child can be admitted to a monastery around the age of 7, and at 21 decides whether to stay or become a householder.
- Monks take 227 vows in Theravada.
- Monasteries are run democratically and by consensus.
- Monks divide their time between communal prayers, study, meditation, meals and services to the lay community.
- Monks support the community through education, funerals and prayers for the dead, and personal advice.
- Laypeople support the monasteries by donating food, clothing and medicine, and by helping to maintain the buildings.
- On festival days, monks and laypeople come together to celebrate.

Chapter 17

MEDITATION IN THERAVADA

Meditation is introduced in the context of the Eightfold Path. The three main methods are presented: samatha, meditations on love, and vipassana. The Buddhist understanding of the benefits that meditation can bring is addressed.

It is better to conquer yourself than to win a thousand battles.
Dhammapada 103

The purpose of meditation in Buddhism

Meditation is the main method used in Buddhism to transform the mind from its present state of confusion, distraction and emotional entanglement to a state of peace and clarity. The Buddha discovered the special value of meditation—he gave up all his other religious practices in the forest in favour of meditating under the bodhi tree—and it was through meditation that he finally gained enlightenment. The importance of meditation in Buddhism is therefore based on the Buddha's personal experience of its benefits.

How should we meditate? And what happens when we do? These days meditation is taught widely in the West by many different groups, some religious and others not, but we should be aware that the term 'meditation' is used to refer to a range of different practices. For some, meditation is about sitting in a particular posture, for others it is about changing one's mood through guided practices of the imagination – feeling good as you imagine you are sunbathing on a tropical beach, for example. Some people meditate by closing their eyes and cutting themselves off from their environment while in other methods one keeps the eyes open. Many people use meditation quite literally as a way of escaping from the complications of life, a way of de-stressing or entering a state of trance. None of this is what Buddhists mean by meditation, so we need to define its precise meaning in Buddhism.

The purpose of meditation in Buddhism is to purify the mind, put a complete end to suffering and its causes, and lead people to enlightenment. Primarily meditation has a spiritual purpose, not a worldly purpose. Even though meditation can help people relax and feel less stressed, these are considered secondary benefits and not the main point. The Sanskrit and Pali term for meditation is *bhavana* which means 'cultivation' or 'development', that is, mental cultivation or development; a way of training the mind. A Buddhist meditates to free the mind of greed and craving, anger, ill-will, laziness, anxiety, sceptical doubts, pride, hesitation and so forth, and to cultivate positive qualities such as concentration, awareness, intelligence, will-power, diligence, confidence, joy and tranquillity.

Ultimately, meditation enables one to cut through thoughts and emotions and see the very nature of the mind, and this is how the highest wisdom, compassion and peace are attained. The Burmese master Ajahn Chah explains:

> *Examining the nature of the mind, you can observe that in its natural state it has no preoccupations. It's like a flag on the end of a pole or like a leaf on a tree. By itself, it remains still; if it flutters, that is because of the wind, an external force. In its natural state, the mind is the same, without attraction or aversion, without ascribing characteristics to things or finding fault with people. It is independent, existing in a state of purity that is clear, radiant and stainless. In its natural state the mind is peaceful, without happiness or suffering. This is the true state of the mind.*[64]

Buddhist meditation is not a way of escaping from life or papering over difficulties, rather it gives us the strength and confidence to face them better and to live life well. The paradox is that even though its main purpose is a long-term one, meditation brings tangible benefits in the short term, too.

It is important to note that meditation was practised in India before the Buddha, and that he learned it from *shramana* teachers in the forest. Meditation is therefore not an invention of the Buddha. However, certain meditation methods were developed by the Buddha and are unique to Buddhism. There are two main types of meditation in Buddhism: *samatha* and *vipassana*. *Samatha* probably existed before the Buddha and is still practised by Hindus today, whereas vipassana was developed by the Buddha himself and is a method practised specifically by Buddhists.

All forms of meditation are usually practised in formal sessions, that is, timed sessions that have a clear beginning and end. The first thing to do is to create a nice environment: make sure the room is clean and tidy and well aired; create an area of the room where you are comfortable; place something inspiring like a flower, a candle or a favourite picture as an object of focus; and make sure you will not be disturbed. You can sit cross-legged on a cushion on the floor, in full lotus posture if possible, or otherwise on a chair. The most important point about the physical posture is to keep the back straight. Make sure you are comfortable and breathe normally.

Traditionally, in Asia, only monks and nuns would meditate regularly, but as Buddhism has spread to Western countries this pattern has changed because most Buddhists here are laypeople. However, laypeople in Asia do engage in chanting, and this has a definite meditative quality arousing joy, calm, concentration and mindfulness. When they do wish to meditate, it is not usual for lay Buddhists to go to temples or monasteries; instead they practise at home where they create a special corner for the purpose. Most Buddhists in the West try to meditate once a day. Beginners are generally advised to meditate only for short periods at a time, say five or ten minutes, because regularity is considered more important than lengthy sessions.

Samatha meditation

Samatha meditation (or *shamatha* in Sanskrit) develops mental concentration and focus and brings about peace of mind. The word means 'calm abiding' and so *samatha* is sometimes called 'tranquillity meditation'; it allows all our busy thoughts to settle of their own accord until we are able to rest spaciously, peacefully and at ease with ourselves.

The first step in *samatha* meditation is the cultivation of 'mindfulness', by which is meant awareness of ourselves and our state of mind. There are four main types of mindfulness practice: mindfulness of body, feelings and sensations, mind, and mental states. One simply focuses on one of these four for a short while and becomes aware of it and of how it feels. Focusing the mind in this manner has the effect of calming both the mind and the body and is a useful preliminary to other meditation practices.

One of the very first methods often taught to beginners is breathing meditation, which can be part of the mindfulness of body. The idea is to rest the mind solely on the breath and not let it get carried away by distracting thoughts and emotions. We can either just notice the breath go in and out, or count the breaths from one to ten, on the out-breath, several times over; or focus on the sensation of the air moving in and out of the nostrils. As soon as we notice that we are daydreaming, that our mind has wandered off and is thinking about something else entirely, we simply bring our focus back to the breathing and begin again.

We can replace the breath with other objects of focus: a candle flame, a flower, a picture, or a statue of the Buddha for example. The object simply acts as a support for concentration. Gradually, thoughts slow down and we become less distracted and more centred. Imagine leaving a glass of muddy water on a table; if you don't stir the water, the mud will gradually settle to the bottom quite naturally and the water will become clear. *Samatha* is like this: our thoughts and emotions slowly settle and the mind naturally becomes clear and undisturbed.

Samatha meditation can be pursued to reach much higher states of consciousness; this occurs in four stages or *jhanas* (Sanskrit *dhyanas*).

- The first *jhana* brings detachment, clarity and concentration
- In the second *jhana* one remains in stillness, rapture and joy
- The third *jhana* brings a more rarefied joy
- The fourth *jhana* is a state of clear, calm consciousness, totally peaceful and undisturbed.

Samatha can then lead on to various mystical states, such as the 'Sphere of Nothingness' and the 'Sphere of Neither Perception nor Non-perception'. However, the Buddha was not satisfied with these states because he found that they do not lead to liberation from samsara. That is why *samatha* is always taught together with *vipassana*.

The meditations on love

> *Just as a mother would protect her only child at the risk of her own life, even so, let him cultivate a boundless heart towards all beings.*
> The Buddha, *Metta Sutta*

You might think that merely focusing on an object is a dry and abstract type of meditation, but there are many other methods, and one of the most popular is the *brahma viharas* or 'divine abidings'. There are four types: meditation on loving kindness, on compassion, on joy and on equanimity. The point of these practices is to help us develop the capacity to love others. We do want to love other people and be kind to them, but all too often our love is blocked in some way and we don't know how to love fully. Maybe we are afraid of getting hurt; maybe we have been traumatised by a past experience of failure or abuse. These meditations aim to help us re-connect with the love deep inside of us and to have confidence in ourselves, so that we are then better able to love others. They enable us to pass from virtuous aspirations to the reality of action, and to extend our love genuinely, equally and impartially to all beings, without prejudice or boundaries of any kind.

- **Loving kindness** or *metta* is the genuine wish that everyone should be happy. The meditation begins with remembering the feeling of having been loved. This love does not necessarily have to have come from your parents or partner; you might have felt most love from your grandparents or a pet, for example. Whatever your experience of the love and kindness of others, however small and however fleeting, you remember that and recognize that you are lovable. Once this is well established you extend that loving feeling progressively, in ever increasing circles, first to those who are dear to you, then to people you feel neutral or indifferent towards, and finally to those you have problems with. Lastly your love embraces all beings in the universe. With each phase of the practice you repeat the following phrase to yourself again and again: "May I/you be happy, may I/you be well."
- **Compassion** or *karuna* is the genuine wish to free all beings from suffering. The meditation focuses on individuals or groups with specific types of suffering. You wholeheartedly put yourself in the other's shoes and generate the resolution to do everything in your power to help them.
- **Joy** or *mudita* is sincere rejoicing at the happiness of others. It counteracts

jealousy. The meditation involves thinking of the happiness of particular individuals and generating sympathetic joy, beginning with situations that come easily and culminating in those you find difficult.

- **Equanimity** or *upekkha* means the loving of all beings equally. This counteracts prejudice and discrimination, likes and dislikes. We extend our love to family and friends, and then systematically extend our love in exactly the same way to others for whom we usually have less sympathy. Equanimity also includes developing even-mindedness throughout the ups and downs of life. There is no virtue in being dragged down or depressed by the misfortunes of others or ourselves.

Each one of these meditations develops positive qualities which act as an antidote to particular negative emotions:

- Loving kindness is the antidote to aggression
- Compassion is the antidote to cruelty
- Joy is the antidote to envy and jealousy
- Equanimity is the antidote to prejudice and resentment.

The 'divine abidings' are so called because they are said to develop the mental qualities of the higher gods, the *brahmas*, and they are also known as immeasurable as they give us a 'big heart'. They are considered very important practices because Buddhism in general lays so much emphasis on having a kind, loving and compassionate attitude. As the Buddha says: "The way is not in the sky; the way is in the heart".[65]

Other subjects of samatha meditation

The fifth century Theravadin scholar Buddhaghosa recommends many other subjects for meditation, particularly the **Ten Recollections**: recollecting the qualities of the Buddha, the qualities of the Dharma, the qualities of the Sangha, virtue, generosity, faith, death, the human body, breathing and peace.

Buddhaghosa recommends that certain topics are particularly suitable for different types of people. For example, meditation on death or on the human body (focusing on what the body is composed of—organs, waste matter and so on) may be appropriate for extrovert people who are attached to material things and worldly pleasures, but it would be quite unsuitable for anyone who was sad and depressed. Cheerful people with strong faith can meditate on the many qualities of the Buddha, the Dharma or the Sangha. Those who are aggressive and full of hatred can meditate on the four *brahma viharas* or aspects of love.

Vipassana meditation

Vipassana (or *vipasyana* in Sanskrit) is often translated as 'insight meditation' as it aims to develop insight into the very nature of things, ultimately leading to wisdom and realization of the ultimate truth of nirvana. *Vipassana* uses our intelligence and our powers of observation and analysis to bring us to a deeper level of understanding. Usually *samatha* is practised first, as the basis for *vipassana;* this is because one needs to be mindful and focused to analyse a topic for any length of time without getting distracted.

The topics that a Buddhist might choose to take as his/her focus for *vipassana* meditation are almost limitless, but in general the main topics are related to the Four Noble Truths. It is also possible to contemplate on any life situations that we wish to understand more deeply and come to terms with. In particular, meditators train their minds to see the impermanence, the suffering quality, and the non-inherent existence of each object of meditation—that is, the Three Marks of Existence applied to specific objects or ideas.

Vipassana cultivates a type of understanding that is neither based on the senses nor on ordinary consciousness, but on what one might call the intuitive mind. *Vipassana* meditation ensures that one's understanding of the Dharma does not remain theoretical but becomes personal and related to experience. In this way, Buddhists develop personal conviction about the truths of the Dharma and believe in them not simply because they have been taught to do so. It is also a way of developing an understanding of life that is in accord with the Dharma.

Because it is important to adapt meditation practice to our state of mind, Buddhism emphasizes the importance of practising under the guidance of an experienced meditation teacher. Learning from books is unsatisfactory because we need advice and guidance when questions or difficulties arise.

The benefits of meditation

Meditation eliminates the Three Poisons of craving, aggression and ignorance. *Samatha* eliminates craving and aggression while *vipassana* eliminates uncertainty and ignorance, but in practice they work together. In addition to eliminating negative emotions, meditation develops positive emotions—for example the *brahma viharas* develop love, compassion, joy and equanimity.

Mental qualities

Each type of meditation acts as an antidote to negative emotions or attitudes and helps to develop the positive counterpart. Sustained meditation practice carried out correctly over many years brings about the corresponding qualities and virtues: mental calm, kindness, love and compassion, joy and equanimity, freedom from doubts and hesitation, clarity and insightfulness. You may wonder how one can tell whether one is meditating correctly or not. Buddhist masters often say that the main sign of successful practice is an increase in love and compassion.

'Magical' powers

Advanced samatha meditation is said to develop supernatural powers such as clairvoyance, clairaudience, the knowledge of others' thoughts and the recollection of former lives. However, Buddhists underplay the importance of such powers, and monks are forbidden to boast of their powers to others or to display their powers in public. The reason for this is that such powers are not considered essential for gaining nirvana; on the contrary, they can become a distraction on the spiritual path because one might become quite attached to them and proud of them. It is interesting to note that similar powers are attributed to holy men in other religions. They are perhaps spoken of in a symbolic way, but Buddhists do believe they are possible to achieve in reality.

One striking example of the type of extraordinary power that meditation can bring was the tragic burning of the Buddhist monk Thich Quang Doc during the Vietnam War. On 11 June 1963 he drove to a busy road junction in Saigon, sat in the road and poured petrol on himself to draw the world's attention to the inhumanity of the war. Watched by a horrified crowd of passers-by and reporters, he lit a match and, over the course of a few moments, burned to death. As he burned he continued to sit in meditation posture and did not move a muscle or utter a sound. His silence and composure were haunting. This event was shown on television around the world and it became a turning point after which Vietnam protests became widespread in the USA. This was not a suicide from desperation but out of self-sacrifice.

Social benefits

Meditation is not only beneficial to the individual, it can also benefit society. Meditation practice has been introduced in prisons, for example, to remarkable effect. The first experiments occurred in Indian jails, where the Burmese teacher Goenka taught ten-day meditation retreats open to prisoners of all religions. The first three days focus on *samatha* and the last seven days on *vipassana*. Meditation helped many inmates come to terms with the crimes they had committed, ask forgiveness of their victims, and gave them the strength to change and begin a new life. This has obvious social benefits. Similarly, meditation has been introduced on a voluntary basis in prisons in the USA and the UK with positive effects. It is acknowledged as a more effective method for bringing about a change of heart in criminals than a penitentiary system that lacks compassion and understanding.

Personal reflection

How do you understand the role of meditation in Buddhism?

Main Points

- In Buddhism, the ultimate purpose of meditation is to purify the Three Poisons, put an end to suffering and its causes, and attain enlightenment.
- Samatha meditation was probably practised in India before the Buddha. It develops focus and concentration, and it pacifies thoughts and emotions so one finds mental calm.
- The meditations on love, compassion, joy and equanimity connect with the qualities we already have and expand them to all beings in the world.
- Vipassana or insight meditation develops mental clarity and an intuitive understanding of the nature of things through focused reflection on different topics.
- Meditation has been shown to bring emotional and mental benefits as well as social benefits.

Chapter 18

CH'AN AND ZEN BUDDHISM

When it spread to the Far East, Buddhism developed a number of traditions that were unknown in its native India. The two traditions that continue to be widely practised today are Ch'an (China) or Zen (Japan), and Pure Land, also known as Amida Buddhism. Both Zen and Pure Land were simple and modest enough to withstand periods of persecution and political upheaval, and to continue as living traditions into modern times. The present chapter gives an historical overview of Ch'an and Zen, and considers their views and meditation practices.

Sentient beings are in essence buddhas.
It is like water and ice.
There is no ice without water,
There are no buddhas outside sentient beings.
Hakuin[66]

Ch'an in China

Ch'an claims to be a special line of transmission of the Buddhist teachings that began with the historical Buddha Shakyamuni. According to the traditional account of its origins, the Buddha was once surrounded by several disciples and at one point he silently held up a flower and turned it in his hand. Only one disciple, Mahakasyapa, understood the message in this gesture, and he smiled in recognition. As a result, the 'special transmission' of which Zen speaks is a silent one, one in which the truth of the Dharma is conveyed in gestures and actions but not in words. It brings a direct, intuitive grasp of reality which is personally transmitted 'from mind to mind' from master to disciple.

The essence of Ch'an is described as follows:

> *a direct transmission of awakened consciousness outside tradition and outside scripture; not founded on words; directly pointing to the human heart; seeing into one's own nature and realizing buddhahood.*[67]

The Ch'an tradition claims that this transmission was passed down individually from master to disciple, and from generation to generation, in ancient India as an alternative, and in parallel, to the scriptural tradition. There are no records of this, however, and thus no evidence to show that this was recognized as a distinct type of tradition in India itself. It is therefore unclear whether Ch'an as a tradition began in India or in China.

Bodhidharma and the patriarchs

The mysterious Indian master Bodhidharma (c. 470-532) is universally accepted as the first patriarch of Ch'an and Zen Buddhism. He is depicted as a rather fierce and ill-tempered man, with bulging eyes and a large beard. Very little contemporaneous information on him exists and the biographies we do have are sometimes contradictory. For instance, one tradition maintains he was born in southern India, in Kanchi, while another claims he was a Persian from central Asia.

Bodhidharma became a monk in India and was the disciple of a certain Prajñatara. Prajñatara advised him to travel to China, and he left by sea and arrived on the southern China coast in around 500 CE. Modern scholars accept that Bodhidharma is likely to have been an historical figure but some put the date of his arrival in China a little earlier, in around 480 CE.

According to legend, he was summoned by the emperor of southern China for an interview. He insulted the emperor by telling him that good deeds, such as sponsoring monasteries and the copying of scriptures, would earn him no merit at all. The Ch'an tradition does not place as much value on scriptural study as it does on meditation practice, and values wisdom more than merit. He then promptly departed from the imperial court and settled in northern China.

He stayed in the Shao-lin Temple, and did a nine-year (some say seven-year) meditation retreat in a cave on Mount Song, above the monastery. It is said that he sat motionless in meditation for the entire period, staring at a wall. Some accounts say that by the end of his retreat his legs had atrophied. He is also said to have cut off his eyelids to keep himself from dozing in meditation.

It is on account of Bodhidharma that Shao-lin has since become famous as the home of kung fu. (This is the temple in which Bruce Lee trained before he made the film *Enter the Dragon*.) During a long retreat, Bodhidharma felt the need to practise some form of physical exercise as a means of maintaining physical health and strength, and as a non-violent way of defending himself against wild animals and brigands. This is how he developed the martial arts. Originally, the martial arts were a Buddhist practice reserved for monks who had eliminated their desire and aggression, and who therefore acted purely in self-defence without hatred for the enemy.

Although Bodhidharma discouraged intensive study of the scriptures, he taught that there are two gates to enlightenment: meditation and study. Meditative wall gazing is a practice mentioned in connection with him. In terms of study, he had a special reverence for the *Lankavatara Sutra* which teaches emptiness *(shunyata)* as well as buddha nature *(tathagatagarbha)*. There are just four publications that are attributed to Bodhidharma himself.

The date of Bodhidharma's death is uncertain; it may have been around 532. Several sources claim that he died at the age of 150 and was buried by his disciple Hui ke. There is also a legend according to which people witnessed seeing him after his death, walking back to India with only one sandal. They then checked his grave and found that one of his sandals was missing.

Bodhidharma founded the northern school of Ch'an, which generally emphasized gradual enlightenment arising as the result of many years of meditation and study, in contrast to the southern school of Ch'an which developed the doctrine of sudden and spontaneous enlightenment.

The written accounts only refer to two direct disciples of Bodhidharma, Dao yu and Hui ke. After Bodhidharma there were six generations of 'patriarchs', the name given to the most important Ch'an master in each period. The fifth patriarch was Hung jen (601–675), who decided to run a poetry competition to choose his successor. The most learned chief monk, Shen hsiu, who was expected to win this title, wrote the following poem:

The body is the bodhi tree
The mind is like a clear mirror
At all times we must strive to polish it
And must not let the dust collect.

This verse was a conventional Buddhist expression of the need to purify the mind of the ignorance that prevents us from seeing clearly. But an illiterate servant named Hui neng, who worked in the monastery kitchen, was also inspired to enter the competition and his poem read:

The bodhi tree is originally not a tree
The mirror has no stand
Buddha nature is always clean and pure
Where is there room for dust?

The mind is the bodhi tree
The body is the mirror stand
The mirror is originally clean and pure
Where can it be stained by dust?[68]

These poems express a deeper level of understanding, because from the enlightened point of view the buddha nature is unchanging, always pure and can never be stained. The 'dust' of karma and ignorance is an illusion, and when we become enlightened we realize that it was never really there. Hui neng was chosen as the sixth patriarch, which was an important step in the history of Ch'an, because he was uneducated. His success vividly demonstrated that scriptural study in itself does not bring true depth of spiritual understanding.

After Hui neng, the northern school of Ch'an died out and present-day Ch'an and Japanese Zen both come from the southern school.

Ch'an survived the persecution of Buddhism in China in 845 CE because it did not depend on large monasteries or vast libraries of scriptures. Its teachings did not require elaborate institutions that needed wealth to support them, and so it escaped political suppression. During the course of the ninth and tenth centuries, Ch'an split into several different schools, the two main ones being Lin chi and Ts'ao tung, which later became the Soto and Rinzai schools of Japanese Zen. These two schools remained separate in Japan but merged in China under the Ming dynasty (1368-1644).

Ch'an continued as a living Buddhist tradition in China until the Communist revolution in 1949. It continues today especially in Taiwan and South Korea. In Taiwan, the eminent master Sheng Yen (1930-2009) taught a new merging of the two Ch'an schools and established the thriving Dharma Drum Mountain monastery.

Zen Buddhism in Japan

Ch'an meditation practices were introduced into Japan as early as the seventh century via Korea, but it was not until the twelfth century that Zen became popular there. The master who established Zen was **Eisai** (1141-1215), a Japanese monk in the Tendai tradition who travelled to China to further his studies, and who later brought back the Lin chi tradition to his homeland which became known there as Rinzai. Rinzai attracted Japan's educated warrior and political classes perhaps because of the way it cultivates toughness, the martial arts, and intellectual riddles called *koans*. But another Tendai monk named **Dogen** (1200-1253) was not satisfied with the Rinzai teachings and decided to go to China himself in search of something more meaningful. He brought back the Tsao tung tradition which became known as Soto in Japan. This is a tradition that emphasizes quiet meditation and a simple life of poverty and peace, uninvolved in worldly intrigue. It is often said that the character of Soto Zen attracted the farmer and peasant classes.

Both Soto and Rinzai schools of Zen continue in Japan to this day. There have been troubled periods in Japanese history when Rinzai monasteries became involved in political rivalries, but the character and teachings of both schools have weathered these difficulties. Several Japanese masters introduced Zen to North America in the 20th century where it is becoming well established.

Dogen and Soto Zen

Dogen (1200-1253) is widely regarded as a genius who made a great contribution to the Dharma. He was a scholar and mystic, a poet, a philosopher and a saint.

Historically, he is acknowledged as the founder of the Soto school of Japanese Zen.

Dogen was born in Japan in 1200. This was a turbulent time in Japanese history because the warrior class had just taken over political power from the emperor, and people were unsettled and confused with the new order. Although Dogen was the son of a famous politician he had a very hard childhood. He could not live with his father because his mother was not his father's first wife, so Dogen lived alone with his mother in the suburbs of Kyoto. When he was two his father died, possibly killed for political reasons, and later, when he was just seven years old, his mother also died. It is said that his early experience of suffering spurred him on to find a way of overcoming suffering and finding a deeper meaning to life.

When he was twelve, Dogen decided he wanted to become a Buddhist monk but his family did not agree. So, one night he left his home secretly and walked to Enryaku temple on Hiei mountain where he became a monk at thirteen. He stayed there for three years and excelled in his studies. This monastery was in the Tendai tradition which emphasized intellectual study of the Dharma, and eventually Dogen was not satisfied with this approach. In particular, he was taught that all human beings are inherently perfect and the human body is naturally splendid, but he wondered why, if this is so, we have to train ourselves in Buddhist practice? He found his studies theoretical and unrelated to his own life experience, and nobody was able to answer his questions.

One day a monk advised him to go to see Master Eisai in Kennin temple. He went there and put his question to him and was startled at the answer: "I do not know whether buddhas in the past, present and future exist, but I know cats and white oxen exist." Dogen stayed with Eisai and studied with him for nine years and appreciated the practical nature of his teachings. However, even after nine years Dogen found it impossible to gain the spiritual goal of *satori,* so in 1224 he travelled to China to further his spiritual journey.

At first, he was disappointed because he found that the teachings in China were the same as those in Japan, but finally he met Master Tendo Nyojo who became his main teacher. Nyojo taught that the most important practice is *zazen,* sitting meditation, which is nothing more than just dropping body and mind. This means that meditation is dropping our awareness of body and our awareness of mind, and just sitting, just acting, in that bare, present moment.[69] Dogen stayed with Nyojo for nine years training in this practice, and then returned to Japan. Upon his arrival he was asked what he was bringing back to

Japan from his travels in China. He replied, "I have not brought anything back to Japan", and then he added, "if I dare say it, I have simply brought back a soft, flexible mind. This is the heart of Buddhism."

Dogen built the first zazen hall in Japan in the suburbs of Kyoto and became a very popular teacher. This success attracted the hostility of Enryaku temple, so he had to move away and established Eiheiji temple in Fukui prefecture, which remains an important Zen temple today. He taught there for ten years, and then became sick and returned to Kyoto where he died in 1253.

Dogen wrote many books in his native Japanese, and many are now available in English. His most important work is the *Shobogenzo* or 'Treasury of the Eye of the Dharma', a presentation of what he saw as the correct view and practice of the Buddha's teaching. This is arranged according to four main principles.

- First, Dogen stresses *bodhichitta* as the foundation for all Buddhist study and practice. If we do not have a willingness to discover the truth, then we can never begin to study Buddhism. Also, by establishing bodhichitta as our prime motivation, any motives for gaining fame or money will disappear on their own.
- Second, we should always respect the law of cause and effect. Some Buddhists may take this law rather lightly and think that they are beyond it, but Dogen saw this as a form of misguided arrogance. The whole universe is governed by cause and effect, and there are no exceptions. This law also relates to moral behaviour, and we should always respect the law of karma.
- Third, Dogen taught that life is just action in the present moment. The past is past, the future is yet to come, all we ever have is the present moment. He expressed this as 'the instantaneousness of the world'. Neither the world, nor ourselves, nor the Dharma, nor anything else is eternal, it simply exists in the present moment, now.
- And fourth, Dogen explained the principle of zazen. By simply reading books on the subject it is impossible to understand or experience any situation in the present moment; that is why the Buddha taught the importance of meditation practice. By relying upon zazen, we can come to experience reality itself.

Dogen's teachings are expressed in action as a way of life. First and foremost, the practitioner should maintain an attitude of non-attachment, not only towards sense objects and worldly pursuits but also to the experiences and goals of spiritual practice. But non-attachment does not mean inaction, it means that one engages with goals and situations without attachment to them. Above all, non-attachment changes the perception of reality in a fundamental way, so that it becomes a constant awareness of the 'buddha nature' that is immanent in all things.

> *If someone, even for one period of time, manifests the buddha nature in physical, verbal and mental action, and sits straight in concentration, the whole cosmos becomes the buddha nature, all of space becomes enlightenment.*[70]

The perception of buddha nature as a fundamental unity immanent in all things, both animate and inanimate, is apparent in Dogen's insistence that beings do not *have* buddha nature, they *are* buddha nature. For example, he said "To see mountains and rivers is to see buddha nature; to see buddha nature is to see a donkey's jaw or a horse's mouth". This realization permeates one's perception of everything and breaks down the idea of things being separate, or of ourselves being different from others, echoing the Buddha's teaching on no self. In a beautiful poem, Dogen says:

> *To what shall*
> *I liken the world?*
> *Moonlight, reflected*
> *In dewdrops,*
> *Shaken from a crane's bill.*[71]

Our entire life becomes 'ceaseless practice in the buddha mind'. In this way, we find the fundamental simplicity of the Dharma encapsulated in Dogen's teaching:

> *There is a very easy way to become a buddha: not doing any evil, having no attachment to birth and death, sympathising deeply with all beings, respecting those above, sympathizing with those below, not feeling aversion or longing for anything, not thinking or worrying—this is called 'buddha'. Don't seek it anywhere else.*[72]

It is this spirit of profound simplicity that characterizes the Soto school founded by Dogen. Soto temples were known as havens of peace and places of modest living, a welcome contrast to the political intrigue, social sophistication and military violence in Japanese society. Above all, Dogen emphasized a strict and simple life of monastic discipline. After many centuries, during which Buddhist monasteries had become rather prosperous and comfortable, Dogen encouraged a life that focused on spiritual practice and the effort to be of benefit to others. He saw this as part of a return to the authentic Buddhism taught by the Buddha.

Meditation in Ch'an and Zen Buddhism

The very term Ch'an (Chinese) or Zen (Japanese) means 'meditation'. It is derived from the Sanskrit word *dhyana*. This in itself reflects the importance given to meditation in this tradition. Zen is founded on the direct grasp of reality that is passed down from master to student and that does not rely on study of the scriptures.

Meditation is accorded more importance than the study of Buddhist scriptures in Zen. Since the ultimate truth is beyond words it cannot be conveyed in ordinary language. Intellectual study is often considered to be a hindrance rather than a help in understanding what is actually non-conceptual. If the scriptures are studied at all, preference is given to the *Lankavatara Sutra*, but the extent to which study is encouraged will vary from teacher to teacher. In the Rinzai tradition students read episodes from the lives of past masters and students in their tradition, and they use these as subjects for meditation.

Bodhidharma emphasized the importance of the mind-to-mind transmission of the ultimate truth from master to disciple. The teacher uses methods that point directly to the student's heart so that he or she can realize his/her own nature there and then. This is the skilful, effective and rapid way of attaining buddhahood according to Ch'an/Zen. The experience that is sought is that of perfect wisdom or *prajñaparamita*, the realization of *shunyata* or the empty nature of all things as described in Madhyamaka, or again the realization of the non-dual nature of things spoken of in Yogachara. Fully realizing this is seeing the world as it really is, and this is enlightenment.

Meditation in Rinzai Zen

The Rinzai tradition emphasizes the sudden approach to enlightenment. The sudden, instantaneous experience of enlightenment is called *wu* in Chinese and *satori* in Japanese. Satori has been likened to the shattering of a block of ice and has also been described as a mystical experience of great unity and peace, with a feeling of really knowing the truth and of having transcended time and space. It is a higher state of consciousness that is impossible to put into words. Many of the methods used in Rinzai aim to bring about satori and produce a sense of shock or surprise in the student which wakens him/her from the sleep of ignorance. The purpose of Rinzai has been described as bringing about 'a revolution in the seat of consciousness' entailing a total shift from confusion to enlightenment. The methods used are eccentric and dramatic. It is believed that gentler methods will not be powerful enough to jolt us out of the deep-seated torpor of ignorance that clouds our minds, and that defilements and negative habits are so strong in this day and age that only dramatic methods will work. These methods are therefore seen as examples of skilful means applied by the Zen master to an individual student.

The other method used in Rinzai is meditation on *kung an* (Chinese) or *koans* (Japanese) which are riddles, and on *mondo* which take the form of questions and answers. Here are some examples of koans.

- What is the sound of one hand clapping?
- If you meet the Buddha on the road, kill him.
- Why did Bodhidharma come from the West?

And examples of mondos include:

- What is the Buddha? Three pounds of flax.
- Is there buddha nature in a dog? Emptiness.

One can attempt some form of explanation for koans and mondos, but the main point is that they cannot really be understood with the rational mind. As students struggle to understand them their minds become exhausted, and in that exhaustion the intellect gives up and an intuitive insight dawns. We could say that all these methods in Rinzai have the effect of purging the mind so the student breaks through from the ordinary mind to the wisdom mind *(prajña)* and the buddha nature.

Meditation in Soto Zen

Soto Zen emphasizes the gradual approach to enlightenment and brings about a progressive understanding of the truth, primarily through intensive daily practice of meditation. Sitting meditation is called *zazen*. The sitting posture is important, with legs crossed in lotus position, the back very straight and the hands resting one upon the other in the lap. Zazen is practised with the eyes open because the material world of the senses is not rejected. Soto monks will often sit in a simple meditation hall in rows with their backs to each other, staring at the blank wall. They practice concentration on the breathing and observation of thoughts similar to the methods of shamatha and vipasyana already described above in Chapter 17. The aim is simply to sit mindfully. Meditation is not seen as a method to reach a goal, it is the goal itself: meditation is the expression of buddha nature.

There is a cartoon that illustrates this. An older monk and a younger monk are meditating together and the younger one says, "Well, I've been doing this for five years now. What's next?" The older monk replies, "What do you mean 'what's next'. This is it!"

Soto students practise meditation in long sessions, and in order to prevent anyone from falling asleep masters traditionally patrolled the meditation hall and tapped anyone who was drowsy with a stick. These ancient methods have now been adapted to modern times. Sitting meditation is alternated with walking meditation *(kin hin)*, when students will walk very, very slowly in a circle round the room or round the courtyard, maintaining mindfulness of every bodily movement and sensation as well as every thought in the mind.

Meditation and the martial arts

Bodhidharma founded the Shao-lin monastery in China which has since become famous as the home of *kung fu*. It is said that while he was in retreat, Bodhidharma felt the need to practise some form of physical exercise and he developed martial arts as a way of expressing meditation in action. Originally, martial arts were only practised by those who had eliminated selfish desires and aggression through meditation practice, and they served as a non-violent form of defence without weapons and completely free from anger, jealousy, greed or any other negative motivation. The integration of martial arts into Zen practice proved very attractive to Japanese warriors following the Rinzai school between the 13th and 17th centuries. Unfortunately, the practice became decadent, to the point where groups of monks were hired as mercenary armies by rival warlords, and the Buddhist values on which martial arts were originally based were forgotten.

The expression of meditation in everyday life

The purpose of meditation is to develop a state of mind beyond thought, the state of 'no thought' where there is no separation between subject and object. Once this state has been attained, it is not confined to meditation sessions but continues throughout the day and night. This pure concentration means that one is completely present and mindful in whatever one is doing, hence the Zen saying 'when I eat, I eat; when I sleep, I sleep'. Zen Buddhists in Japan also developed formal ways of expressing the peaceful and harmonious qualities of meditation in life. These formal expressions include calligraphy, painting and drawing, archery, the tea ceremony, gardening and flower arranging *(ikebana)*. These are all examples of how Buddhism infuses the Japanese culture.

Eisai popularised the drinking of tea, arguing that it would be better for warriors than drinking alcohol. Zen monks also found it helpfully refreshing. "Whenever one is in poor spirits, one should drink tea", said Eisai. During the civil unrest in Japan in the 14th and 15th centuries, Soto Zen monasteries developed the tea ceremony, a ritual lasting several hours and performed in complete silence, involving the preparation of a large pot of tea by the Zen priest. The atmosphere of the ceremony is one of total peace and calm, every movement and gesture is graceful, mindful and harmonious, and all those who look on remain in meditation throughout.

Both gardening and flower arranging are ways of taking natural elements such as landscape, trees, plants, flowers, stones, water and so on, and combining them in such a way that a sense of balance and harmony is created. The spirit of these activities was influenced by Taoism in China and by Shinto in Japan, and their closeness to nature. The result is a garden or a flower arrangement that naturally inspires meditation.

Personal reflection

Which elements of the Ch'an/Zen tradition do you find appealing?

Main Points

- Ch'an (Chinese) or Zen (Japanese) is one of the main Mahayana traditions that still flourishes in the Far East today.
- It claims to originate with Buddha Shakyamuni but was probably not a distinct tradition in ancient India.
- The founder of Ch'an/Zen as a tradition was the Indian master Bodhidharma (c. 470-532) who introduced it to China.
- From China Ch'an spread to Korea (5th century) and from Korea to Japan (6th century).
- This tradition emphasises meditation rather than scriptural study.
- There are two approaches in Zen:

    - the Rinzai tradition founded by Eisai (1141-1215) teaching the sudden approach using dramatic methods to bring about immediate realisation of enlightenment *(satori);* and
    - the Soto tradition founded by Dogen (1200-1253) teaching a gradual approach based on meditation *(zazen)* and a simple life.

- In Japan, Zen was influenced by the indigenous nature religion called Shinto. The spirit of Zen pervades the whole of Japanese culture, and is expressed in painting, calligraphy, drama, gardening, flower arranging and the martial arts.

Chapter 19

PURE LAND BUDDHISM

Pure Land Buddhism emerged as a distinctive tradition in China and later spread to Japan. It is perhaps the simplest of all Buddhist approaches and is based on devotion rather than scriptural study. It survived political upheavals and is widely practised in the Far East today.

The origins of Pure Land Buddhism

A Mahayana Sutra of Indian origin tells the story of a monk named Dharmakara who vowed, in the presence of a buddha, that when he attained enlightenment he would create a perfect paradise out of compassion for the suffering of beings. One of his vows was that beings only have to think of him and he will lead them to this paradise after death. His vows are expressed in a poem by Tz'u min:

That Buddha in his bodhisattva stage made the universal vow:
"When beings hear my Name and think on me, I will come and welcome them.
Not discriminating at all between the poor and the rich and well born,
Not discriminating between the inferior and highly gifted;
Not choosing the learned and those who uphold pure precepts,

Not rejecting those who break precepts and whose evil karma is profound,
Solely making beings turn about and abundantly say the Name
I can make bits of rubble change into gold." [73]

Dharmakara attained enlightenment and became known as Buddha Amitabha (Sanskrit) or Amida Buddha (Japanese), meaning 'the Buddha of limitless light'. He created a perfect heaven called Sukhavati or 'the land of bliss or happiness'. The Pure Land tradition of Buddhism is one that is based on devotion to Buddha Amitabha, and one of the goals of the tradition is to achieve rebirth in his pure land of Sukhavati.

The founder of the Pure Land tradition is said to be the Chinese master Hui Yuan (4th century CE), but the school's first patriarch is Tan lu'an (6th century) who was inspired by a vision of Buddha Amitabha. He taught that meditating on Amitabha and reciting his name are an unfailing path to liberation for all but the very worst sinners. Then Tao cho (562-645) added to this doctrine the principle that it is the only method that is suitable for this morally decadent age when the Three Poisons are extremely strong. Traditional methods, including scriptural study, will not work with beings as defiled as we are now, nor do our lives allow us the time to pursue spirituality as the only focus of our lives. In such circumstances, devotion is the only method that is powerful enough to bring about liberation.

Pure Land became extremely popular in China, especially with the masses who could not pursue philosophical studies. It also attracted people with morally questionable livelihoods such as fishing, which, according to the classic Eightfold Path, would be seriously discouraged because it involves killing fish. Pure Land teaches that genuine devotion is more effective than virtuous action as a means to attain Sukhavati. It remained the most popular form of Buddhism in China until the 20th century, and it is estimated that in the 1930s almost 70% of Chinese Buddhists followed Pure Land Buddhism.

Figure 19.1 – Buddha Amitabha

In Japan, the recitation of Amida Buddha's name, the *nembutsu,* was integrated into existing Buddhist meditation and study in the 9th century, but Pure Land became a distinct school only in the 13th century. The founder of the Pure Land school, Jodoshu, was **Honen** (1133-1212) a scholar-monk who taught that Buddhist institutions had become corrupt and the only way to salvation was devotion to Amida Buddha. He believed that the long programmes of scriptural study in the Tendai school were too difficult for most and taught 'the easy path' of devotion. The Tendai authorities did not appreciate his criticism of orthodoxy and Honen was forced to disrobe and was banished from Kyoto. He simply continued to teach in the countryside. He did not himself found a new school, this was done by his followers. Most of his followers remained celibate monks and led a simple life.

Honen had an important disciple named **Shinran** who founded the True Pure Land school or Jodo shin shu, sometimes known as Shin Buddhism. Shinran believed that his was the only correct understanding of Honen's teaching. He criticised the principle of gaining merit through virtuous action, saying that this only leads to pride and self-importance. We are all hopeless sinners and have no power of our own to bring about enlightenment; instead we must rely entirely and wholeheartedly on the power of Amida Buddha to help us. Shinran discouraged practices of devotion and respect to any Buddhist figure other than Amida Buddha. Furthermore, Shinran had a dream in which he had a vision of the Buddha of compassion, Kwannon, who advised him to get married. As a result, priests in the True Pure Land school can marry, have families and also have jobs so there is no monastic tradition in this school. The responsibilities of the priest are usually handed down through heredity, from father to son. Shin Buddhism is the most popular form of Buddhism in Japan today.

Honen and the Pure Land School (Jodoshu)

Honen (1133-1212) was the only son of a small clan chieftain in Japan. His father was assassinated, and on his death bed is reported to have told his son, "Don't hate the enemy but become a monk, and pray for me and for your liberation". Honen was ordained at the famous Mount Hiei temple and studied there for nearly thirty years. He gained a reputation as a scholar and could have risen in the monastic ranks, but at the age of forty he decided to break with the Tendai tradition and leave the monastery. He followed in the footsteps of the shamans of his day and went to live alone in a mountain hermitage.

It was at that time that he wrote his most important treatise, *Senchaku-shu,* which later became the foundational text of the Pure Land School. He emphasized the moral degeneration of the age, called *mappo* in Japanese, and taught the *nembutsu* as the only method one needed in order to be free of suffering. His teaching attracted a large following, and he began to teach people in Kyoto.

Honen broke with tradition in the sense that he taught the Dharma to people from all walks of life. Until then, laypeople had been rather like spectators while the heart of Buddhist life was in the temples. Honen taught both men and women, and also taught people from all social classes. His critics claimed that he attracted 'butchers, prostitutes and fortune-tellers' who otherwise would not have had a place in the Buddhist sangha. Nevertheless, his genuine holiness, coupled with his personal appeal and the simplicity of his teaching, made him more and more popular.

This did not please either the political leaders or the Tendai authorities, and in 1207 the Tendai monks succeeded in banning the teaching of the nembutsu in Kyoto. Honen was expelled from the sangha, forced to disrobe and was banished to the countryside. Passions were so strong that some of his followers were executed. He continued to give his teachings in small villages until 1211 when the ban was lifted and he was allowed to go back to Kyoto as a layperson. He did so and died there in the following year.

Buddhist histories usually honour Honen as the founder of the Pure Land (Jodo) school in Japan, but in fact he never began a school. The school developed later with his followers. Honen himself was humble and more concerned about solving the problems of everyday life than about philosophical theories.

The Pure Land school of which Honen was the inspiration emphasizes devotion to Buddha Amitabha but it also allows devotion to other buddhas and bodhisattvas, too. The Pure Land school also teaches that the point of praying for rebirth in Sukhavati is that this speeds up one's path to enlightenment. If we succeed in being reborn in Amitabha's Sambhogakaya heaven, we are able to meet other pure beings who will inspire us, and we can also hear Dharma teachings given by various buddhas and bodhisattvas. It is therefore an experience that will strengthen our determination to practise Dharma in our future lives. Then after a certain time one leaves Sukhavati, and one is reborn again within the wheel of samsara to continue the path until full enlightenment is reached.

The Sutras contain vivid descriptions of life in Sukhavati that serve to inspire the faithful.

This world system of Sukhavati, the heaven of Buddha Amitabha, is rich and prosperous, comfortable, fertile, delightful and full of many gods and men. In this world system there are no hells, no animals, no ghosts, no asuras and none of the inauspicious places of rebirth.

This world naturally emits many fragrant scents, it is rich in many flowers and fruits, adorned with jewel trees frequented by various birds with sweet voices, all of which the Buddha has conjured up through his miraculous power.

And the beings in Sukhavati do not eat gross food, like soup or sugar, but whatever food they wish for they perceive as eaten and it satisfies them. Whatever perfumes they wish for the whole buddha field becomes scented with just that kind of perfume; but if someone does not wish to smell that perfume then the perception of it does not reach him. In the same way, whatever they wish for comes to them.

And all the beings who have been born, who are born and who will be born in this buddha field are all focused on the correct path to liberation until they have reached nirvana.

Sukhavativyuha Sutra, 15, 16, 19, 24

Shinran and the True Pure Land School *(Jodo shinshu)*

One of Honen's chief disciples was Shinran (1173-1263) who was born into the aristocratic elite near Kyoto. He lost his father when he was four and his mother when he was nine, so his uncle sent him to Mount Hiei in order to advance his career through education rather than through marriage. He studied there for some twenty years but lost heart with the complex and difficult practices they taught there.

He claimed to have a vision of Kwannon, the bodhisattva of compassion, who directed him to find a Buddhist monk called Honen. So, in 1201 he left Mount Hiei and joined Honen in Kyoto. He remained with him until they were forced into exile in 1207 with the official banning of nembutsu practice. Shinran was banished separately to Echigo, present-day Niigata, and never saw Honen again after this. As a result of the official ban he had been forced to disrobe, and at that point he called himself 'the foolish, bald-headed one', reflecting his unease at being neither a monk nor a layperson. He claimed that he had another vision, this time advising him to marry. In around 1210 he married Eshinni and had six children with her.

Shinran wrote many treatises and commentaries in simple Japanese, not classical Japanese, so that ordinary people were able to read them. His major work was published in 1224 and is entitled *Kyogoshinsho* or 'The True Teaching, Practice and Realization of the Pure Land Way'. It is a selection of sutra passages. He regarded his teaching as an expression of the true meaning of Honen's teaching, and therefore called his school True Pure Land or *Jodo shinshu*. Shinran himself lived a humble life, and the school was organised by his disciple Rennyo.

However, even though he claimed to be faithful to Honen's teaching, Shinran developed some of his master's principles much further than Honen did himself, to the extent that there are significant differences between these two schools of Pure Land Buddhism.

- Shinran taught the nembutsu practice but, at the same time, said that it was ultimately unnecessary. He said that faith in Amida Buddha is sufficient in itself to ensure that one would not be reborn in samsara, one could purify all one's karma, and one would be reborn and attain enlightenment in the Sukhavati heaven. Such faith leads to *shinjin* or spiritual awakening.
- Shinran was extremely sceptical about the Buddhist teachings on ethical conduct. He felt that human beings are helplessly full of passion and depravity and are ignorant of what is truly good and bad. Even in the case of those who try to follow a path of virtue, ethical action only becomes a source of pride and self-importance and causes them to lose faith in the power of Amida Buddha himself. The only way to make spiritual progress is to put one's total reliance on the power and blessing of Amida Buddha.
- He said 'even a good man will be received in Buddha's land, how much more a bad man' — emphasizing the mercy of Amida Buddha. By relying on him we remain humble in the thought that we ourselves do not have the power to effect the personal transformation necessary to attain enlightenment.
- Unlike Honen, he discouraged practices of devotion and respect to any Buddhist figure other than Amida Buddha.
- In Shin Buddhism there is no monastic celibacy. A small number of married clergy perform certain rituals and ceremonies, but there are no traditional monastic ethics based on the Vinaya. The responsibilities of the priest's role are usually handed down from father to son.
- Finally, Shin Buddhism teaches that rebirth in Sukhavati is the final and ultimate goal, the equivalent to nirvana or buddhahood in the classical

three Vehicles of Buddhist teachings. So, unlike Honen, he did not teach that rebirth in Sukhavati was merely a step on the way to enlightenment, but enlightenment itself. This may sound far removed from the original teaching given by the Buddha in ancient India, but it is seen as a form of skilful means *(upaya)* appropriate for an age when confusion and negativity are widespread, and most people no longer have the time to spend many years on study or in retreat.

There were occasional disputes within the sangha of Shinran's followers, but the most tragic is the incident with his eldest son Zenran. Zenran provoked a split in the sangha; he accused several faithful followers of heresy and claimed to have a special teaching that his father had taught him alone. It seems he also encouraged Shingon (Tantric) practice and emphasized virtuous deeds and the importance of merit. In all these ways he conspired against the authority of his father, so in 1256 Shinran publicly disowned him, making it clear that he had never shared any special teaching with him that he had not given to his other disciples. Shinran died at the age of ninety.

Meditation in Pure Land Buddhism

Pure Land began in China in the fourth to fifth centuries CE and by the seventh century it taught five main practices:

1. reciting the name of Amida Buddha
2. reciting the Mahayana sutras
3. meditating on the wonders of the Pure Land, the heaven of *sukhavati*
4. paying respect to statues of Amida Buddha
5. singing Amida Buddha's praises.

These five practices were not continued for very long, however, and the path in Pure Land Buddhism gradually became limited to *nien fo* or reciting the name of Amida Buddha. When Pure Land was introduced into Japan in the ninth century, the recitation of Amida's name and singing his praises were practised by the Tendai sect alongside their own forms of practice. But when Pure Land was established as a separate school in Japan by Honen and Shinran, the recitation of the name of Amida Buddha became virtually the sole practice.

Pure Land Buddhism emphasizes devotion and teaches reciting the name of Amida Buddha as the main vehicle for expressing that devotion. It is called the *nembutsu* and in Japanese is *Namu Amida Butsu* meaning 'I bow to Amida Buddha'. The *nembutsu* is recited over and over again throughout the day and can be recited whilst one is carrying out one's daily activities. It is a way of keeping the presence of Amida Buddha in mind at all times and continually asking for his protection and help.

Some scholars claim that the nembutsu is a meditation method and not only a devotional practice. At the outset, one acknowledges the darkness of one's ignorance and, with the nembutsu, one calls out to Amida Buddha for transformation by means of his immeasurable light. Taitetsu Unno writes that constant recitation of the nembutsu asks us to become authentically real as human beings by awakening to the boundless compassion that sustains us, and which is embodied by Amida Buddha. Philosophically speaking, Unno says that the nembutsu is "the self-articulation of fundamental reality", and by reciting it one transcends ordinary ways of thinking and comes to realize reality as it is.

> *At the core of nembutsu experience is a noetic element that enables us to see things as they are, so that we are no longer fooled or agitated by delusions.*[74]

Through this practice one can come to embody the *dharmakaya*, the ultimate reality that is beyond words, and one's whole being becomes vibrant with the boundless compassion of Amida Buddha. It is an experiential process that requires great self-discipline and mental focus just as meditation does in other Buddhist traditions.

There are two differences between nembutsu practice and meditation in other traditions. First, the benefits of nembutsu recitation do not depend only on one's own efforts but also on the blessings of Amida Buddha which infuse the bodies and minds of devotees. This practice combines meditation and devotion together and is not only an own-powered practice but an other-powered practice. That means that the power of the practice arises not only from one's own mind but from a buddha who is seen as external. And, second, the nembutsu does not have to be recited only in formal sessions, sitting in a particular posture, but can be called out at any time and during ordinary periods of daily activity. This makes nembutsu practice very flexible and easily adapted to the busy working lives of laypeople.

The crucial role of devotion in Pure Land Buddhism indicates that this practice is closer to Vajrayana than to Mahayana. Indeed, nembutsu recitation plays the same role in Pure Land as the recitation of mantras in Vajrayana.

Personal reflection

Do you agree that devotion can be a powerful and accessible method on the spiritual journey?

Main Points

- Pure Land Buddhism became a distinct tradition in China between the 4th and 6th centuries CE.
- It offers a simple path based on devotion to Buddha Amitabha (Amida Buddha in Japanese). Devotion is seen as the most effective method for these morally decadent times when moral discipline and the determination to study are weak.
- The key practice of Pure Land Buddhism became the recitation of the name of Amitabha, which is said over and over again. This is called *nembutsu.*
- The goal of Pure Land Buddhism is to be reborn in Sukhavati, the heaven of Amitabha.
- From China, Pure Land was introduced to Japan in the 12-13th centuries, where it divided into two schools:
    - Pure Land was founded by Honen (1133-1212)
    - True Pure Land was founded by Shinran (1173-1263). This is also known as Shin Buddhism.

Pure Land still flourishes in the Far East today. It is popular with the masses since it requires no special learning and is easily adapted to busy working lives.

Chapter 20

MEDITATION IN TIBETAN BUDDHISM

All three Vehicles are taught and practised in Tibetan Buddhism. This Chapter reviews the characteristic ways in which meditation is taught and especially how it relates to compassion and bodhichitta.

The characteristics of meditation in Tibetan Buddhism

Tibetan Buddhism incorporates Nikaya, Mahayana and Vajrayana forms of Buddhism. All schools of Tibetan Buddhism teach that we have buddha nature *(tathagatagarbha)* and that meditation and other practices are ways of uncovering this buddha nature and allowing it to reach its full potential. Generally speaking, Tibetan Buddhism teaches the gradual approach to enlightenment in a similar way to other forms of Buddhism.

In the Tibetan tradition, meditation is just one of a range of methods that are used to train and transform the mind, and it is not necessarily taught straightaway. First, students are given an understanding of the teachings so that they develop the wish to want to follow the path. And then, once they have basic knowledge of the Four Noble Truths, the Four Seals and so on, they engage in a structured set of practices that transform the mind gradually and systematically from its present state of confusion to the state of liberation and full enlightenment. Every school, every tradition and every master has their own way of presenting the stages of the path. In this Chapter, we will follow the stages described by the 8th century Indian master Kamalashila. The Dharma was newly established in Tibet at that time, and he wrote an explanatory treatise to ensure that Tibetans were clear about the right path to follow. This work is entitled *Bhavanakrama II,* or the middle-length *Stages of Meditation,* and in English there are commentaries on it by H. H. the Dalai Lama[75] and Khenchen Thrangu Rinpoche[76]. The *Bhavanakrama* is a classic text that is respected by Tibetans of all schools.

Three main stages of the path

Kamalashila says that there are three main stages that we need to follow, in the correct order, if we wish the path to be effective in transforming the mind thoroughly and bringing us to complete enlightenment. They are:

a. developing compassion
2. generating bodhichitta, and
3. practising meditation.

Developing compassion

Love and compassion are extremely important as the basis of the spiritual path. A disciple of the Buddha asked him one day what the main principles of spiritual training are. The Buddha replied that it is not necessary to train in many different things, and in fact one main one will do: the training in compassion and kindness. This is why students of Mahayana begin by training in compassion.[77]

Although compassion is valued in every culture and religion, the Buddha taught it in quite a unique way. He was not content with seeking peace and liberation only for himself but wished always to be of help. He valued compassion because he took delight in being of benefit to sentient beings. This is why compassion is the cause of achieving buddhahood because without it we can only achieve our own liberation.

It is true that we do already have compassion right now but it is limited and biased. For example, we may have compassion for human beings but not for animals; or for animals but not for insects; or for people from our own country but not for foreigners. We tend to draw a line somewhere, as though we only have a certain capacity for compassion. However, the Buddha said that all beings need compassion equally, so we should extend our love and compassion to them all. Anyone who wishes to train on the spiritual path needs to extend that compassion until it becomes 'immeasurable', that is, until it is so vast and limitless that it cannot be measured.

The practices that are taught for this are called 'the four immeasurables'. They are based on the *brahma viharas* practised in Theravada: love, compassion, joy and equanimity (see Chapter 17). One trains to make each one of these vast and without preferences of any kind.

Compassion is defined as the wish to free all beings from suffering and its causes. There are two ways of developing compassion. First, we can apply insight and wisdom, and reflect on the fact that all beings suffer because of ignorance. Every single one wants to be happy but they don't know what to do to create that happiness, and instead they only bring about suffering for themselves. As Shantideva says:

> *Though longing to be happy, in their ignorance*
> *They destroy their own well-being as if it were their worst enemy.*
> *Although they long to be rid of suffering,*
> *They rush headlong towards suffering itself.*[78]

The second method is to reflect on the various qualities of the suffering of beings. This is done by focusing on beings in each of the six realms in turn, or on one's friends and family, or one's enemies or rivals, and extending the practice to strangers and finally to all beings. We try to put ourselves in others' shoes and when our compassion has become immeasurable it is called great compassion.

Generating bodhichitta

English translations attempt to capture the breadth of meaning of this term: the 'mind of awakening', the 'mind of enlightenment', the 'enlightenment mind', the 'heart of the enlightened mind' but we leave it untranslated. Asanga defines bodhichitta as follows:

Bodhichitta is, for the sake of others, longing to attain complete enlightenment.[79]

Bodhichitta is developed on the basis of immeasurable compassion and has two aspects: relative and ultimate. The first step, according to Kamalashila, is to develop relative bodhichitta which can be divided into two: the bodhichitta of aspiration and the bodhichitta of action.

Relative bodhichitta

The bodhichitta of aspiration is the cultivation of our initial thought to attain complete enlightenment for the sake of all beings, and also involves taking the bodhisattva vow formally in order to stabilise that motivation (see Chapter 15). There are two causes that threaten to make bodhichitta decline: a self-centred attitude and becoming angry. The result of either of these is that we abandon the wish to help others in favour of our own life interests, and at the same time we abandon our wish to attain buddhahood. On the Mahayana path, one has constantly to refresh and re-inspire one's bodhichitta of aspiration.

One trains the mind systematically by considering others as equal to ourselves; by exchanging ourselves with others and putting ourselves in their shoes; and by considering that others are more important than we are. Bodhichitta cannot be cultivated overnight; it takes time, many lives even, but it can be done.

It is not enough merely to aspire to benefit beings, one actually has to do something practical in order to relieve their suffering and bring them happiness. One therefore trains in **the bodhichitta of action** which is presented in terms of five *paramitas* or 'perfect' actions (sometimes translated as 'transcendental actions'). Literally, this means actions that 'reach for the other side', to the state beyond suffering. In other words, the paramitas cause us metaphorically to reach the other bank of the river that is free of the extremes of samsara and nirvana. The five paramitas are: generosity, moral discipline, patience, diligence and meditation.

Each action is 'perfected' when it is joined with the wisdom of emptiness which is the sixth paramita *(prajña paramita)*. In other words, the bodhisattva performs the action while recognizing that the action, the doer and the person that is benefiting are all empty in nature. In this way, his or her actions are selfless, without any self-interest, completely free from any hope and any fear, and performed entirely for the welfare and ultimate benefit of the other person. The bodhisattva trains in each one of these in turn.

- Beginning with generosity, then, he or she starts by giving small things, then gives more valuable things, and so on until, at a very advanced stage, he is able even to give his life for the sake of others.
- The training in moral discipline means following the ethical guidelines outlined in Chapter 15, refraining from negative actions and cultivating positive ones.
- Patience means not getting upset, being able to bear any hardships for the sake of the Dharma. Hardships can be environmental, for example, it might pour with rain while you are outside listening to a teaching, or they can come from other people who wrong you or criticise you unfairly. Whenever sufferings like this come, the bodhisattva meets them with patience and with a longterm view.
- Diligence means delighting in virtue, being enthusiastic about the path that one is following, and rejoicing in all the benefit it brings. As a result one puts energy and effort into practising the Dharma.
- Meditation refers to *shamatha* or concentration, training the mind so that it is free of distractions.
- Wisdom is the ability to discern the true nature of all things.

Ultimate bodhichitta

The sixth paramita, the paramita of wisdom, is ultimate bodhichitta, whereas the first five paramitas are relative bodhichitta. The supreme wisdom of the bodhisattva sees the empty nature of all things, the fact that nothing exists independently, permanently and as a single, undivided entity. While relative bodhichitta develops from compassion, ultimate bodhichitta arises from meditation. This shows where meditation fits on the bodhisattva path.

Practising meditation

The first step in shamatha meditation is the cultivation of 'mindfulness', by which is meant awareness of ourselves and our state of mind. There are four main types of mindfulness to practise: 1) mindfulness of body, 2) of feelings and sensations, 3) of mind and 4) of mental states. We simply focus on one of these for a short while and become aware of it and of how it feels. Mindfulness calms both the mind and the body and is a useful preliminary to shamatha meditation (see also Chapter 17).

Kamalashila says that there are five conditions that must be present for shamatha meditation to be successful.

1. We must practise in a place that is conducive to meditation – a place that is not too busy and noisy, with people who try to interrupt us.
2. We should reduce our desires and be content with what we have.
3. We don't become involved with lots of activities that will distract us.
4. We abandon other activities and focus on meditation instead. We should be happy to give meditation a central place in our life; maybe we even do a retreat for a brief period.
5. We should follow the ethical guidelines (see Chapter 15) which create the situation for meditation to happen.

We focus our mind on an object. We can begin with anything, like a stone, or something more inspiring like a picture of the Buddha. Whenever the mind wanders off, we bring it back mindfully to the object of our focus. We continue doing this, and gradually our practice will make the mind stronger, less prone to distraction, and quicker in becoming aware that it is distracted. We meditate spaciously, neither trying too hard nor becoming too relaxed.

Inevitably distractions will arise, and we will find it difficult to concentrate. The reason for this is because we actually find the distractions very interesting; we almost invite them to come and, once they have appeared in our mind, we enjoy following after them. The way to overcome this is by learning to like meditation more than we like being distracted![80]

Meditation is therefore a process of getting to know our tendencies and working with them until the mind is less of a wild elephant and it will actually focus on what we ask it to focus on. Once we have mastered shamatha with an object of focus, we can practise it without any specific object and simply rest peacefully, the only focus being the peaceful mind itself.

Vipasyana meditation

Vipasyana, or insight meditation, cultivates a type of understanding that is neither based on the senses nor on ordinary consciousness but on what we might call the intuitive mind. Meditators train their minds to see the impermanence, suffering quality and non-inherent existence of each object of meditation.

Kamalashila identifies three conditions that are necessary for vipasyana practice.

- First, one needs to rely on a master or sangha friend who is experienced in meditation and qualified to guide us. It is rather like setting out on a journey and asking directions from someone who has already made the same journey herself. In the absence of such a guide one may make mistakes and it will take much longer.

- Second, one needs to hear many teachings so that one has a sound understanding of the meditation methods to be used and of the state one is aiming to achieve.
- And third, one needs to contemplate deeply on the teachings one has studied, and test them against one's logic and experience, until one is personally convinced that they are authentic and true. If one contemplates correctly, doubts will evaporate.

Once a meditator is able to remain in calm abiding, instead of placing the mind single-pointedly on an object he or she begins to examine it. The point of this analysis is to discover the true nature of the object. Two types of object are distinguished: persons and inanimate phenomena. In both cases the analysis is similar and aims to establish that the object has no inherent essence or 'self'.

The benefit of vipasyana meditation is that one's understanding of the Dharma does not remain theoretical but becomes personal and related to experience. In this way, Buddhists develop personal conviction about the truths of the Dharma and don't believe in them simply because they have been taught to do so. Finally, having accomplished all three stages of the path, the student generates the highest wisdom and becomes a buddha.

Mantras and visualisation

A number of meditational methods are characteristic of Tibetan Buddhism, in particular the use of mantras and visualisations.

Mantras are sacred words of power, almost always in Sanskrit, the recitation of which has a deeply transformative effect on the practitioner. Each buddha and deity has his or her own mantra, so the mantra is like a name that invokes the being one is praying to and causes the mind of the practitioner to 'tune in' to his/her presence, qualities and power. Buddhas and bodhisattvas are not seen simply as external beings but as reflections of the qualities of one's own mind, so mantra recitation is a method for awakening the corresponding qualities in one's mind so that, ultimately, one's mind and that of the buddhas becomes one and the same. This is the meaning of *yoga* in Vajrayana Buddhism: the merging or union of one's mind with the enlightened mind of the buddhas or the lama. *Guru yoga* lies at the heart of Tibetan Buddhism and reflects the importance given to devotion as a method for attaining enlightenment.

The musical quality of chanting mantras is said to have a significant healing effect and calms the emotions in a similar way to the effects of certain musical chords. Mantra practice is therefore sometimes used as a preliminary to shamatha or vipasyana meditation because it helps the mind become relaxed and peaceful quite quickly and effortlessly, making further meditation much easier.

Mantras are recited over and over again either within formal meditation sessions or informally, in everyday life. Most Tibetan laypeople would recite mantras quietly to themselves all day long as they went about their work, especially the mantra of Chenresig, the Buddha of compassion, which is *Om mane padme hum*. It is traditional to print mantras on to cloth and hoist them as *prayer flags* in the belief that the wind will carry the blessings of the mantra far and wide.

Mantras are usually combined with visualisation of the buddha or deity concerned. A detailed description is given of the being to be visualised, often depicted in Sambhogakaya form, and the practice entails focusing mentally on the image until one can see it effortlessly in the mind's eye. Visualisation practice is therefore a form of shamatha concentration. Traditionally, visualisation practice combined with mantra was far more common in Tibetan Buddhism than the simple practice of sitting meditation that is practised, for example, in Theravada, Ch'an and Zen.

To help practitioners develop their ability to visualise, there are paintings or *thangkas* depicting these beings in full and inspiring detail. It is always emphasized that visualisation is not simply a way of developing the imagination, or of fabricating images that have no relation to reality, nor is it a way of white-washing ordinary life by superimposing a perfect reality that is simply a form of wishful thinking. On the contrary, visualisation is understood as a method for developing our ability to perceive the Sambhogakaya dimension of reality, a way of expanding our minds so they are in touch with dimensions of being that are unknown to the ordinary human mind.

The direct approach

The Dzogchen tradition taught by the Nyingma school – the earliest Buddhist school in Tibet – teaches the direct approach as well as the gradual approach. The direct approach requires devotion to a lama, which enables the lama to transmit his or her wisdom mind directly to the student either silently, through gestures or in words. This is called 'the transmission of the nature of mind' and it can happen very subtly in apparently quite normal situations. Devotion is important because unless the mind of the student is completely open, he or she will not be able to recognize and realize what is being transmitted. The highest meditation is simply resting in, and abiding by, this recognition of the nature of mind. The 20th century master Dudjom Rinpoche describes it like this:

No words can describe it
No example can point to it
Samsara does not make it worse
Nirvana does not make it better
It has never been born
It has never ceased
It has never been liberated
It has never been deluded
It has never existed
It has never been non-existent
It has no limits at all
It does not fall into any kind of category.

Benefits of meditation

Tibetan Buddhists have been particularly active in exploring the physiological and mental effects of meditation from a scientific point of view. Lamas have volunteered for experiments in Harvard, Wisconsin and New York universities. As a result, there is now documented evidence of a wide range of physical benefits arising from meditation. Some findings provide measurable evidence for emotional benefits, too. For example:

- The journal *Stroke* published a study of 60 African-Americans with artherosclerosis or hardening of the arteries who practised meditation for 6-9 months. The meditators showed a marked decrease in the thickness of their artery walls while non-meditators showed an increase. Meditation brought about a potential 11% decrease in the risk of heart attack and an 8-15% decrease in the risk of stroke.
- Researchers at Harvard Medical School have monitored the brain activity of meditators. They have found meditation activates the sections of the brain

in charge of the autonomic nervous system which governs bodily functions we cannot normally control, such as digestion and blood pressure. This may explain why meditation helps to ward off stress-related conditions such as heart disease, digestive problems and infertility.

- The British journal *New Scientist* reported brain-scanning experiments on experienced Buddhist meditators in the University of Wisconsin, USA. Both during meditation and afterwards they showed persistent activity in the left prefrontal lobes which are associated with positive emotions and good moods.
- Research at New York University suggests that Buddhist mindfulness practice might tame the amygdala, a subcortical area of the brain involved in relatively automatic emotional and behavioural responses. This would explain why meditators in the experiment did not become as flustered, shocked or surprised as ordinary people by unpredictable sounds, even those as loud as gunshots, and did not become as angry.

Paul Ekman of University of California San Francisco Medical School has concluded, "The most reasonable hypothesis is that there is something about conscientious Buddhist practice that results in the kind of happiness we all seek."

Engagement in scientific research on the effects of meditation has also brought about a re-evaluation of what consciousness is and how it functions. Mingyur Rinpoche, a Tibetan lama who has taken part in several scientific experiments, speaks about how more clarity about the functioning of the mind is important for anyone on a spiritual path.

> *Whether looked at subjectively through mindful observation taught by the Buddha, or objectively, through the technology available in modern laboratories, what we call the mind emerges as a constantly shifting collision of two basic events: bare recognition (the simple awareness that something is happening) and conditioning factors (the processes that not only describe what we perceive, but also determine our responses). All mental activity, in other words, evolves from the combined activity of bare perception and long-term neuronal associations.*
>
> *One of the lessons repeated again and again by my teacher Saljay Rinpoche was that if I wanted to be happy, I had to learn to recognize and work with the conditioning factors that produce compulsive or trait-bound reactions.*[81]

Scientific findings on the effects of Buddhist meditation have been instrumental in the development and success of the 'mindfulness movement' in the 21st century. They have helped to make the practice of secular mindfulness acceptable in professional and educational contexts. Even though mindfulness is based on Buddhist meditation it is not exactly the same and does not have the same objectives. It focuses on the physical, emotional and mental benefits that mindfulness can bring over relatively short time periods, whereas the focus of meditation in Buddhism is soteriological: it frees the mind from the Three Poisons and is the way to be free from samsara altogether.

Personal reflection

What do you think are the advantages of cultivating compassion before we engage with meditation?

Main Points

- According to Kamalashila (8th century), there are three stages to the Mahayana path:
  - o developing compassion
  - o generating bodhichitta
  - o practising meditation.

- To develop compassion one practises the Four Immeasurables: immeasurable love, compassion, joy and equanimity.
- Bodhichitta is: for the sake of others, longing to attain enlightenment. It has two aspects: relative and ultimate.
- Relative bodhichitta is cultivated through compassion:
  - o *aspiration:* taking the bodhisattva vow, constantly refreshing that intention
  - o *action:* cultivating the paramitas of generosity, moral discipline, patience, enthusiasm and meditation.

- Ultimate bodhichitta is cultivated through meditation:
  - o cultivating the paramita of wisdom, the realization of *shunyata.*

- All Tibetan schools teach the gradual path and the Nyingma school also teaches the direct, instantaneous path.
- In recent times, Tibetan Buddhist lamas have engaged as candidates in scientific research on the effects of meditation practice.

Chapter 21

THE FOUR PHILOSOPHICAL SCHOOLS OF BUDDHISM

Starting in India in the early centuries of the Common Era, and later continuing in Tibet, Mahayana scholars have identified four main schools of Buddhist philosophy. The Vaibhashika and Sautrantika schools represent the Nikaya traditions and a realist view, while the Yogachara and Madhyamaka schools represent Mahayana and a non-realist view. This chapter introduces the tenets of each of these schools in accessible terms and makes connections to life experience so the subject does not remain abstract and theoretical.

It should be noted that this presentation of four main philosophical systems is drawn from Indian and Tibetan sources. It simplifies the Nikaya tradition by selecting two out of the eighteen Nikaya schools as representative of that approach. It notably does not include the Theravada school.

Who are you and what do you know?

Imagine that, right now, there is a beautiful flower growing in the middle of the desert. There is nobody in this desert at the moment, so nobody has ever seen this flower. Does it make sense to say that the flower exists? If you answer 'yes', I would have to ask on what basis you can state that it exists? Nobody has ever seen it, so how can you (or anyone else) know that it is there? And if nobody knows that it exists, what does it mean to say that it does indeed objectively exist? We could make the question broader and ask: how can one assert that anything exists independently of our knowledge of it?

One of the big debates in both East and West, is just this: does the world exist independently of us? Is there a pre-defined world out there that exists before I come to know it, and that continues to exist in the same basic way whether I know about it or not? If this is not the case, then what are the alternatives? Perhaps the world is a figment of someone's imagination, or a complete illusion; or maybe it is all a dream? We could say that philosophy begins when we start to ask such questions.

The Buddha expressed reservations about the value of philosophy. He thought that metaphysical questions about the origin of the world, and so forth, are a waste of time because they miss the main point which is freeing ourselves from suffering. We might therefore object and ask: is it not an internal contradiction for Buddhism to have a philosophy at all? Did the Buddha himself not indicate that philosophy is not necessary for enlightenment? (See Chapter 9 on the questions of Malunkyaputta)

All traditions agree that it is perfectly possible to be a genuine Buddhist without knowing the difference between the Vaibhashikas and the Sautrantikas. The main point of the Dharma is transforming the mind through meditation practices, and one can do this without philosophy. The Zen and Pure Land schools of Buddhism both minimise the role of philosophy. And yet it was the Buddha who taught the seeds of Abhidharma philosophy, one of the three categories of Buddhist scripture (see Chapter 8). Over the centuries philosophy, when combined with meditation, has developed into an effective method for developing wisdom, and enlightenment is nothing other than wisdom and limitless compassion. In Buddhism, the purpose of philosophy is always soteriological; it serves to identify and eliminate mistaken views of reality, and thereby counteracts the ignorance and confusion that are the root of samsara.

Philosophy can play a useful role in training people to ask good questions and find sound arguments to answer those questions. Unless a Buddhist has some understanding of the way Buddhism articulates its views, whenever she faces difficult choices and decisions she will be incapable of applying the Dharma to that situation. She will only know how to think about it in a conventional way.

These days, philosophy is sometimes associated with ancient theories which nobody believes in anymore, or with language that is so technical it is impossible to understand. Many would argue that philosophy is now far removed from the 'love of wisdom' which is the original meaning of the word in Greek. I hope to show that the Vaibhashikas, Sautrantikas, Yogacharas and Madhyamikas of ancient India did not propose antiquated theories that have been superseded by modern thought. They represent four different approaches to understanding the world that are still relevant today, and that relate directly to the way each one of us interprets our experience of life. It is therefore helpful not to study these views only in order to refute them philosophically, but in order to identify our own views and, along the way, to discard any views we hold that prove, upon analysis, to be incoherent or unaligned with reality.

Common sense (naive realism)

Buddhist thinkers begin by examining the common-sense views that people usually take for granted. They find that we all base our lives on the assumption that we are real and the world in which we live is real. If anyone starts imagining that they don't really exist, or that other people are merely imaginary, we would quickly jump to the conclusion that they are mentally unstable, or that they are hallucinating because they have a fever or are taking drugs. The very fact that there is general agreement about what is real and unreal is extremely reassuring. It enables us to believe that things exist objectively as we perceive them. If everyone in the town agrees that there is a tree by the river, then it's reasonable to say that a tree objectively exists there, independently of any single person's perception of it. If anyone were to disagree and claim that there is no tree there, we might explain their position by saying that they were short-sighted or blind, or perhaps that it was a misty day, and we would say their perception and knowledge were mistaken.

We probably don't ask ourselves too often what we mean by reality but Buddhist thinkers encourage us all to do so. How should we define real and unreal? What is it that makes one thing real and another thing unreal? If we reflect on this for a moment, we might conclude that anything that we can see with the eyes, hear with the ears, smell with the nose, taste with the tongue and touch with the body, has real and proven existence. From the point of view of common sense, the main proof that something exists is that it can be perceived with the senses. That is why ordinary people believe that objects like tables, houses, trees and people are real. As the saying goes, 'seeing is believing'.

Common-sense assumptions go further than this, and manifest as the belief that things exist exactly as we perceive them to be. If I hear bees buzz as they fly from flower to flower, I think that buzzing is a thing that bees do; I don't think that it's just me and my human friends who hear it that way. We assume there is a natural law that guarantees that what we perceive corresponds to reality. Distortion is only possible if there is something wrong with our sense faculties, with our mind or with the circumstance (for example, when it is too dark to see things clearly). If there were no such natural law it would be impossible to know anything correctly. This state of affairs we simply take for granted.

Common sense works very well in everyday life and gives us all a shared basis for interacting with each other and accomplishing our daily tasks. Philosophical questions would just get in the way and make us inefficient. Imagine that I am in the middle of cooking the family dinner and I start to ask myself whether the vegetables and the spices are really real. Are potatoes more real than carrots? And is my knife more real than the vegetables? If I want to feed my family then it's better not to ask such questions and just get on with it. That is exactly what we usually do; most of the time we avoid asking searching questions and stick to common sense.

From the perspective of common sense, for something to be real, and therefore an ultimate truth that we can believe in and rely upon, it needs to be more than just perceptible to the senses. It must also be independent, meaning that its quality does not vary in dependence on a reference point. If pure Indian silk, for example, changed every time it moved to a different shop, then at which street number could we accept it as pure and where would we decide it was fake? To be real it must be pure all the time, independently of circumstance and also independently of my mood or what I think about it. This principle gives rise to the idea of truth that is objective.

Another aspect of the common-sense view is that we have a kind of blind faith in the validity of language. If a word exists we assume that the object to which the word refers must exist, too. If there were not such things as rabbits and chickens we would not have words for them. A few words refer explicitly to fictional realities such as unicorns, Batman, Pokemon and Yogi Bear; but everyone knows that they are not real. In general, we assume that, if a word exists, this is sufficient proof that the object to which it refers must exist.

For ordinary people in every part of the world, existence is quite simple. The world is as we perceive it, and our minds are such that they are able to understand it correctly. Our intelligence enables us to use natural laws to do things that really work.

Questioning common sense

One only questions common sense when it does not fully explain things. In certain moments we discover that common sense has its limits. For example, there are many disappointments in life: we lose people or things that we held very dear and we are faced with the death of loved ones. At times such as these we might wonder about the nature of existence. What can we rely on, not just in the short term but in the long term, too? What can we believe in? When the existence of people and things comes to an end, how are we to understand the nature of life and existence? Is this all a dream? Is life really as insubstantial as it sometimes feels?

Here are some examples of the limitations of common sense identified in Buddhist thought.

- *Lack of general agreement*
  There are occasions when people disagree about what they perceive. Some people claim to have seen ghosts, for example, whereas others have never seen a ghost and therefore don't believe that they exist. They think ghosts must be imaginary. If there is disagreement, how can one decide who is right and who is wrong?

- *Perception is unreliable*
  Sometimes perception can be deceptive and can lead one to think something that is not the case. Take two well-known examples: when a straight stick is placed in a body of water, it will look crooked; and if salt is poured into water and stirred, it becomes invisible even though you know it is there. There is a discrepancy between what one perceives and how things are. Given examples like these one might wonder how reliable any perceptions are, and one might call into doubt the validity of sense perception as the foundation of all knowledge. On what basis can one distinguish between reliable and unreliable perceptions?

- *Is knowledge always objective?*
  It is possible for two people to experience the same situation in quite different ways. I might think that Mary is very beautiful, whereas you don't think she is special at all. Who is right? Is Mary beautiful or is she not beautiful? Is beauty an objective truth or merely a subjective one? If beauty is 'in the eye of the beholder', does this principle extend to other qualities as well? To what degree is all experience subjective?

- *The case of dreams*
  Common sense is based on the physical world of the senses, but it does not account for dreams. In dreams I can experience very powerful situations—terrifying nightmares that make my heart pound, or blissful, pleasurable feelings that linger even after I wake up. While I am dreaming, these experiences appear to be real yet they are mental and not related to the physical senses; so how can we explain them? Does this mean they are without meaning or value or truth?

- *Belief in essences*
  Even though the general rule is that things only exist if we can perceive them, many people nevertheless have a strong belief that certain things, and especially people, have an 'essence' that continues after they are destroyed or die. Many refuse to accept that death is the end; they feel there must be something that continues, even if we cannot perceive it. This belief defies common sense insofar as there is no hard evidence to support it, and yet it is part of the common-sense view.

Four Buddhist approaches

There were at least eighteen Buddhist schools in ancient India, and there was a lively culture of debate between them. Each school formed organically over time by honing its views against the views of opponents in debate. It is only with hindsight that one can define anyone as the founder of a school, or a particular text as marking the beginning of a school. Although some Indian scholars such as Bhavya (500-570) began identifying schools as self-conscious traditions of thought, the framework presented here was developed by later Indian Madhyamikas and then adopted by Tibetans.

The Tibetans simplified everything into four main schools of Buddhist thought, two representing the Nikaya approaches and two representing the Mahayana. While this is a useful tool for approaching the subject, it is important to point out that Tibetan scholars were not familiar with the Theravada tradition, so Theravada views are not included. Tibetans were following a certain Indian tradition on this matter. For us today, this is an historical oversight, and complete knowledge of Buddhist philosophy needs to include the Theravada system. Furthermore, no Yogachara master transmitted the views of that Mahayana school in Tibet so Tibetans tend to critically evaluate Yogachara from the point of view of Madhyamaka. Yogachara was transmitted to China, however, where, in contrast to Tibet, Madhyamaka was introduced but relatively weak, so today the Yogachara tradition is followed only in the Far East.

Figure 21.1 – Indian Philosophical Masters

APPROACH	SCHOOL OF PHILOSOPHY	KEY INDIAN MASTERS
Nikaya	**Vaibhashika**	Vasubandhu (4th century)
	Sautrantrika	
	According to scripture	Vasubandhu
	According to reasoning	Dharmakirti (600-660)
Mahayana	**Yogachara**	Asanga (4th century) Vasubandhu
	Madhyamaka	Nagarjuna (2nd century CE) Bhavya (500-570) Chandrakirti (600-650) Shantarakshita (700-785)

In this chapter, we present these four main philosophical systems of Buddhist thought with a focus on two topics:

a. Does the external world really exist?
b. What is the process of knowledge?

The general Buddhist view of the world was presented in Chapter 10, The Three Marks of Existence, and that chapter should be read alongside this one. Here, we go into more detail and discover that Buddhist scholars do not all agree. When we look more closely beyond the basic principles, we find there is not just one single Buddhist answer to any questions about the world, or one straightforward Buddhist view that can be distinguished from non-Buddhist views. The four major schools of Buddhist philosophy each developed a slightly different system. In Tibetan colleges the study of Buddhist philosophy usually takes all four of these approaches into consideration.

One of the most important frameworks of all Buddhist thought is called the Two Truths: conventional or seeming truth, and ultimate truth. Every school makes a distinction between these two but each school defines them differently. In general, we can say that ultimate truth represents a particular school's understanding of the highest truth or reality, while conventional truth refers to a lesser truth such as the truths that are commonly accepted in a given society and that may work well on a transactional level, but not from every point of view. For example, from one perspective I could say that my television is real because it functions as a television should; the proof is that I can watch the news every night. From another perspective, I could say that it is not really real because it can easily be destroyed by a hammer and then there is no television left.

We should be aware that one of the big differences between the Nikaya philosophies and the Mahayana ones is that the former argue that the external world does ultimately exist, while Mahayana scholars claim that it does not.

Figure 21.2 – Buddhist views on the existence of an external world

- The Vaibhashikas say we perceive an objective external world:
  'My mind is real, and the world is real'
- The Sautrantikas say that perception implies that an external world exists:
  'I perceive it, so it must exist'
- The Yogacharas say we can only know what is mental in nature:
  'Life is like a dream'
- The Madhyamikas accept an external world on the conventional level:
  'The universe and its inhabitants are interdependent'

Vaibhashikas: Ultimately, my mind is real and the world is real

The view of the Vaibhashikas is more subtle than common sense. They accept that the objects of our everyday world do exist as we perceive them, but only in a conventional way and not in an ultimate way as ordinary people think. A Vaibhashika tenet is that ultimate existence means unchanging, indestructible existence; only things that are unchanging and indestructible are truly real. Anything that can be destroyed either physically (e.g. with a hammer) or mentally, through analysis, exists only conventionally.

Through analysis, we break down both things and people into the parts that make them up until they become unrecognisable. This analysis investigates everyday objects such as tables and chairs, and animate objects such as horses and people. The investigation consists in taking objects one by one and analysing them to find what parts they are made of. And then one continues the analysis further and analyses the parts themselves, and so on and so on, until one ends up with the smallest possible indivisible particles from which everything is made. This reductionist approach is similar to that of modern science with regard to physical objects, but Buddhism is unique in applying the same kind of analysis to persons, too. What is the point of this exercise for Buddhists? It helps to counteract the common-sense view that something is real because it is a single, distinct thing. The Vaibhashikas hold that anything that can be reduced to parts, either physically or mentally, only exists on the conventional level.

Buddhists do not carry out this analysis in laboratories but on their cushions. It is a type of analytical meditation, developing a deeper insight into what and who things are. The great Abhidharma scholars of the past claim to have perceived clusters of seven indivisible material particles in states of meditation, and on this basis they assert that partless particles exist because they have perceived them.

Likewise, the mind is mentally dissected into its thoughts and emotions in analytical meditation. The person is found to be made of five *skandhas* or aggregates, which can each be broken down into partless particles and indivisible moments of consciousness (see Chapter 10). For example, the body is not one thing: it is made of legs, arms, a trunk, a neck and a head. Each one of those is itself made of many different parts, and so on. We then ask ourselves what we mean by 'my body'? Would it still exist if it lacked one or other of these parts?

The Vaibhashikas conclude that the entire world of everyday experience exists only in conventional truth. There are only two factors that exist in ultimate truth, in an unchanging and indestructible way: partless particles and indivisible moments of consciousness. These two are the building blocks of the physical and mental worlds, respectively. This view holds that the consciousness that perceives the world is real, and the particles that make up the world are real. Both subject and object are ultimately real, even though this is true only on the subtlest level of indivisible realities. Gross objects like cars and motorbikes are not real, only the particles that compose them.

This view implies that objective knowledge is possible. Humans are able to know the existence of objects directly, and the natural laws of perception guarantee that what appears to our minds correlates with what exists out there.

Breaking things down to their parts is a useful practice on the Buddhist path because it helps to dissolve emotional attachment to things and to oneself. After all, we only become attached if we think something is real. My brother might be very attached to his new motorbike, but if he analysed it in this way he would find it difficult to feel attached to bits of metal and a heap of atoms.

Sautrantika: I can perceive it, so it must exist

So far, we have analysed object and subject separately; we have not yet explored the relationship between the two. Doing so leads to the second philosophical approach, that of the Sautrantikas. When we set out to investigate the process through which knowledge is possible, we make some surprising discoveries.

Imagine that we are in the mountains, and we can see a herd of cows on the other side of the valley. As we are sitting and watching them, we can hear them moo quite clearly. But when we observe more closely, we find that we only hear their mooing a few moments after we can see their mouth opening to make the noise. It takes a few more seconds for the sound to travel across the valley and hit our eardrums than it does for light rays to hit our eyes. In everyday life this does not normally present a problem, but for an apprentice philosopher it certainly does. If there is a time lag between the arising of a sound and the moment I hear that sound, this means that I am not perceiving what is there in the moment of perception; I am hearing something that existed in the past, not something that exists in the present.

There are many other examples that show that one does not perceive the world as it is in the present moment, even though ordinary people take it for granted that we perceive what is there. For instance, when people look up at the night sky and see many beautiful stars, they naively assume that all those stars are actually there, out in space. Yet scientific calculations show that because of the time it takes for the light from the stars to reach us across millions of miles, what we are seeing is how the stars were at some point in the (distant) past. Most of those stars will have since moved, or grown bigger or smaller, or perhaps disintegrated altogether; to know how and where the stars are in the present moment is impossible. Therefore, what appears to us does not correspond to present reality. This is a key insight of the Sautrantikas.

If the process of perception requires time because it occurs in a sequence of cause and effect, the perceiver is necessarily removed from the object he is perceiving. This is very different from the Vaibhashika view that holds perception to be instantaneous. The more we investigate the perception process, and examine modern scientific research on the subject, the more elements we find to support the Sautrantika view that there is, indeed, an 'epistemological gap' between subject and object.

What exactly happens when I see something? Three things must be present for any perception to take place at all: the object, a sense organ capable of perceiving that object, and an awareness. Let's say I am seeing a house. The form and shape and colours of the house travel on rays of light that leave the object and hit my eye. This information is communicated by the eye to the mind so that I become aware that I am seeing a house. Yet what precisely is it that I see? A house is at least 30 foot (10 metres) tall and it is too big to fit into my eye. How can a large physical house be perceived by a small delicate eye?

The Sautrantikas explained that it is not the house that I see but a mental image representing the house. The information about the house travels on rays of light and my visual faculty translates that into an image that resembles the house. This image is a mental image, not a physical reality. This is called a representational model of perception.

According to this view, we do not perceive the external world as it is, in its physical reality; we perceive mental representations of it. The way we know things is indirect. Mental images act as an intermediary between the physical and mental worlds, and they relate the two together. We can therefore infer that the image in my mind is produced by the corresponding external object, even though I am unable to know that object directly. For example, if I perceive a hamburger on the table in front of me, that image does not arise out of nowhere; it must be produced by a hamburger out there. The logic is therefore that the object, a hamburger, must exist because only something like a hamburger could have produced the image of hamburger that I have in my mind. However, I only know of the world's existence indirectly, through inference; I can never directly apprehend a hamburger, or anything else.

At the time the Sautrantikas expressed this view in ancient India it was very radical. The Vaibhashikas, along with most Hindu scholars—as well as ordinary, common-sense people—believed that the mind was able to perceive the world directly. They were afraid that if this were not the case then valid knowledge would be impossible. Sautrantika philosophy was truly cutting-edge and it also happens to fit well with some modern theories of perception.

In the seventh century, the logician Dharmakirti[82] elaborated on the Sautrantika theory and described knowledge as a three-step process. In the first moment, the senses perceive the object directly, without any concepts, filters or anything else getting in the way and creating a distortion. In the second moment, the mental image is formed with some distortion from past habits and tendencies, but this is still non-conceptual. In the third moment concepts enter in and we identify, label and evaluate the object in relation to all the other things we know.

The difference between forests and trees

Dharmakirti also explored the way humans use language. The question he wanted to answer was this: does each word refer to a particular entity in the world that really exists out there? That would be the common-sense view, but is it valid? Put another way, if words are signifiers, is it the case that what they signify necessarily exists?

According to the views considered so far, things are real if we are able to perceive them. Many words do indeed point to objects that we can perceive: rabbits, cows, horses and so on, can all be considered real in this respect. The big question, then, is whether or not there are words that refer to entities that cannot be perceived, because that might mean that some words refer to things that don't exist.

Buddhist thought identifies three mistakes that are commonly made with regard to conceptualisation: (1) conceptual constructs expressed as universals; (2) category mistakes and (3) mistakes in relation to time. The mistake in point is believing that these words refer to reals when they do not.

Conceptual construction expressed as universals

Sautrantika philosophers identified a category of words that they claim do not refer to anything real or perceptible. They draw a distinction between two broad categories of words: universals and particulars. Universals denote types of things or concepts, while particulars denote specific, identifiable objects. Examples of universals include: tables (in general), chairs (in general) and so on, as well as collective nouns such as forest, herd, flock and crowd. Abstract concepts include ideas like beauty, justice, fairness and fun. Particulars are specific objects in our world: my red cup, my old wooden chair, her blue silk dress, the eucalyptus tree outside my house, and so on. To put it very simply, Sautrantika Buddhists assert that particulars are words that denote unique, real, perceptible things whilst universals denote ideas that are conceptually constructed; they do not refer to anything in the world that can be perceived or that has functionality. Universals cannot therefore be considered real.

This theory of language is another way of showing that the ordinary way we understand the world is unreliable. The problem is that we are generally unaware of the subtleties involved, so we behave as though universals exist even though there is no evidence they do. Imagine that we decide to join an environmental group to save forests from destruction. Our thinking would be closer to reality if we realized that there is no such thing as a forest, there are only trees. 'Forests' are a conceptual construct. One does not perceive a 'forest', one perceives a group of individual trees. It is a certain number of trees that we need to save.

Category mistakes

In the case of categories, some Hindu thinkers, and some in ancient Greece, believed that categories exist independently of the individual objects they characterize. For example, they believed that there is such a thing as roundness (we have a word for it, after all) and when roundness pervades an object it becomes round rather than square. I can have a general idea of 'chairs' and each individual chair is simply a particular instance of universal 'chairness'. 'Chairness' is what all chairs have in common. Buddhists do not believe that categories exist separately, over and above the objects that instantiate them. They hold that category words are conceptually constructed, for convenience, and do not refer to reals.

As these so-called universal realities have never been perceived by anyone, Sautrantikas say there is no good reason for asserting they exist. It is worth taking some time to reflect on this point because so many of our concepts are like this. What is time, for example: can you perceive time? What is space? The difficulty becomes more evident when we use universals in the plural.

Whenever we speak of 'horses', 'men', 'women', 'politicians', 'Americans', and so forth, our words refer to conceptually constructed ideas, or generalisations, not to objective realities that we have apprehended.

Mistakes in relation to time

A third type of mistake relates to time. In addition to conceptual constructs and to categories that pervade objects located anywhere in space, the third mistake is to think that the computer in front of me is the same as it was last week. Failing to apprehend subtle momentary change, we use the word 'computer' to refer to an object that is constantly changing, even though the word and my image of it remain the same. This is another example of the way language is imprecise in the way it points to referents.

As a result of these reasonings, Sautrantikas define the real in a different way from the Vaibhashikas. For them, reality is not related to the idea of wholes and parts, it is a question of functionality. An object is real if it is able to perform a function. Function can occur in two ways: (1) producing the next moment of its own momentary continuum, and (2) producing a cognition. Only unique specific objects fit the criteria for functionality. Universals have no continuum that would need sustaining, neither do they cause a cognition to arise in the mind. I do not see a herd, I see cows; there is no 'herd' there producing sense perception.

Yogachara: a detailed model of the dynamic processes of the mind[83]

Can we ever know the external world?

The viewpoints presented thus far have one key factor in common: they are all based on the belief that the external world exists. There is a real world out there; it is not our imagination. Whether we know things directly or in a mediated way, through mental representation, they function in a predictable manner—planes take off and fly in the sky, they don't suddenly do something else entirely—and people consider that this proves they follow natural laws and have their own existence, independent of you and me. Our whole life is underpinned by this assumption.

This assumption masks two fundamental questions: Is there such a thing as an objective world? And, if so, can we ever know it 'objectively' just as it is? Is objective truth possible, understood as a set of facts that pertain to an object and that are always true? Is grass always green, for instance, and is the sun always round?

Or is truth sometimes—or always—subjective and contingent, meaning that it is relative to the person who knows, and to circumstance? For example, doesn't the colour of grass vary according to whether one looks at it in the daytime or at night? Or according to whether or not it has rained in the last month?

If one claims that truth is objective, then there is only one truth about a thing. Grass is green, that is how it is, and this is a fact. If someone says otherwise they must necessarily be wrong. However, if we argue that truth is subjective and contingent, then we may have to accept that there are as many truths as there are people. What is true for you may not be true for me or, indeed, for anyone else. The fact you believe there is a man on the moon does not mean that I believe there is one, yet you might go out at night in order to talk to the man on the moon because you believe he is wise. Instead, I might believe there are rabbits on the moon or, if I am an astronaut, I might believe that there is not a single living thing on the moon at all. We can't all be called mistaken if there is no single objective truth that is right; instead, maybe each one of us is right in our own way. But is truth always subjective? Is there no hope of finding a truth that is true for everyone?

Buddhist scholars agree that the gross objects of our experience do not truly exist as independent entities in the way they appear to us but Buddhists disagree on the status of our objects of knowledge.[84] One of the main differences between the Nikaya and Mahayana schools is just this: Nikaya scholars hold that particles and indivisible moments of consciousness are real, while Mahayana scholars do not.[85] For this reason, Nikaya Buddhism is classified by Mahayanists as realist.

The Mahayana view turns common-sense upside down. It encourages us to question absolutely everything we hold as true. If the external world does not really (ultimately) exist, either on a macro level or on a micro level, then the awareness stimulated by perception does not really exist either, which means that neither objects nor subjects exist independently of each other or have any unique defining characteristics. The questions we started with remain unanswered: what is there? Is knowledge possible at all?

Life is like a dream

The Sautrantika view was just one step away from concluding that the world we perceive is a mental construct, and the Yogacharas take that extra step. Every object we perceive and have a word for is simply the result of the arbitrary way our mind has of dividing up data. We never see reality as it is because our perceptions depend on the filtering and structuring processes of our mental apparatus. The world we apprehend is our projection. That is why the way I experience the world is unique, and different from the way anyone else experiences the world; none of us are dealing with objective reality. We are in our own bubble or, in more philosophical terms, our own cognitive closure.

For the Yogacharas, there may be a material world out there, who knows? The point is that, with our ordinary minds, we are incapable of ever knowing it directly and without distortion. Yogacharas say that mind can only relate to what is mental in nature and cannot be in direct contact with matter, if there were such a thing. For example, when I feel the softness of my new cotton shirt what I am feeling is not the shirt but the sensations of pleasure produced within my nervous system and within my consciousness.

We might wonder how images can be created in the mind if there are no external objects producing them. The Yogachara answer is that they are created by the mind itself from all the memories, associations, karmic seeds and so on that are stored there. If I see a table as a flat square with four legs, that image has more to do with the way my human mind structures sense data, and it does not mean that a table exists 'objectively' like that. We are always perceiving and relating to our own projections. Life is like a movie, and our mind is the bulb that lights up the film reel of karma and habit to create the illusion of a real situation.

This viewpoint is particularly useful in accounting for two problems that are unsolved by common sense or by the Nikaya philosophies: a) the process of dreams and b) the differences in perception between different types of being.

If we accept that the images in our minds are produced by our minds themselves, and not by external objects, then dreams are easy to understand. The reason that I dreamt of a rampaging elephant last night is because my memories and associations and emotions surfaced in that particular way. There is no need for a real elephant to enter my bedroom to explain why I had an elephant nightmare. Rather than being aberrations or exceptions, dreams are used as the main model to explain the mind's functioning. It is therefore no coincidence that Yogacharas say that the whole of life is like a dream. It is not said that life *is* a dream, in the sense that it's illusory and ultimately meaningless; rather life is *like* a dream. The way we perceive things and know things in life is similar to the way we perceive and experience things in dreams. The mental processes are the same. There are just two main differences. First, in our waking state, our perception is roughly shared by other members of the same species. And second, objects perceived correctly when we are awake function in the way they are supposed to whereas in dreams they don't. For example, in life a glass of water will quench my thirst, but a dream glass of water will not.

Yogachara scholars derived their theory of reality from insights they gained in meditation. Through meditation one can begin to recognize consciously that one's mind, and the experiences or objects that one's mind perceives, are one and the same.

> *The practice of meditation over a long period dissolves artificial distinctions between subject and object—which in turn offers the perceiver the freedom to determine the quality of his or her own experience, the freedom to distinguish between what is real and what is merely an appearance.*
>
> *Dissolving the distinction between subject and object, however, doesn't mean that perception becomes a great big blur. You still continue to perceive in terms of subject and object, while at the same time recognizing that the distinction is essentially conceptual. In other words, the perception of an object is not different from the mind that perceives it.*[86]

The Tibetan teacher Mingyur Rinpoche explains that to understand the world in this way is like lucid dreaming: recognizing that you are dreaming while you are dreaming. You realize that the dream is merely occurring in your own mind, and this recognition is sufficient to free you from experiencing things as real. To return to our previous dream example, you won't be afraid because you know that it's not a real elephant. In the daytime you continue to experience situations as before but you are no longer caught by the experience, and you no longer grasp on to anything, or on to yourself, as though they were real. The automatic response mechanism that makes ordinary people see things as real is out of order.

Through meditation and other related practices, the Buddhist path can free us of this automated response so that the grasping between subject and object is dissolved. Once the mind is freed of this habit then, and only then, is it able to directly intuit things as they are through its own natural enlightened wisdom.

Reality is not out there

Yogachara asserts that the objects of knowledge can never be anything other than mental. Knowledge is a mental experience. They negate the existence of real objects out there through three basic approaches: (1) breaking objects down into their parts; (2) analysing the causal relationship between objects and our perception of them, and (3) recognizing the fundamental subjectivity of every appearance and experience.

We are familiar with the first approach, which is also that of the Nikaya schools. The difference here is that no ultimate partless particle is found. Once we conclude that there are no identifiable outer objects, then our experience of such outer objects is understood as a projection of the mind, similar to dream experiences.

When we consider personal perception, we can only speak of the existence of an object once we perceive it. As long as we do not perceive it, we have no way of directly knowing whether there is such an object. For this reason, the object and the subjective consciousness that is aware of it occur simultaneously. However, if there were objects that existed external to our mind and that were the cause of our perception of them, they would have to exist before the perceptions that are their results. Causation is sequential; causes must precede their results and cease to exist once the results arise. But if the perception process is subject to such causal laws it means that the object is already gone at the time of perception. What do we actually perceive then? This dilemma leads Yogacharas to deny the existence of outer objects as causes for perceptual knowledge.

The third approach concerns the subjectivity of perception. Upon investigation, we see that every perception is only an experience in the mind of the perceiver. This point echoes the findings of the Sautrantikas detailed above. Yogacharas state that all our perceptions are alike in that they are nothing but immaterial appearances in the mind. In other words, what appears to the mind is no different from the cognizing consciousness. The mind can only know what has the same nature as itself and cannot directly know anything material, if such a thing exists.

The three natures and the eight consciousnesses

In addition to distinguishing two levels of truth, ultimate and conventional, Yogacharas developed a model of three realities or three 'natures'. The ultimate level corresponds to the 'perfect nature' which is the pure, luminous clarity of awareness uninvolved with objects, non-dual and non-conceptual. The conventional level is divided into two: the imagined nature and the dependent nature. The imagined nature consists of our projections and labels, while the dependent nature refers to 'mere cognition': the images that appear in the mind and the mind to which they appear. These latter two are differentiated because the imagined nature is not functional whereas the dependent nature has functionality.

The three natures are not fixed entities, they are dynamic processes that constantly interact. At the time of enlightenment, the imaginary nature and dependent nature dissolve and only the perfect nature remains. We should note that the perfect nature is not a permanent soul; it is a stream of awareness and not an entity of any kind. The Buddhist path consists of realizing, first, that the imaginary nature of words and projections is nothing other than just that: it is not an external reality. And, second, one realizes that the cognizing mind itself is not real either because, if its objects are not real, then the subject apprehending them is not really produced. Finally, one abides in the luminous clarity of the nature of the mind, which is the nature of all things.

To explain the psychological processes at work on the path, the Yogacharas developed a model of eight types of consciousness which constitute the dependent nature. They are the five sense consciousnesses, the mental consciousness, the afflicted consciousness and the *alaya* or 'storehouse' consciousness. The first six consciousnesses are largely the same as they are in the Nikaya model of six consciousnesses (see Chapter 10) except for the important point that they are not triggered by external objects but by imprints stored in the alaya consciousness. One can understand how this works by referring to dreams.

The seventh consciousness *(klistamanas)* is associated with the dynamic of ego-clinging and, crucially, this is the aspect of consciousness that can be transformed, through spiritual practice, from being defiled to being pure and undefiled. The eighth consciousness *(alaya)* is the subtlest aspect of consciousness and one that is continuous and not dependent on whether or not we are alive. The *alaya* is the consciousness that continues from one life to the next. It is the stream of karmic seeds and habits accumulated over aeons, and when those seeds mature they are appropriated by the seventh consciousness, and then by the other six consciousnesses, and manifest as thoughts and projections.

According to this view, our delusion stems from the way the seventh consciousness, in moments of self-awareness, takes the eighth consciousness to be real and permanent, and in that process the *alaya* is reified and conceptualised as a permanent 'self'. The path for Yogacharas therefore consists of freeing oneself from this mistaken view of self which manifests as the move to identify with the subtlest level of the mind. One eventually realizes that neither body nor mind, neither coarse nor subtle, truly exist as a basis for personal identity. *Shunyata* in this system is defined as freedom from the polarised apprehension of subject/object, grasping and the grasped; in meditation, one experiences the state where the mind of which one is aware does not exist as a separate 'object' of awareness, and one transcends duality altogether.

Madhyamaka: The universe and its inhabitants are interdependent

The whole purpose of Madhyamaka is to prove that everything we think is wrong
Dzongsar Jamyang Khyentse Rinpoche

The fourth philosophical view, considered the highest view by most Tibetans, is that of the Madhayamaka or 'middle way' school. Madhyamika philosophers warn against possible misunderstandings of Yogachara, where one holds that phenomena don't even exist conventionally and are merely mental fabrications. This goes against common sense, and Madhyamikas believe it's very important for any philosophy to take account of common sense, at least on the conventional level of truth, otherwise people will dismiss it out of hand.

There is a story that illustrates their point. A wealthy man has two expensive matching Chinese vases in his home. A friend accidentally knocks one of the vases over and breaks it. The owner is extremely upset because the vases were very precious to him; not only did they cost a lot of money but they had sentimental value as well. He is beside himself with rage. But his friend follows Yogachara and he is surprised at this reaction. "But your vase was not real in the first place", he says reassuringly, "there is no need for you to be upset." At these insensitive words the owner grows even more furious. In a flash of anger, he picks up the remaining vase and smashes it over his friend's head. "You say that my vases are not real?" he shouts. "What nonsense! I wonder what you think now. Maybe you think that your headache and the blood running down your face aren't real either, eh?" He had made his point.

Madhyamikas formulate things a little differently. Literally, 'madhyamika' means someone who follows the middle way. Madhyamikas tread their own Middle Path between the extreme of believing that things truly exist and the other extreme of believing that things are completely non-existent. However, Nagarjuna emphasizes that one 'should not dwell in the middle' either: one should not hold to a so-called 'middle way' view because then that simply becomes another target for attachment and fixation. A genuine Madhyamika does not hold to any view at all, either in ultimate truth or in conventional truth.

To establish the emptiness of inherent existence *(shunyata)* Madhyamikas apply three fundamental principles to everything in the universe, with no exceptions. These principles define what they mean by inherent existence. They are:

a. Impermanence and change
b. Lack of unitary existence (nothing is a single, self-contained entity, everything is composed of many parts and particles)
c. Lack of independent existence (things are defined in relation to each other)

Anything or anyone that can be shown to fit these criteria are said to be empty of inherent existence. Madhyamikas set about analysing one object after another in relation to these criteria and asking themselves whether they apply to the object or not. If they do, then the object is shown to be 'empty'. According to this view, every single possible thing in the universe, both animate and inanimate, as well as the universe itself, is indeed empty of inherent existence. There are no exceptions at all. *Shunyata* is the ultimate nature of all things.

Emptiness can also be explained as interdependence, and this may be easier to understand. Interdependence points to the way that things depend on each other for their existence in a relation of mutual dependence. For example, the bare fact that I exist is dependent on my parents and on the right conditions for my conception and birth. The fact that I am still alive today fifty years later depends on many, many factors: food and drink, heat and cold, the care received from other people, and so on. My state of mind right now also depends on a host of conditions: I feel relaxed because my neighbours are quiet tonight; I feel happy because my home is cosy and warm; I am joyful because I am with people I get on with, and so on. It makes no sense to imagine my existence as something independent of, or separate from, circumstance.

My existence *is* the coming together of all these factors.

In particular, Madhyamikas apply the principle of emptiness to the mind itself. My mind, and its thoughts, emotions and feelings, depend on factors such as stimuli. My states of mind change, they are not fixed, immutable entities.

Thoughts, for example, arise, stay and dissolve like clouds in the sky. They should not be taken too seriously because they are empty of inherent existence. And likewise, the fundamental ground of mind from which thoughts and emotions arise is also empty in nature. There is nothing at all we can hang on to as fixed and 'real', neither the world, nor our body, nor our mind.

The point of Madhyamaka reasoning is to bring about an understanding of the no-self of phenomena and of the person. By showing that the way we usually think of ourselves and our world is riddled with contradiction and absurdity, Madhyamaka exhausts our ability to understand things logically and steers us towards non-conceptual breakthrough.

A good example of the way commonly-held notions are shown to be absurd is the case of causality. According to Madhyamaka, in ultimate truth we cannot distinguish between a cause and its effect; between agent and action; between thinker and thought, and so on. None of these exist separately from the other. If we take the first example, a cause cannot exist separately before the arising of its effect because how could we explain the actual joining of the two in the process of production? For production to take place, there must be a moment in which both 'cause' and 'effect' exist side by side, simultaneously. If this were not the case, there would never be a connection between the two. It follows that the idea of sequential causation is absurd.

At the same time, ordinary people do perceive objects and they do find that things function in particular ways according to the laws of cause and effect, so Madhyamikas accept this way of seeing things as a conventional level of truth. That does not mean they believe in it themselves (because they know that things are not really like this) but they accept it as a useful view for living in the world alongside other people who share this view.

Words are simply concepts that help to structure reality, but they do not withstand investigation and do not refer to distinct objects and entities that actually exist. To understand the true nature of things, which is *shunyata*, we have to find a way of apprehending non-conceptually because concepts just get in the way. That is why Madhyamaka does not assert anything on the conventional level of truth, because doing so would be misleading. Instead, conventional truth in this system refers to whatever is held to be true by people conventionally, in any given society and culture. This is accepted as 'truth' simply for the purpose of dialogue and communication. For example, a Madhyamika could discuss the existence of a soul with you because you believe in the existence of a soul, but he indirectly makes clear that souls are not asserted on his side. He does this by dismantling your views, showing their contradictions and inconsistencies, without asserting anything in their place.

It is because concepts and thoughts are traps in the search for ultimate truth that Dzongsar Jamyang Khyentse Rinpoche says provocatively that "the whole purpose of Madhyamaka is to prove that everything we think is wrong". Language can lead us to the truth, but we have to go beyond language to understand it deeply. Madhyamaka is utterly radical: it is a philosophy that urges us to go beyond philosophy.

Finally, we should note that both Yogachara and Madhyamaka make the distinction between relative and ultimate truths according to the viewpoint of the subject, and not according to the object that is observed. Ultimate truth is the enlightened view whilst conventional truth is the view of deluded beings.

Figure 21.2 – Madhyamika arguments concerning particles

1. Madhyamikas say that it makes no sense to say that particles can be partless. They occupy three-dimensional space, have a top, bottom and sides, and can move.
2. To say that objects would not exist at all if the particles that compose them did not exist, is absurd. In the moment that B is produced by A, A ceases to exist; therefore the cause, A, is not permanent. It is not logical to insist that particles must be permanent (so truly existent) just because objects exist.
3. It is impossible to prove the existence of partless particles by saying that they can be perceived in meditation. If they have no top, bottom and sides then they are immaterial so, by definition, they are invisible.
4. The Abhidharma argument that wholes do not truly exist because they are made of parts, can be turned on its head. Madhyamikas argue that wholes do not truly exist because they are *not* made of parts! By this they mean that particles and parts do not truly exist either, so there are no truly existing parts for things to be made of.
5. In fact, we see objects, not partless particles, so particles are not perceived by the senses. If something cannot be perceived it does not exist conventionally.

Summary

The following is a summary of the four Buddhist philosophical views.

1. The Vaibhashikas believe that there are two separate types of entity, matter and mind, and each really exists. The mind perceives material objects directly and nakedly, without any intermediaries and without distortion. Knowledge is therefore objective.

   But how can we explain the connection between matter and mind, between subject and object? They are opposites. The object of knowledge must be of the same nature as consciousness. The Vaibhashika system is flawed.

2. The Sautrantikas argue that if we want to accept the existence of external objects, the only way of making sense of knowledge is to say that it takes place through mental representations produced from sense data. This explains how matter and mind connect.

   But this theory only makes sense if we assume that mental representations reflect accurately and precisely the objects that they represent, just like objects are reflected in a mirror. If this were not always the case the validity of our knowledge would be uncertain.

   Dharmakirti explains that, in the first moment, our senses do perceive external objects directly as they are. It is only in the second and third moments that reality is hidden by the image we make of it and the conceptual understanding we attach to it.

   Delusion is the mistaken belief that what is perceived is the object itself when, in fact, it is only a representation of it. We take the perceived and conceptualized world to be the real world.

3. Yogacharas accept that knowledge takes place through mental representations, but they say these representations are not produced by external objects but rather by the mind itself. The mere presence of an image in the mind is not sufficient to establish the existence of an outer object because in dreams we have mental images with no external object. Mind can only know an object that is mental in nature, thus the existence of an external reality is unproven.

   The eighth consciousness or *alaya* is not engaged with objects in the way the other seven consciousnesses are. It is the stream of karmic seeds that produce what appears to the mind, and it is the mental continuum that goes from life to life.

4. Madhyamikas avoid falling into the extreme views that hold to existence or non-existence. Ultimate truth is ineffable and beyond all such dualistic distinctions. Conventional truth is merely what is accepted for the sake of communication with others. Madhyamikas themselves do not assert anything on the level of conventional truth because doing so could imply reification, which is unwarranted.

   Some Madhyamikas (and many scholars in the Nyingma and Kagyu schools of Tibetan Buddhism) combine the Yogachara and Madhyamaka views. They accept the Yogachara explanation on the conventional level, for describing the knowledge process and the liberation process to someone on the path. But on the ultimate level, knowledge is beyond language and concepts, beyond ideas like cause and effect, producer and produced, mind and matter, subject and object. This indescribable, ineffable knowledge is the wisdom of an enlightened being and Tibetans believe it is best taught in the Madhyamaka system.

Concluding points

When we take these four philosophical views together, we might be tempted to conclude that Buddhism is inconsistent and has internal contradictions. It is clearly impossible to say, for example, that 'Buddhism is realist', and also impossible to say that it is not realist; it is both, which is self-contradictory if Buddhism is taken as a single system of thought. Likewise, its different ways of understanding the ultimate and conventional levels of truth could prompt critics to argue that Buddhist thought is unclear and indecisive; one cannot pinpoint a single perspective as representing Buddhism as a whole. This might feel frustrating and unsatisfactory; for some, it could be disappointing to find that Buddhism cannot be presented as a clear and coherent view of the world.

In earlier chapters, we presented some of the key principles of Buddhist thought that *are* shared by all traditions and that do indeed characterize Buddhism as distinct from other bodies of knowledge. It is only on the level of detail and of philosophical discussion that the differences emerge; most practising Buddhists would be unaware of these subtleties. Arguably, there is more common ground between traditions than there are points of contention.

When evaluating the philosophical systems within Buddhism, it is important to remember that the purpose of philosophy is invariably considered to be soteriological. Each set of tenets describes the viewpoint one has on the basis of a particular mindset and a particular stage of the path. Vaibhashika realism reflects the understanding of someone who has cultivated a particular level of meditation, while the three natures of Yogachara express the viewpoint of someone on a different level of meditation. There is therefore something intrinsically subjective about all the philosophical systems of Buddhism. They are not speculative theories. Each system is about how one sees the world, and each view plays two roles: first, it is the view that one cultivates on the Buddhist path and, second, it is the view that one fully realizes by practicing that path. If philosophy is understood as an ally of meditation and an integral part of the Buddhist path, and something that evolves naturally with spiritual development, then it is acceptable for Buddhism to teach a number of different tenet systems without necessarily entailing internal contradiction.

Personal reflection

Do you believe that there is an external world out there? Why, or why not?

Main Points

- Tibetan scholars identify four main philosophical schools in Indian Buddhism:

    - Two realist schools: Vaibhashika and Sautrantika (Nikaya Buddhism)
    - Two non-realist schools: Yogachara and Madhyamaka (Mahayana Buddhism)

- Realism in Buddhism denotes the view that the building blocks of reality are real: they are partless particles for physical matter, and indivisible moments of consciousness as the basis of experience.
- Yogachara asserts that an external world cannot be known by the mind. What ordinary people believe exists 'out there' is merely a projection of the mind.
- Madhyamaka makes no assertions in ultimate or conventional truth so as to be consistent with its view that truth is beyond concepts and reification of any kind.
- The purpose of all systems of Buddhist philosophy is soteriological.

Chapter 22

SIGNIFICANT PEOPLE

There are countless individuals who have made tremendous contributions to the spread and continuation of Buddhism over the centuries. Here we select just three significant figures by way of example: Emperor Ashoka, the Dalai Lama, and S. N. Goenka.

Emperor Ashoka

Ashoka was one of the greatest emperors of India. He came to the throne in 268 BCE and died in 239 BCE. For the first time in Indian history (and the only time until the arrival of the British) Ashoka united the whole subcontinent except the extreme south under a single leader. He is famous in Buddhist tradition as one of the most powerful patrons the religion has ever had. He single-handedly ensured that Buddhism grew from being a minority religion in northern India to a world religion. During his reign missionaries spread the Dharma far and wide both to the West (Syria, Egypt, Macedonia, central Asia, Kashmir) and to the south and southeast (Sri Lanka, Myanmar and other parts of southeast Asia), as well as throughout the Indian empire. Furthermore, his reign is extremely important to historians since it offers us the first dated historical records of Buddhism and of Indian history. And finally, Ashoka's conversion to Buddhism led to his applying Buddhist values and ethics to social, economic and political life with far-reaching consequences. His contribution to the history and development of Buddhism is therefore enormous.

We possess detailed information about Ashoka's achievements because archaeologists have discovered 32 of the edicts that he had carved into rock faces or pillars throughout India. These edicts are inscriptions ranging from records of historical events, to imperial proclamations, to decrees exhorting his people to behave morally and live together in harmony. One of these edicts (Rock Edict XII) tells us that Ashoka initiated a climate of religious tolerance in India, and we know separately that he supported the institutions of all religions, not only of Buddhism.

> *"One should not honour only one's own religion and condemn the religions of others, but one should honour others' religions for this or that reason. So doing, one helps one's own religion to grow and renders service to the religions of others too. In acting otherwise one digs the grave of one's own religion and also does harm to other religions. Whosoever honours his own religion and condemns other religions, does so indeed through devotion to his own religion, thinking, 'I will glorify my own religion'. But on the contrary, in so doing he injures his own religion more gravely. So concord is good. Let all listen, and be willing to listen to the doctrines professed by others."*

The ethical advice given on the edicts never claims to be Buddhist, and this is why some modern scholars like Basham argue that Ashoka's ideas were not Buddhist at all. According to Buddhist tradition, however, the values encouraged by Ashoka were inspired by, and based upon, Buddhism but since Buddhist values have a universal truth there is no need to couch them in sectarian terms, especially for a man in Ashoka's position trying to unite his country. So for example, Ashoka exhorts his subjects to behave responsibly, to obey parents and superiors, to help the poor and the sick, to be fair to servants and employees, and to be generous to holy men. These values are not unique to Buddhism or to Indian culture and are followed throughout the world even today, but in the Indian context we can see that Ashoka could well have learned them from Buddhism though not necessarily so. Ashoka also wanted his subjects to develop personal moral qualities so he advised them to be truthful and honest, merciful, and not too concerned with material possessions. In particular, he asked people to refrain from killing or harming any living being. We know that Ashoka banned animal sacrifices (which were still carried out at that time by the Vedic-influenced Hindu religion) and that he also banned hunting which even in India was 'the sport of kings' and of the aristocracy. It is possible that Ashoka also banned the death penalty. This last set of policies, at least, appears to bear the hallmark of Buddhist thinking because although similar non-violent values are taught in Jainism there is no indication that Ashoka was a Jain.

Many of these ideas may seem quite ordinary to us today, but that is mainly because early Christianity played a similar role in applying compassionate religious values to social and political life in Europe. In Ashoka's day, however, these ideas were totally revolutionary since the model of kingship was completely hierarchical, and the leader's role was mainly a military one of protecting his people and his territory from outside enemies and destabilising influences. Kings, after all, belonged to the *kshatriya* class of warriors. Ashoka radically changed the very notion of kingship and extended the role to one of protecting his people morally, through kindness and social justice, and actively directing resources to meet the everyday needs of a peaceful civil society. This was completely new – a form of socialism before its time! It is also an example of what is today called 'engaged Buddhism'.

Ashoka initiated many social projects throughout the Indian empire. He set up medical and veterinary centres, constructed wells and reservoirs, planted trees for fruit and shade, and also provided welfare services and temporary financial support for ex-prisoners. He established the first rest-houses for travellers (especially needed once pilgrimages became a regular feature of life). Officials were encouraged to look after old people and orphans, and to ensure equal judicial standards throughout the empire. Ashoka also banned torture.

One of the principal ethical values upheld by Ashoka was *ahimsa* or non-violence, and we have already seen how he applied this to both humans and animals. In time it seems that the entire royal household was asked to become vegetarian. Non-food animals such as birds and fish were protected. Gentleness, sexual morality and contentment were recommended. In modern jargon we could say that Ashoka tried to create a 'compassionate society', and historically this is the first instance of any large scale attempt to apply Buddhist values on the level of society as a whole. It provides a good blueprint for what Buddhism in action can mean, especially in the context of the laity, and still today Ashoka's experiment is looked to as a model of its kind.

In addition to these activities Ashoka offered a great deal of support specifically to Buddhists. Some of his rock edicts, for example, commemorated events in the history of Buddhism, a notable example being the rock pillar in Lumbini indicating that Lumbini was the Buddha's birth place. Without such evidence we would have little or no proven knowledge of this fact. Ashoka also had many Buddhist stupas built throughout India which became places of pilgrimage. Instead of going hunting he himself would go on pilgrimages. Also, Ashoka donated state resources towards the building of Buddhist monasteries and the upkeep of the monks, thus allowing the religion to establish itself firmly in many new parts of India.

After Ashoka the dynasty declined and India split up again into several kingdoms, but Buddhism continued to be supported by kings and other wealthy patrons for centuries. It is also often claimed that the longterm impact of Ashoka's missions to spread Buddhism outside of India effectively secured the survival of the religion until today since in India itself it disappeared in the 12th century.

The Dalai Lama

The Dalai Lama is the religious leader of the Tibetan people. The reason he is considered a significant person in the development of Buddhism is due to the role he has played in helping establish Buddhism in the modern world. This has not been merely a question of transplanting ancient cultural traditions into the West, but rather of adapting the way Buddhism is taught and practised so that it meets the needs of men and women from all walks of life. Part of this effort lies in cultural exchanges, for instance by way of the dialogues he has initiated between Buddhist thinkers on one side and scientists, politicians and other religious leaders on the other side so as to explore ways in which Buddhist thinking can make a creative contribution to modern life.

Dalai Lama

The Dalai Lama was born to a peasant family in a small village of northeastern Tibet in 1935. At the age of two he was recognized by religious dignitaries as the reincarnation of his predecessor the 13th Dalai Lama, the previous leader of Tibet, and so was educated and trained from the age of six to take on this role once he came of age. It is a Tibetan tradition to recognize the reincarnations of great lamas and then to educate them so they are able to carry on the work they began in previous lives. The case of the Dalai Lamas is special in that they are considered human embodiments of the Buddha of Compassion, Chenresig, who chose to take birth as human beings to serve humankind. This is why the Western media have called him a 'God King' but this is not an accurate understanding of the Buddhist principle involved here. From the Buddhist point of view, the Dalai Lama is the Nirmanakaya manifestation of the Sambhogakaya Buddha Chenresig.

In 1950 some 80,000 Chinese soldiers invaded Tibet, and this political crisis led to the Dalai Lama assuming full political power at the young age of 15. His efforts to bring about a peaceful diplomatic solution to the Sino-Tibetan conflict were thwarted by Beijing's ruthless policies in eastern Tibet which sparked popular uprising and resistance, first in the east of the country and then in many other parts of Tibet. In 1959, the Tibetan National Uprising in the capital, Lhasa, was brutally crushed by the Chinese, and the Dalai Lama escaped over the Himalayas and was given political asylum in India. Some 80,000 Tibetan refugees followed him into exile. Since that time the Dalai Lama has lived in Dharamsala, northern India, the seat of the Tibetan government-in-exile. Tibet itself remains under Chinese control, and especially in the 1980s the Red Army was responsible for destroying almost all the Buddhist monasteries, scriptures and artwork in Tibet, and also for killing, imprisoning or torturing tens of thousands of monks.

As the Tibetan leader in exile, the Dalai Lama has tirelessly pursued a pacifist strategy to persuade China to allow autonomy for Tibet. He has always spoken out against violent resistance, and believes that the Buddhist value of *ahimsa* has definite longterm benefits even if the situation remains difficult in the short term. Violence, he says, only breeds resentment and mistrust for generations. In 1989, the Dalai Lama gained worldwide recognition for his efforts and was awarded the Nobel Peace Prize in Oslo. He accepted the prize on behalf of oppressed peoples everywhere, saying that "the prize reaffirms our conviction that with truth, courage and determination as our weapons, Tibet will be liberated. Our struggle must remain non-violent and free of hatred."

The Dalai Lama has actively participated in ecumenical dialogue and has met many times with the Pope and other leaders of the Catholic and Anglican churches and the Jewish community. He explains his reasons for religious tolerance as follows:

> *"I always believe that it is much better to have a variety of religions, a variety of philosophies, rather than one single religion or philosophy. This is necessary because of the different mental dispositions of each human being. Furthermore, each religion has certain unique ideas or techniques, and learning about them can only enrich one's own faith."*

In the course of giving Buddhist talks and teachings in the West, the Dalai Lama has also called for agreement on a universal code of ethics, independent of any particular religious denomination yet compatible with all religions, and therefore acceptable to the vast numbers of people in the modern world who follow no religion at all. He believes that certain basic ethical values are common and applicable to the whole of humanity – values such as love and compassion for others, respect, tolerance and individual responsibility – and should not be seen as religious in a narrow sense. Scientists and politicians, journalists, doctors and so on, whether they follow a religion or not, would benefit the whole community by applying values such as these in their work. When asked to summarise the essence of his religious belief, the Dalai Lama said once: "My religion is simple; my religion is kindness."

The Dalai Lama has also given great importance to environmental questions, and in addressing these he refers to Buddhist principles such as dependent arising (or interdependence) to explain why human activity in one part of the globe affects the situation in another. He has also called on every individual to nurture a sense of universal responsibility, realizing that the actions of each one of us have consequences far beyond the limits of our personal lives. We all bear some measure of responsibility for the future of mankind and of the planet.

Finally, the Dalai Lama has been interested in science and technology from a young age. As a boy he would take his telescope, camera and car apart and put them together again to understand how they worked. He has initiated conferences with scientists to explore the connections between science and Buddhist wisdom especially in the sciences of the mind such as neuro-biology, psychology and psychiatry. One of his conclusions has been that scientific approaches to the mind are based on the assumption that mind cannot exist or be active independently of matter, and this assumption he claims is unproven. He has been behind a series of laboratory experiments in North American universities testing the effects of longterm meditation on the brain and other health indicators (see Chapter 20). Initial results show significant and longterm benefits in physical and mental wellbeing. He is very open to using scientific methods wherever they can be helpful, even in religious areas. He believes that open-minded rational inquiry is essential for sound human understanding in any field of knowledge, and in this respect Buddhism is very close to science.

Some scholars think the Tibetans, including the Dalai Lama himself, have been instrumental in communicating Buddhism to the world at large without distorting or diluting it for the sake of popularity. In Europe, the Dalai Lama has attracted audiences of over 10,000 people for public talks, and in the USA he attracted 100,000 people at certain events. It may well be that, in the future, the Dalai Lama will be seen to have played a historic role in the development of Buddhism across the world.

S.N. Goenka

S.N. Goenka (1924-2013) was a leading master of the Theravada tradition and notable for being a layman, not a monk, in a tradition that has always been dominated by the monasteries. He has been very successful in teaching samatha and vipassana meditation to people of all faiths in both Asia and the West, and he is especially known for his work in introducing meditation within prisons. There are now Vipassana Meditation centres following his teachings in many countries around the world including India, USA, Canada, Germany, the UK, Australia and Japan. He was also a prominent figure promoting the message of peace and religious harmony, emphasizing that outer peace is only possible on the basis of inner peace.

Goenka was born in Myanmar, then Burma, in 1924. He joined his family business in 1940 and rapidly became a pioneering industrialist with several manufacturing corporations in the country. In 1969, he retired from business and devoted his life to teaching meditation for the benefit of humanity. He was trained for 14 years by the renowned Buddhist teacher Sayagyi U Ba Khin (1899-1971) in the tradition of Ledi Sayadaw. Goenka started teaching in Myanmar and India, and in 1979 began travelling more widely, in the East and to the West. He trained over 600 assistant teachers who carry on his work around the world. Neither he nor his assistants receive any financial gain from their courses.

Goenka found that vipassana meditation is easily accepted by people everywhere because its benefits are universal and it can be taught in a totally non-sectarian way. Whatever a person's socio-economic background or religious beliefs, vipassana provides a way of finding inner peace, reconciling with life's difficulties and transforming negative emotions into positive ones. It also gives a direction and meaning to life. In communities divided by caste and religion, vipassana is able to bring everyone together.

Goenka was invited to lead ten-day vipassana retreats in a number of jails in India, and in 1995 he gave the largest retreat ever in modern times, attended by 1000 prisoners in Tihar jail, New Delhi. The results have been both moving and astounding, so much so that the Indian government has since recommended that every prison in the country should organise similar retreats for both wardens and inmates. As a result, hundreds of prisoners continue to attend vipassana retreats every year, and thousands of Indian police officers have followed courses too. Results include improved integration into society after prison and a reduction in recidivism, not to mention thousands of cases where offenders were able personally to come to terms with their past.

The effectiveness of vipassana as a tool for prisoner rehabilitation has led to courses being offered in jails in the USA. Studies there have shown that vipassana is effective in reducing drug and alcohol addiction among inmates, and in one prison in Seattle, Washington state, the number of inmates re-admitted within two years in 2002 was 47% for men and 28% for women among those who meditated compared with 75% for those who did not. Goenka's assistants also offer vipassana programmes for school children, drug addicts, the disabled, homeless children and business executives.

In 1981, S.N. Goenka established the Vipassana Research Institute in India to support research into the Pali Buddhist scriptures. One of the centre's key achievements is to have completed the computerisation of the Pali Canon which is now freely available to scholars everywhere in Sanskrit, Pali, Burmese, Khmer, Mongolian and Thai languages. This is a major contribution to Buddhist scholarship.

Goenka emphasized the universality of the Buddha's message, saying that the Buddha never taught 'Buddhism' as an 'ism', nor did he teach any kind of sectarian religion; he taught Dhamma, the way to liberation, which is universal and belongs to whoever wishes to follow it. This non-sectarian approach is one of the main reasons for his appeal, along with his firm conviction that Buddhist methods are of immediate and practical benefit. Thus he said: "May the stream of pure Dhamma keep flowing in the world, for the happiness of everyone, for the benefit of all."

Conclusion

Although these three significant figures in the story of Buddhism are each very different, it is interesting to note that they all have one characteristic in common. Each one, in his own way, realized that the message of Buddhism is universal and carries a truth and a benefit that go far beyond the limitations of sectarian religion. It is this universality of the Dharma that each has succeeded in communicating, thereby changing the attitudes and lives of countless people. This they see as the real point of the Buddha's message: their aim is not to convert people but to benefit their lives and bring them a greater measure of happiness.

Personal reflection

Is there a Buddhist figure who you personally find significant and inspiring?

Main Points

- **Emperor Ashoka** of India (r.268-239 BCE) established Buddhism as a state religion and supported its propagation throughout the country.
- He sent missions to Sri Lanka and central Asia as well as to the West, and is credited with turning Buddhism into a world religion.
- He applied Buddhist principles to governance, society and culture.
- **The Dalai Lama** has been instrumental in making Buddhism known to hundreds of thousands of people all over the world.
- He initiated the Mind and Life Institute and its series of dialogues between scientists and Buddhist scholars.
- **S.N. Goenka** has had a tremendous impact through teaching vipassana in India and all over the world.
- He introduced ten-day meditation retreats in Indian prisons to great effect.

Chapter 23

RELIGIOUS AUTHORITY

Western philosophy of religion identifies four sources of religious authority: tradition, scripture, reason and religious experience. We consider the question of how these four apply to Buddhism, past and present.

Introduction

Philosophy of religion, as it is taught in the West, identifies four sources or types of religious authority: tradition, scripture, reason and religious experience. In principle, this model can be applied to any of the world's religions. Each religion defines these areas, and the balance between them, in specific ways. For example, the so-called 'religions of the book' (Judaism, Christianity and Islam) consider their scriptures to be more authoritative than reason, while within Christianity some churches emphasize religious experience and others do not. In this chapter we look at how each source of authority is considered in Buddhism, and at the issues raised by the question of religious authority in contemporary Buddhism.

Figure 23.1 – Religious Authority in Buddhism

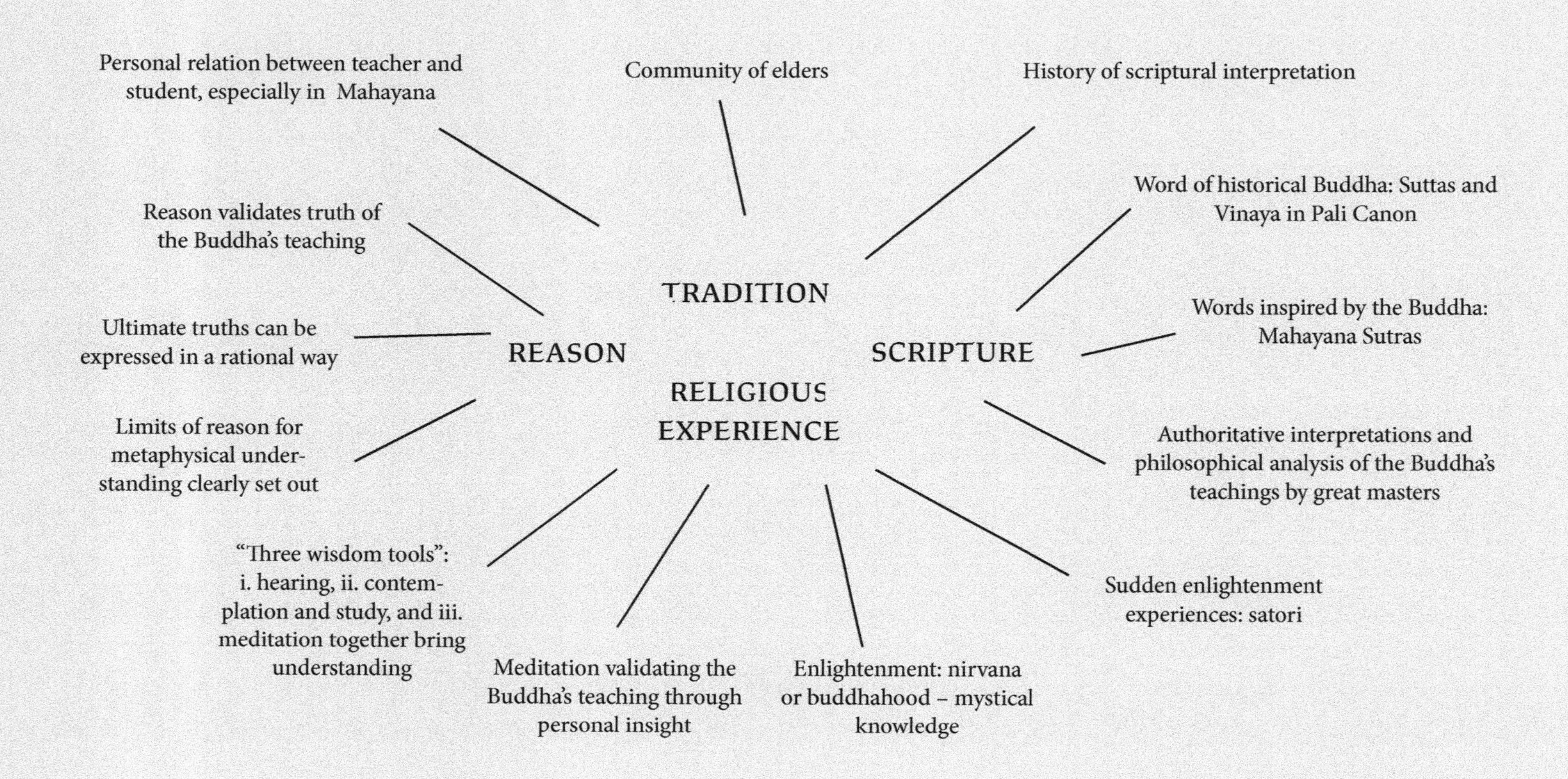

While Buddhism accepts all four of these sources of authority, it considers that some sources are more important than others. For example, in Theravada, the commentator Buddhaghosa presents their order of priority as follows:

- Scripture
- What is in conformity with scripture
- The commentaries by great scholars
- Personal interpretation based on reasoning and religious experience.

Scripture is without doubt the most important source of authority, and the other three must be in accord with the scriptures to be authoritative.

In Mahayana this is presented slightly differently but scripture remains the most important source of authority. Based on Indian Mahayana sources, Buddhist sources of authority are given by Deshung Rinpoche in his *The Three Levels of Spiritual Perception* (2003) as follows:

- Scripture
- The commentaries by great scholars
- The spiritual teacher
- Religious experience.

This is the order in which they are presented in the texts, but in terms of a person's experience the order is reversed. First, one develops some valid experience which leads to appreciating the importance and value of a teacher. Respect for the teacher brings more respect for the commentaries he or she is teaching from, and finally for the original scriptures taught by the Buddha.

Although Buddhism expresses itself differently on the sources of authority that it recognizes compared to Western models of thinking, the differences are not critical. We will therefore look at authority in Buddhism according to the four areas identified earlier to make it easier to compare Buddhism with the other faiths examined in philosophy of religion.

Scripture

Chapter 8 offers an overview of the Buddhist scriptures and explains which scriptures are considered authoritative by each tradition and school. In the present chapter we summarise the main points concerning the authority of the various collections of scriptures and then we consider some philosophical discussions about how and why scripture is authoritative in Buddhism.

The Pali Canon, the scriptures of the Theravada school, comprises three categories of scripture: the Vinaya, the Suttas and the Abhidhamma. The Vinaya and the Suttas are considered authoritative by all traditions of Buddhism because they are believed to contain the words of the historical Buddha. The Abhidhamma is considered authoritative by most Theravadins because it contains philosophical analysis by scholars who are accepted as great masters of the tradition. In addition, some believe that the Abhidhamma was originally taught by the Buddha himself when, using his supernatural powers, he visited his deceased mother in the Tushita heaven during the teaching phase of his life. Those who believe in this account also accept the authority of the Abhidhamma on the grounds that it is the word of the Buddha.

The Mahayana Sutras are accepted as authoritative only by the followers of Mahayana and Vajrayana Buddhism. These followers believe that they contain words inspired by the Buddha, or taught by the Buddha in Sambhogakaya form, and their authority therefore derives from this. Some Mahayana Buddhists also believe that the doctrine of these Sutras was also taught by the historical Buddha during his life time, and recent textual discoveries may attest to the existence of Mahayana teachings much earlier than first thought by modern scholars.

In Buddhism, therefore, the authority of the scriptures is relative to the specific scriptures accepted by each tradition. In other words, a particular text may be accepted by one tradition and not by another. But the whole of Buddhism follows the principle laid down by the Buddha, which says that scripture is never to be accepted blindly on trust but tested against reasoning and religious experience. Buddhists do not follow any of their scriptures dogmatically, instead they systematically set out to validate their truth by applying logical arguments and by examining their meaning in the light of their meditational insights. In Buddhism, the authority of scripture is intimately connected with the authority of reason and the authority of religious experience.

Philosophical justification for scriptural authority

In ancient India, Buddhists were engaged in debates with members of other schools of Buddhism and also with followers of Hinduism, Jainism and other non-Buddhist Indian systems. In the course of such debates, they were sometimes tempted to cite their scriptures in order to validate their arguments, and this was problematic when the opponent in the debate did not accept those scriptures as authoritative. As a result, generations of Buddhist scholars looked into the question of what makes scripture authoritative. Dignaga and Dharmakirti identified a set of three criteria that any authoritative scripture needs to fulfil.[87]

1. A scripture is valid if its statements are not contradicted empirically by direct perception and observation.
2. A scripture is valid if its statements are not contradicted by correct logical inference.
3. It is valid if it does not contain internal contradictions regarding trans-empirical matters.

In Buddhism, scripture is not regarded as authoritative if it defies empirical experience based on everyday observation, or if it goes against inferences used in correct logical reasoning. Scriptural texts therefore lend themselves to investigation on both these counts, and this is why the foundations of Buddhism are held to be rational and empirical, in a similar way to the foundations of modern science. According to Dharmakirti, basic teachings of Buddhism like the Four Noble Truths can be validated by reference to either perception or inference so they are eminently accessible to ordinary people.

There is, however, a category of topics that is classified as trans-empirical and that eludes both reason and sense perception. Buddhism distinguishes three types of phenomena: those that can be perceived by the senses, those whose existence can be inferred through logic, and those that are trans-empirical and to which neither perception nor inference apply. For example, billowing smoke is a phenomenon that can be seen by the eyes and maybe also smelled by the nose. On the basis of seeing smoke one might infer that fire is present even though one cannot perceive 'fire' as such (let's say the smoke is some distance away). In this case, fire would be a phenomenon that can be inferred through reasoning. Examples of trans-empirical phenomena are karma, rebirth and enlightenment. Why should we trust a scripture that teaches subjects such as these?

Buddhist scholars identify two arguments that can be put forward to assert that the trans-empirical type of content is reliable. The first argument is that a text is reliable when the source of that text is considered trustworthy. The second argument is that the text is not of human origin so its validity is somehow inherent in it. Most Buddhists follow the former option and many other religions follow the second option.

In the case of the sutras, then, any trans-empirical content would be validated by the belief that the Buddha is a trustworthy source of knowledge. So the next question is: what qualities does a person need to have to be considered a trustworthy source of knowledge? There are four.

- The person must be motivated by genuine compassion for the well-being of all. This is the safeguard against teaching with the intention of manipulating the audience or pushing one's own agenda. Out of compassion he teaches what is best for his listeners.
- The person must be knowledgeable and thus able to speak and explain the truth.
- He or she not only teaches that truth but explains the methods that others can use to realize it themselves.
- The person makes every effort to teach so that others will truly benefit.

If the source of a scripture meets these criteria, then the text can be accepted as authoritative. It follows that even if some teachings are obscure and trans-empirical, one can have confidence in their reliability because other topics which are readily understandable have proven to be true. The idea is that one develops trust on the basis of what one *can* understand, and one can then accept the more difficult points on trust.

The problem with this line of reasoning is that the mere fact that some of what is said proves to be true (either through perception or through inference) is no guarantee that everything that is said is true. Inconsistencies could be possible. It is at most grounds for thinking that the scripture in question is worthy and reliable as far as we can judge. If we do choose to accept the scripture in this case, we do so because we want to, or because we need to do so for our spiritual goals. The three criteria set out above do not therefore compel anyone to accept a scripture's authority on radically inaccessible, trans-empirical matters. Such matters lie beyond the cognitive scope of the ordinary mind and can only be apprehended in states that are free of the Three Poisons. Their acceptance therefore requires not so much trust in a particular scripture but rather trust in the Buddhist path.

Tradition

Tradition is generally held in high esteem in Asian cultures, and this attitude applies in Buddhism as well. Tradition is regarded as a safeguard of authenticity, and a way of counteracting any tendencies towards individualism that would be detrimental for realizing the truth of no-self.

Buddhism has no church or other institution that has the authority to decide about what is orthodox and what is not, and what is accepted by the tradition and what is not. Instead, there are three factors that safeguard the authenticity of tradition: the community of elders, the historical lineage of scriptural interpretation and, in Mahayana and Vajrayana Buddhism, the personal relationship between teacher and student.

The Community of elders

The 'community of elders' refers primarily to the monastic community, and to some extent it refers to the community of each monastery rather than of all Buddhist monasteries in general. As we have seen in previous chapters, the role of the monastics is to uphold religious traditions such as ceremonies, festivals and other rituals. Monks and nuns uphold the traditional values of Buddhism by keeping all their precepts and vows and being living examples of ethical behaviour. They also keep knowledge of the religion alive by studying the scriptures. All these traditions are accepted as authoritative by the Buddhist community as a whole because most of them were first established by the Buddha himself, and because they have been continued from one generation to the next since the Buddha's time.

Within each Theravadin monastery, authority is conferred democratically upon the abbot or head of the monastery who is usually elected on the basis of his knowledge of the scriptures and his length of continuous monastic service. All but the most critical decisions are taken by the body of monks (in practice either all the monks within a given monastery or an elected group) on the basis of consensus, and both monks and laypeople accept the authority of this mechanism because it stems from the time of the Buddha. However, in Tibetan monasteries authority is often less democratic since the head *lama* of each monastery has more power and authority than anyone else.

History of scriptural interpretation

Scriptures are authoritative in Buddhism, but just as important as the texts themselves is the way they are interpreted. Each Buddhist school has one or more traditions of scriptural interpretation, and these are considered to be the only authoritative ways of understanding scripture. This means that, in Buddhism, the scriptures are not completely open to individual interpretation, and since there are ancient traditions that establish the meaning of each text there is also no room for anyone to speculate about their meaning. Should anyone choose to re-interpret scripture outside of this tradition, their views would not be considered authoritative.

When a monk studies the scriptures, he will be taught to interpret them in the way that his own teacher was taught, and the 'lineage' of interpretation that he thus joins goes back for generations. In one sense, this is similar to the way we might learn at university in the West when we learn the approach and the views of our professors. In another sense it is quite different from this, because in India tradition is prized far beyond individual innovation in all areas of philosophy and religion; the student self-consciously aims to belong to a tradition rather than to create a distinct viewpoint of his very own. For Buddhists, holding tenaciously to one's personal views is just another form of attachment and needs to be abandoned like all other forms of craving and attachment. Consistent with the doctrine of *anatta*, it is tradition that is authoritative in Buddhism and not the individual. As a result, when new ideas do emerge they are presented as reassessments of what earlier texts or traditions 'really meant'.

The teacher–student relationship

In previous chapters we have seen how important the teacher–student relationship is in Ch'an/Zen and in Tibetan Buddhism. This is because the teacher transmits the mind of enlightenment directly to the student, one-to-one, and it is believed that enlightenment is impossible to achieve without the transformative blessing of the teacher. The tremendous authority wielded by the teacher rests on his or her ability to effect this transmission and keep the lineage alive, so that the truth retains its full power and is not just a dead set of ideas.

The other reason for the lama's authority in Tibetan Buddhism is that he or she is considered to be a living embodiment of the qualities of the enlightened mind. This is why the lama is an object of Refuge. The lama is a spiritual guide, like the Buddha; his teachings and advice are the Dharma; and he is a friend on the path, fulfilling the role of the sangha. In spiritual terms, therefore, there is nobody higher or more important than one's own lama.

Both in Zen and in Tibetan Buddhism, the student cultivates devotion to the teacher, meaning an openness of heart and mind, and a surrender of the 'ego' that gets in the way of that openness. The student will view the teacher's words and actions as so many skilful means *(upaya)* of expressing the Dharma, and will take them as opportunities for learning and personal development. The teacher is accepted as completely authoritative, and as representing the Buddha, Dharma and Sangha, but teachers themselves must always abide by the Dharma during this teaching process. The authority of the teacher ultimately rests on his or her own spiritual attainment comprising both knowledge and compassion.

Reason

Reason plays a more important role in Buddhism than perhaps in any other of the world's religions. An underlying assumption in Buddhist thought is that the truth – even truths that are ultimate and beyond words – can be pointed to in rational language. In the case of ultimate truths, rational language will only be able to convey an approximation of those truths at best, but the principle remains that nothing can be accepted as true if it is irrational, illogical or somehow goes against valid reasoning. In other words, even the highest truths are always compatible with reason.

How can we account for the prominent role of reason within the Buddhist religion? It is connected with the fact that neither the doctrine nor the scriptures of Buddhism are considered divine in origin, and consequently there is nothing intrinsically non-human about them, and nothing in them that is inherently inaccessible to the human mind. There is therefore no justification within Buddhist thought for arguing that ultimate truths must be unfathomable mysteries by definition.

The Buddhist understanding of enlightenment is that it is the attainment of freedom from ignorance. This implies that once ignorance has dissolved then knowledge will arise and indeed knowledge, along with the qualities of compassion or *bodhichitta*, is one of the characteristics of both nirvana and buddhahood. For human beings, knowledge is intimately related to reason and, even for philosophies that acknowledge the limits of reason, reason is nonetheless an indispensable tool for gaining at least some degree of knowledge. Buddhism is therefore internally consistent in the way it sets out the limits of reason for knowing metaphysical truths, while at the same time valuing reason on the conventional level as a method for helping us reach the point when we can transcend reason altogether.

Zen Buddhism, and especially Rinzai Zen, may be exceptions to some of the points made above. The Zen approach tends to be one that does not accept the value of rational discourse as a stepping stone for understanding higher, non-conceptual truths. Instead, when language is used it employs paradox and riddles which, on the face of it at least, are far from logical and rational.

The four reliances

Human beings are intelligent and yet we need to be educated so we know how to use reasoning correctly. Buddhism sets out guidelines that must be adhered to for reasoning and logic to be regarded as authoritative. One important set of guidelines is called 'the four reliances'. They identify the basic discernments necessary when inquiring into the nature of reality.[88]

1. When analysing a particular claim, we must not draw conclusions based on the renown of the person making the claim. Rather, we should draw conclusions on the basis of his or her message.
2. We should not deduce the truth or falsity of a statement from its literary merits or the quality of the writing; the content of the message is more important than its form.
3. We should not put our trust in statements that have conventional and provisional validity with respect to a particular expedient purpose, but rather we should give more importance to the definitive meaning of a text that pertains to the actual nature of reality. This point can also be rendered as the principle of not believing the culturally-conditioned meaning but the definitive meaning.
4. With respect to the definitive meaning, we should accord greater importance to the observations of direct perception and not be content with conjecture or understanding simply on the level of the words.

Irrespective of the topic one is studying, and whether or not one is studying Buddhism or some other subject, these four conditions should be applied when we engage in analysis. Taken together, they mean that we should beware of believing in someone's words simply because they are charismatic, good talkers or famous; we should not jump to conclusions too quickly on the basis of the literal meaning alone but reflect upon it deeply; we should know how to tell the difference between a statement that is made with a particular goal in mind and one that is made about the truth of reality (that is, the difference between conventional and ultimate truths); and finally, we should discern between truths that are based on direct perception and statements that are speculative and not validated in experience.

Religious experience

Religious experience has enormous authority in Buddhism. The authority of the Buddha himself, both during his life and ever since, is due entirely to his enlightenment experience; without this Shakyamuni would be a human being like any other, albeit perhaps a very wise one. The teachings of Buddhism arise from the insights gained during his enlightenment, which means that the authority of the scriptures is ultimately validated by the Buddha's religious experience. This has important implications for Buddhism as a whole, especially since the Buddha was not divine but human, and therefore his experience is not unique but can be shared by any one of us. Lewis Lancaster explains it this way:

> *While the followers of the Buddha considered that his words possessed special power, the idea that the teaching arose from insights achieved in a special state of yogic development, a state open and available to all who have the ability and the desire to exert the tremendous effort needed to achieve it, meant that the words based on the experience need not be considered as unique or limited to one person in one time.*[89]

Mahayana develops this idea to the full when it teaches that the goal of Buddhism is full buddhahood, and when it accepts that a number of Buddhist masters since the Buddha's time have become enlightened in their turn, and hence have become authoritative. It also helps to explain the authority accorded Buddhist teachers in Vajrayana when they have attained very high stages of spiritual realization.

The authenticity of a person's religious experience is not taken for granted in Buddhism, and there are various ways in which it can be verified. For instance, the insights gained would have to accord with scripture; and the nature of the experience would need to be attested by a meditation master with more experience and, preferably, with long-standing knowledge of the person concerned.

Defining religious experience

In Western philosophy of religion, there are two main definitions of religious experience. Some thinkers such as Schleiermacher describe religious experiences as feelings. They are affective rather than cognitive experiences. In Buddhism we certainly find examples where religious experiences are described in terms of feelings; nirvana, for instance, is described as an experience of bliss and peace. Other thinkers such as William Alston define religious experiences as a type of perception and therefore as cognitive experiences. This, too, applies in Buddhism. The description of the enlightenment of the Buddha explains how he perceived certain truths in each of the three watches of the night: he saw all his past lives in detail, he understood the karma of all beings and the nature of all things.

However, there are differences in what these terms mean when used in Buddhism. If we apply the idea of 'perception' to the Buddha's enlightenment, for instance, we are stretching its usual meaning because we would not be referring to sensory perception but to types of mental perception based on states of meditation. Nevertheless, enlightenment is understood as a cognitive experience. Furthermore, when Rudolf Otto speaks of perception in the context of numinous experiences he defines it as 'apprehension of the wholly other' which certainly does not apply in Mahayana Buddhism. The whole point of enlightenment is to realize that the nature of subject and object is the same; all boundaries between 'I' and 'other' dissolve, indeed the sense of 'I' dissolves completely *(anatta)*. Buddhahood is not 'other' and unattainable, it *is* our very being. In Theravada, on the other hand, nirvana is presented as the opposite of samsara and is radically different from our deluded self. In this sense, from the perspective of a samsaric being, it could justifiably be called 'the wholly other'.

To present the Western range of definitions of religious experience very simply, some emphasize the affective while others emphasize the cognitive. But there are several problems associated with both these models. For example, it can be argued that feelings depend on concepts and are conditioned by them; feelings are culturally bound, so, for instance, my cultural background may lead me to experience a particular type of feeling as important or as unimportant. In the case of cognitive experiences, the belief systems present within one's culture and society provide a framework for the way one accounts for experiences. The very fact that there is such a diversity of religious experience from one culture to another might imply that this diversity depends more on interpretation than on the experiences themselves.

The Buddhist understanding of the cognition process resolves these problems (see Chapter 21). One classic Buddhist presentation of cognition based on the works of the Indian scholar Dharmakirti asserts that conceptual interpretation occurs after the first moment of sense perception. Sense perceptions themselves are non-conceptual and apprehend things as they are.

However, conceptual interpretation arises extremely quickly so it is very difficult to experience the difference between these two moments. These two phases of cognition can only be distinguished in advanced meditation. Meditation has the effect of slowing down the process and increasing its visibility to consciousness, and with repeated meditation practice the conceptual reflex no longer operates. Importantly, it is held that the undeluded, non-conceptual mind can perceive reality as it is, as an instance of advanced meditational insight. This is termed yogic perception.

For Buddhists, authentic religious experience is a mental cognition of reality as it is, undistorted by language and culture. It is a cognition of the undeluded mind purified through the process of the spiritual path; it is not a mental cognition of the ordinary deluded mind subject to strong emotions and conceptual judgments, and limited by language. The framework of the spiritual path explains how an apprehension of reality is possible.

In Buddhism, noetic religious experiences are not confined to the attainment of enlightenment itself. If this were so, only buddhas would be able to have religious experiences. Practitioners can have glimpses of reality at any time along the path to enlightenment; instances of this are *vipassana* insights and *satori* in Zen. However, glimpses such as these may be transient and the point of continuing on the path is to stabilise these glimpses until wisdom-perception becomes continuous, both in meditation sessions and during the rest of the day and night. This is enlightenment.

Grounds of knowledge claims

If we accept that religious experience in Buddhism has a cognitive element, then we have to ask whether it provides adequate grounds for knowledge claims. Consider the following points:

- In Mahayana, enlightenment and glimpses of enlightenment are a non-dual experience, beyond subject and object, and therefore transcend conceptual conditioning.
- In Theravada, enlightenment and glimpses of enlightenment are not a non-dual experience, but they do transcend concepts.
- They are verifiable experiences since they can be checked by other meditation masters.
- They can be replicated since they can be experienced by anyone following the same Buddhist path.

- They do not occur haphazardly since there are specific methods like meditation for attaining enlightenment.
- Enlightenment is internally consistent with the Buddha's teachings both in terms of being a state of highest realization and in terms of the methods used to attain it.
- Enlightenment is absence of ignorance, and absence of ignorance gives religious insight. Enlightenment *means* liberation from ignorance.

Types of religious experience

Many different types of religious experience are identified in Western philosophy of religion, in particular visions, numinous experiences, mystical experiences, conversions and revelations. Most books on this subject address religious experience in purely theistic terms and this may be misleading in the sense that readers may imagine that religious experience therefore does not apply to Buddhism at all. This is not so, but of course we need to re-define each type of experience accordingly.

Visions

If we take the story of the Buddha's experience of Mara as symbolic then it can be understood as a series of visions, although it is not actually described as a vision in the scriptures. The experience was also noetic (a source of new knowledge) which is a characteristic of authentic visionary experience. Visions are certainly recounted in the Buddhist literature, especially in the biographies or autobiographies of great yogis. In Mahayana and Vajrayana Buddhism, visions are understood as the apprehension of the Sambhogakaya dimension of reality.

Numinous experiences

Numinous experiences are defined as those that bring both fear and wonder at the overwhelming power of an unknown force. When they are not theistic they are related to nature, or places, or another human being. It seems that nothing in the Buddha's experience fits this description.

Mystical experiences

This category comes closest to describing enlightenment. Some Christian descriptions of mystical experience are extremely close to Buddhist descriptions of enlightenment: "He knew that the light was within himself" (Richard Bucke); "distance and nearness become blurred into one, without and within glide into each other"; and "his understanding and that of God are now both one" (St John of the Cross). But the phenomenological object of mysticism in Buddhism is not God or a permanent substance or force underlying the existence of all things, but the nature of things which is beyond time and space, and beyond the ideas of existence and non-existence.

William James[90] identifies four characteristics of mystical experience: ineffability, noetic quality, transience and passivity. Do they apply to mystical experience in Buddhism?

- *Ineffability* Both nirvana and buddhahood are said to be beyond words.
- *Noetic quality* This certainly applies to all forms of enlightenment since the goal of Buddhism always combines wisdom and knowledge together with compassion.
- *Transience* This does not apply to nirvana or buddhahood. It is said that once one has attained enlightenment there is no going back, it is a realization that is present every minute of the day and night and that continues after death. But transience would apply to glimpses of reality and other insights on the path.
- *Passivity* In one way this does not apply to Buddhism and in another way it does. The descriptions of the Buddha's enlightenment do not convey the impression he was overwhelmed by his experience, on the contrary: he emerges in complete control. On the other hand, nobody can bring about such experiences at will. There is no meditational button we can press to attain instant enlightenment whenever we want it, and in this sense we do not have any control over it. In some Mahayana traditions such as Pure Land Buddhism, the other-powered nature of religion is strongly emphasized so that there is a significant degree of passivity in religious attainment, all attainment being due entirely to the compassion and blessing of Amida Buddha.

Many of the problems that Western thinkers have with mysticism do not necessarily apply to Buddhism. For example, A.J. Ayer is concerned that indescribability means that one cannot say anything rational about mystical experience. In Buddhism, there is an underlying belief that logical reason is not incompatible with mystical knowledge even though the two are distinct. Reason can help us explain and understand mystical knowledge. Ayer also argues that mystical experience yields no knowledge of the external world, only knowledge of the mystic's own mind. Buddhists would counter this in a number of ways: first, mystical experience occurs when subject and object have dissolved (in Mahayana), so the dichotomy between the external world and the mystic's own mind no longer applies. Second, Ayer assumes that without the senses the mind's understanding can only be subjective. Buddhism distinguishes between the confused mind which is indeed subjective, and the wisdom mind that apprehends things as they actually are. Third, Ayer states that true knowledge must be empirically based, meaning it should be derived from the senses and be verifiable by the senses. Buddhism contends that no cognition involves the senses alone; even sense perception involves the corresponding sensory consciousness. Both the senses and the mind are valid sources of cognition, and the mind can cognise reality without the mediation of the five physical senses. It is clear that the assumptions and perspectives of both sides are very different.

The role of mystics and mysticism is very important in Buddhism. After all, the Buddha himself was a mystic and the goal of the religion is a mystical experience. Buddhism has no church or overall institutional authority in a position to condemn mystics; instead, mystics have played a mainstream role in the development of many Buddhist traditions. Indeed, mystics like Nagarjuna have actually been the source of new scriptural traditions.

Conversions

William James defines conversion as follows: "To say a man is 'converted' means that religious ideas, previously peripheral in his consciousness, now take a central place, and that religious aims form the habitual centre of his energy." In other words, a conversion experience changes your life. The example that springs to mind in Buddhism is the moment that the Buddha decided to leave the palace and follow a religious life. The process of seeing the Four Signs or Sights revealed his natural interest for religious questions and formed what nowadays we might call a time of 'spiritual crisis' when he questioned all his values and his very way of life. The result was a radical change in his outlook and a decision to make religious aims the central focus of his life. In all these ways, this event in the life story of the Buddha might be called a conversion experience.

The Buddha's life story also contains many examples of the way the Buddha's disciples were converted, mostly after meeting with him or speaking with him. The stories of Sunita and Angulimala are examples of this (see Chapter 2). The experience changed their lives and they immediately decided to become monks or nuns. So, although we cannot interpret conversion in a theistic way, we can say that conversion experiences exist in Buddhism.

Revelation

If we define revelation in theistic terms as an active communication from God or other external source, it is not an accepted experience in Buddhism. However, it is possible to re-define revelation in a way that does fit with Buddhist thinking. In the Buddhist sense, 'revelation' is *parivartina* – turning something over, explaining it, making clear what was previously hidden. The Buddha can be said to 'reveal' the truth of the Dharma insofar as he uncovers what was hidden from our view due to ignorance and other mental defilements. When we listen to Buddhist teachings we may find certain truths resonate with us, they click with us, and at such moments it is as if we recognized something that had been confused or hidden before, as if a hood had been pulled from our head and we see something clearly. We could call these 'moments of personal revelation or personal insight', and they are important on an individual's path.

Religious experience as proof of the religion's tenets

In Buddhism, religious experience is never used to prove the existence of God. In fact, the reverse is the case: it is because neither the Buddha nor any Buddhist master since the Buddha, has ever found God through their religious insights and experience that his existence is denied. We could say that this lack of experience of God is used as proof for his non-existence, along with reasoned arguments (see Chapter 24).

Authority in contemporary Buddhism

Some issues around religious authority have surfaced over recent years as Buddhism begins to take root in Europe and North America. These problems stem mainly from the cultural conflict involved in overlaying Western ways of thinking on to Buddhist ways of thinking. This is a vast subject so here we just take two examples to illustrate this type of cultural difference.

Scriptural interpretation

First, some Westerners – especially academic scholars of Buddhism – find it hard to accept the authority of traditional scriptural interpretation, and the idea that there is no individual freedom to read the texts and interpret them as one wishes and as one understands them. They argue that this Buddhist custom was determined by the lack of printed texts in ancient times, which meant that one was literally unable to gain access to scriptures and read them outside of a monastic setting. In those days there were no bookshops or public libraries or internet. This question has arisen especially in relation to Tibetan Buddhism where a ritualised approach to textual study still exists today. For example, unless one listens to the oral recitation of a text by a qualified scholar, it is believed that one will not be receptive to the transformative blessing of the text when one studies it.

In response, a Buddhist might argue that the 'liberal' way of interpreting scripture stems specifically from Christian Protestantism which encouraged personal reading of the scriptures, free of the constraints of the Church. It is interesting to explore the arguments of both sides in this debate, and to separate out what is historically and culturally specific from what is essential to the integrity of the religion.

Given the modern situation of free access to texts, it is probably inevitable that some readers will propose new interpretations of their own. There are no institutions in Buddhism that prohibit the free expression of ideas, but the question is: what conditions need to be in place for such new ideas to be considered authoritative? Does John Smith's personal understanding of a Buddhist text, or of a particular point in the texts, simply represent his own subjective and possibly idiosyncratic view? Or can it be taken to have authority? In response, we can apply some of the criteria mentioned above: the person in question should be trustworthy, his or her interpretation should not contradict experience or logic, and it should not contradict the Buddhist scriptures either literally or in meaning; and finally, the new analysis should conform with the four reliances.

This controversy is a live one in the early 21st century and deserves to be considered in depth. Writers and teachers of secular Buddhism, for instance, are frequently accepted as authoritative outside the Buddhist tradition where the culture encourages free thinking and where academic credentials may suffice. From the viewpoint of the tradition itself, however, rigorous criteria apply before religious authority is granted. If such criteria are not met, one is only dealing with personal opinion.

Issues around patriarchy

Second, some Westerners reject the way that Buddhism has always tended to give more authority to men than to women. The monastic code for nuns enshrines the principle that nuns have a lower status than monks and must show respect to them at all times. In all Buddhist countries throughout Asia, there have always been a greater number of monks than nuns. Furthermore, almost all the Buddhist masters and scholars revered by the tradition are men, and even today most of the Buddhist teachers of all traditions are men.

While these facts are indisputable, it must be remembered that the superior social status of men has been a universal fact in all areas of the globe for millennia, barring a few short-lived exceptions. It is only in the last hundred years or so that women have actively stood up for equal rights as we understand them today. It should therefore be no surprise that Buddhism, which began many centuries ago, does not teach the social equality of men and women in the way we might wish.

However, Buddhism certainly does teach that men and women are spiritual equals. In Mahayana and Vajrayana, enlightenment can be attained by both men and women equally. At the time this idea was introduced in India it was very radical, but it is fair to say that the idea of spiritual equality was not reflected in social equality. Many Buddhist traditions are today adapting to the modern world by accepting women on socially equal terms with men. In this respect the tradition is in the process of evolving with the times.

Personal reflection

What gives anyone authority in your view?

Main Points

- Buddhists respect the authority of scripture but consider its value to be instrumental, not inherent.
- Scriptures are investigated in relation to experience and logical reasoning.
- Tradition is highly regarded partly as a means of counteracting individualism.
- Tradition includes the role played by the community of elders, the traditions of scriptural interpretation and the relationship between student and teacher.
- Reason is encouraged so followers have an intelligent understanding of the teachings.
- Religious experience plays an important role since both the foundation and the goal of the religion is mystical experience.

Chapter 24

THE EXISTENCE OF GOD

In Western thought, religion is defined as a form of belief in God. Buddhism does not fit this definition because it refutes the existence of a creator God. This chapter examines the main arguments put forward by Buddhist scholars in support of their views on theism.

What do we understand by 'God'?

A significant part of Western philosophy of religion is concerned with arguments for and against the existence of God. Paradoxically perhaps, very few Buddhist texts address this question, and it is an assumption of most Buddhist doctrine that God does not exist. One of the few treatises that does set out the Buddhist arguments on this question is the *Tattvasamgraha* by the 8th century Indian scholar Shantarakshita. This work is like an encyclopaedia of Buddhist thought and has been compared to Thomas Aquinas' *Summa Theologica* for its thorough and comprehensive treatment of philosophical questions. The present chapter is based on this work.[91]

It is important to know how God is defined to appreciate why Buddhists refute his existence, because the Buddhist refutation is a logical and precise one. We have to remember that, in the Indian context, Buddhist scholars were refuting the Hindu idea of God and not the Judeo-Christian idea of God. The following characteristics were commonly ascribed to God by Indian theists and are those that define the 'God' that Buddhists refute.

- **Creator of the universe.** The theist argument for this is based on the idea that insentient matter cannot produce itself, therefore the cause of the universe cannot be material and must be intelligent and mental/spiritual. In ancient India no distinction was made between theist and deist conceptions of creation, that is, one where God remains involved in his creation and one where he does not.
- **Omniscient.** This theist argument follows from the previous one: if God created the universe, then he knows everything it contains.
- **Eternal.** The meaning given to this divine characteristic is that God has no beginning and no end, and he is not produced by anything else.
- **Distinct from the soul.** Some Indian philosophers argue that God is distinct from the soul since he is both eternal and omniscient and the soul is neither of these.
- **First cause and only efficient cause.** As Creator of the universe God is the First Cause, meaning that the chain of causality begins with him. All the other physical and mental factors that are involved in the creation of things – such as atoms, virtue, lack of virtue and so on – are only contributory causes. The example given is that God causes things to arise just like a potter creating a pot. God is an intelligent cause.

There are two other theistic arguments cited by Shantarakshita for the existence of God:

- **The first** is that the world is a place of suffering only because it is controlled by an intelligent being or cause. Suffering cannot be produced by unconscious matter. The very existence of suffering is therefore a proof of the existence of God.
- **The second** concerns the idea that what exists is what is known, and only God can know all things in their entirety. Humans cannot perceive all things all the time, only God is able to do this. So the very fact that all things in the universe exist means that God must exist.

The Buddhist refutation

The following points present the key arguments used by Buddhist scholars to refute the existence of God as defined above.

God and the natural order

- Buddhists do not accept the notion that the world must have an intelligent First Cause simply because there is a natural order, that is, simply because there appears to be an intelligent arrangement of its parts.
- Even if one accepts that there is a natural order in the universe, Buddhists claim that this argument could equally be used to *disprove* the existence of God. If things function harmoniously according to natural laws, they say, then what need is there to posit the existence of God?
- For a Buddhist, the existence of things is unproven (example of the chariot: see Chapter 10) and the existence of a thing's parts is also unproven (see the Mahayana sections in Chapters 10 and 21). Buddhists do not hold the universe to be ultimately real.

God as Creator of all things

- The metaphor of God as a cosmic builder is predicated by theists on the analogy of an architect who builds a house. Buddhists argue that there are no good reasons to extend this analogy to the natural world. For example, there is no evidence to suggest that mountains and so on are 'built' in the same sort of way as houses. And in the case of houses, the architect does not build them alone but employs many builders to help him; so how would this analogy work with the idea of God as the sole universal builder? If God needed the help of other agents to produce the universe then he would not be the Supreme Creator.
- Another refutation of God as Creator is that there is no certainty that the creator of one thing must be identical with the creator of another thing. For example, the architect of one house is not necessarily the same person as the architect of another house. The assertion that there must be one Creator of the whole universe, and only one, is unproven.

Likewise, there is no certainty that the creator of a thing must be unitary and single rather than many. For example, there are many people involved in the building of a house, not just one, so why could this analogy not be applied to the universe? Could it not be the case that the universe was created by several gods?

God as eternal Being

- It is impossible to prove the existence of an eternal being. Such a being would be unitary and would be an eternal substratum embracing all things and consciousness itself. It follows that our consciousness could not conceive of such a being or prove his existence because he would be beyond the capacity and limitations of our minds.
- It is a contradiction to say that an eternal being created the world. Eternal things cannot produce effects because the notions of consecutive time and concurrent time are mutually contradictory with eternity. The Indian idea of 'eternity' means 'out of time' or beyond time, so this contradicts an act of creation because such an act necessarily occurs in time. If the universe has a beginning, then the Creation must happen at a particular time. Buddhists argue that it is irrational to say that a Being who is beyond time acts within time because the two are mutually exclusive.

God as omniscient

- Following on from the preceding argument, if objects exist consecutively then they must be known consecutively. In other words, something cannot be known until it exists. This contradicts the idea of God's omniscience because it would make it impossible for him to know all things at once, in any single moment.
- God's omniscience is justified by his creatorship of the world. As Buddhists reject the latter they reject the former as well.

Other difficulties with the creation process

- Buddhists argue that if God is an unobstructed, all-powerful cause, and if nothing can conceivably obstruct his ability to create, then he would have to produce everything simultaneously. This is because there can be no reason *not* to produce something, and there can be no reason to produce a thing at one time rather than another. If a theist responds by saying that it is the auxiliary factors involved in causation that constitute the reasons for producing things at one time rather than at another, then Buddhists reply that, if this is the case, it means that God's power to create is constrained by these other factors, and if God is all-powerful no kind of constriction should occur. The conclusion is therefore that the idea of God as an all-powerful Creator has internal contradictions. It would imply that God could never be *dependent* on auxiliary causes.

- Some theists respond to the previous argument by saying that the reason God creates different things at different times is simply because he wishes to do so, and this is a sufficient reason. Buddhists dismiss this argument on a number of counts. First, they say that the notion of 'wishing' is irrelevant here; a wish in itself is ineffective unless one has the power to create, and therefore the issue here is not God's wish but God's power to create. Second, they point out that there is ample evidence in the natural world for things being produced without any wish being involved. For example, a sprout appears without the wish of a seed. Wishing is therefore not a necessary factor in the process of causation.

Taken together, these Buddhist arguments are designed to show that the theist's position is flawed by self-contradiction. For Buddhists, theistic arguments are irrational in that they defy logic. Buddhists suppose that the truth of things is always compatible with reason, for if this were not the case we could never know anything at all. This is why Buddhism does not accept the existence of God in the sense of an omniscient, all-powerful, eternal Creator.

It may be useful to add, however, that some masters have expanded on the traditional Buddhist presentation as a result of Buddhism's recent contacts with Christianity. One modern interpretation of the Buddhist view is to say that Buddhists do not accept the existence of God as a *person* who acts, creates, judges, rewards and punishes in a similar way to the way human beings act. This is too much of an anthropocentric view of God, an understanding that describes God in the image of Man. Buddhists think it is a mistake to think of God as a person and it is more consistent to think of him as a universal principle. The Buddhist equivalent of this is the Dharmakaya, the body of truth out of which all things naturally manifest first as energy and light (Sambhogakaya) and then as matter (Nirmanakaya). And the Dharmakaya mind of enlightenment is characterized by clarity and lucidity on the one hand, and by boundless compassion on the other hand. In this sense, then, Buddhism does not reject the idea of an intelligent and loving principle at the heart of the world, and many Buddhists may have no objection to calling this 'God' provided that no hypostatisation was implied by this term. The Three Kaya principle is one Buddhist answer to the question of how the world and everything in the world arise.

The role of God in ethics

Questions around the existence of God are not only matters of theological debate; they have a tangible impact on the way religion is lived and experienced. For example, for those who believe in God, God plays a vital role in safeguarding ethical conduct. Human psychology is such that it is easier to abide by ethical guidelines when one thinks that almighty God will reward or punish accordingly than if one thinks there are impersonal causal laws that determine the results of moral action, and there is nobody to whom one is accountable. One's personal relationship with God is a motivator of moral discipline, just as it is a comfort in difficult times.

Some might feel that without a God who fulfils these two human needs, religion would become meaningless and ineffective. This is an important facet when considering the existence of God in Buddhism: most human beings are not moved by theological debates but they are moved by emotional needs, and faith in a just and loving God fulfils some of the deepest needs of humanity.

One might wonder, therefore, whether Buddhism can ever fulfil this level of human need and offer people the support required to lead a virtuous life and find strength in times of suffering. In other words, one might wonder whether Buddhism warrants being called a religion at all. Certainly, Buddhism places the focus squarely on personal responsibility. In practice, however, Buddhism does play the supportive role of a religion but in ways that are different from theistic religions.

- The *sangha* or religious community plays a constant supportive role. This applies to the support given by monks, nuns and spiritual teachers as well as to the human support of fellow Buddhists. One is not alone.
- In Mahayana and Vajrayana especially, devotion to the buddhas, bodhisattvas and masters of the lineage serves as a channel for prayer. Psychologically, this functions in a similar way to prayer to God and to saints, but the understanding behind it is different. A Buddhist knows that buddhas, bodhisattvas and spiritual masters do not exist in ultimate truth. Prayer is effective due to the meeting of the power of one's focused heart and mind on one side, and the power of the aspirations of the buddhas and bodhisattvas on the other. On the conventional level, Mahayana and Vajrayana Buddhism function like other religions in this respect.

With regard to the motivation for moral discipline, the Abhidharma texts explicitly mention two mental factors that are instrumental in keeping people on track. They are shame and embarrassment, and they are regarded as virtuous mental factors for this reason. Shame refers to being sensitive to public judgement of one's actions and embarrassment refers to being sensitive to the promptings of one's own conscience. Both serve to restrain a person from committing harmful actions. They make an ethical life possible without reference to God.

Personal reflections

How do you understand the idea that an eternal, all-powerful person created the universe? Does this make sense to you? Why, or why not?

Main Points

- The Buddha refuted the existence of God philosophically with specific reference to the ideas of God prevailing in India in his time.
- Buddhists refute God as First Cause, as Creator of all things, as eternal Being, and as omniscient.
- The principal reason underlying this refutation concerns the Buddhist analysis of causality.
- Buddhism succeeds in functioning as a religion despite its refutation of God.

Chapter 25

BUDDHISM AND SCIENCE

Buddhist thought is founded on logic and reasoning on the one hand, and on meditative experience on the other. Such an approach is not dissimilar to that of the modern sciences. Over the last thirty years, landmark conferences organized by the Mind and Life Institute have brought together Buddhist scholars and scientists from different fields to discuss questions related to consciousness and the physical universe. This book concludes with an overview of the relationship between Buddhism and science, which can be as illuminating as it is contentious.

Buddhism and science are not conflicting perspectives on the world, but rather differing approaches to the same end: seeking the truth.
His Holiness the Dalai Lama[92]

The dialogue between science and Buddhism

The Dalai Lama has suggested three avenues for overcoming the challenges of the modern world: ecumenical dialogue, agreement on a universal code of ethics, and dialogue between Buddhists and scientists. Just as Buddhist thinkers once debated with Hindus and Jains in India, with Taoists and Confucianists in China and with Shinto priests in Japan, in a similar way we are now witnessing an exciting, dynamic and ground-breaking interaction between Buddhism and contemporary culture as it moves west. Science is so dominant in modern culture that it is inevitable, if Buddhism is to become fully established in the West, that it engages with scientific thought. Foreseeing the importance of building bridges with science, the Dalai Lama has spearheaded a series of cross-cultural conferences with top scientists to explore the connections between science and Buddhist wisdom. Beginning in 1987, they have been organised by the Mind and Life Institute, an American-based association of businessmen and scientists who are personally interested in forging links that can benefit both sides.

It is a pervasive fact that the modern world does not believe in religion, it believes in science. Over one billion people in the world today do not follow a religion at all[93], but everyone accepts the truths and successes of science at least to some degree. From the Western point of view, these dialogues are revolutionary because for the last 500 years religion—meaning Christianity—and science have often been viewed as incompatible. While the scientific approach is seen as rational and based on experimentation and logic, the religious approach is characterized as irrational and based on myth or mystification. This perceived conflict stems from the way the Catholic church rejected a number of important scientific discoveries on the grounds that they undermined Christian teachings: for example, Copernicus' astronomical theory that the earth turns around the sun rather than the other way around; and Darwin's biological theory of the evolution of species. As a result, the very idea that religion and science could complement one another in humanity's search for the truth is, in itself, quite startling to many Western-educated thinkers. For theologians and philosophers, the mere possibility of a dialogue with science means that the very concept of religion has to be redefined.

There is hardly a country left on the planet where thinking has not been influenced by the materialist worldview that results from the rejection of religion as a source of truth. To engage in dialogue with holders of that worldview we need to begin by characterizing scientific materialism.

- Its thinkers focus on the *object* they wish to study and ignore the *subject* who is carrying out the study. They don't entertain the possibility that the way I understand an object might depend, to some extent, on my mind or state of mind. The idea of truth being objective, rather than subjective, is held in great esteem.

- An important method of analysis is to break things down into the parts that compose them, and while this is very useful it means that knowledge becomes fragmented and over-specialised, and nobody has the complete picture. For example, if one reduces the brain to its cells and molecules, this narrow vision will prevent one from seeing global processes occurring in different regions of the brain.
- Materialists believe that there is only one basic type of reality in the world, and that is matter. This is not proven, it is an assumption, but belief in this principle prevents them from considering other possibilities. Subjective experience is therefore of no interest because only the objective world is considered real.
- Most scientists are not open to the possibility of any form of non-physical causation. Even if they acknowledge that something non-material exists (and many don't accept this) they believe that it has no influence on the physical universe. All phenomena and their interactions are reducible to the laws of matter.

The population at large has been brought up to accept these ideas and assumptions. They have come to shape modern thinking in every field of activity. Hardly anyone in Europe and North America believes in fairies, ghosts or spirits, for example, whereas only two hundred years ago their existence was taken for granted. Economics accounts for events entirely in material and behavioural terms, without any room for more subtle levels of explanation such as moral causation.

These ideas have led some people to take a stand against religion in general. A political theory such as Communism, for example, is anti-religious; for Marx and Mao tse tung, religion suppressed intelligence, responsibility and progress, whereas work and science were the way to find truth and happiness. 'Modern culture' is not confined to Western countries; India believes passionately in science and China believes passionately in economics.

The dialogue with scientists is important from a Buddhist point of view. The Dharma is being introduced into societies where people believe that science holds the truth; if scientists have proved that something is the case, then it must be the case. If a doctor can explain a chemical formula which shows why a particular toothpaste is better for your teeth, thousands of people are likely to believe him and buy some. Even though we ourselves don't understand the details of what scientists are saying, mainstream thinking gives them the benefit of the doubt. In this context, it makes sense for Buddhist teachers to connect with this cultural consensus.

In recent years, minority viewpoints have emerged that are skeptical about science in general. Creationists prefer the Biblical account of Creation to the theories of cosmology and evolution; anti-vaxxers passionately attack the achievements of modern medicine. Although they have influence, such views are not based on rationality, or an alternative set of logical arguments; they are rooted in religious or emotional responses. This makes dialogue and debate improbable.

What is science?

How is science defined? In a general sense, science can be defined as any system of acquiring knowledge that is based on scientific method, defined as observation and logic. There are two main types of science: the natural sciences and the human sciences.

- *The natural sciences* investigate the observable world and include physics, chemistry, biology, geology, optics and so on. They are systems of knowledge based on controlled experiments that can be repeated and give the same results each time. The scientific method combines careful observation with the mathematical logic needed to make theories and laws.
- *The human sciences* investigate humans and society, and include ethics, politics, sociology, psychology and so on. They are based on observation and mathematical logic, but also on interpretation. For this reason, the knowledge they produce is only probable and uncertain.

Following this definition, Buddhism itself can be considered a science. The Buddhist approach to understanding the mind, for example, is based on open-minded rational inquiry and establishes truths that are validated by repeated experience and by logic. So, Buddhism *is* a science and the Dalai Lama believes that this is what justifies the dialogue between Buddhists and scientists: it provides some shared common ground. At the same time, however, Buddhism is also categorized as a religion so this is confusing if one holds to the view that religion and science are autonomous and their domains of concern are mutually exclusive.[94]

> *Because of Buddhism's emphasis on self-creation, there is no creator-deity, and thus some people consider it, strictly speaking, not to be a religion. A Western Buddhist scholar told me, "Buddhism is not a religion; it is a kind of science of mind." In this sense, Buddhism does not belong to the category of religion. I consider this to be unfortunate, but in some sense it means that Buddhism becomes closer to science. However, from the pure scientist's viewpoint, Buddhism is a type of spiritual path. It is unfortunate that we do not seem to belong to the category of science either. Buddhism thereby belongs to neither religion nor pure science, but this situation provides us with an opportunity to make a link, or a bridge, between faith and science.*[95]

A growing number of scientists are intrigued by Buddhism for these reasons. One of the first was Albert Einstein who wrote:

> *Buddhism has the characteristics of what would be expected in the cosmic religion for the future: it transcends a personal God, avoids dogma and theology; it covers both the natural and the spiritual, and it is based on a religious sense aspiring from the experience of all things, natural and spiritual, as a meaningful unity.*[96]

Understanding the mind

A number of the insights contained in the Buddhist Abhidharma concerning the mind and the process of perception have recently been corroborated by scientific experiments. Some would say that these insights have been *validated* by scientific experiments while others consider that Buddhism does not require the validation of science to be held as true: it has a rigorous epistemological and logical system of its own. The field of research is fast moving, so here we select a small number of topics that are of interest.

Pliability and neuroplasticity

The Mahayana teachings on *lojong* (see Chapter 20) offer methods that transform negative and self-centred thoughts and emotions into altruistic, positive ones.

These methods are based on the principle that emotions, thoughts, attitudes and habits are transformable. We might be angry quite often but this does not mean that we will be angry forever or all the time; with the right training we can change. Buddhism supports this possibility by invoking the principle of interdependence, and the idea that the mind is not a static, permanent entity but an ever-changing process that can be influenced by many factors. It argues that negative mental tendencies result largely from conditioning and are not inherent. Furthermore, *lojong* can only be practised once meditation is well established because meditation makes the mind pliable (see Chapter 17) which means that it is no longer stuck but open to new possibilities.

Discoveries in the brain sciences provide a scientific basis for all the above arguments. The brain is made of nerve cells, and until the 1990s it was thought that nerve cells did not change or grow after birth. In the last few years it has been found that this is not the case. The brain continually changes as a result of experience, and this phenomenon is called neuroplasticity. One example of how this works is seen in a study of London taxi drivers. It was discovered that after their first six months of driving through the complicated web of London streets, the areas of the brain that enable them to navigate become more developed.[97]

It has been shown that the connections between neurons (nerve cells) that structure the way we experience the world are created through experience and conditioning, and they are not inherent. Each moment of perception produces its own neural connections and pathways. It's only with repetition that a particular way of behaving becomes someone's temperament.

Learning and repeated experiences either create fresh connections between neurons or they produce new neurons.[98] There is therefore scientific proof that through training in developing positive thoughts and feelings, it is possible to transform negative habits and tendencies to the point that they have been completely replaced by the new ones.

Progressive stages of mastery

In most traditions, the Buddhist spiritual path is described as a gradual one. To begin with, progress is impossible without effort and discipline, but gradually positive states of mind become more and more natural and frequent. This progression from effort to effortlessness is found in many different Buddhist practices, whether one is developing shamatha, mindfulness, compassion, patience and so forth. Why is it that positive thoughts don't come naturally from the outset? Why does it require effort and discipline to generate them each time?

The scientific evidence now explains that this is because we are establishing new neural connections that were not there before. With repetition positive feelings will arise more and more effortlessly and spontaneously, because in the process the meditator has created new neural pathways. The neurobiologist Francisco Varela explains:

> *The interesting thing about the neurobiological evidence is that the sense of familiarity and effortlessness comes from the fact that our bodies have changed. The brain has rearranged itself, and we are a different being because of those changes. The familiarity has resulted in lasting changes in the brain.*[99]

Showing that the mental poisons are harmful

In Buddhism, it is a fundamental tenet that the mental Poisons of confusion, craving and aggression are harmful and cause suffering. Not everyone agrees with this view, however. There are people who argue that it can be healthy to express one's anger rather than to suppress it, that aggression is quite natural because it's essential for survival, and that desires are the juice of life. Some psychotherapists encourage their patients to view all emotions equally without any judgement and without labelling some as 'good' and others as 'bad'. During the Mind and Life conferences the Dalai Lama was particularly interested to see that, without needing to refer to religion, or God, or nirvana, there is a sound basis in science for saying that certain emotions are harmful and others are beneficial.[100]

For example, we know that anger is directly harmful to health: research has shown that it raises blood pressure, weakens the heart and shortens the lifespan. Repeated playing of violent computer games has been shown to change children's behaviour so they become aggressive, erratic and mistrustful. Following the same principles, experiments have shown that meditating on compassion increases neural activity in the left prefrontal lobe of the brain, and that activity in this zone is associated with feelings of happiness, enthusiasm, joy, high energy and alertness. A study of children in Bangladesh has shown that people with a compassionate attitude are better able to recover from stress or trauma. This shows that compassion brings benefits not only to others but also to oneself. In addition, meditation has been found to enhance concentration, reduce anxiety and strengthen the immune system.

Extending the limits of science

Another outcome of these dialogues has been that the sciences of life and the mind are changing as a result of their contact with Buddhism.

- The Dalai Lama observed, in 1991, that some scientists assume that the mind cannot exist or be active independently of matter, and he claimed that this assumption is unproven. Since then, more refined research is taking place to look at the mind-body relationship.
- Western psychology has focused almost exclusively on investigating mental illness or abnormality, and it has also examined negative emotions in detail. However, the area of positive emotions such as compassion was totally unexplored and no studies had ever been made of people with exceptionally positive and lucid qualities. This has changed as a result of the dialogues. Extensive experiments are taking place on meditators to understand the effects of positive thoughts and emotions on the brain.
- Until 1991, the mind was studied only from the point of view of an outside observer. High-tech machinery was used to probe the brain, while psychologists studied behaviour. These methods have now undergone a revolution so that subjective experience is now taken into account. Methods are being developed to study experience scientifically, and one such example are the methods used to study meditators.[101]

Understanding the universe

We will focus on two of the topics addressed during the Mind and Life conferences: how the universe began and the nature of matter.

How the universe began

Drawing from ancient Indian theories on time and the cosmos, the Buddhist Abhidharma describes the development of the world in terms of vast cycles of time. Worlds come into being and go through four different phases of evolution, at the end of which they degenerate and disintegrate. Then, after a period of inaction, another world appears and goes through a similar cycle.

> *Buddhist sources describe how the world first comes to form, then abide, disintegrate, and become empty, and how during the empty stage there*

remains space or empty particles. It is from these particles that another new world comes to form that abides, disintegrates, and becomes empty. In this way, in a repeated cycle, the universe is said to retain its endless continuity.[102]

Tibetans identify four different Buddhist theories explaining the origin and configuration of the universe. This is interesting in itself because it shows that Buddhism does not have one single account of these events. This is a subject that pertains to the conventional level of truth so a plurality of explanations is not philosophically problematic. The four theories are presented in Jamgön Kongtrul's *Treasury of Knowledge.*[103] While a core explanation is the same in all the theories there are some significant differences.

- In the cosmology of Nikaya Buddhism, the universe is described as mathematically finite and the number of worlds is limited. The force that creates the world is the 'winds' or energies that arise from the collective actions *(karma)* of beings, and it is these energies that form the bridge between mind and matter. These same forces also destroy the world. The world is static, with the cosmic mountain of Mount Meru in the centre, surrounded by various 'continents' and realms.
- Mahayana cosmology presents the universe as an infinite number of buddha fields. World systems come into being partly due to the actions of beings (as in the previous system) and partly because of the interconnections between buddhas and sentient beings. Buddhas and bodhisattvas are instrumental in the manifestation of the universe since through their compassion, vows and aspirations they can create innumerable worlds. The world is dynamic and is essentially composed of the infinity of space and light.
- The cosmology that is special to the Kalachakra ('Wheel of Time') teachings of the Vajrayana establishes a subtle correlation between the human body and human breath on one side, and the motion of the planets and stars on the other. The cosmos coherently integrates macrocosm and microcosm. The Kalachakra explains that what remains after a world has been destroyed is particles of matter scattered in space (sometimes called 'space particles') which coalesce to form new planets, stars and so forth in the next cycle of creation.
- The non-cosmology of Dzogchen, the highest teachings of the Nyingma school of Tibetan Buddhism, teaches that the primal creative cause of the universe is *rigpa,* a state of pure and total awareness, the ground of being

> itself. The delusion of cyclic existence – of worlds and lives – is simply the reification of the spontaneous expression of the ground of being; compassionate manifestations of energy and light are mistakenly taken to exist separately from *rigpa* and to be real. Influenced by karma, perception then solidifies these manifestations and views them as a physical world.[104]

These different views of the world are directly related to the stage of spiritual maturity of beings, meaning that we see the world according to our spiritual capacity to do so. This means that, in Buddhism, there is no one single objective universe out there that can be described; rather the world appears and is understood relative to the observer. It also means that there is no single, representative Buddhist view of how the universe began that we can compare with scientific views. The Dalai Lama often chooses to refer to the Kalachakra system when he speaks on these matters.

According to current scientific theories in astronomy, the universe had an absolute beginning, and this is called the 'Big Bang'. In this explosion, different points moved away from each other much faster than the speed of light, so it almost instantly gave rise to a huge universe, 100 billion light-years across.[105] (A light-year is the distance travelled by light in a vacuum in the course of a year.) The Big Bang was a centreless explosion that took place here, and everywhere. It occurred 12 billion light-years ago.

Scientists believe that time began with the Big Bang, so time is finite. However, they do not yet know for certain whether space is finite or infinite. This is because there are many events in the universe we cannot see because they are too far away, and the light signal from them has not had time to reach us. We are therefore unable to see to the edge of space because it is 100 billion light years across. However, scientists have discovered the afterglow produced immediately after the Big Bang and before galaxies were formed. It is a very regular light that is almost the same in every direction, with no structures but with some differences in temperature. They believe that it is from these temperature differences that galaxies were later born. By studying the afterglow more carefully they hope to be able to know whether or not the universe is finite.

The Dalai Lama asked scientists what they believe caused the Big Bang, and they admitted that they do not yet know. He also asked whether it was scientifically possible that there was not just one Big Bang, but that there could be a series of big bangs with universes being created and destroyed in a cycle—as in the Buddhist view. It was accepted that this is a possibility. The idea of sequential big bangs is called an 'oscillating universe'. The evidence that is required for better knowledge of this depends on a principle of Einstein's: if there is more than a critical amount of matter then the universe will oscillate, and if there is not then a single universe will persist forever. Researchers have recently realized that there is much more matter in the universe than they can see through their telescopes. They can't see it because it does not emit light, but they know it exists through implication, because they have found that it exercises a gravitational pull on other bodies which are visible. Since this matter is invisible they call it 'dark matter', and it is currently believed that some three-quarters of all matter in the universe may be dark matter. By applying Einstein's principle, scientists think they will soon have evidence to show whether or not there were several big bangs.

In making the connections between Buddhist and scientific cosmologies, one fundamental difference stands out, and that is that scientists in this field assume the objective existence of the universe they are studying. Unlike Jamgön Kongtrul, they do not admit that the cosmos we perceive depends in a fundamental way on the mind of the observer. A second key difference is that scientists assume that there exists only a physical universe, so all causes and connections are material and measurable. That assumption rules out the possibility that the origin of any given world could be mental, as stated in Buddhism and other religions.

The nature of matter

The connections between the Buddhist and scientific understandings of the nature of matter are clearer and easier to establish. In Chapter 21 we reviewed the differences between the main Buddhist philosophical views of matter and it is interesting to see that these views are closely echoed by scientific theories.

Classical physics and Abhidharma

First, the view of Nikaya Buddhism echoes that of classical physics. The Abhidharma analyses material phenomena and breaks them down into indivisible parts called *dharmas*. Dharmas are considered ultimately real in the sense that they cannot be analysed further or divided further. Furthermore, these dharmas are strictly momentary, lasting only a split-second before producing another dharma in the next moment. Dharmas have their own-nature which determines the qualities of the objects they form (i.e. their colour, texture and so on). Dharmas are the building blocks of the whole of the physical world, and they combine to form material objects as we know them.

Classical physics has a similar approach.[106] By 'classical physics' we mean the physics that was developed from Galileo in the 17th century up to Einstein in the early 20th century, and that is often characterized by the work of Isaac Newton. It gave birth to the idea that the physical universe can be explained as unchanging particles of matter which interact by means of forces that can be described by mathematical laws. If we know the laws governing these forces—the laws of electromagnetism, thermodynamics, optics and so on—then we can predict how things will behave and interact with each other. This means that the laws are deterministic and things are predictable.

The similarities between Abhidharma and classical physics can be summarised as follows:

- Both reduce the world to impersonal, relatively simple units of analysis which are causally related to each other. Physical objects and living beings are just combinations of these simple units.
- Both Abhidharma and classical physics agree that statements like 'there is a book on the table' are only conventionally true. In physics, both the book and the table are collections of atoms interacting by means of forces, while in Abhidharma they are collections of *dharmas* that influence each other according to certain causes and conditions.
- The fundamental units (particles and forces) that constitute the material world are considered to be ultimately real in both systems. They are believed to be objectively there. The purpose of both Buddhist Abhidharma and of classical physics is to understand the nature of what objectively exists, out there.
- In both the Abhidharma and in physics, the fundamental units that compose the world are known only indirectly, so their existence is established by inference. In the Abhidharma, individual *dharmas* cannot be perceived by ordinary consciousness, and in physics, the existence of particles and forces is proved through theories that are found to be consistent with an experiment, and that are expressed through mathematics.

There are some important differences as well. For instance:

- Dharmas are closer to our experience than the particles and forces of physics. Buddhist scholars maintain that small clusters of dharmas can be perceived by human beings in certain states of meditation, so they are directly verifiable through experience. In physics, by contrast, particles are detected indirectly thanks to the use of certain machines, like electron microscopes. Without machines they could not be known.
- Most dharmas are mental, whereas physics deals exclusively with the physical world. This reflects the spiritual aim of the Abhidharma, and the fact it is just as concerned with our *experience* of the world as it is with the world itself.

- Dharmas are momentary (changing from moment to moment) while atoms are unchanging. In classical mechanics, change is due to the motion of unchanging atoms, and to the forces that produce that motion. There is therefore a sharp duality between what is static and what is mobile, hence the distinction between particles and forces.

It is interesting to note that the most recent findings in physics are also relevant to the Abhidharma view of ultimate partless particles. Scientists currently believe that there are building blocks of our world that are smaller than the atom. Some of these sub-atomic particles are made up of even smaller constituents, while others cannot be broken down further into anything else. The latter type are called fundamental particles. One of these fundamental particles is called a muon; it is similar to an electron but more than 200 times heavier. Fundamental particles might possibly meet the definition of a partless particle in the Abhidharma.

Madhyamaka and quantum theory

Madhyamaka philosophy teaches that everything in the universe, both physical and mental, is 'empty' of inherent existence. Emptiness *(shunyata)* can be defined as absence of independent existence, of permanent existence, and of existence as an indivisible unit. This principle is applied not only to the gross objects of our experience, such as books and tables, but also to the particles that make them up. In Madhyamaka logic there are therefore no ultimate building blocks of reality, there is nothing at all we can point to and say 'this is real'. Yet this does not imply that things do not exist at all. It implies that nothing exists independently, permanently and indivisibly. The phenomena of our experience arise through the laws of interdependent origination which govern both the production of objects and our perception of them.

In Madhyamaka, both objects and their qualities are always relative to context. For example, in Abhidharma it is said that heat is the intrinsic nature of fire, but in Madhyamaka this idea is questioned. The precise amount of heat generated varies from one fire to another depending, for example, on what type of fuel is burned. So Madhyamaka accepts the Abhidharmic analysis but only on the conventional level, not ultimately.

Since all phenomena exist only in relation to each other and not in isolation, everything depends for its existence on causes and conditions. The existence of each particular *dharma* is sustained by *dharmas* other than itself. Nothing, neither objects nor particles, is self-sufficient. This leads to a paradox:

> *If we focus on a particular dharma in an effort to distinguish its own intrinsic nature from that of other dharmas, we find that it disappears. The process of excluding from consideration everything but the dharma in question removes the very conditions on which its existence depends.*[107]

The similarity between this view and the findings of quantum physics is very striking. Quantum theory is based on Einstein's theory of relativity (first published in 1905), and was developed by Niels Bohr, Werner Heisenberg and others in order to explain certain phenomena which could not be accounted for through classical physics. They found that the laws of classical physics do not explain events at the subatomic level, that is, the dimension of reality that is found when we break down atoms and study the nature and interactions of their parts. These are some of the key principles developed in quantum physics.

- In many circumstances, there is only a certain range of possibilities for the physical quantities of energy or momentum that an object can have. For example, when an electron is orbiting an atom's nucleus, it can only have certain discontinuous energies which means that some orbits are possible and others are not. This contrasts with classical mechanics according to which an electron can theoretically follow any orbit around the nucleus.
- In classical physics, there are waves and there are particles, but nothing can be both. In quantum theory particles such as electrons can sometimes behave like waves, while electromagnetic waves can sometimes behave like particles. Yet even in quantum theory, nothing behaves as a wave and a particle at the same time. One can choose do to experiments that bring out either the wave nature of an object or its particle nature. So an electron can't

be defined either as a wave or as a particle. It can be said to have a wave nature or a particle nature only in relation to a given experimental situation.

- In classical physics all the properties of a particle are well defined, but according to quantum theory it's impossible to determine both the position and the momentum of a particle simultaneously and accurately. This is not due to limitations in our scientific instruments or our powers of observation. It is not the case that the electron actually has a determinate position and momentum but we cannot know them; rather, the electron's position and momentum are objectively indeterminate or 'fuzzy'. This is called the uncertainty principle.
- The laws of quantum theory are not deterministic as in classical physics. They predict probabilities not certainties.
- In classical physics, one thinks that the world is composed of separate and distinct physical objects that interact with each other. This implies that each object has its own location in space. When we add the theory of relativity to classical physics, we can say that none of the information that passes between objects can travel faster than the speed of light. This means that a distant object cannot influence another object in less time than it takes light to travel the distance between them.
- In quantum physics things are more complex. If two objects interact with each other, move off in different directions and later become widely separated, in quantum theory they remain in a strange way intertwined, subtly influencing each other in every moment. Since quantum theory deals with probabilities, these influences cannot be controlled. Moreover, these influences seem to be transmitted faster than the speed of light, yet no matter or energy is transported between the two objects. So rather than there being 'something' travelling from one distant object to another, it may be that the objects are somehow not separate, that they are somehow fundamentally connected even though they are separate in space. This is called nonlocality.[108]

On the basis of this summary, we can identify a number of connections between the views of Madhyamaka and quantum physics.

Both reject the idea that anything has an intrinsic nature. However, Madhyamaka is more complete in its negation because it denies the intrinsic existence of both matter and mind—both subject and object, observer and observed—whereas quantum physics deals only with the physical world. Furthermore, quantum physics is less exhaustive in its negation than Madhyamaka because, for instance, certain properties of an electron, such as its mass, are considered to be intrinsic to it, while others are not.

Both accept that there is an interdependence between subject and object, observer and observed. In quantum theory this is called a 'participatory universe'. The observer does not simply study an objectively existing electron, rather he or she is partially responsible for determining what the electron is (i.e. a wave or a particle). Madhyamaka is more thorough than quantum science in establishing this interdependence because, in physics, not all the properties of an electron are affected by the conditions of observation whereas in Madhyamaka, subject and object are fully relative.

Concluding points

How can we reconcile the differences among the truth claims of the different religions and of science? One approach is to take a position of cultural relativism, and to say that any given set of beliefs is valid and useful for the adherents of that system but that does not make them so for anyone else. Some might extend this approach further and consider that all religious truths are culturally relative in this way in contrast to scientific truths which are uniquely and universally valid because they depict reality as it is.

Buddhism does not define itself as either a science or a religion, and it makes no distinction between religious truths and scientific truths. The recent series of volumes on *Science and Philosophy in the Indian Buddhist Classics* cites a large number of scriptural passages that address questions that we would normally say pertain to the domain of science. For example, the scriptures detail the nature, role and effects of micro-organisms living in different areas of the body. The dichotomy between religious and scientific domains becomes even more untenable when it comes to the nature of human existence and the nature of the mind. The notion that science and religion do not overlap is indefensible.

Alan Wallace[109], a Buddhist teacher who is also a qualified physicist and who has taken part in Mind and Life dialogues, proposes a different approach to evaluating the truth claims of Buddhism. He warns against the Orientalist way of gaining knowledge about the culturally distinct (and colonized) 'other' without listening to the voice of the other. Dialogue is only possible if both sides are open to working with all voices in the process of understanding.

Wallace also points out that the outcome of dialogue should not be restricted to knowledge about another system of thought, but it should also serve as a way of re-evaluating one's own system of thought.

> *In terms of the interface between Buddhism and science, we must be self-conscious of the assumptions we bring to Buddhist studies, while entertaining the possibility of learning about the world from Buddhism, as opposed to studying this tradition merely as a means to learn about Buddhism.*

For the Dalai Lama, one significant way in which science could learn from Buddhism is by considering the ethical consequences of research and implementation. Many people in the modern world assume that the scientific view of the world is the only basis for valid knowledge. Scientific theories lead to technology and we believe that technology is the true producer of miracles: rockets that go to Mars, computers that correct our grammar, beautiful buildings that are 200 storeys high, robots that switch the heating on, wish-fulfilling aspirins that can cure any illness. But technology is the fruit, or expression, of a particular way of understanding the world, and the danger is that the view on which it is based leads to a narrow vision bounded by materialism and nihilism. Many of the dimensions of the full reality of what it is to be human—art, ethics, spirituality, goodness, beauty and above all, consciousness—are either reduced to chemical reactions or are considered purely imaginary or simply dispensable. It is not difficult to see that the meaning of life and morality have no place in this world view. What then is the difference between a robot and a human being?

It is of utmost importance for our future that humanity rediscovers the true meaning of spirituality, which is the meaning of life itself. This will automatically bring with it a sense of morality, and it is perhaps in the field of morality that this cross-cultural dialogue will bring its most decisive benefit. "This is critical," argues the Dalai Lama, "because unless the direction of science is guided by a consciously ethical motivation, especially compassion, its effects may fail to bring benefit. They may indeed cause great harm. Humanity may end up serving the interests of scientific progress rather than the other way around."[110] We need only think of Hiroshima, Chernobyl, Bhopal or the climate crisis for examples of what can happen when things go wrong. Technology is powerful so, in the Buddhist view, scientists have a moral responsibility to ensure that science serves the interests of humanity in the best possible way. The Dalai Lama concludes:

My plea is that we bring our spirituality, the full richness and simple wholesomeness of our basic human values, to bear upon the course of science and the direction of technology in human society. Science and spirituality have the potential to be closer than ever, and to embark upon a collaborative endeavour that has far-reaching potential to help humanity meet the challenges before us. We are all in this together. May each of us, as a member of the human family, respond to the moral obligation to make this collaboration possible. This is my heartfelt plea.[111]

Main Points

- The Dalai Lama believes science and Buddhism are simply two different ways of seeking the truth and has initiated dialogues between the two under the Mind and Life Institute.
- Buddhism and science share common ground in the way they establish validity through experience/experimentation and through logical reasoning.
- There is convergence between Buddhism and science on: mental pliability, the possibility of training the mind and the harmful nature of certain emotions.
- Buddhism presents four ways of understanding how the universe began. They all include the theory of the arising and destruction of universes in a perpetual cycle, consonant with modern theories of an oscillating universe.
- The views of Nikaya Abhidharma can be compared to those of classical physics while the view of Madhyamaka is closer to quantum physics.

GLOSSARY

Abhidhamma (Abhidharma) scriptures containing philosophical and psychological analysis
Amitabha (Skt.) Amida (Japanese) the buddha of infinite light and life, devotion to whom ensures rebirth in his pure land after death. He is the main buddha revered by the Pure Land School.
Anatta (Pali), anatman (Skt.) the doctrine that there is no permanent, inherent essence to anything that exists
Anicca (Pali), anitya (Skt.) impermanence, change
Arhat (Skt.) literally 'worthy one', one who has attained nirvana (nibbana), the highest level in Theravada
Aryans people who invaded India from central Asia c. 1500 BCE
Asuras 'demi-gods'; powerful and jealous beings who dwell in one of the six realms of samsara
Atman (Skt.) the impersonal essence of a person according to Hinduism
Bardo (Tib.) literally 'interval', and specifically the intermediary period between the end of one life and the beginning of the next in Tibetan Buddhism
Bhikkhu monk
Bhikkhuni nun
Bodhichitta (Skt.) literally 'awakened mind' or 'mind of enlightenment'; the mind that strives to realize enlightenment for the sake of all beings in Mahayana Buddhism
Bodhidharma Indian master considered the first patriarch of Ch'an (Zen) Buddhism, who brought Ch'an from India to China (c. 470-543)
Bodhisattva (Skt.) in Mahayana: a person motivated by *bodhichitta* who follows the path in order to liberate both themselves and all others. Advanced bodhisattvas may deliberately choose to be reborn in one of the six realms to help suffering beings; some are considered to be present in Sambhogakaya form and are objects of prayer and devotion
Brahma the supreme personal God of Hinduism
Brahman the supreme impersonal principle that governs the universe in Hinduism
Brahmin priest in the Vedic religion and also in Hinduism

Brahminical social or religious order where brahmins are dominant
Canon collection of scriptures
Dharmakaya (Skt.) the 'body' of truth, the enlightened mind
Dharmakirti considered instrumental in establishing the Buddhist tradition of logic and epistemology (c. 600-660)
Dignaga a disciple of Vasubandhu and the formaliser of Indian Buddhist logic (c.480-540)
Dogen considered to have introduced the Soto school of Zen into Japan (1200-1253)
Dukkha (Pali), duhkha (Skt.) the first of the Four Noble Truths; suffering, pain, frustration, insecurity, anxiety, angst, unsatisfactoriness
Eisai considered to be the founder of the Rinzai school of Zen in Japan (1141-1215)
Ekayana literally 'one vehicle'; a doctrine in the Lotus Sutra that asserts all Buddhist Vehicles lead to the same ultimate goal and can therefore be considered elements of a single over-arching Vehicle
Four Seals Mahayana presentation of four key tenets of Buddhism: impermanence, suffering, no-self and nirvana.
Hinayana literally 'lesser vehicle' referring to the eighteen early schools of Buddhism in India (see Nikaya Buddhism)
Karma (Skt.), kamma (Pali) literally 'action', this also refers to the universal law of cause and effect that governs the moral results of intentional actions, including rebirth
Kathina festival at the end of the rains retreat in Theravada
Koan a seemingly paradoxical riddle or statement used as a training method in Zen Buddhism to force the mind to abandon logic and conceptual thought
Lama (Tib.) spiritual teacher or master in Tibetan Buddhism
Madhyamaka literally 'the middle way', a school of Indian Mahayana philosophy which taught the doctrine that all things are empty of inherent existence *(shunyata)*
Mahayana literally 'Great Vehicle', one of the three major traditions of Buddhism teaching *bodhichitta*, *shunyata* and the *bodhisattva* path
Mantra phrases composed of sacred syllables (usually in Sanskrit) representing the speech and mind of a particular buddha or bodhisattva; in Vajrayana they are repeated as meditation aids and for prayer
Merit the store of wholesome karma created by the performance of virtuous deeds
Nagarjuna founder of the Madhyamaka school of Mahayana philosophy (2nd-3rd century CE)
Nembutsu (Jap.) the Pure Land practice of reciting the name of Amida Buddha 'Namu Amida Butsu'
Nidanas the twelve 'links' of dependent origination that perpetuate samsara
Nikaya Buddhism literally Nikaya refers to 'collections' of scriptures and the term also refers to the eighteen early schools of Indian Buddhism
Nirmanakaya (Skt.) the 'body' of manifestation, the physical dimension of reality
Nirvana (Skt.), nibbana (Pali) literally 'extinguishing, blowing out'; the goal of Theravada Buddhism, which is liberation from the cycle of rebirth and suffering
Pali sacred language of Theravada Buddhism
Pretas 'hungry ghosts', beings with excessive greed who suffer in one of the six realms of samsara
Samanera novice monk
Samatha (Pali), shamatha (Skt.) calm abiding meditation
Sambhogakaya (Skt.) the 'body' of enjoyment, the dimension of energy and light in Mahayana and Vajrayana
Samsara (Skt.) the cyclic existence of birth, death and rebirth characterized by suffering
Sangha the third of the Three Jewels; this generally refers to the monastic community, but nowadays also to the lay Buddhist community

Sanskrit sacred language of India, especially of Mahayana and Vajrayana Buddhism, and of Hinduism

Satori (Jap.) sudden glimpse of spiritual insight or enlightenment in Zen Buddhism

Sautrantika literally 'those who follow the sutras' rather than the Abhidharma, a philosophical system in Nikaya Buddhism specialised in epistemology

Shunyata (Skt.) literally 'emptiness', the doctrine that all things are without essence and arise in dependence upon causes and conditions; characteristic of Mahayana philosophies

Stupa (Skt.) religious monument that may house the relics of buddhas or saints

Sukhavati (Skt.) literally 'land of bliss', the pure land or heaven of Buddha Amitabha (Amida Buddha)

Suttas (Pali), sutras (Skt.) discourses of the Buddha on meditation, the Four Noble Truths and so on

Tathagatagarbha (Skt.) 'buddha nature', the potential of enlightenment that exists in everyone according to Mahayana

Theravada literally 'Way of the Elders', the only surviving school of Nikaya Buddhism

Tipitaka (Pali), Tripitaka (Skt.) The Three Baskets or categories of the Buddhist scriptures: Vinaya, Sutta (Sutra) and Abhidhamma (Abhidharma)

Tulku literally, the Tibetan translation of 'Nirmanakaya' also used to refer to 'incarnate lamas' whose rebirth is considered to be a voluntary choice free of karmic determination

Upanishads Hindu scriptures composed from 7th century BCE

Upasaka layman

Vaibhashika literally 'those who follow the Vibhasa', the seminal treatise of a philosophical system in Nikaya Buddhism teaching the reality of partless particles and indivisible moments of consciousness

Vajrayana literally the 'Diamond Vehicle', one of the three major traditions of Buddhism, also known as Tantric Buddhism

Vassa rains retreat in Theravada

Vedas scriptures of the Vedic religion

Vedic religion religion believed to have been introduced into India by the Aryans from around 1500 BCE

Vihara monastery (Theravada)

Vinaya scriptures on monastic discipline

Vipassana (Pali), vipasyana (Skt.) insight meditation

Wesak festival celebrating the birth, enlightenment and passing away of the Buddha (Theravada)

Yana literally 'vehicle', referring to the three major traditions or vehicles of Buddhism: Nikaya Buddhism (Hinayana), Mahayana and Vajrayana

Yogachara a philosophical system in Mahayana teaching the Three Natures and a model of eight consciousnesses

Zazen (Jap.) sitting meditation in Zen Buddhism

STUDY QUESTIONS

Chapter 1 The Indian context

1. What social and religious factors led people to become followers of the Buddha during his lifetime?
2. What were the major influences on the thinking of Gautama the Buddha?
3. 'The Buddha was greatly influenced by the religious thought of the time.' To what extent do you agree with this view?
4. In which sense was the Buddha radically different from other religious leaders of his time?

Chapter 2 Gautama the Buddha

1. 'Stories of the Buddha's life show that he must have been a supernatural figure and not an ordinary human being.' How do you understand the Buddha?
2. Examine and comment on the influence that luxury and asceticism had on the subsequent life and teachings of the Buddha.
3. What lessons can Buddhists learn from the Buddha's life story? What is the significance of his death?
4. Examine Buddhist beliefs about the Buddha and Christian beliefs about Christ.

5. Identify three religious experiences of the Buddha and assess how they can be described in the language of Western philosophy of religion.

Chapter 3 The Buddha's disciples

1. How significant are a teacher's disciples for the development of a religion?
2. Describe the life and accomplishments of one of the Buddha's main disciples.

Chapter 4 A Brief History of Buddhism

1. Assess the view that Ashoka's contribution to the development of Buddhism was on balance a positive one (refer also to Chapter 22)
2. Give an account of how Buddhism has spread to the West.

Chapter 5 Buddhism in the Far East

1. Analyse the factors which facilitated the expansion of Buddhism in China or Japan.
2. Evaluate the claim that Buddhism underwent radical changes in the process of its expansion in the Far East.

Chapter 6 Buddhism in central Asia and the Himalayas

1. What distinctive features did Buddhism develop when it spread to Tibet and to Mongolia?

Chapter 7 The Three Vehicles

1. Explain the framework of the Three Vehicles.
2. Describe the stages and perfections of the bodhisattva path.
3. In what sense do the Theravada and Mahayana understandings of enlightenment differ?
4. 'There is only one vehicle'. Examine this quotation from the Lotus Sutra and assess its significance for Mahayana teaching on liberation.
5. Compare and contrast the arhat and the bodhisattva as Buddhist ideals.
6. 'Mahayana Buddhism is so different from Theravada Buddhism that it is hardly the same religion.' Examine the main differences between

Theravada and Mahayana Buddhism. To what extent do you agree with this statement?
7. What do Theravada Buddhism and Mahayana Buddhism have in common?

Chapter 8 The Buddhist Scriptures

1. How significant are sacred texts for Buddhists of different schools of thought?
2. On what basis do Mahayana Buddhists consider their scriptures to be authoritative?
3. Assess the view that the scriptures hold little authority in Buddhism today.

Chapter 9 The Four Noble Truths

1. Evaluate the advantages of a moderate or 'middle way' approach to life and to happiness.
2. What 'extreme' ways of life can you identify within society today? What is the underlying assumption or understanding of each about the nature of happiness? Do these ways of life succeed in bringing about their respective forms of happiness or not? How can you tell?
3. Modern society has many different explanations for the causes of suffering; for example psychology, psychoanalysis, psychotherapy, sociology, politics, economics, genetics and religions each have theories on this. Consider some of these accounts and compare their validity to the teachings of Buddhism.

Chapter 10 The Three Marks of Existence

1. Outline the Buddhist teachings on the three characteristics of existence.
2. Assess the view that the three Marks of Existence are all of equal importance for Buddhists.
3. 'The three marks of existence are really *anicca* described in three different ways.' Discuss.
4. Explain how the Buddha came to the conclusion that everything is *dukkha.*
5. What is the Buddhist understanding of *dukkha*? Does it make Buddhism gloomy and pessimistic?
6. Why do Buddhists consider happiness to be a form of suffering or *dukkha*?
7. What are the five aggregates? Discuss the significance of the belief that each

of these constituents is 'impermanent and so ultimately leads to suffering'.
8. 'It makes no sense to talk of a person without a soul.' Discuss with reference to Buddhism.
9. Describe and assess the Theravada analysis leading to the claim that all things are dependently arising.
10. Why does understanding no-self lead to happiness?

Chapter 11 The cycle of birth and death

1. Explain the relation between *kamma* (karma) and rebirth.
2. Compare the Buddhist view of life after death with one or more Western views.
3. Analyse the philosophical concepts associated with belief in life after death in Buddhism, and evaluate the strengths and weaknesses of the belief.
4. 'Belief in karma and rebirth means that evil and suffering present no philosophical problems'. Discuss.
5. 'Karma and rebirth are not acceptable ideas in a modern scientifically-based world view.' Critically address this statement.

Chapter 12 Karma and the causes of suffering

1. Explain the relationship between karma and samsara in Buddhist teaching.
2. "You are the owner of your *kamma*, you are the heir of your *kamma, kamma* is your friend and your refuge." (Pali scriptures) Explain what Buddhists believe about *kamma*.
3. What do the Four Noble Truths say about the causes of suffering?
4. "Buddhists believe that each person is responsible for his or her own suffering, so there is no need to take pity on the less fortunate." Is this the Buddhist view?
5. "Buddhist thought falls apart without karma and rebirth." Discuss the critical role played by karma and rebirth in the Four Noble Truths.

Chapter 13 Samsara and Nirvana

1. Explain the six realms of samsara. What questions does this teaching address?
2. How would a Buddhist approach what in Western terms is called the 'problem' of evil and suffering?

3. Explain the terms *anatta* and *nibbana (nirvana).* What is the relationship between them?
4. '*Nibbana* is not a worthwhile goal, as it promises nothing but emptiness.' Discuss.
5. Outline the understanding of nibbana found in Theravada Buddhism and assess the claim that nibbana cannot be defined with any degree of accuracy.
6. Describe the relation between nirvana and the Buddhist path.
7. Outline Nagarjuna's teaching on samsara and nirvana. Assess the view that Nagarjuna's teachings are a radical departure from the traditional teachings of the Buddha.
8. 'Nirvana is unconditioned, free from self, suffering and change.' Analyse and evaluate this claim.

Chapter 14 The Three Refuges

1. Explain what is meant by taking refuge in the Dharma and assess to what extent taking refuge in the Dharma is sufficient to gain enlightenment.
2. Discuss the meaning of the Refuges as a conscious expression of religious identity.
3. What do Buddhists mean when they say 'I go to Buddha for refuge'?
4. Explain what Buddhists mean by the term 'Dhamma/Dharma' and by the term 'Sangha'.
5. 'Buddhism is based on faith in the Buddha.' Do you agree with this view?
6. Is taking refuge really an elaborate form of escapism?
7. Explain the meaning and teaching of the Three Refuges. Evaluate the claim that the Refuges are the essence of Buddhism.

Chapter 15 Buddhist ethics

1. 'Actions themselves are neither good nor bad.' Evaluate this claim in the context of Buddhist ethics.
2. Describe and explain what Buddhists mean by Right Action.
3. Explain what Buddhists mean by the Middle Way. How useful is the concept of the Middle Way in helping Buddhists know how to behave?
4. Buddhism is often associated with the principle of non-violence. Discuss the Buddhist arguments for this position.

5. Analyse the distinctive features of ethics in Buddhism and evaluate their significance within that religion.
6. Explain the nature of the five precepts.
7. Outline and comment on ways in which Buddhists apply beliefs about karma to (a) social justice and (b) family life.
8. What are the features of Buddhist ethics for the laity? How do they compare with the moral precepts taken by monks and nuns?
9. For what reasons should a Buddhist behave morally?
10. How would a Buddhist view the ethics of (a) abortion and (b) vegetarianism?
11. Explain how belief in *ahimsa* influences attitudes to the embryo and the unborn child.
12. "For both Buddhism and virtue ethics, genetic engineering is wrong." Critically examine and evaluate this claim with reference to the dialogue between Buddhism and virtue ethics.

Chapter 16 Society and the Buddhist way of life

1. Describe the main features of life as a Buddhist monk in a Theravada monastery.
2. Explain the relationship between a monastery and its lay community. How has this relationship evolved in modern times?
3. Assess the claim that monastic Buddhism is too remote from lay people to have any impact on them.
4. Explain the nature and role of the Sangha in Buddhist life.
5. 'The Sangha puts more into the Buddhist community than it takes out.' Discuss.

Chapter 17 Meditation in Theravada

1. Explain the aims and methods of meditation in Theravada.
2. Discuss the importance of meditation for the achievement of *nibbana.*
3. Describe how Buddhists practise *samatha* meditation and explain its spiritual benefits.
4. Explain the role and purpose of meditation in the context of the Three Higher Trainings.
5. What is the point of *vipassana* meditation?

Chapter 18 Ch'an and Zen

1. Describe how Ch'an and Zen became established in China and Japan.
2. Explain the differences between Soto and Rinzai traditions.
3. What is the role of meditation in the Ch'an/Zen tradition?
4. 'Many different methods but only one aim'. To what extent is this a fair assessment of Buddhist meditation?
5. Explain the distinctive features of Zen meditation.
6. Explain why Zen meditation is completely different from samatha and vipassana as practised in Theravada.

Chapter 19 Pure Land Buddhism

1. Examine the ways to liberation taught by Pure Land.
2. To what extent could it be argued that Pure Land does not follow the main principles of the Buddha's teaching?
3. Explain the differences between Pure Land and True Pure Land.
4. Critically examine the teachings about methods to liberation in Pure Land and Zen Buddhism. To what extent, if any, are these teachings opposed to each other?
5. Do you agree with the assertion that Zen and Pure Land are so different that they cannot be considered to be part of the same religion?

Chapter 20 Meditation in Tibetan Buddhism

1. What role does meditation play in Tibetan Buddhism?
2. Describe three characteristic features of meditation in the Tibetan tradition.

Chapter 21 The four philosophical schools of Buddhism

1. Outline four views in Buddhist philosophy on the existence of the external world.
2. According to Buddhist philosophy, can we ever know anything objectively?
3. Explain the Yogachara model of perception. To what extent is this similar to views in cognitive science?
4. What is meant by conventional and ultimate truths and how can we know them?

5. What arguments do Buddhists use to explain no-self?
6. Discuss the view that Madhyamaka is a philosophy that goes beyond philosophy.

Chapter 22 Significant people

1. Consider critically the contribution made by one person in Buddhism to the development of social justice.
2. Critically examine the contributions that Ashoka made to the early development of Buddhism.
3. Evaluate the reasons for arguing that Ashoka's influence was fundamentally good for Buddhism as a whole.
4. Evaluate the contribution made by two 20th century Buddhist leaders to the evolution of Buddhism.

Chapter 23 Religious authority

1. "One of the main characteristics of the twentieth century was that people were accustomed to challenging authority no matter from where it may have been derived."
   a. Examine some of the sources of authority which Buddhists might have believed to be important.
   b. Explain some of the ways religious authority has been challenged in Buddhism and assess how effective these challenges have been.
2. Critically examine the Buddhist view of scripture as a source of religious authority.
3. In what circumstances is reason considered authoritative in Buddhism?
4. Analyse Buddhist attitudes to tradition and assess their value in the 21st century.
5. In which sense can nirvana be classified as a mystical experience?
6. How does nirvana or enlightenment differ from any type of religious experience in a theistic religion? You may choose one particular theistic religion to illustrate your answer.
7. Explain the relationship between religious experience, faith, religious practice and moral behaviour and assess the importance of religious experience within Buddhism.

8. Comment critically on the Buddhist understanding of the nature of religious experience.
9. "It is not reasonable to believe that religious experiences happen." Critically examine and evaluate this view with reference to the dialogue between Buddhism and philosophy.

Chapter 24 The existence of God

1. It is a central tenet of Christianity, Judaism and Islam that God created the world. Discuss this causal claim in the light of Buddhist philosophy.
2. 'The fact of our existence demonstrates the existence of a creator God.' How might a Theravada Buddhist respond to this statement?
3. How would a Buddhist refute the ontological argument for the existence of God?
4. Do you agree that Buddhism should be considered a religion despite its refutation of a Creator God?

Chapter 25 Buddhism and science

1. Do you consider that scientific explanations present a serious challenge to the Buddhist teaching on karma and miracles?
2. Assess the dialogue between science and Buddhism in terms of their shared ground for discourse.
3. Consider three examples of the convergence between scientific and Buddhist truths.
4. Discuss the Dalai Lama's view that scientists need to become morally responsible for the outcomes of their research.

RESOURCES

Books

Scriptures

Dhammapada: Carter, J.R. and Palihawadana, M., transl. (1987) Oxford University Press; Easwaran, E., transl. (1985), Nilgiri Press, USA; and Mascaro, J. (1973), Penguin Classics
The Lotus Sutra, Watson, B., transl. (1993), Columbia University Press, New York
Buddhist Scriptures, Conze, E. transl. (1959), Penguin Classics
The Questions of King Milinda, ed. N.K.G. Mendis, Buddhist Publication Society, Kandy, Sri Lanka, 1993.

Selected books

Bechert H. and Gombrich R., eds., (1984) *The World of Buddhism,* Thames and Hudson, London
Buswell R.E. and Lopez, D.S., *The Princeton Dictionary of Buddhism,* Princeton University Press, 2014.
Chah, Ajahn (2001) *Being Dharma,* Shambhala, Boston and London
Conze, E., (1993) *A Short History of Buddhism,* Oneworld, Oxford
Coward, H., (2000) *Scripture in the World Religions,* Oneworld, Oxford
Cush, D. (1993) *Buddhism,* Hodder and Stoughton, London
Dalai Lama, (2000) *The Meaning of Life,* Wisdom, Boston
Dalai Lama, (1991) *Mind Science: an East-West Dialogue,* Wisdom, Boston
Embree, Ainslie T, ed., (1988) *Sources of Indian Tradition,* Columbia University Press, New York
Emmanuel, S.M., ed., (2013) *A Companion to Buddhist Philosophy,* Wiley Blackwell
Encyclopedia Britannica: sections on *Buddhism, Jainism, Hinduism,* and *Indus Valley civilisation*
Gethin, R., (1998) *The Foundations of Buddhism,* Opus, Oxford
Gombrich R., (1988) *Theravada Buddhism,* Routledge, UK
Hanh, Thich Nhat (1988) *The Heart of Understanding,* Parallax Press, Berkeley California

Harvey, P., (1990) *An Introduction to Buddhism,* Cambridge University Press
Harvey, P. (2000) *An Introduction to Buddhist Ethics,* Cambridge University Press
Jinpa T., ed. (2017) *Science and Philosophy in the Indian Buddhist Classics,* vol.1 *The Physical World,* Wisdom Publications.
Jinpa T., ed. (2020) *Science and Philosophy in the Indian Buddhist Classics,* vol.2 *The Mind,* Wisdom Publications.
Keown, D., (1996) *Buddhism: A Very Short Introduction,* Oxford University Press
Keown, D., (2000) *Contemporary Buddhist Ethics,* Curzon, UK
Rahula, W., (1959) *What the Buddha Taught,* Oneworld, Oxford
Reat, N.R., (1994) *Buddhism: A History,* Asian Humanities Press, Berkeley California
Saddhatissa, H., (1997) *Buddhist Ethics,* Wisdom, Boston
Strong, J.S., (2001) *The Buddha: a short biography,* Oneworld, Oxford
Thomas, E.J., (1993) *The Life of the Buddha as legend and history,* Motilal Banarsidass, Delhi
Tillemans, T.J.F., (1999) *Scripture, Logic, Language,* Wisdom Publications, Boston.
Unno, T. (1998) *River of Fire, River of Water: an Introduction to the Pure Land Tradition of Shin Buddhism,* Doubleday, New York
Williams, P. (2000) *Buddhist Thought,* Routledge, London

Websites (in alphabetical order)

The following websites offer a range of resources free of charge

http://www.accesstoinsight.org
Access to Insight, a reliable website on Theravada Buddhism with translations of suttas from the Pali Canon and transcripts of talks on key topics.
https://www.bbc.co.uk/religion/religions/buddhism/
https://www.bbc.co.uk/ethics/guide/
These BBC sites address topical issues in relation to all world religions and offer many points that can stimulate discussion. It should be noted that Buddhism is not always described accurately, for example it is said that the soul takes rebirth.
http://www.buddhanet.net
BuddhaNet has many different study resources covering especially Theravada and Chinese Buddhism.
http://www.dharmanet.org
Dharma Net International offers articles and videos from all Buddhist traditions.
https://dharmasun.org/
Talks, courses and other resources on Buddhism from teachers in the Tibetan tradition.
https://middlewayeducation.org/
A website dedicated to school teachers and students with articles, videos, audios, lesson plans, worksheets and more.
http://www.tricycle.com
Tricyle offers articles, videos and podcasts from one of the leading magazines on Buddhism in North America. Access to many longer articles requires subscription.
http://www.windowsintobuddhism.com
Educational resources by topic and age group.
https://wisdomexperience.org/
A quality website with book reviews, Dharma talks and online courses led by speakers of all Buddhist traditions.

CREDITS

All maps, line illustrations and photographs in this book are reproduced with permission from the Terton Sogyal Trust, UK unless otherwise indicated.

The photograph of the Buddha lying down in parinirvana is by Detlef Hansen and reproduced under a Creative Commons Attribution-Share Alike 4.0 International licence. https://commons.wikimedia.org/wiki/File:358401_Gal_Vihara.jpg

The photograph of the novice monk is by Mlenny/iStock.

The translation of the Heart Sutra is reproduced with permission from the Nalanda Translation Committee, Canada.

ENDNOTES

1 *Dhammapada* 153-4.
2 *Dhammapada* 353.
3 *Lalitavistara Sūtra,* XXV, 1.
4 See Thich Nhat Hahn, *Old Path, White Clouds,* Parallax Press.
5 *Buddha,* p. xviii.
6 See R. Malhotra, *Being Different.*
7 Paul Williams, *Buddhist Thought,* p.22.
8 Compiled by the Buddhist Society, London.
9 This chapter is primarily based on *Great Disciples of the Buddha,* Nyanaponika Thera and Hellmuth Hecker, Wisdom Publications, Boston, in collaboration with the Buddhist Publication Society, Kandy, 1997.
10 *Great Disciples of the Buddha,* pp.21-22.
11 Edward Conze, *A Short History of Buddhism,* Oneworld, Oxford, 1993.
12 Thomas Laird, *The Story of Tibet,* Atlantic Books, London, 2006, p.94.
13 ibid., p.95.
14 According to the Vinaya scriptures of the Mulasarvastivada school of Nikaya Buddhism.
15 The Dzogchen teachings are followed within the Nyingma school, the oldest school of Tibetan Buddhism.
16 *The Words of My Perfect Teacher (Kunzang Lamé Shalung),* Shambhala, Boston, 1998, p.338.
17 John Reynolds, *The Golden Letters,* Snow Lion, Ithaca, New York, 1996, pp.211-212.
18 Atisha is also known as Dipamkara Shrijñana.
19 *Dhammapada* 183.
20 'Nirmanakaya' in *The Princeton Dictionary of Buddhism.*
21 'Dharmakaya', ibid.
22 Shantideva, *Bodhicaryavatara* 10.55.
23 *Kalama Sutta,* in *Anguttara Nikaya* i.188 in the Pali Tripitaka; III.6.5 and 6.6 in the Thai Tipitaka. References to the *Kalama Sutta* are based on the translation by

Thanissaro Bhikkhu, www.accesstoinsight.org

24 ibid.

25 Coward H., *Scripture in the World Religions,* Oneworld, Oxford, 1988, 2000, pp.138-158.

26 See the *Majjima Nikaya*, 63 and 64 in *The Middle Length Discourses of the Buddha,* transl. Bhikkhu Nanamoli and Bhikku Bodhi, Wisdom Publications, Boston, 1995.

27 Ajahn Chah, *Being Dharma.*

28 *The Foundation of Buddhist Thought: Part I, The Four Noble Truths* by Geshe Tashi Tsering, pp.2-3.

29 Walpola Rahula, *What the Buddha Taught,* p. 17.

30 Walpola Rahula, *What the Buddha Taught,* p.18.

31 Rupert Gethin, *The Foundations of Buddhism,* p.142-3.

32 *Majjhima Nikaya*, 1.262-264.

33 Ajahn Sumedho, *The Mind and the Way*

34 Robert Thurman, *Inner Revolution.*

35 Sogyal Rinpoche, *The Tibetan Book of Living and Dying,* p.13.

36 Reported by A. Wells in the *Journal of Near-Death Studies* (1993).

37 Reported by A. Wells in the *Journal of Near-Death Studies* (1993).

38 See *Establishing Validity,* Karmapa Chodrak Gyatso and Dharmakirti, KTD Publications, Woodstock, New York, 2016. This work is a translation of, and commentary upon, a chapter in Dharmakirti's *Commentary in Verse on Validity (Pramanavarttika karika).*

39 ibid., p.61.

40 Shantideva, *Bodhicharyavatara,* 8.129.

41 P.A. Payutto, *Good, Evil and Beyond: Kamma in the Buddha's Teaching,* Buddhadharma Foundation, Bangkok, 1995, p.1-2.

42 *Anguttara Nikaya,* III.415 in *The Numerical Discourses of the Buddha,* transl. Bhikkhu Bodhi, Wisdom Publications, Boston, 2012, p.963.

43 Patrul Rinpoche, *The Words of My Perfect Teacher,* Shambhala, Boston, 1998, pp.112-117.

44 *Dhammapada* 71.

45 *Dhammapada* 1-2, transl. Eknath Easwaran.

46 *Dhammapada* 173.

47 Walpola Rahula, *What the Buddha Taught,* p.21.

48 *Dhammapada* 119.

49 Rupert Gethin, *The Foundations of Buddhism,* p.119.

50 *Dhammapada* 1, transl. Easwaran.

51 *Samyutta Nikaya,* IV.252.

52 *Nagarjuna, Mula madhyamaka karika,* XXV.19. See *The Fundamental Wisdom of the Middle Way,* transl. Jay Garfield, Oxford University Press, 1995.

53 *The Four Noble Truths* by H.H. the Dalai Lama, Thorsons, London, 1997, p. 126.

54 *Dhammapada* 380.

55 *Turning Suffering and Happiness into Enlightenment* by Dodrupchen Jigmé Tenpé Nyima.

56 *Samyutta Nikaya,* III.120.

57 *Dhammapada* 118.

58 *Karma Chakme's Mountain Dharma* by Khenpo Karthar Rinpoche, vol. 1. p. 151.

59 Walpola Rahula, *What the Buddha Taught,* p.46.

60 *Dhammapada 5.*

61 *Sigalaka Sutta,* 'Advice to Lay People', Digha Nikaya 31.

62 *The Buddhist Scriptures,* transl. E. Conze, Penguin, pp.203-206.
63 Peter Harvey, *An Introduction to Buddhist Ethics,* Cambridge University Press, 2000.
64 Ajahn Chah, *Being Dharma.*
65 *Dhammapada* 254.
66 *Essential Zen*, ed. Kazuaki Tanahashi and Tensho David Schneider, Castle Books, Edison, New Jersey, 1996, p.67.
67 Dumoulin H., *A History of Zen Buddhism.*
68 Bercholz S. and Kohn S., *Entering the Stream*, Rider, London, 1994, pp.192-204.
69 See Watts A., *The Way of Zen,* Arkana, London, 1990, pp.142-4 for a summary of Dogen's teaching on time.
70 Nishiyama K. and Stevens J., transl., *A Complete English Translation of Dogen Zenji's Shobogenzo,* San Francisco, Japan Publications Trading Company, 1975, vol. II, p.16; slightly modified.
71 Heine S., transl., *The Zen Poetry of Dogen: Verses from the Mountain of Eternal Peace.*
72 Cleary T., transl., *Shobogenzo: Zen Essays by Dogen,* University of Hawaii Press, Honolulu, 1986, p.123.
73 Unno T., *River of Fire, River of Water: An Introduction to the Pure Land Tradition of Shin Buddhism,* Doubleday, New York, 1998, p.16-17.
74 ibid.
75 *Stages of Meditation* by H.H. the Dalai Lama, Rider, London, Sydney, Auckland, Johannesburg, 2001; and Snow Lion, Ithaca, New York, 2001.
76 *Essential Practice* by Khenchen Thrangu Rinpoche, Snow Lion, Ithaca, New York, 2002.
77 *Dharmasamgiti Sutra,* quoted by Kamalashila.
78 *Bodhicharyavatara,* I.28.
79 *Abhisamayalankara* by Asanga/Maitreya.
80 *Stages of Meditation* by H.H. the Dalai Lama, p.75.
81 Yongey Mingyur Rinpoche, *The Joy of Living,* Harmony Books, New York, 2007, p.115-6.
82 See John Dunne, *Foundations of Dharmakirti's Philosophy,* Wisdom Publications, Boston, 2004.
83 I am indebted to Karl Brunnholzl for clarifications on Yogachara. See *The Compendium of the Mahayana,* transl. Karl Brunnholzl, Snow Lion, Boulder, Colorado, 2018.
84 *The Yogacara-Svatantrika-Madhyamaka School of Buddhism and its influence on Nyingma doctrine with special reference to Shantarakshita's Madhyamakalamkara* by Dominique Messent Side, University of Bristol, 2003, Chapter 7.
85 The following arguments are taken from Aryadeva's *Four Hundred Verses.*
86 Yongey Mingyur Rinpoche, *The Joy of Living*, p.82-3.
87 See Tom Tillemans, *Scripture, Logic and Language,* Wisdom, Boston, 1999, pp.27-51; John Dunne, *Foundations of Dharmakirti's Philosophy,* pp.231-245; and David Karma Choephel, *Establishing Validity,* KTD Publications, Woodstock, NY, 2016.
88 H.H. the Dalai Lama, 'Introduction' in *Science and Philosophy in the Indian Buddhist Classics*, vol.1, p.10.
89 Lewis Lancaster, *Buddhist Literature.*
90 William James, *The Varieties of Religious Experience,* Routledge, London, 2002.
91 *The Tattvasangraha of Shantarakshita*, transl. G. Jha, Motilal Banarsidass, Delhi, 1986.
92 Foreword by H.H. the Dalai Lama in *Destructive Emotions* by Daniel Goleman, p. xiii.
93 *The World Factbook*, Central Intelligence Agency, USA, 2004.
94 See 'Introduction: Buddhism and Science – Breaking Down the Barriers' by B. Alan Wallace, in *Buddhism and Science,* ed. B. Alan Wallace, pp.1-20.
95 H.H. the Dalai Lama, *The Meaning of Life,* p.67.
96 Albert Einstein, *The Human Side.*

97 Scientific results reported in *Destructive Emotions* by Daniel Goleman, p.285.
98 ibid., p.21 and p.334.
99 ibid., p.286.
100 ibid., p.342-5.
101 ibid., p.312-4.
102 H.H. the Dalai Lama, 'Introduction' to *Science and Philosophy in the Indian Buddhist Classics*, vol.1, p.15.
103 This is translated into English as *Myriad Worlds* by Jamgön Kongtrul Lodrö Thayé, Snow Lion, Ithaca, New York, 1995.
104 *Myriad Worlds*, pp.40-56.
105 Zajong, Arthur, ed., *The New Physics and Cosmology: Dialogues with the Dalai Lama*, Oxford University Press, Oxford, 2004, p.176-195.
106 Ames, William L., 'Emptiness and Quantum Theory' in *Buddhism and Science*, ed. B. Alan Wallace, pp.283-302.
107 ibid., p.300.
108 ibid., p.293-298.
109 B. Alan Wallace, *Buddhism and Science*, p.27.
110 H.H. the Dalai Lama, *The Universe in a Single Atom*: *How Science and Spirituality can Serve our World*, Little Brown, London, 2005, p.9-11.
111 ibid., p.220-1.

This book is printed on paper from sustainable sources managed under the Forest Stewardship Council (FSC) scheme.

It has been printed in the UK to reduce transportation miles and their impact upon the environment.

For every new title that Matador publishes, we plant a tree to offset CO_2, partnering with the More Trees scheme.

For more about how Matador offsets its environmental impact, see www.troubador.co.uk/about/

About the Author

Dominique Side is a practising Buddhist and experienced teacher of Buddhism. She has a Ph.D. in Buddhist philosophy and has edited numerous publications, including two books by the Dalai Lama. She is the author of *Buddhism* (2005) and a founder of the *Windows into Buddhism* website providing educational resources for all age groups.